Jean Sibelius's Legacy:

Research on his 150th Anniversary

Jean Sibelius's Legacy:

Research on his 150th Anniversary

Edited by

Daniel Grimley, Tim Howell,
Veijo Murtomäki and Timo Virtanen

Cambridge
Scholars
Publishing

Jean Sibelius's Legacy: Research on his 150th Anniversary

Edited by Daniel Grimley, Tim Howell, Veijo Murtomäki
and Timo Virtanen

This book first published 2017

Cambridge Scholars Publishing

Lady Stephenson Library, Newcastle upon Tyne, NE6 2PA, UK

British Library Cataloguing in Publication Data
A catalogue record for this book is available from the British Library

ISBN (10): 1-4438-9860-0
ISBN (13): 978-1-4438-9860-7

To the memory of Einojuhani Rautavaara (1928–2016)

TABLE OF CONTENTS

III Analysis and Instrumental Practices

1. Modality and Compositional Techniques

2. Instrumental and Notational Practices

3. Analytical Essays

PREFACE

The 150th anniversary of Sibelius' birth in 2015 was a momentous occasion, celebrated worldwide through numerous concerts, performances, broadcasts, recordings, and discussions of his music. There were approximately three thousand concerts and events—half of them in Finland, the rest abroad. Cycles of Sibelius' symphonies were played in Berlin, London, Seattle, and several cities and towns in Finland. As part of this broad, celebratory atmosphere, a number of Sibelius scholars gathered together in his home town, Hämeenlinna, for a four-day conference leading up to his birthday on December 8: the Sixth International Jean Sibelius Conference. Some 64 participants assembled to listen to 42 presentations by Sibelius experts—young and old—drawn together by their common enthusiasm for the music of one of the world's greatest composers.

The current volume, *Sibelius' Legacy: Research at his 150th Anniversary*, draws directly upon this collective knowledge, and draws together the diverse viewpoints and overwhelming admiration for his music that emerged from this international gathering. But it is more than a simple account of that occasion—this is not a straightforward record of conference proceedings, though it is certainly a reflection of those events. Overall, the 25 chapters in this book represent a selection of the possible contributions on offer, grouped into sections according to topic. With this degree of focus, the opportunity to develop ideas that might only have been outlined within the context of a conference paper has now resulted in broader, chapter-length discussions that are more developed and expansive. Collectively, they offer a snapshot of current thinking within the field of Sibelius research, providing new perspectives and in-depth considerations of a wide range of issues.

Perhaps what is most striking about this book is the sheer diversity of its contents. To help locate a sense of focus within this wealth of material, the individual submissions have been grouped into three larger research areas: history and reception, aesthetics and style, and analysis and instrumental practices. The book therefore moves from general, wide-ranging concerns towards more detailed and focused studies, providing some sense of direction through the collection as a whole.

These studies essentially cover all of the genres in Sibelius' production: symphonies and other orchestral works, incidental music, and piano and chamber music, as well as songs, including both well-known works and rarities, and even some recently discovered findings. In addition to demonstrating the vivid and expanding field of Sibelius research, the chapters in this book are also a welcome reminder of the manifold sources of inspiration—including the music of his contemporaries, nature, literature, and visual art—the versatility of Sibelius' output, and the richness of his creative imagination.

There are still several open questions and challenges in regard to Sibelius' personality and life as well as his extensive oeuvre. On the one hand, Sibelius has for a long time been held, both in Finland and elsewhere, as the foremost Finnish composer, describing its history, myths, and nature, living in the forest and fighting musically for his Fatherland during many critical phases of the early- and mid-twentieth century. Thus, he could easily have been viewed as a conservative national hero. On the other hand, more recent research has tried to respect the urban and cosmopolitan character of Sibelius and the modernity of his music, which was progressive in a way that has only lately been fully recognised. This inner conflict or tension within our current image of Sibelius can still be observed in writings about him and his music. These features, alongside other issues, are discussed in the "Introduction" and the first main section of the book, "History and Reception."

The idea of Sibelius as a versatile composer, writing both *Gebrauchsmusik* and independent art music, has always been a problem—even a stumbling block—for many scholars. Both aspects are covered in this anthology: Sibelius wrote dozens of occasional compositions for friends, colleagues, and institutions, and his music also served as popular music. However, his symphonies and other large orchestral works belong to the central repertoire of the early twentieth century, and putting them into a contemporary context is one of the most important goals of this anthology. The reception of his music in Europe and the United States is a fascinating story of both the ease and difficulty with which it has been accepted and adopted as a model for composing, and also rejected for different reasons. More recently, Sibelius' relationship with the politics of his time and the use of his music for patriotic and military purposes in Finland and elsewhere has become a sensitive and contradictory research field, in which scholarly and intellectual conflicts have arisen. These discussions will likely continue for many years to come.

A deeper perspective emerges in the second section "Aesthetics and Style" and the third section "Analysis and the Instrumental Practices" in relation to Sibelius' works themselves: the compositions, their background ideas and style, compositional techniques (including orchestration), harmony, and structure (including voice-leading). Sibelius and the styles and "isms" of contemporary music and other arts provide as fruitful a source for discussion as it is inexhaustible. Likewise, his unique way of employing tonal and modal harmony and the highly characteristic sonic design of his music represent an endless and rewarding source for research. Studies of compositional processes and various versions of Sibelius' works have revealed that the qualities in his music that we consider to be highly individual and apparently spontaneous were very probably the result of painstaking reassessment and revision.

The editors of *Jean Sibelius' Legacy* cordially thank The National Library of Finland (Helsinki) and The National Archives of Finland for their help in using archive materials, the Legal Successors of Jean Sibelius, who permitted the use of original manuscript materials, copy-editors June Huuha and Andrew Barnett for their significant contributions, and especially Anna Krohn for her indispensable work during the many challenges of both organising the Conference itself and compiling this anthology. Also, we would like to thank the Sibelius Birth Town Foundation for organising the Sixth International Jean Sibelius Conference, which was one of the major events of the anniversary year in Finland.

As this volume goes to press, we learn the sad news that Einojuhani Rautavaara has died at the age of 87. In 1955, as part of his 90th birthday year, Sibelius was asked to select the most promising young Finnish composer for a grant from the Koussevitzky Foundation to study in America: he nominated Rautavaara. With Rautavaara's music standing as testimony to the enduring nature of Sibelius' legacy, it seems appropriate to dedicate this book to his memory.

The Editors,
August 2016
Oxford, York, Espoo, and Helsinki.

INTRODUCTION

"EITHER/OR?" NO: "BOTH–AND"! CURRENT CHALLENGES OF THE SIBELIUS IMAGE

VEIJO MURTOMÄKI

Introduction

The image of a composer is often in a state of fluctuation and change, and a "new" paradigm of interpretation often breaks through after 30 years or so. This means that every generation has its own ideas and seeks to redefine that image. In the case of Jean Sibelius, there have been at least four or five phases of looking at him as a person and composer and listening to his music.

Initially, the young Finnish nation as an "imagined community"[1] had to establish its right of existence with its own language and culture, which resulted in the creation of a national epos (*Kalevala*) and the support of great national heroes in the fields of literature (Aleksis Kivi, Juhani Brofeldt/Aho, Eino Lönnbohm/Leino), the arts (Albert Edelfelt, Axel Gallén [Gallen-Kallela], Erik/Eero Järnefelt, Pekka Halonen), and in music (foremost Jean Sibelius). Thus, the nationalist movement first linked the *Kalevala*, the alleged Finnish Karelian history, and Finnish nature to form a paradigm for the reception of Sibelius' music. His music also became politicised, whether he wanted it to or not. Next, in the early twentieth century Sibelius turned towards a more "European" or German-Austrian tradition, starting to compose symphonies and creating an important violin concerto. During this time, he and the supporters of his music begun to emphasise the "absolute" essence of his oeuvre, although patriotic interpretations were still maintained.

During the 1930s and 1940s, Sibelius was again heavily politicised as he willingly supported the Finnish-German alliance against the Soviet Union and the "comrade-in-arms" (*Waffenbrüderschaft*) policy. After the war, the writing of Theodor W. Adorno challenged the fame of Sibelius

---

[1] Benedict Anderson, *Imagined Communities: Reflections on the Origin and Spread of Nationalism*, rev. ed. (London & New York: Verso, 2006).

and influenced the reception of his music, especially in the German-speaking countries. This resulted in another change in Sibelius' image, trying to emphasise and create a paradigm of the "universality" of his music, although its national bases were not entirely rejected. Towards the end of the twentieth century, Sibelius was discovered by some French, English, American, and even German composers, who held his formal and textural inventions to be exemplary and worth following. Sibelius' ecological and postmodern qualities were also discovered.

However, it is interesting that, now and then, something like a "battle" breaks out, as some influential people or scholars are inclined to declare what is a "wrong" or "proper" image of Sibelius or his music. During this "battle" the question is: who has the "right" or the "power" to determine and define the "relevant" or "politically correct" image of Sibelius? This kind of inquiry or argument is of course possible and most welcome, as Sibelius' music easily evokes different and even controversial interpretations, because these kinds of discussion allow us to focus our thinking in ways that otherwise would not have been considered.

Thinking in the mode of either/or is largely a result of the German dialectic tradition based on "binarisms." Consequently, everything in this world has to be presented as exclusive dichotomies. Richard Taruskin has criticised in a provocative way this kind of philosophy of Carl Dahlhaus,[2] who asked, as reformulated by Taruskin: "Is art history the *history* of art, or is it the history of *art*?" Taruskin continues: "What a senseless distinction!" Other examples of Dahlhaus' dichotomies are:

> Does music mirror the reality surrounding a composer, *OR* does it propose an alternative reality? Does it have common roots with political events and philosophical ideas; *OR* is music written simply because music has always been written and not, or only incidentally, because a composer is seeking to respond with music to the world he lives in?[3]

These questions consist "of a veritable salad of empty binarisms" according to Taruskin."[4]

This kind of extending one's mind to choose between extreme alternatives—instead of saying "both and"—does not represent a Western

---

[2] Carl Dahlhaus, *Grundlagen der Musikgeschichte* (Köln: Musikverlag Hans Gerig, 1977), 36–7.

[3] Richard Taruskin, "Music from The Earliest Notations to the Sixteenth Century," in *The Oxford History of Western Music* vol. 1 (Oxford: Oxford University Press, 2010), xix; reformulated citations from Carl Dahlhaus, *Foundations of Music History*, trans. J. B. Robinson (Cambridge: Cambridge University Press, 1997) 19.

[4] Ibid.

culture of argumentation. An absolute claim says more about the attitude and thinking of its proposer than the object of the statement itself, and leads easily to anachronisms, reflecting modern ideas back into history, as has also occurred with the concept of so-called "absolute music." Jim Samson has written in an elucidating way on this subject, citing Jacques Derrida who has stated that, "contraries, unlike contradictories, do not exhaust the range of possibilities."[5] Fortunately, Dahlhaus' later idea is based on the conviction that the reception history of a musical work becomes an essential part of the work itself.[6] Thus, the production of or creating a work is as important a form of cultural activity as its reproduction or performing, and its reception or deciphering when listening. Consequently, it is reasonable to take into account all the phases of the life of a particular musical work: its reception in the context of its creation; its reception during the historical reception process; and its present reception against the background of what has happened during its long reception history.

In order to clarify the current thinking about Sibelius, I have divided its topics into ten dichotomies or "binarisms" that dominate, although mostly unconsciously, the present discussion. These preliminary dichotomies are as follows (more can be found, of course):

(1) Sibelius as European/Finnish composer
(2) Sibelius as political/apolitical composer
(3) Sibelius as urban/nature-oriented composer
(4) Sibelius as "absolute"/expressive or poetic composer
(5) Sibelius as symphonist/miniature composer
(6) Sibelius as earnest/humoristic composer
(7) Sibelius as non-erotic/amorous composer
(8) Sibelius as Christian/pagan composer
(9) Sibelius as composer without a "method"/with his "own path" or "method found"
(10) Sibelius as conservative/progressive composer

[5] Jim Samson, "Either/Or," in *Rethinking Musical Modernism. Proceedings of the International Conference Held from October 11 to 13, 2007* (Belgrade: Institute of Musicology, 2008), 15–25, the quote is from p. 22. I am indebted to Helena Tyrväinen for informing me about this source.

[6] Carl Dahlhaus, *Die Musik des 19. Jahrhunderts*, Neues Handbuch der Musikwissenschaft, vol. 6, ed. Carl Dahlhaus (Wiesbaden: Akademische Verlagsgesellschaft Athenaion, 1980).

Sibelius the European/Finnish Composer

Most recently, the Finnish conductor Atso Almila stated that "according to investigations there is nothing especially Finnish in the music of Sibelius" because he was "a global fellow," and thus "at the global level a reformer of the symphony" who suffered "from being a national icon."[7]

It is true that by the time of his Fourth Symphony Sibelius wanted to be appreciated as a European symphonist, not just a Finnish national composer. In his academic lecture in 1896 he said that:

> A composer immersed in his home country's folk music must naturally … [and sought] his gratification in art in quite different ways than others. Therein lies to a large extent his originality. In his works he must liberate himself from the local as much as possible—especially as far as the means of expression are concerned. He will succeed in this to the extent that he has a distinguished personality.[8]

We know that Sibelius achieved this: his orchestral works have taken their place in the standard repertoire all over the world. However, there is no conflict between his international status as an "absolute" composer and his Finnish origin and use of Finnish themes, topics, and intonations. He once put in his diary the following confession: "How Finnish I am in in the bottom of my heart/my soul!"[9] Why should this be otherwise? Verdi is an Italian composer, Debussy French, Falla Spanish, Grieg Norwegian, and Mussorgsky Russian: are their national characteristics faults, or have they harmed the reception of their music or prevented its performance abroad? Sibelius himself admired the Sicilian essence of Pietro Mascagni's *Cavalleria rusticana*, the French features of Georges Bizet's *Carmen*, and the Bohemian quality of Bedřich Smetana's *The Bartered Bride*.

There are dozens of examples of the Finnish quality of Sibelius' music, such as the *Kalevala* compositions and the pieces linked to Finnish history and nature. Among those based on the Finnish epic are: *Kullervo*, Op. 7 (1892), *"Karelia"* music, JS 115, Tableau I, *Karelian Home* (1893), *The*

---

[7] *Taideyliopiston Sibelius-Akatemia. Tapahtumakevät 2015*. Concert programme booklet of The University of Arts Helsinki, Sibelius Academy, Spring 2015.

[8] Jean Sibelius, "Some Viewpoints Concerning Folk Music and Its Influence on the Musical Arts," trans. Margareta Martin, in *Jean Sibelius and His World*, ed. Daniel M. Grimley (Princeton, Oxford: Princeton University Press, 2011), 315–25, quote from p. 324.

[9] Fabian Dahlström (ed.), *Jean Sibelius Dagbok 1909–1944* (Helsingfors: Svenka litteratursällskapet in Finland, 2005), 275, diary entry June 25, 1918; in orig. Swedish: "Huru finsk är jag ej in i själen!"

Boat Journey, Op. 18 No. 3 (1893), *Rakastava* ["The Lover"], Op. 14 (1894), *Music for the Press Celebration Days* No. 2, *A Song for Väinämöinen*, Op, 31 No. 1 (1899), *Tiera*, JS 200 (1899), *The Origin of Fire*, Op. 32 (1902), *Kyllikki*, Op. 41 (1904), *Luonnotar*, Op. 70 (1913), and *Väinämöinen's Song*, Op. 110 (1926). In addition to these, Sibelius used motifs, figures, and turns derived from *runo* singing and *kantele* melodies, of which the song *The Dream*, Op. 13 No. 5, *"Karelia"* music, JS 115, Tableau I, *Karelian Home*, *Pohjola's Daughter*, Op. 49, the second theme in B minor of the first movement of the Third Symphony, and *Tapiola*, Op. 112 offer good examples. Finnish and Karelian-Russian folk dances can be found in his music, especially in the Six Impromptus for piano, Op. 5, and in the F major Piano Sonata, Op. 12. Sibelius' method of building his musical language, at least partially, on folk modes found in the singing and playing of Karelian musicians, as well as his ways of harmonising the modes, are innovative.[10] All these features form both part of his unequivocally international compositions and the Finnish substance of his music.

There are numerous works in which Sibelius uses modes found in Karelian music; besides, he used these modes to avoid being erroneously identified with the so-called "church modes" in a different way than was customary in nineteenth-century modality, as Sibelius' "neo-modality"[11] was derived from the folk music where there was not necessarily any *finalis* or tonic. In addition to the Aeolian mode or the "Scandinavian mode" (*Lemminkäinen in Tuonela*, the middle section of which is in A Aeolian mode), the Dorian mode or the "Kalevala mode" is very common in Sibelius' music. The entire Sixth Symphony is based on the Dorian mode, although it is too often understood to be in D minor, which is absolutely false, as there are no V–I cadences either in the D-centred first, third, or fourth movements or in the G-centred second movement. Very important modes are also the Aeolian-Ionian mode or the minor-major mode, found for instance in his *Six Finnish Folk Songs Arranged for Piano*, JS 81,[12] and the Ionian-Aeolian mode or major-minor mode used in

---

[10] See Veijo Murtomäki, "Modal techniques in Sibelius' op. 114," in *Musurgia* XV/1–3 (2008): 71–81.

[11] About "neo-modality" see Juhani Alesaro, *The Apparition from the Forest. A Treatise on* Satz *in the Music of Jean Sibelius*, Studia Musica 66 (Helsinki: University of Arts Helsinki. Sibelius Academy, 2015), 39–40, 52–57, http://ethesis.siba.fi/files/nbnfife2015110516083_copy1.pdf.

[12] Veijo Murtomäki, "The Influence of Karelian *runo* Singing and *kantele* Playing on Sibelius' Music," in *Sibelius in the Old and New World*, eds. Timothy L.

his opera *The Maiden in the Tower*, Scene No. 3 with chorus. Ionian and Mixolydian modes are common besides the major mode or key, the preceding ones deviating from the major keys in their characteristic chord progressions, avoiding the V–I cadences.[13] He invented ways of harmonising the modes without following a mainly functional harmony: the basic harmony was often a ninth-chord, which can be either "consonant" or "dissonant"; parallel seventh-harmonies appear without any need to be resolved, as in the music of Debussy, for instance.

When listening to some new music in Berlin in 1914, Sibelius made the following diary entry: "It is strange how few composers can create something living based on [church] modes. I am closer to them owing to my 'birth and habit by nature' and thus somehow made for them."[14] Of course, he was a cosmopolitan composer, as his Symphonies, the Violin Concerto, and other orchestral works are "European." Knowing some contemporary music, and being influenced by it, also makes him a European. A number of direct influences on Sibelius are relevant here: Mahler on *In memoriam*, Op. 59 (1910); Debussy on *The Dryad*, Op. 45 No. 1 (1910), and *The Oceanides*, Op. 73, especially the Yale version (1914); and Schoenberg on *The Lizard*, Op. 8 (1909), the Fourth Symphony (1911) and *Everyman*, Op. 83 (1916). Even Stravinsky and Prokofiev lurk in Sibelius' *The Tempest*, Op. 109 (1925), and in his *Kullervo*, Op. 7 (1892) Sibelius used "music on white keys." Scriabin's influence can be felt in Sibelius' *Rêverie*, Op. 58 No.1 (1909) and especially in his last piano and violin pieces, Opp. 114–116.

Sibelius was also inspired by the Swiss symbolist painter Arnold Böcklin (1827–1901), an influence which can be seen, for instance, in the recurring "swan theme" in his orchestral works and songs. He composed two songs, Op. 51 Nos 4–5, based on the Austrian expressionist Richard Dehmel's (1863–1920) poems, and wrote incidental music for the dramas of some leading contemporary writers (and one older one): *Pelléas et Mélisande*, Op. 46 (1905) for the play by Maurice Maeterlinck, *Swanwhite*, Op. 54 (1908) for August Strindberg's theatrical piece, the ballet pantomime *Scaramouche*, Op. 71 (1913) for Poul Knudsen's libretto, *Everyman*, Op. 83 (1916) for Hugo von Hofmannsthal's play, and

---

Jackson, Veijo Murtomäki, Colin Davis, and Timo Virtanen (Frankfurt am Main: Peter Lang, 2010), 199–218.

[13] Alesaro, *The Apparition from the Forest*, 122–9.

[14] Dahlström, *Jean Sibelius Dagbok*, 183, diary entry January 26, 1914 in Swedish: "det är förunderligt huru få nutida tonsättare kunna skapa nå'nting lefvande baseradt på kyrkotonarterna. Jag som står dessa närmare på grund af 'födsel och ohindrad vana' är som skapat för dem."

finally *The Tempest*, Op. 109 (1925), to enhance William Shakespeare's masterpiece.

Sibelius the Political/Apolitical Composer

Recently, one Finnish musicologist wrote that:

> in the Finnish writings on music during the early 20th century the ideals of freedom and independence were undoubtedly expressed in both noble and trivial ways. The last ones can be found in those interpretations according to which the culmination towards the end of the Second Symphony is a symbol of forthcoming independence.[15]

Although such patriotic formulations may seem old fashioned and naive when viewed from current aesthetic and listening practices, the world was a different place then and the task of music and other arts was much more important in society than now. Today, composers can choose to be free from becoming socially engaged, and freedom from social engagement was an exception rather than the norm in music history. War has always had a special impact and often provoked reactions from creative artists. Most recently, for instance, Kaija Saariaho's *Adriana Mater* (2004) deals with the Balkan War, and Sir Peter Maxwell Davies has confessed that his Ninth Symphony (2012) is a protest against the invasions of Afghanistan and Iraq. In addition to this, the idea that a contemporary audience would have listened in the "wrong" way to the new music they heard for the first time seems somewhat strange, and anyway such an attitude would be historically anachronistic.

Contemporary critics gave patriotic interpretations of Sibelius' music at the outset of the twentieth century, which the composer accepted, at least indirectly, as he did not deny them. Kajanus, who was also active as a critic, wrote in his review after the premiere of Sibelius' Second Symphony how the second movement seemed to be:

> like the most crushing protest against the injustice that in our time threatens to steal us the sunlight and the scent of the flowers ... the scherzo is a picture of a hasty preparation ... for what is at stake ... and it forms an immediate bridge to the finale ... This allegro moderato begins with a

[15] Matti Huttunen, "Ideasta ideologiaksi: Kansallisen musiikin käsite ja sen kohtalo 1930-luvun Suomessa," manuscript February 23, 2015; when published later in a revised form, after the editorial process this passage was omitted from the article in *Trio* 1 (2015): 25–45, abstract on p. 113, https://www.uniarts.fi/sites/default/files /Trio_1_2015_fin_web.pdf.

> manly resolution and powerfully speaking motif, rounded off by proud and victorious fanfares. At the same time, the principal motif forms the main content of the movement and leads into a triumphal ending, which evokes in the listener's mind imagines of bright and trustful views of the future.[16]

Additionally, the scherzo of the Second Symphony contains a citation from a well-known song of Hungarian origin which was sung, in Sibelius' early years, with Finnish lyrics and by Finnish students. In the song, a pair of melodic phrases appear twice and are sung in this "Song of Oath" (*Valalaulu*) with the words "Thee will we protect/ With our blood preserve … Thy rock will not waver/ it will repel the attacks." This was one of many messages that Sibelius addressed to the nation.

There are dozens of pieces by Sibelius that are closely linked to the Finnish independence fight: *The Maiden in the Tower*, JS 101 (1896); *The Broken Voice*, Op. 18 No. 1 (1898); *Finlandia*, Op. 26 (1899) originally *Finland Awakes*, No. 7 from the *Press Celebrations Music*; *The Breaking of Ice on the Oulu River*, Op. 30 (1899); *Song of the Athenians*, Op. 31 No. 3 (1899); Symphony No. 1, Op. 39 (1899); *To the Fatherland*, JS 98a (1900); *March of the Björneborgers*, JS 152 (1900); *Snöfrid*, Op. 29 (1900); *Hail O Moon!* Op. 18 No. 2 (1901); Symphony No. 2, Op. 43 (1902); Overture in A minor, JS 144 (1902); Impromptu, Op. 19 (1902/10); *The Origin of Fire*, Op. 22 (1902/10); *Have You Courage?* Op. 31 No. 2 (1904/11); *My Brothers Abroad*, JS 217 (1904); *The Captive Queen*, Op. 48 (1906); *Pohjola's Daughter*, Op. 49 (1906); *Night Ride and Sunrise*, Op. 55 (1908); *In memoriam*, Op. 59 (1909/10); *March of the Finnish Jäger Battalion*, Op. 91a (1917); *My Own Land*, Op. 92 (1918); *Skyddskår's March*, JS 173 (1925); and *Patriotic March/Karelia's Fate*, JS 108 (1930).[17]

Of course, when Finland had censorship imposed by Russian officials, all messages to the nation to awaken the resistance of the Finnish people had to be concealed. Sibelius carried out these hidden political messages in pieces mostly with an allegorical content and refined allusions: the themes included issues like captivity, slavery, hunger, mist, coldness, frost, ice, winter, storms, darkness, and night either in the titles of the compositions or in the texts of the vocal works. The positive expectations of the nation

---

[16] Robert Kajanus, "Jean Sibelius' andra sinfonia," *Hufvudstadsbladet*, March 13, 1902.

[17] See Veijo Murtomäki, "Sibelius: Composer and Patriot," in *Sibelius Forum II. Proceedings from the Third International Sibelius Conference Helsinki December 7–10, 2000*, eds. Matti Huttunen, Kari Kilpeläinen and Veijo Murtomäki (Helsinki: Sibelius Academy, Department of Composition and Music Theory, 2003), 328–37.

were expressed by the longing for and return of the spring, the breaking of ice, sunrise, the origin of fire, and the dawn.

Sibelius also made statements and diary entries in which he acknowledged his important role for Finland. For instance:

> If I could give up composing and if I were rich, I would choose to be a patriot, among the leaders of our own army.[18]

> Will do anything for our country.[19]

> Maybe my life and that of Gallén have been devoted to our native country.[20]

> I envy their battle [= of the German comrades-in-arms] for freedom, and I would like also to fight, if I were not too old.[21]

Sibelius sometimes regretted not having composed more patriotic works.[22] He often cooperated with the Finnish Ministry of Foreign Affairs. For instance, we know that, "Sibelius was ready to do PR work for his homeland when war was at the door."[23] The most important of his international statements for Finland comes from 1941, when newspapers in the United States published the following text:

> In 1939 my fatherland was attacked by the Bolsheviks. Enlightened American people then realized we were fighting not only for our freedom but also for all the Western civilization and they gave us valuable assistance. Now that the barbaric hordes of the East are again attacking us in their attempt to Bolshevize Europe, I am convinced that freedom-loving, intelligent American people will rightly understand and appreciate the

---

[18] Dahlström, *Jean Sibelius Dagbok*, 272; diary entry May 13, 1918.

[19] Sibelius' telegram, October 19, 1919, to Sigurd Wettenhovi-Aspa to support Finland's (rather than Sweden's) right to own the Åland islands; see Erik Tawaststjerna, *Sibelius Volume III: 1914–1957*, trans. Robert Layton (London: Faber and Faber, 1997), 173; in Swedish: "Redo till allt för fosterlandet," in *Jean Sibelius. Åren 1920–1957*, ed. Erik Tawaststjerna (Keuru: Söderström & C:O Förlags AB, 1997), 24.

[20] Dahlström, *Jean Sibelius Dagbok*, 326; diary entry September 10, 1926.

[21] Sibelius' statement to composer Einar Englund as given in the latter's memoires *I skuggan av Sibelius. Fragment ur en tonsättares liv* (Jyväskylä: Söderström & C:o Förlags Ab, 1996), 51.

[22] Sibelius' statement to his son-in-law, see Jussi Jalas, *Elämäni teemat* (Helsinki: Tammi, 1981), 70.

[23] Interview with Sibelius in autumn 1939, see Vesa Sirén, *Aina poltti sikaria. Jean Sibelius aikalaisten silmin* (Helsinki: Otava, 2000), 521.

present situation, realizing that the Bolshevization of Europe would annihilate freedom and civilization in this continent.[24]

During the war, Sibelius gave several interviews to the German press in which he supported the "comrades-in-arms" policy, saying, for instance:

> I am happy to live at precisely the time that will bring justice to the world, especially as I know so well Germany and the Germans. I wish you from the bottom of my heart a prompt victory. I do not doubt that you will accomplish it!

After the war, on February 9, 1945 Sibelius did at first prevent some Communists, including the composer Dmitri Kabalevsky, from coming to Ainola for a visit! It was only after some obvious pressure from the Ministry of Foreign Affairs that he had to open his door to the Soviet visitors, who finally arrived on February 15, 1945.[25] However, a little later he said willingly, after listening to broadcasts of Soviet music, of which he especially appreciated the Seventh Symphony of Shostakovich: "There is a great deal of fertility coming from Russia."[26]

Sibelius the Urban/Nature-oriented Composer

According to the Finnish-German musicologist Tomi Mäkelä, "the nature associations make the core/essence of the composer almost incomprehensible," and "his interest in the migratory birds has been exaggerated."[27] It is easy to understand the reason for this kind of a reaction: earlier, in the reception of his music in the United Kingdom, North America, and especially Nazi Germany, Sibelius was regarded as a composer of a thousand lakes and forests of Finland, and consequently references to nature were regularly found in his music. Theodor W. Adorno was highly allergic to this kind of reception of music. Of course, it is often all too easy to understand Sibelius' works in terms of nature—and it is thus as easy to misunderstand the specific content of some piece(s). To some extent, we have to rid ourselves of the notion of the omnipotence of nature in his music. And of course, there are many central pieces in his

---

[24] Jean Sibelius, "Sibelius Appeals to U. S. To Understand Finn Case," *New York Times*, July 13, 1941.

[25] Sirén, *Aina poltti sikaria*, 584.

[26] Santeri Levas, *Jean Sibelius: A Personal Portrait* 2nd ed., trans. Percy M Young (London: J.M. Dent & Sons, 1972), 78.

[27] Tomi Mäkelä, *"Poesie in der Luft." Jean Sibelius. Studien zu Leben und Werk* (Wiesbaden etc.: Breitkopf & Härtel, 2007), 71, 105.

output that don't have any relationship with nature: e.g. the Seventh Symphony, most of his incidental music, and numerous piano and violin pieces. Sibelius spent a good part of his life in the metropolises of Europe and travelled abroad some 41 times, composing as easily during his travels as when he was at Ainola. He composed the Second Symphony and *Tapiola* in Italy, started composing *Kullervo* in Vienna, *Voces intimae* was finished in London, the principal ideas for the Third Symphony were born in Paris, and the first sketches for the *Night Ride and Sunrise* were written when he was looking at the Colosseum in Rome at night.

However, although it is not scientific proof, all the living members of the Sibelius family say that it is not possible to overestimate the role of nature in Sibelius' life and his composing.[28] After all, he was living in the countryside from 1904. Walking daily and observing birds and other phenomena around him were stimulating creative impulses, as the following diary entries show:

> A wonderful day. Walked around and enjoyed the voices of the flying cranes—these sounds that are the most kindred spirits of my soul.[29]

> Saw today before eleven o'clock 16 swans. One of the greatest impressions in my life! O God this beauty! The voice is about the same type as that of the cranes, but without tremolo. The singing/voice of the swans comes closer to trumpet, although the sound of the sarrusophone is apparent. Having a low refrain that resembles a small baby's cry. Nature mysticism and life's suffering! The Finale theme of the V Symphony, tromba, legato in trumpets!! Good Lord! Nature mysticism + romanticism and God knows what.[30]

> The swans are always in my thoughts and give splendour to life. Nothing in this world, in the arts, in literature, nor in music can have such an effect on me like these swans + cranes + bean geese. Their voices and appearance.[31]

Still later, probably in the 1940s or 1950s, he confessed to his private secretary Santeri Levas that he was "crazy about the swans"[32] and that he

---

[28] For instance, the granddaughters of Sibelius, the violinist Satu Jalas and the oboist Aino Porra, made this kind of statement in their public presentations in 2015.

[29] Dahlström, *Jean Sibelius Dagbok*, 97; diary entry October 8, 1911.

[30] Ibid., 225; diary entry April 21, 1915 includes a sketch for "the Swan theme," the Finale of the Fifth Symphony.

[31] Ibid., 226; diary entry April 24, 1915.

[32] Santeri Levas, *Järvenpään mestari* (Porvoo–Helsinki: WSOY, 1986), 340–1.

described "the call of the crane as the *Leitmotiv* of my life ... Nobody has any idea what the flight of the migrant birds in the spring and autumn means to me."[33] In addition to the swans, cranes, and bean geese, Sibelius mentions other birds in his diary: nightingales, cuckoos, skylarks, starlings, eagles, wild ducks, thrushes, and kestrels.[34]

Whom should we believe more: a musicologist or the composer himself? The famous conductor Eliahu Inbal of the Frankfurt Radio Symphony Orchestra (1974–90) said in an interview that:

> Sibelius' works are ecological music: man is in harmony with nature, forests and lakes. It is music of dreams and hope. It addresses young people, who seek solutions to the problems of the world and a new sense of community.[35]

It is easy to agree with this point of view. What could be wrong in this, except in the opinion of Adorno and many of his followers, who always linked nature in music with primitivism—and even Nazism?

Sibelius the "Absolute"/*Ausdruck* Composer

Sibelius' late statements seem to give support to the "absolute" essence of his symphonies. "Sibelius always particularly wished to emphasize that all his seven symphonies were pure, absolute music, and exclusively fashioned from his own musical ideas. They had no programme element at all."[36] However, in 1894, in the midst of his Wagner phase and crisis, he said, obviously paraphrasing Wagner's *Musik und Drama* (1850), "I believe that music alone, that is to say absolute music, is in itself not enough ... Music is like a woman, it is only through man that she can give birth and that man is poetry."[37] "Also: really I am a tone painter and poet."[38]

---

[33] Levas, *Jean Sibelius*, 49–50.

[34] I am indebted to Timo Virtanen for giving me his unpublished manuscript "Sibelius ja linnut."

[35] Hannu-Ilari Lampila, "'Sibelius on ekologinen säveltäjä.' Kapellimestari Eliahu Inbal uskoo Sibeliuksen puhuttelevan nuorta yleisöä," *Helsingin Sanomat*, October 20, 1994.

[36] Levas, *Jean Sibelius*, 84.

[37] Sibelius' letter to the poet and librettist J. H. Erkko, July 8, 1893, see Erik Tawaststjerna, *Sibelius Volume I 1865–1905*, trans. Robert Layton (London: Faber and Faber, 1976), 141.

[38] Ibid., 158; letter to Aino Sibelius, August 19, 1894.

Of course, the thinking of an artist can undergo remarkable changes over time. However, there is not necessary any conflict in either the young or the old Sibelius' ideas about the essence of his music in general and symphonies especially, although the last statement sounds a little strange from a composer who had written many pieces based on the *Kalevala* and semi-programmatic symphonic poems. He was probably referring to his symphonies after *Kullervo* and the *Lemminkäinen* Legends.

When composing his Fourth Symphony, Sibelius said: "A 'symphony' is not just a composition in the ordinary sense of the word; it is more of an inner confession at a given stage of one's life."[39] Thus, the symphonies contain expressions of his thoughts, experiences and feelings of life connected to music. Although it is true that the symphonies don't have any literary sources behind them, neither do they exclude his personal thoughts about life. Therefore, when listening to his symphonies, we—at least some of us—cannot escape the external images or associations that are embedded in the music. We know that the Third Symphony was built upon the foundations of the unfinished "Marjatta" oratorio, about the life, funeral, and resurrection of Christ, based on the last Canto of the *Kalevala*. There are chorales in the two first movements, sacral characteristics appear now and then, and the finale is based on the gradual crystallisation of a theme called "Bönen till Gud" ("Prayer to God") by the composer.[40]

According to the composer, in the background of the Fourth Symphony lurks the Koli mountain: "*At Koli*! One of the greatest impressions in my life. Plans for 'La montagne'!"[41] In the first and third movements we can find traces of Wagner's *Parsifal*: the *Abendmahl* and *Wunde* motifs, and the finale has swallowed Sibelius' sketches for an orchestral song on Edgar Allan Poe's *The Raven*, to mention just some of its most distinctive associative features.

The swan associations of the Fifth Symphony are common knowledge.[42] Less well known is the fact that the slow movement was based on early thoughts on Viktor Rydberg's poem "The Song of the Goths."[43] The influences of both Renaissance music and the Finnish essence of the Sixth Symphony with its Dorian basis have been discussed

---

[39] Dahlström, *Jean Sibelius Dagbok*, 59; diary entry November 5, 1910.

[40] Timo Virtanen, *Jean Sibelius, Symphony No. 3. Manuscript Study and Analysis*, Studia musica 26 (Helsinki: Sibelius Academy, 2005), 125–40.

[41] Dahlström, *Jean Sibelius Dagbok*, 36; diary entry October 3, 1909.

[42] See footnote 30.

[43] Tawaststjerna, *Sibelius Volume I 1865–1905*, 5.

by many writers.[44] The Seventh Symphony can be seen as a "Symphony of Life" with its slow "birth," the long "Palestrina" section, the sacral or ancient trombone theme, the "Hellenic Rondo," and the *Valse triste* citation in the end. Thus, in the same way as, for example, the symphonies of Brahms (with "Clara" motifs, FAF, AEF motifs, and Wagner associations), those by Sibelius can be read and understood as being at the same time both "absolute" and "poetic" expressions, as there are plenty of links, beyond the so-called "pure" or "absolute" music, with real life. After all, the idea of "absolute music" is very problematic when adopted as an interpretative model for the work of most composers, and it is itself a historical product of a certain situation: a result of the German idealistic philosophy and hegemony.

Sibelius the Symphonist/Miniaturist

The status of Sibelius as one of the most significant symphonists of the twentieth century has generally been accepted. His Violin Concerto in D minor is one of the most recorded violin concertos of the century. However, there is no shortage of writers on music according to whom Sibelius' greatness must be seriously challenged because he wrote so many, even too many, smaller pieces that are just "salon music" or otherwise trivial and without any real value, only "bread and butter" pieces, as he himself used to call them. For instance, Guy Rickards describes Sibelius as, "an abstract symphonist of imposing classical severity yet the perpetrator of light music pot-boilers of embarrassing vacuity," with the apparent result that, "an embarrassing emptiness of a large section of his output is often held to have diluted the value of the whole of it."[45] Elsewhere, I have tried to investigate this aspect of aesthetic

---

[44] Simon Parmet, *The Symphonies of Sibelius: A Study in Musical Appreciation*, trans. Kingsley A. Hart (Cassel: London, 1959), 92–4; Lionel Pike, "Sibelius' Debt to Renaissance Polyphony," *Music & Letters* 55 (1974): 317–26; John Amis, "Sibelius via Legge," *Gramophone* 77 (794) (July 1989): 152; Veijo Murtomäki, "Symphonic Unity: The Development of Formal Thinking in the Symphonies of Sibelius," trans. Henry Bacon, *Studia musicologica universitatis helsingiensis* 5 (Helsinki: University of Helsinki, Department of Musicology, 1993), 193–241; Tim Howell, "Restricting the Flow: Elements of Timescale in Sibelius' Sixth Symphony," *Dutch Journal of Music Theory* 5 (2) (2000): 89–100; James Hepokoski, "Rotations, Sketches, and the Sixth Symphony," in *Sibelius Studies*, eds. Timothy L. Jackson and Veijo Murtomäki (Cambridge: Cambridge University Press, 2010), 322–51.

[45] Guy Rickards, *Jean Sibelius* (London: Phaidon, 1997), 12, 204.

misevaluation of small-scale music.[46] The underestimation of miniatures is difficult to understand, and is the result of the nineteenth-century German aesthetics and its particular reverence for large-scale forms. However, in the oeuvre of most nineteenth-century composers, miniatures have an important role, and Sibelius said: "One must be able to combine large and small. This means symphonies and songs … See things on a grand scale. Style in everything."[47]

Of course we can ask whether a pine is "better" than a rose, or a tiger "better" than a mouse, but these are unnecessary questions as "Auch kleine Dinge können uns entzücken."[48] I think that most of us wouldn't like to be without the impromptus of Schubert, intermezzi of Brahms, or lyric pieces of Grieg. The same is true also with Sibelius: in his total output, the major part of which consists of smaller pieces, there are examples which, by their very existence, make our life more comfortable: *Caprice*, Op. 24 No. 3; *Valse*, Op. 24 No. 5; *Romance* in D flat major, Op. 24 No. 9; *Polonaise*, Op. 40 No. 9; *The Spruce*, Op. 75 No. 5; *Étude*, Op.76/2 for piano; *Romance* in F major, Op. 78/2; *Mazurka*, Op. 81/1, and *Rondino*, Op. 81/2 for violin and piano. In addition to these favourite pieces, there are others that contain lasting challenges for performers, listeners, and scholars as well. Just take his last Opuses 114 to 116, or Op. 58 for piano: they also give us intelligent pleasures.

Sibelius the Earnest/Humoristic Composer

The image of Sibelius as an earnest composer "who never smiled" is connected with the busts and statues, foremost those by the Finnish sculptor Wäinö Aaltonen in the late 1930s, or photographs taken especially by Yousuf Karsh in 1949 of the elderly man from his later years at Ainola. According to the Finnish composer Einojuhani Rautavaara, who on Sibelius' recommendation won the Koussevitzky Prize in 1955 to study in the United States, in his old age, "Sibelius was afraid, subconsciously even horrified of becoming fossilized into a monument, which had already happened … this man was not even a living being anymore."[49] We know

---

[46] Veijo Murtomäki, "Sibelius and the Miniature," in *The Cambridge Companion to Sibelius*, ed. Daniel M. Grimley (Cambridge: Cambridge University Press, 2004), 137–53, 253–4.

[47] Dahlström, *Jean Sibelius Dagbok*, 44; diary entry May 16, 1910.

[48] "Also small things can attract us," poem by the German writer Paul Heyse (1830–1914).

[49] Einojuhani Rautavaara, *Omakuva* (Porvoo–Helsinki–Juva: WSOY, 1998), 117–18.

that Sibelius normally stiffened before the photographers, which is, after all, not exactly uncommon. At that time, taking a photo was not yet like a Hollywood shoot, in which people not only smile but even laugh. The moment of taking a picture was a serious business as you had to adopt a particular pose, though we have some pictures where Sibelius is either very humorous or even laughing. There are many accounts of Sibelius, in small social groups, being an amazing storyteller and generating humorous reactions in others.[50]

Certainly, Sibelius, as a symphonist, was a great aesthete and humanist in the spirit of ancient Greece and Rome. But this cannot characterise all his output. For instance, he wrote some 18 Humoresques, six of them being the important Humoresques for violin and orchestra. Humorous moments can be found also in his piano pieces, choral music, and the incidental music for *The Tempest.* Of course, the humorous quality of music has rarely been the criterion to define the greatness of a composer: just think of the music of Liszt, Bruckner, or Wagner (*The Mastersingers* perhaps being the exception).

Levas cites some really interesting anecdotes about Sibelius as host; this is one of them:

> I was in Ainola with a young Brazilian journalist (whose field was culture) who had come to interview Sibelius. In the course of the conversation the journalist told how a single tribe of man-eaters still lived in a primeval forest in Brazil. The government allowed them to live in peace, although all missionaries were eaten up by the cannibals …
>
> Sibelius had been listening attentively, and suddenly his face took on a roguish expression. He laughed and said: "I have had need of man-eaters in recent times. The romance of the last century more and more disappears. Much was lost when the Turkish harems were closed, and the cannibals certainly belong to the good old days."
>
> Later Sibelius still added in the best of moods: "How splendid that there are still cannibals."[51]

[50] See, for instance, Olof Mustelin, *Euterpe. Tidskriften och kretsen kring den. En kulturhistorisk* skildring (Helsingfors: Svenska Litteratursällskapet i Finland, 1963), 113: "It was a joy without comparison to see him in a cheerful mood and to listen to his freely running conversation, full of his ingenious thoughts. His is an admirable, charming, considerate and understanding personality."

[51] Levas, *Jean Sibelius*, 34–5.

Sibelius the Non-erotic/Amorous Composer

In the 1920s and 1930s Sibelius' fame, both in Britain and North America, was based not only on the music itself but also to a large extent on his image as "a striking and characteristic example of a man from the North—a Viking type" with "ice-blue eyes,"[52] and thus "a hero" who was "clean" and whose "music was of intense masculinity, from which the erotic element … is entirely absent."[53] As Byron Adams puts it:

> For these critics [i.e. Rosa Newmarch, Cecil Gray, Ernest Newman, Constant Lambert, David Cherniavsky, and Donald Francis Tovey], the influence of the Finnish composer's masculine "rootedness" offered a way of purging from English music the lingering perfume of post-Wagnerian decadence.[54]

Sibelius' music was thought to be able to purify and integrate those young men in Britain who had pacifist, socialist, and homosexual inclinations, instead of being faithful and military-minded soldiers of the Empire. Later, this alleged aspect of Sibelius and his music was adopted by the Nazi government. Instead of apparent sensual or erotic characteristics, it is possible to find austere and ascetic features in his music which would strengthen the military capacity of the German army. According to Petra Garberding, Nordic music was of such remarkable importance for the Germans because it was thought to be a source to purify the Germanic race, and it is due to this attribute that the music of Nordic composers (including Sibelius) was regularly exploited for the purposes of Nazi propaganda.[55]

However, the possible erotic or non-erotic content of Sibelius' music depends on the genre and the age of the composer. A symphony, for instance, has not very often been evaluated on the basis of its possible erotic dimensions. And Sibelius' sensual or erotic music can be mostly found in his works from the 1890s: *Balettscen*, *Kullervo and His Sister*, *Lemminkäinen and the Maidens of the Island*, *The Wood Nymph*, and the

---

[52] Rosa Newmarch, *Jean Sibelius. A Short Story of a Long Friendship* (Boston MA: C.C. Birchard Co., 1939), 16.
[53] Glenda Dawn Goss, *Jean Sibelius and Olin Downes: Music, Friendship, Criticism* (Boston: Northeastern University Press, 1995), 26–7.
[54] Byron Adams, "'Thors Hammer:' Sibelius and British Music Critics, 1905–1957," in *Jean Sibelius and His World*, ed. Daniel M. Grimley (Princeton and Oxford: Princeton University Press, 2011), 135.
[55] Petra Garberding, *Musik och politik i skuggan av nazismen. Kurt Atterberg och svensk-tyska musikrelationerna* (Lund: Sekel Bokförlag, 2007), 37 and 58.

opera *The Maiden in the Tower*, as in all of these pieces extremely dramatic culminations hinting at sexual climaxes can be found. In the half-fictitious novel *A Book About a Man* (*En bok om en människa*, 1891) by Adolf Paul, the "ingenious child Sillén" (i.e. Sibelius) is described as having been "the best skirt hunter of us" who "read a woman like a lascivious book." Later still, in the ballet *Scaramouche* (1914), there's an impressive scene where Scaramouche seduces the main female protagonist Blondelaine, wife of the innocent Leilon. So: both and.

Sibelius the Christian/Pagan Composer

Many Finnish writers, some decades ago, wanted to see Sibelius as a Christian or even Lutheran composer. Amongst the evidence, proof might be found in the chorale "We Praise Thee, Our Creator" from the *Cantata for the University Graduation Ceremonies of 1897*, Op. 23 No. 6a, and several chorale-like melodies in his early chamber music as well as in *Finlandia*, the Third and Fourth Symphonies with their hymn-like passages, the incidental music to Hofmannsthal's *Everyman*, etc. His organ piece *Intrada*, Op. 111a (1925), *Three Introductory Antiphons* (1925), and the popular *Andante festivo*, JS 34b, although originally composed for the celebrations of the Säynätsalo factory in 1922 (as JS 34a), can easily been understood either as church or otherwise solemn music. Interestingly, Sibelius' *Masonic Ritual Music*, Op. 113, with its obvious spirituality, was later called (or renamed) "Musique religieuse" (1926–7). Indeed, chorale or hymn-like characteristics penetrate much of Sibelius' music.

Supporters of the Aryan "Nordic Thought" (*Nordische Gedanke*) saw in Sibelius a composer representing a pagan or non-Christian culture because of works like *Kullervo*, *En saga*, and the *Lemminkäinen* Legends, which could be seen to depict ancient soldier heroes and their merciless attitude towards their enemies, "kein Mitleid wissend."[56] These kinds of writing are typical of many German authors, but also, and interestingly, of some Americans. For instance:

> No one but a Norseman could have written this work [*Tapiola*]. We were all enthralled by the dark pine forests and the shadowy gods and wood-

[56] See Lucien Price, "Portrait of Sibelius at Järvenpää," in *We Northmen* (Boston: Little, Brown, and Company, 1936), 354–66.

> nymphs who dwell therein. The coda with its icy wind sweeping through the forest made us shiver.[57]

> His music harks back to the Eddas, the sagas and the runes. It is a conversation of Odin and Thor in our time. The music maker of the northern spirit, Sibelius gives us a glimpse of what might have been had the upsweep of Mediterranean culture been turned back, and Vikings and Norsemen been allowed to go their own way and express their own thoughts in music.[58]

Paraphrasing the American journalist and writer Lucien Price (1883–1964), who himself promoted the non-Christian ideology, in 1944 the Finnish-American publicist and translator Paul Sjöblom wrote an article based on Price's thoughts, presented in the *Yale Quarterly Review* "some years ago" for the Finnish magazine *Suomen Kuvalehti*, in which Sjöblom says:

> The spiritual heritage of the Jews, which the Bible has spread around itself, has penetrated the Western culture and all its art forms. Beethoven and other German masters did not succeed in liberating themselves from its influence. The veneration of the Christian church is sounding everywhere in their works. In Germany a pure man of the North cannot be found. Not until in the symphonies of Sibelius the world hears for the first time the voice of Nordic man's spirit, liberated from the oriental mysticism. Only now for the first time the world can have what the Nordic art can develop freed from the directing influence of the Semitist-Christianity ... Mr. Price emphasizes the greatness of the *Kalevala*'s influence—as totally pagan and Nordic and totally released from the oriental contamination—on the art of Sibelius.[59]

The truth lies again somewhere in between.

---

[57] Letter of the conductor Walter Damrosch to Sibelius, January 3, 1927. Finnish National Archive's Sibelius Family Collection, box 19.

[58] Carleton Smith, "Sibelius: Close-Up of a Genius," in *The American Mercury*, LII (206) (1941): 144–50; the quotation is from page 147.

[59] Paul Sjöblom, "Sibelius—Pohjolan profeetta," in *Suomen Kuvalehti* 50 (1944): 1456–7.

Sibelius the Composer without a "Method"/ with his Own "Path More and More Found" or with Method Embedded in the Music

It has been claimed that, because Sibelius did not write any treatises or textbooks on composition, he did not have any "method." Instead, he composed instinctively, from personal fantasy, which implies that he was not at all a rational person or composer. However, if the existence or non-existence of a composer's compositional method is the ultimate criterion of its quality—or consequently a proof of his intellectuality or naivety— it is easy to see that we would have to exclude many masters from the canon or repertoire of Western music. Not all important composers wrote about their techniques or methods or musical aesthetics; those who did so mostly wanted to promote or propagate their new inventions, i.e. Berlioz, Liszt, Wagner, Strauss, Schoenberg, Debussy and Messiaen. Brahms, Bruckner, Tchaikovsky, and Mahler, on the other hand, did not write theoretical texts to any great extent. With regard to his writing about musical ideas, Sibelius later confessed to his lifelong friend Georg Boldemann:

> When I started my career, I made a clear decision to be productive only in my music. I have always—as you know—kept to this decision. Even when the big world-wide newspapers (for instance the *Times* and *New York Times*, to mention the biggest ones) have asked me to publish my opinions on musical matters ... I have thus absolutely rejected all attempts to publish my private thoughts in any newspaper.[60]

Then there's one very important possibility that has hardly ever been taken seriously: the "method" can be embedded and thus discovered in the music of a great composer. It is true, though, that Sibelius often doubted his own "method" and tried to find a proper way to work:

> How far away I am from the rational way of working, which gives life and joy to an artist and those around him.[61]

> You, wonderful Ego, comfort yourself with the thought that you work in "your" way. But the result would be ten times greater if the working method would be more rational.[62]

---

[60] Sibelius' letter to Georg Boldemann, October 20, 1943, in Tawaststjerna, *Sibelius Volume I*, 338.

[61] Dahlström, *Jean Sibelius Dagbok*, 37; diary entry October 23, 1909.

[62] Ibid., 59, November 6, 1910.

> Worked in my own way. I am worried about my capacity to come with something really important. I even doubt my way of working—this "plein air" manner—so far removed from the working method of the Germans! As far as I can see, they have made science of the *art* of composition.[63]

> If only I could work!! But my way to work, based on inspiration, is not something close to the "bourgeois" art.[64]

However, when struggling with his compositional thinking and principles he was slowly finding himself, although the doubts and hopes kept alternating for a long time:

> I have great plans. I think that you will recognize that my art by and by will give an impression of being both convincing and "joyful" as far as technique is concerned. For I have suffered and learned a lot.[65]

> I have seen and heard much. I have been able to learn from all this—things that weren't clear to me before are so now. My personal meetings with Debussy and d'Indy, Bantock, Barth and Dale and other composers, together with many new works, among them Elgar's new symphony—also Bantock's *Omar Khayyam*, Debussy's new songs and the orchestral suite "Nocturnes" etc., *have all confirmed my thoughts about the path I have taken, take and have to take!*[66] (emphasis added)

> Bright hopeful thoughts! Worked in my own way. I believe that with the quartet [Op. 56 (1909)] I've gained my master's certificate. Set the course for the open sea. You've achieved "something"![67]

> I have not developed in the style of the German critics. However, my own conviction is still of some value! They have no idea of the wholeness and the calm mastery that my compositions breathe.[68]

> My new composition is wonderful. You know, my darling, it is as if I find more and more of myself. The Fourth Symphony was the beginning. But in

---

[63] Ibid., 84, July 18, 1911.
[64] Ibid., 197, September 19, 1914.
[65] Letter to Axel Carpelan, November 12, 1908. Fabian Dahlström, *Högtärade Maestro! Högtärade Herr Baron! Korrespondensen mellan Axel Carpelan och Jean Sibelius 1900–1919* (Helsingfors: Svenska litteratursällskapet i Finland, 2010), 228.
[66] Letter to Axel Carpelan, March 27, 1909; ibid., 234.
[67] Dahlström, *Jean Sibelius Dagbok*, 43; diary entry April 27, 1910.
[68] Ibid., 87; diary entry August 21, 1911.

this [*The Oceanides*], there is everything even more.[69]

Actually it is easy for me to compose nowadays.[70]

I think I have found a little light regarding work—that's to say, working methods.[71]

I see deeply nowadays what concerns my genius and skills.[72]

And actually, in following the artistic credo of his academic trial lecture in 1896, Sibelius was able to integrate so-called "Western" music, the expanded harmonic tonality from Liszt to Debussy, Scriabin, and early Schoenberg, with his own findings based on the Finnish-Karelian modality and its inherent possibilities.

Sibelius the Conservative/Progressive

If only *Tonhöhenstruktur* [pitch structure] is regarded as the most important dimension of music and its "progression," then the line from Wagner to Schoenberg to Boulez is the only possible direction of "evolution." And then it is easy to see that Sibelius—among other contemporaries like Edward Elgar, Richard Strauss, Hans Pfitzner, Christian Sinding, Serge Rachmaninov, and Hugo Alfvén—belongs to the same group of many "conservative" late- or post-romantic composers, at least in some works such as his early miniatures and songs. Sibelius never abandoned harmonic tonality, although he developed new ways of composing and expanding traditional tonality with his own "neo-modal" musical language. However, a "progressivity" or lack of it at some certain moment of history can always be later reconsidered, and after some generations an absolute up-to-date "modernism" loses its significance, as, in the final analysis, it is only the quality of the music that matters. Composers like J. S. Bach and Brahms were in a way "out of their period," but their appreciation grew in time—and then nobody asks if some piece of music by Bach was written in 1700, 1725, or 1750, or one by Brahms in 1850, 1870, or 1890.

---

69 Letter to Aino Sibelius, May 30, 1914, see SuviSirkku Talas, *Syysilta. Aino ja Jean Sibeliuksen kirjeenvaihtoa 1905–1931* (Helsinki: Suomalaisen Kirjallisuuden Seura, 2007), 266.

70 Dahlström, *Jean Sibelius Dagbok*, 234; diary entry July 11, 1915.

71 Ibid., 245; diary entry February 18, 1916.

72 Ibid., 279; diary entry October 2, 1918.

Sibelius was a "progressive" composer in the 1890s: he used inversions of ninth chords in the first version of *En saga* (1892) several years before Schoenberg's scandalous *Verklärte Nacht* (1899).[73] Additionally, the *Lemminkäinen* Legends contain a highly-chromatic, post-Wagnerian musical language. Again, in the 1910s Sibelius' Fourth Symphony was up-to-date and extremely "progressive," described and also rejected as "cubistic," "futurist," and "ultramodern" in New York in 1913,[74] and the Fifth Symphony was called "cacophonic" and again "futurist" in Stockholm in 1920.[75] Sibelius' own "progressive" path was based on the idea of combining folk music modes and their harmonisation with functional harmony, thus creating a language in which either the harmonic tonality or Sibelius' own neo-modality can govern a piece. In the final analysis, the degree of "conservatism" or "progressiveness" disappears or ceases to be a criterion, because musical life decides what is a vital force in the community and what is not.

Sibelius' handling of temporality, form, and orchestral textures has been admired by contemporary composers in different countries, which reveals much about a new level of appreciation of Jean Sibelius. Among those composers that can be mentioned, in Finland are Einojuhani Rautavaara, Magnus Lindberg, and Kaija Saariaho; in England Sir Peter Maxwell Davies, the brothers Colin and David Matthews, and Julian Anderson; in France Gérard Grisey, Tristan Murail, Pascal Dusapin, and Eric Tanguy; in Germany Wolfgang Rihm; in the United States Steve Reich and John Adams; and in Scandinavia many names from Per Nørgård to Anders Hillborg and Sunleif Rasmussen.

---

[73] Veijo Murtomäki, "Sibelius' Symphonic Ballad Skogsrået: Biographical and Programmatic Aspects of his Early Orchestral Music," in *Sibelius Studies*, edited by Timothy L. Jackson and Veijo Murtomäki (Cambridge: Cambridge University Press, 2001), 95–138; see especially 128–9, and the Ex. 6.11. on *En saga* (1892).

[74] Nicolas Slonimsky, *Lexicon of Musical Invective. Critical Assaults on Composers Since Beethoven's Time*, 2nd ed. (Seattle and London: University of Washington Press, 1984), 178–9.

[75] Tawaststjerna, *Sibelius Volume I*, 194.

I

History and Reception

1. Case Studies

SIBELIUS' "LOULOU ANDANTINO"— A SOUVENIR COMPOSITION WITH A MYSTERY

ANNA PULKKIS

The Young Composer at the Spa

> I have not played much, but composed all the more, among other things songs and waltzes for young ladies, as souvenirs. They have rewarded me with sweet smiles and compliments, laurel wreaths and flowers.[1]

Jean Sibelius wrote these words to his uncle Pehr Sibelius from Lovisa on July 6, 1889. During that summer, Sibelius stayed for several weeks in the coastal town east of Helsinki, where the family still owned Sibelius' father's old home.

Wattenkuranstalten i Lovisa, the local spa which had begun operating in 1866, was the centre of the small town's social and musical events. The bourgeoisie gathered there to enjoy health treatments and the pleasures of social life. Among the guests were the 23-year-old Jean, or Janne. He had recently graduated from the Helsinki Music Institute with outstanding grades in composition and violin playing. His chamber music compositions, performed at the Music Institute's concerts, were already being acknowledged by the press in Helsinki. In the autumn he was going to continue his studies in Berlin. The handsome and eccentric young composer attracted the attention of many young ladies.[2]

The Sibelius brothers, Jean and Christian, played music in soirées and matinées. Their repertoire included a number of new works by Jean. In a letter to his friend Axel von Bonsdorff on August 22, Christian recorded

---

[1] "Spelat har jag inte mycket, men destomera komponerat, bland annat visor och valser åt unga damer, som souvernir [*sic*]. De hafva belönat mig med ljufva småleenden och tacksägelser[,] lagerkransar och blommor." Jean Sibelius' letter to Pehr Sibelius, dated July 6, 1889 in Lovisa (the City Archives of Hämeenlinna); see Glenda Dawn Goss, *Jean Sibelius. The Hämeenlinna letters. Scenes from a Musical Life 1874–1895* (Esbo: Schildts, 1997), 106, 181.

[2] A contemporary description of the social life at the spa and Jean Sibelius' role in it can be found in Alma Söderhjelm, *Min värld* I (Stockholm: Bonnier, 1929), 377–84.

that he had sailed, swum, paddled, danced, sung, played, read, and taken part in "spa life." He then described his brother's new compositions:

> During this summer, Janne has composed a sonata for piano and violin, a great fantasy for cello, and a number of smaller pieces (waltzes etc.). I have played that fantasy at the spa twice ... When we had played it, the audience truly went wild. Another composition by Janne that I have played at the spa is a waltz, the "Lulu" waltz; I had to repeat it, too. In addition, Janne has composed some pieces for the local brass septet.[3]

The largest compositions from the summer of 1889 are the Violin Sonata (JS 178) and the Fantasy for Cello and Piano (JS 79). Only the cello part of the Fantasy has survived, as a manuscript probably in Christian Sibelius' hand.[4] In the letter to his uncle on July 6, Jean Sibelius mentions playing the accompaniment of the Fantasy on the piano, while his brother performed the cello part. This is one of the rare occasions when Sibelius performed in public as a pianist. He is known to have been fonder of improvising freely on the instrument; at the spa he played dance music on the piano, but got so carried away that the result was "more interesting than it was suitable for dancing."[5]

Further compositions from summer 1889 include *Valse* (JS 1), a rather extensive waltz for piano; an overture for brass septet (JS 146); and the "Lulu Waltz," most likely *Tempo di valse II* (JS 194) for cello and piano.

The Mysterious "Lulu"

The manuscript of the "Lulu Waltz" (*Tempo di valse II*, JS 194) bears the date August 19, 1889 and, judging from Christian's letter of August 22 (quoted above), the piece was performed immediately at the spa. Later in that year, the "Lulu Waltz" was mentioned a couple of times in the correspondence between Jean and Christian Sibelius and also in a note that

---

[3] "Janne har i sommar komponerat en sonate för piano och violin, en stor fantasi för violoncell, samt en mängd smärre stycken (valser o.s.v.). Den der fantasin har jag 2 gånger spelat på badhuset ... Då vi spelat den voro åhörarena alldeles som vilda. Af Jannes kompositioner har jag vidare spelat på badhuset en valse, 'Lulu' valsen; den fick jag också spela 2 gånger. Janne har dessutom komponerat för härvarande hornseptett några stycken." Christian Sibelius' letter to Axel von Bonsdorff, dated August 22, 1889 in Lovisa (the National Archives of Finland, Sibelius Family Archive, file box 121).

[4] The manuscript material of the Fantasy and the Violin Sonata are preserved in the National Library of Finland.

[5] "mer intressant än det var lämpat att dansa efter," Söderhjelm 1929, 381.

Sibelius wrote on the manuscript of another piece for cello and piano, *Adagio* (JS 15). However, none of these sources shed light on the identity of the mysterious "Lulu."[6]

In February 2012, the conductor and violinist Pekka Helasvuo, who also works for Jean Sibelius Works, sent an enquiry to various libraries and archives in his search for manuscript materials relating to the Impromptu for string orchestra. The enquiry produced unforeseen results from Harvard University in the USA: a previously unknown composition by Sibelius, an Andantino in D major. The cover page of the manuscript bears the dedication "Till ("To") Emma Kristina Marie-Louise Berndtson | Lulu," and the first page of music (Ex. 1) includes the date July 28, 1889.[7]

Ex. 1. The autograph manuscript of the "Loulou Andantino," Eda Kuhn Loeb Music Library of the Harvard College Library, US-CAe Merrit Mus 806.4.419, fol. 2r.

[6] Christian Sibelius' letters to Jean Sibelius dated September 18, October 1, and November 20, 1889 (the National Archives of Finland, Sibelius Family Archive, file box 28). The manuscript of *Adagio* (JS 15) is preserved in the City Archives of Hämeenlinna, and the manuscript of the "Lulu Waltz" in the Sibelius Museum in Turku.

[7] For facsimile images of the entire manuscript see Anna Pulkkis (ed.), *Jean Sibelius Works V/4: Works for Piano Without Opus Number* (Wiesbaden: Breitkopf & Härtel, 2014), 135–9.

A list of guests staying at the Lovisa spa, published in the newspaper *Finland*, mentions "Mrs Marie Louise Berndtson, Helsingfors." Mrs Berndtson was in her mid-30s and married to Axel Berndtson, a journalist, writer, and art dealer. The actual dedicatee of the piece, however, was probably their baby daughter, born on June 24, 1889.[8] The name of the daughter was also Marie-Louise, and whether the full name Emma Kristina Marie-Louise belonged to the mother or the daughter remains unclear. In any case, baby Marie-Louise was called Loulou. The little Loulou—or "Lulu"—was probably the recipient of both the Andantino and the "Lulu Waltz."[9]

Sibelius and the Berndtsons became lifelong friends and, according to a later letter from Axel Berndtson, Sibelius was Loulou's godfather. The letter, written in the form of a humorous congratulatory poem for Sibelius' birthday, includes the line: "You, the godfather of my little Loulou | Forgive me, who is sometimes crazy."[10]

Loulou—the younger Marie-Louise—later moved to the UK. In 1921, she married Royal Navy officer Charles Forbes, who became Sir Charles Forbes, Admiral of the Fleet, during the Second World War. In the 1990s, the manuscript of Andantino was purchased by the Eda Kuhn Loeb Music Library of Harvard University. Loulou and Charles Forbes had one daughter, but whether the manuscript came to Harvard directly from the family is unknown.

Sibelius' Musical Souvenirs

Sibelius' works, those without opus number in particular, include many compositions that were intended as gifts or souvenirs. The "Loulou Andantino" counts as one of them. The manuscripts of these compositions are typically beautifully written and include a dedication to a specific person, date, and the composer's signature. Souvenir compositions were seldom meant to be performed in public, but were of a more private nature. Some of them can be described as small compliments, while others are rather large in scale.

---

[8] A birth announcement was published in *Nya Pressen* on June 26, 1889.

[9] Axel Gallén (later Akseli Gallen-Kallela) painted a portrait of Loulou when she was five months old. The painting "Portrait of a Child (Loulou Berndtson)" (1889) belongs to the permanent collection at Turku Art Museum.

[10] "Du, gudfar till min lilla Loulou | Förlåt mig, som ibland är hullu." Axel Berndtson's letter to Sibelius, undated but likely from the 1930s (the National Library of Finland Sibelius Collection, Coll. 206.3).

Souvenir compositions should by no means be considered insignificant or secondary. They can reflect specific aspects in the composer's relationship to the dedicatee. *Valse* (JS 1) was a gift for Betsy Lerche, a senator's daughter who attracted Sibelius' attention during the summer of 1889. Lerche was a piano pupil of Ferruccio Busoni, and the eloquent and passionate waltz might offer a glimpse of Lerche's temperament as a pianist. *Florestan* (JS 82), a piano suite from spring 1889, highlights the interest in E. T. A. Hoffmann shared by Sibelius and his fellow student Adolf Paul.

Souvenir compositions can also be connected to other works. *Adagio* (JS 13) for piano shares material with the third movement of the *Voces intimae* String Quartet (Op. 56), which Sibelius completed two years later. The manuscript is dated February 3, 1907 and is signed by Sibelius, but the dedicatee remains unknown. However, the layout of the manuscript and the fact that it had found its way into private possession in Germany suggest that it was a gift to someone.[11]

Of particular interest is the *Adagio* for piano four hands (JS 161), which Sibelius gave as a birthday present for his wife Aino on August 10, 1931. He dedicated the composition "To Beloved Aino." The bold and spare piece is one of the final statements of the aging composer, and also a practical gift—the spouses could play it together.

The Empty Staff

The "Loulou Andantino" is a pleasant piece of music, hardly revolutionary but nevertheless a fine example of the light, fresh chamber music of the young composer. One feature, however, is strikingly unique: the music is written for the piano, but Sibelius reserved an empty staff with a treble clef, a key signature, and bar lines above the piano staves (see Example 1).

The paper contains braced staves for piano and a solo instrument, or solo voice. The manuscript was trimmed, possibly at Harvard, and the Breitkopf & Härtel papermark is only partly visible. The paper resembles type B&H.Nr.5.*A*, which Sibelius used, for example, for the solo song *Drömmen* (Op. 13 No. 5), composed in Vienna in 1891.

By choosing this paper type and moreover by consistently adding the bar lines, key signatures, and clefs for the solo staff, Sibelius revealed that he hardly had a solo piano piece in mind at the start. The music, however, is entirely satisfactory as solo piano music—the piano part stands on its

[11] In 2012, the manuscript was purchased from Sotheby's by the National Library of Finland.

own. Other options are few; a solo violin could double the uppermost line in the piano part nicely, but this would hardly be meaningful without changing the piano part in the manner of an accompaniment, and an improvisational solo part would be truly unique in Sibelius' output.

The Andantino is in triple time. It may invoke associations with a slow waltz, but a waltz character is much less obvious here than in the "Lulu Waltz" or *Valse* (JS 1), which includes a generic waltz accompaniment. The key is a steady D major, with a contrasting middle section in B minor. The introductory bars could at first sight seem an odd formal feature in a solo piano piece, but in fact many of Sibelius' early piano works contain such introductory passages. Examples include *Valse* (JS 1) and the first two Impromptus (Op. 5).

A motivic feature that has some importance is the 5–6–5 motion, or alternation, between the pitches A and B. This feature is very clearly highlighted by the bridge (bb. 35–40) that leads to the return of the D major material after the contrasting B minor section, with the pitches accompanied by D major and B minor triads (Example 2).

Ex. 2. Alternation between the pitches A and B in the "Loulou Andantino," bb. 35–40.

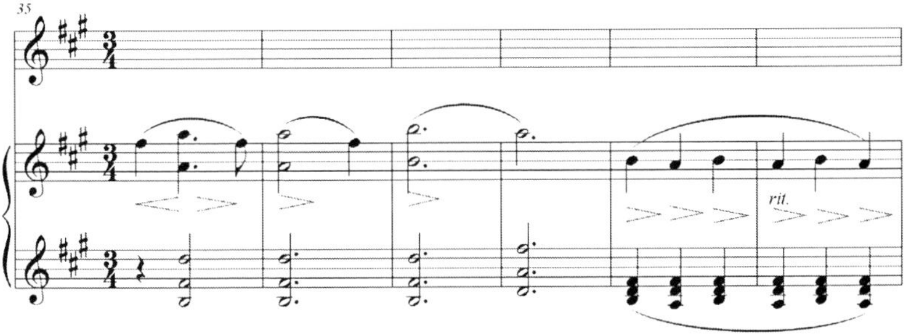

The Andantino was probably composed quickly, in an impression. It shares some common features with *Valse* (JS 1) for Betsy Lerche, completed about a month earlier. One such feature is the rhythmic figure with a triplet, dotted crotchet, and quaver (Example 3). Another common feature is the scalar motif rising from the fifth to the third scale degree (Example 4, which shows the melodic lines only). However commonplace such figures might be, they are reminiscent of the fact that the Andantino was not created in a vacuum but relates to other works from the same period.

Ex. 3. Similar rhythmic figures in the "Loulou Andantino" and *Valse* (JS 1).

"Loulou Andantino"

Valse (JS 1)

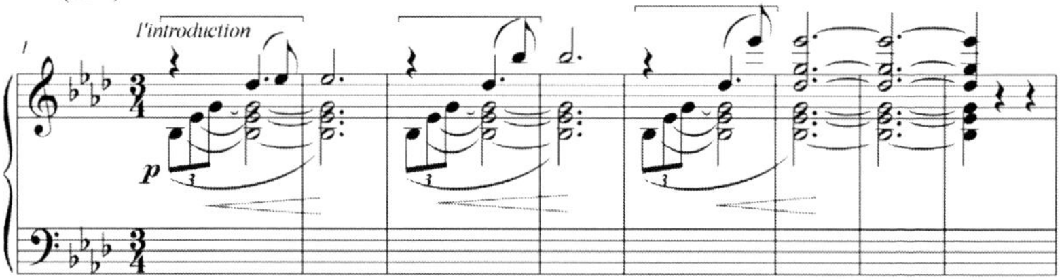

Ex. 4. Melodic figures rising from the fifth to the third scale degree in the "Loulou Andantino" and *Valse* (JS 1).

"Loulou Andantino"

Valse (JS 1)

The "Loulou Andantino" thus reveals some of its mysteries and yet still conceals others. Despite the curiosities of its layout it remains a piano piece and an outstanding example of what might still be found in private or public archives around the world.

WAR SYMPHONIES AND PEACE SYMPHONIES: SIBELIUS' FIFTH

FERRUCCIO TAMMARO

The First World War's Impact on the Symphony

"This wretched conflict will leave us old men"[1] Jean Sibelius wrote to his friend the journalist Wentzel Hagelstam in 1915, while in a diary entry written the previous year, shortly after the outbreak of World War I, he expressed his sense that an era was drawing a close: "The War! Probable end of our civilization,"[2] showing he had understood the extent to which his times would be affected by the conflict. In fact, by the end of the War many composers had severed their ties to the late-Romantic period, and for many of them this entailed rejection of the symphony—a monument to a time-honoured and venerable tradition that had come to be seen as compromised.

The Russian Alexander Glazunov, for example, composed eight symphonies before 1906, but left his Ninth, begun in 1910, unfinished. He continued to create other works, but never composed another symphony. Another Russian composer, Reinhold Glière, wrote three symphonies between 1899 and 1910. Although he lived until the mid-1950s, after the Bolshevik revolution he never returned to the genre, despite the fact that the symphony was one of the Soviet regime's preferred musical forms.

The same is true of several Scandinavian musicians. After composing two symphonies, Wilhelm Stenhammar left his Third (1918–19) incomplete, probably as a result of the cultural upheaval caused by the war. Another Swede, Natanael Berg, stopped composing symphonies after his Fifth (1924): another coincidence that doesn't seem totally casual. Although he lived until 1964, the Danish composer Hakon Børresen's last

---

1 To Wentzel Hagelstam October 28, 1915. Ferruccio Tammaro, *Sibelius* (Torino: Eri, 1984), 357.

2 Diary, August 18, 1914; Fabian Dahlström (ed.), *Jean Sibelius Dagbok 1909–1944* (Helsingfors: Svenska litteratursällskapet i Finland; Stockholm: Atlantis, 2005), 194.

symphony was his Third (1925–6). The Finnish musician Erkki Melartin completed his Sixth in 1924 (the same year that Berg composed his Fifth); he later began two other symphonies, but left both unfinished. After his Second (1919), another Finn, Aarre Merikanto, worked in more modern genres; only in the 1950s did he compose a new symphony, a work that differed little from his early compositions. In other countries, the German Richard Wetz stopped after his Third (1920–2) and, after composing his Third, the Romanian George Enescu left two further symphonies, begun after the war, incomplete. In other words, for many composers the war appears to have been a psychological Hadrian's Wall beyond which the symphony didn't matter anymore.

Sibelius grappled with similar problems. Influenced by the ferment being experienced in Europe between 1912 and 1914, in the period immediately after he had completed his Fourth, he was increasingly coming to doubt whether it still made sense to compose symphonies. This is the same dilemma that Gustav Mahler would have had to come to grips with, had he not died before war broke out. In fact, writing in 1912, Sibelius observed: "Often it seems to me that this symphonic yearning of mine is useless." However, he then went on to state: "But this exercise and this yearning will have great educational value for me;"[3] later, in 1917, he commented: "My progress in composing has led me to a blind alley,"[4] and in 1919 he added: "This idealism of mine that keeps me working on a symphony and wasting time and money and time for something that in other people's eyes is worth nothing—is really subtle."[5]

Obviously, not all his contemporaries reacted to the war in the same way. Many of them continued to compose symphonies, following the same late-Romantic path they had set out on previously, seemingly unaffected by the cataclysm taking place around them. Their loyalty to tonal music and the symphony in particular was meant to be a statement of trust: they had not been vanquished by the war and felt they could attempt to reattach the threads connecting them to tradition that had been severed by the conflict; that, in fact, they actually had a duty to do so.

An extreme example is the Dutch composer Julius Röntgen, who composed 24 symphonies (only three of them before the war), while all of his 21 post-war works were composed between 1922 and 1932 when Röntgen was between the ages of 67 and 77. Another Swede, Josef Otto af Sillén, who died at the age of ninety, only began to write symphonies after the War had ended, while others, Hugo Alfvén and Kurt Atterberg for

[3] Diary April 19, 1912; ibid., 134.
[4] Diary January 12, 1917; ibid., 256.
[5] Diary March 7, 1919; ibid., 285.

example, continued to write in the same style found in their early work until the end of their lives. Other examples are the Danish composer Rued Langgaard, who wrote the first of his 16 symphonies in 1911, and the last 40 years later in 1951; to the list could be added other composers out of Scandinavia like Ralph Vaughan Williams in Great Britain and Felix Weingartner in Austria.

Moreover, many composers in the younger generation wrote their first symphonies during the war years. For example, in 1915 the Czech Miroslav Krejčí composed the first of his five and the North American Henry Cowell the first of his 21; in 1916 the Russian Andrei Filippovich Pashchenko (who also composed four sinfoniettas) began the first of his 15 symphonies; while in 1917 the Dutchman Willem Pijper finished *Pan*, the first of his three symphonies, and the Swede Hilding Rosenberg completed the first of his seven. In other words, a new symphonic genre was emerging from the ashes of the old and the ruins left by the war. Dmitri Shostakovich significantly composed and presented his first shortly after Sibelius had finished his last.

Types of War Symphonies

Of course, the symphony was not the only musical genre affected by the war. We need only think of Maurice Ravel's *Le tombeau de Couperin*, Claude Debussy's *Noël des enfants qui n'ont plus de maison* and *Berceuse héroïque*, Gian Francesco Malipiero's *Pause del silenzio*, Edward Elgar's *The Spirit of England*, or Arthur Bliss' *Morning Heroes*. But the use of a genre like the symphony, endowed with such a stately legacy, allowed the composer to ennoble his message.

Many composers, especially those in countries involved in the conflict, were appalled by what was happening and used the symphony to react against the war. Composers in other countries were less influenced by events on the battlefield: the Dane Langgaard, mentioned above, began or composed three symphonies (his Third, Fourth, and Fifth); the Swedish Karl Yngve Sköld composed his First in 1916, when he was still an adolescent; another Swede, Oskar Lindberg, completed his only symphonic work, his Symphony in F major, Op. 16, during the war years (1914–17). Only in the finale of Lindberg's work do we find dramatic incisiveness interpretable as an effect of the war.

Even the work of some composers whose countries were involved in the war might reflect little interest in the events taking place. Instead, like Sibelius, they were clearly more absorbed by personal concerns. Examples include the German Richard Wetz, whose three intense Brucknerian symphonies were composed between 1917 and 1922, and the Pole Karol Szymanowski, who was seemingly oblivious to events in the world around him and in his Third ("The Song of the Night") chose to surround himself in an oriental atmosphere. In other words, for many composers, even in a time of war, the symphony's significance remained unchanged; they continued to see the symphony as a world closed in on itself, distant from the events of their times. By placing his Third ("Same-Ätnam"), composed between 1913 and 1915, in Lapland, the Swede Wilhelm Peterson-Berger seems to try to distance himself as much as possible from the war setting, while his countryman Hugo Alfvén's Fourth ("From the Outskirts of the Archipelago"), composed in 1918–19, seems for its part to be sheltering in the Baltic mists.

Sibelius' Fifth does not belong to any of the main categories of symphonic composition associated with the war. It is not a patriotic symphony whose purpose it was to instil nationalistic feelings in the listener. It is known that many of Sibelius' works like the *Jääkärien marssi* ("March of the Finnish Jäger Battalion") and the cantata *Oma maa* ("My Own Land") bore witness to the tragic events of the war years; nevertheless; Sibelius knew that his symphonies had also indirectly contributed and would continue to contribute to patriotic aims. It is true that the composition of his Fifth coincided with the struggle for Finnish independence, but Sibelius' intentions are different and, even in his First and Second symphonies, possible references to the political situation in Finland were, if not unconscious, certainly not deliberate. Sibelius' annotated project plans, from which both these symphonies sprang, confirm it, and the same goes for the Fifth.

Other composers instead sought to encourage national pride by including folk and national motifs in their work. This is true of Vincent d'Indy's Third Symphony (*Sinfonia brevis de bello gallico*) (1916–18), which includes evocations of mobilisation at the beginning of the war, the battle of the Marne, and moments of soldierly gaiety at the front, as well as passages contrasting inferior contemporary German music with superior music in France, and ends with the hymn of Saint Michael used as a victory song.

In a similar vein, the Dutchman Cornelis Dopper's Seventh Symphony (1917) contains numerous folk songs drawn from Adriaen Valerius' collection *Nederlandsche Gedenck-Clanck* ("Dutch Memory Songs"), which, inspired by Holland's struggle to gain independence from Spain, was published in 1626. Dopper began composing the symphony, entitled "Zuiderzee" (the bay of the North Sea on which Amsterdam lies), during Germany's World War I invasion of the Netherlands; Mengelberg performed it again when Germany attacked the country at the beginning of World War II.

Not all patriotic symphonies were composed in Europe. In 1919, the Brazilian Heitor Villa-Lobos composed a triptych of symphonies (his Third, Fourth, and Fifth), respectively entitled "War," "Victory," and "Peace." Unfortunately, the Fifth has been lost, but the other two amply demonstrate the composer's attention to the war, albeit in a stiffly formal way.

Although other composers working during these years were not directly involved in the war, they felt called upon by the circumstances to write patriotic symphonies. In his Second (1919), named *Mitt Land* ("My Country"), with three movements entitled *Sagan* ("The Fairy Tale"), *Skogen* ("The Forest"), and *Drömmen* ("The Dream"), the Swede Ture Rangström is open to the nature, fantasy world and legends of his native land. Similar themes are found in Kurt Atterberg's Third (1914–16) and Fourth (1918). Both the first of these, entitled *Västkustbilder* ("West Coast Pictures"), with movements subtitled *Soldis* ("Sun Smoke") and *Storm* and *Sommarnatt* ("Summer Night"), are imbued with national folk themes. In other words, their worlds and sources of inspiration were similar to those found in Sibelius' youthful works like *Kullervo* and *En saga*, two pieces joined together by the same national spirit.

A further category comprises symphonies of a meditative nature, reflections on the dramatic events of the war. The Fourth and Fifth Symphonies (1917–19) of Nikolai Myaskovsky are explicit examples of works by an artist involved in the conflict and the Bolshevik Revolution: in the Fourth, the first two movements, *Andante, mesto con sentimento* and *Largo, freddo e senza espressione*, lead to a radiant finale. While at the beginning of Myaskovsky's Fifth, the atmosphere is quiet and pastoral, the symphony ends with a dramatic, positive rush. With rational coldness and objective formalism, Myaskovsky shows that the war, although tragic, would contribute to the success of the new-born USSR, and his optimism allowed him to be academically constructive. A similar vision of the war was expressed in the First Symphony (1918–19) by the young Ukrainian Borys Mikolayovich Lyatoshynsky. Its deeply reflective second movement is redeemed by a finale that is not only dynamic, but even heroic, in close conformity with the tastes of emerging Soviet symphonism. The case of another Russian composer, Sergei Lyapunov, is different but equally meaningful; his Second Symphony, composed in 1917, is dramatic but not swaggeringly triumphal. Listening to it, we realise that its composer would not embrace the changes brought about by the revolution. In fact, he left the Soviet Union in 1923.

Composed at the end of the conflict which had only marginally affected life in his country, the Swiss composer Volkmar Andreae's Symphony in C major, Op. 31 (1919) nevertheless preserves an echo of the war in the first movement's funeral march and in the "Trio" of the Scherzo, where we can glimpse something that resembles Mahlerian sarcasm, although Andreae was too far removed from the world of war to indulge in mocking bitterness.

Another Swiss composer, Hermann Suter, wrote his only symphony in the early months of the war. His Symphony in D minor, Op. 17, is a meditative work and on the autographed last page Suter wrote the emblematic words "Inter arma silent musae," which explain the character of the work's second movement (*Capriccio militaresco, alla Marcia*), where we can glimpse probably unconscious allusions to Georg Grosz's or Otto Dix's paintings. The expressive planning of Enescu's Third is similar, upset by a strong strain in its glittering, lively first movement, with scraps of marches in the second, while in the third the angel-like voices of the chorus announce deliverance from the horrors of war.

Meditation as escape from the war is clear in the Austrian Emil Nikolaus von Reznicek's Third and Fourth, both composed in the same years (1918–19). The Third is "in the old style," as if von Reznicek did not want to cut his ties with the past and hoped to keep the work somewhat light-hearted by injecting optimistic energy. The Fourth contains a "Funeral March on the Death of a Comedian," whose intentionally unnaturally stiff tempo is intended to be sarcastic, yet is so devoid of causticity that the symphony closes aseptically with a series of variations on its own theme. A further two meditative symphonies, composed when the war had ended, have little in common. While Matthijs Vermeulen's Second (1920), entitled *Prélude à la nouvelle journée*, is not always serene, Vaughan Williams's Third (*Pastoral*), composed between 1920 and 1922, is a pensive reflection in four predominantly slow movements.

Sibelius' Fifth is not a pensive symphony written in memory of people he knew, while Madetoja's Second is. It was composed on the wave of emotion caused by the deaths of his brother Yriö and colleague Toivo Kuula in the Finnish Civil War of 1918. Sibelius wrote in his diary[6] that he had been impressed by Madetoja's symphony (in fact, the first and the second movements are strongly Sibelian in some ways). Yet, although he was troubled by similar losses (not for war reasons: Faltin and, above all, Carpelan), he shunned references to death and grieving in his own symphony.

---

6 Diary December 20, 1918; Dahlström, *Jean Sibelius Dagbok*, 281.

Maurice Emmanuel's First, composed in 1919 in memory of an aviator killed in action, is also free of mournful or epic tones. In the first movement, *Tranquillo molto*, a dimension of aerial lightness prevails and, in the *Allegro leggero e giocoso* that follows, the lively atmosphere is full of French-style vitality. In the third *Adagio molto* movement bombast is avoided, and the final movement, *Allegro con fuoco*, ends serenely, without a real apotheosis.

In no way does Sibelius' Fifth even attempt to seek shelter in the world of the playful music. Thus, it does not resemble Sergei Prokofiev's *Classical Symphony*, composed during the dramatic events that occurred during the Russian Revolution: "Classical" was for him an entirely different matter. Nor is it similar to Paul Hindemith's *Lustige Sinfonietta* (1916), composed in memory of the poet Christian Morgenstern, known for his poems tinged with gallows humour. The shambling, ironic accents Hindemith employed in this symphony seem intended to offer solace to those who had experienced the tragedy of war.

Franz Schreker's Chamber Symphony, created for the Vienna Musical Academy in 1916, also belongs to this group: it has a prevalently unstrained character consistent with the festive occasion for which it was composed but, like the works of Prokofiev and Hindemith mentioned above, the orchestral reduction of the instruments seems to mirror a (perhaps unintentional) wish to avoid excessive rhetoric—precisely the sort of rhetoric the war was sweeping away.

The uniqueness of Sibelius' Fifth is also clearly seen in his eschewal of references to eschatological questions. For him, coming to terms with the devastation of war did not mean embracing religion, as it did in the symphonies of the French composer and organist Charles Tournemire, for example. Between 1900 and 1924, Tournemire composed eight symphonies which exemplify his confidence in the power of religious faith. His Sixth, composed in 1918, uses texts he based on the Psalms. It begins by invoking God's help, and in its closing movement the religious comfort sought arrives via "Christ's Voice." Tournemire's Seventh, begun in 1919 and completed in 1922, is also imbued with a desire for transcendence. Its title, *Les danses de la vie*, indicates that Tournemire saw life's highest aspiration as progressing toward divinity. Sibelius' Fifth, like most of his work, instead seeks deliverance only in itself, eschewing fideistic support of any kind. Sibelius does not even turn to philosophy for solace, as did the Danish Louis Glass in his theosophic Fifth (*Svastika*), written in 1919. The North American Charles Ives, who progressively stopped composing during the war, after his "transcendentalist" Fourth continually reworked his unfinished *Universe Symphony*.

A Difficult Birth

The gestation of Sibelius' Fifth Symphony is known to have been long and complex. No other symphony of his demanded so much tiring work—not even his Fourth, composed at a time when he was suffering from both physical and emotional problems. It was a particularly difficult period for Sibelius. He was appalled by the World War and Finnish Civil War, haunted by long-standing financial problems, and upset by the public debate on his family's origins. He was also drinking heavily and experiencing hearing problems and tensions with fellow musicians.

But it was principally a spiritual crisis that troubled Sibelius, complicated by the increasingly widespread rejection of the symphony as a genre by fellow composers. He decided, however, that the symphony did indeed have a place in the modern world, and his Fifth and later Sixth and Seventh Symphonies, are the works of a composer who was fully at peace with himself. The war interrupted his Europeanisation process, and at the same time drove him to withdraw more into himself. Starting from his Fifth, Sibelius was becoming less concerned with problems in the world around him. For example, while Finland was in the throes of a Civil War he wrote in his diary:

> Again murders and murders that destroy morale and set our nerves on edge. My brother Christian was arrested, but is now free again. One thing is certain: these murderous gangs must be stopped, otherwise nothing will remain of poor Finland, a country without cultural traditions.—It seems darker than ever. And without hope.

However, he continued: "Marvellous winter weather and +6° [C]! Unforgettable atmosphere with the moon. I am working on my Fifth Symphony."[7] And when his house was searched by the Red Guards he wrote: "Going out for a walk forbidden! Splendid! But what does all that have to do with my symphonies?"[8] In other words, Sibelius once more showed that a genre he had defined "not a 'composition' in the common sense, but a profession of faith [*trosbekännelse*] at different moments in our lives"[9] could not be contaminated simply by fortuitous circumstances. As Peter Revers has explained, for Sibelius:

> "The Classical" means … emancipation from any theatre-like, from any pathos, the consequent pursuit of an inner musical logic that is embedded

[7] Diary February 17, 1918; Dahlström, *Jean Sibelius Dagbok*, 271.
[8] Diary February 5, 1918; Dahlström, *Jean Sibelius Dagbok*, 269.
[9] Diary November 5, 1910; Dahlström, *Jean Sibelius Dagbok*, 59.

in the musical motifs and themes ... "classical" thus in the meaning of timelessness and independence from fashionable modes.[10]

For Sibelius, classicism made it possible to enter a world that was without history, eternal and incorrupt.

From this point forward, Sibelius' music, like that of so many other great composers, reveals a substantial separation between man and artist. It is clear that the artist Sibelius is another person, totally different from the man Sibelius with all his weaknesses, defects, and insecurities. What his diary, his letters, and the external biographical events of his life tell us fail to explain his music entirely, precisely because, for an introspective artist like him, internal and external life rarely coincide. Only through his music can we really enter what he called in the diary a "jardin secret." This is what Sibelius' Fifth, and a little later also his Sixth, Seventh, and *Tapiola*, make clear.

Vitality in the Natural World

The Fifth is a substantial affirmation of the vitality which Sibelius absorbed from his intense relationship with nature. "A truly beautiful day. Fantastic poetry. In the evening I went for a walk. I would not like to leave life on a day like this. Suicide would be impossible,"[11] he wrote one day in his diary. But his is once more a totally individual vitality, one that is not descriptive and very different from that of other composers. It coincides with the idea that the directly symphonic is "det tvingande," i.e. the directly symphonic is the "compelling vein" that, Sibelius felt, "goes through the whole. This in contrast with the depicting."[12]

His Danish colleague Carl Nielsen reacted to the carnage of war by composing a strong assertion of life in his Fourth Symphony, "The Inextinguishable" (1914–16). His vitality is highly physical, almost physiological, however. In his symphony, meditative moments have only a

[10] Peter Revers, "'Musik wie klares, kaltes Wasser.' Zu den Symphonien Nr. 5–7 von Jean Sibelius," in *Jean Sibelius und Wien*, edited by Hartmut Krones [Wiener Schriften zur Stilkunde und Aufführungspraxis, ed. Hartmut Krones, Sonderband 4] (Wien, Köln and Weimar: Böhlau Verlag, 2003), 140; "'Klassisch' ist ... die Emanzipation von jeder Theatralik, von jeglichem Pathos, die konsequente Verfolgung einer inneren musikalischen Logik, die den musikalischen Motiven und Themen immanent ist ... 'klassisch' also im Sinne von Zeitlos und Modeströmungen unabhängig."

[11] Diary 17 April, 1913; Dahlström, *Jean Sibelius Dagbok*, 170.

[12] Karl Ekman, *Jean Sibelius. Life and Personality of an Artist*, trans. Edward Birse, (Helsingfors: H. Schildt, 1935), 232.

contrasting function, and the wasteland left by the war found at the beginning of the second movement serves merely to prepare for the "timpani duel" that will happen in the finale, allowing what is "inextinguishable" to assert itself in a wholesome and almost Straussian climate.

In fact, Strauss expresses a similar, healthy exuberance in his *Alpensymphonie* (1915), equally permeated by nature absorbed in a solid and concrete way (a Nietzschean exaltation of the "Antichrist"), as if the composer wanted to escape the horrors of war by going to breathe pure mountain air. Felix Weingartner's Fourth, albeit immersed in a wholly different world, was defined by its composer as being "bucolic," and in fact it seems to be trying to forget the war with the waltz rhythms of its first and third movements and the amicable clarity of its second and fourth. Darius Milhaud's brisk Chamber Symphonies were composed in part to counterbalance the excesses of the late-Romantic symphony. The first two (1917–18), with the titles "Spring" and "Pastoral," the first a nonet and the second a septet, display the anti-Romantic detachment from nature typical of this French composer.

Sibelius occasionally used the image of a mountain to symbolise the slow, fatiguing progress of his work. While working on his Fourth, he often had to push himself to continue and began to use the word "Himalaya"[13] to describe the effort he needed to make. While composing the Fifth, he wrote to Axel Carpelan the famous letter: "Deeply discouraged again. But in the darkness I have already perceived the mountain I will *surely* climb. God is opening His door for a moment and *His* orchestra is playing the Fifth Symphony."[14] In other words the mountain was not simply synonymous with going on an outing to enjoy the sunrise and sunset, meadows and glaciers, woods and flowers. After the excursion he made to Koli in September 1909, Sibelius was so impressed by the mountain landscape that he decided to write a work entitled *La montagne*. But he subsequently transformed his ideas for this work and possibly incorporated them in the Fourth Symphony's *Il tempo largo*. The significance the mountain had for Sibelius is far different from the importance attributed to it in Tournemire's long Fifth Symphony

---

[13] Diary December 27, 1909 and April 29, 1910; Dahlström, *Jean Sibelius Dagbok*, 2005, 38, 43.

[14] Jean Sibelius' letter to Axel Carpelan, September 22, 1914; in Fabian Dahlström, (ed.), *Högtärade Maestro! Högtärade Herr Baron! Korrespondensen mellan Axel Carpelan och Jean Sibelius 1900–1919* (Helsingfors: Svenska litteratursällskapet in Finland; Stockholm: Bokförlaget Atlantis, 2010), 370.

(1914), known as "La montagne" because of its composer's use of the mountain and ascending a mountain as a religious metaphor.

Natanael Berg's Straussian Third Symphony (1917–18) is another work which, with its title *Makter* ("Forces"), has definite energy, whereas the German Paul Büttner's Fourth (1918) is even more striking and strong-willed, preceded by the epigraph, "My soul is like a metal mirror. Your worlds are reflected in it, and it resounds in the thunder of your storm." Although it is a symphony underpinned with resolution and security, and admits neither doubts nor hesitations, it is nevertheless the work of a man who is not at peace with himself.

Moreover, to express his imperative vitality, Sibelius made no use of the contrapuntal procedures loved by Melartin and used in his Fifth (1916), in which the theme of the third movement is heard in counterpoint with the theme of the first, and the fourth movement is in turn a quadruple fugue. Sibelius did not feel the need to cling to the handrail of this technique to maintain his certainties and preserve his inner self-confidence.

For Sibelius, the vitality of the Fifth Symphony was nonetheless subject to the laws of time and to the instability of emotions. In this regard, Marc Vignal has pointed out that in this symphony, "three superimposed tempos—fast, slow and static—can be discerned at the same time. More than the themes themselves, it is the working with the tempos—and with the sound material itself—that determines the form."[15]

The beginning is pastoral in tone (an explicit reminiscence, with his intervals of perfect fourth and fifth, of the widely-used *ranz des vaches*), but soon the atmosphere, which is dramatised by passages rich in tension, changes several times. This occurs not only because the composer wished to introduce variety, but also because Sibelius was trying to suggest how much effort it takes to reach the security of the constant, deliberate vitality that is found in the second part of the movement (a hypothetical "scherzo," which for this reason is directly connected to the first one and at the same time separated from it).

The second movement, as David Hurwitz has written, is also "decidedly pastoral in tone" but "with an occasional darkening of both orchestration and harmony for contrast."[16] According to Vignal, "it is

[15] Marc Vignal, *Sibelius* (Paris: Fayard, 2004), 789; "Trois tempos superposés—rapide, lent et statique—sont parfois perçus en même temps. Plus que les thèmes eux-mêmes, c'est ce travail sur les tempos—et sur la matière sonore elle-même—qui détermine la forme."

[16] David Hurwitz *Sibelius. The Orchestral Works. An Owner's Manual* (New Jersey: Amadeus Press, 2007), 116.

dominated by the tendency of superimposing the slow [movement] on the fast one."[17] In this way it differs from the central movements of Nielsen's Third and Melartin's Fourth, each of which uses vocalises to increase the bucolic scenery. Here, in the *Andante mosso, quasi allegretto*, nothing is really descriptive; rather, we hear what Sibelius meant when he compared the symphony to a river[18]; the symphony must first of all have "water," i.e. spiritual substance, and it must flow following the natural meanderings of intuition rather than the penstock of rationality. In this movement, the simple scales of the first theme are "the small brooks that look for each other," and finally the "river" reaches its estuary in the "sea" of the last movement, whose thundering vitality provides the key for understanding the whole symphony. But is the finale really fully triumphant and cathartic? We must focus our attention not only on the famous theme of "swans in flight," which Sibelius had noted on the edge of a page of his "spittoon" [*crachoir*] (the term he used for his diary),[19] but also on the pensive, rather unhappy countermelody of the woodwinds and cellos. This wonderfully eloquent theme communicates the beauty of the swans and the other migratory birds Sibelius—like many other Finns—loved, but also the fact that he saw this beauty as transient. The birds come again, and again leave Finland's lakes; they represent the possibility of peacefully crossing borders closed by the war, and therefore also represent the freedom and timeless strength of nature. But the birds cannot stay and summer is short; in other words, life and the world's loveliness are fleeting. The swans go and come back, and one day, after seeing them, Sibelius wrote in his diary: "My soul is full of sadness and admiration (*vemod och dyrkan*) in regard to nature."[20] To him, the "sadness and admiration" evoked by nature were closely connected and one did not exclude the other, as a further diary entry shows: "Nature's mysticism and life's troubles. The final theme of the Fifth Symphony, romanticism and only God knows."[21] And Sibelius referred to his elegant *Humoresques* for

---

[17] Vignal, *Sibelius*, 789: "[il] a plutôt la tendance à superposer le [mouvement] lent au rapide."

[18] "I would like to compare the symphony to a river. It springs from a great number of little brooks that look for each other. And so the river rolls broadly and mightily toward the sea. But today people dig broad and mighty river beds, in other words they build rivers. But where should they get the water?" Diary August 1, 1912. Ferruccio Tammaro, "'L'imperativo' nella musica di Sibelius," in *Nuova Rivista Musicale Italiana* VIII (1) (1974): 29; Dahlström, *Jean Sibelius Dagbok*, 147.

[19] Diary February 11, 1915; Dahlström, *Jean Sibelius Dagbok*, 217.

[20] Diary September 10, 1916; Dahlström, *Jean Sibelius Dagbok*, 252.

[21] Diary April 21, 1915; Dahlström, *Jean Sibelius Dagbok*, 225.

violin and orchestra, Op. 87 and Op. 89, composed during the same period, as "clouds and flashes of sunlight."[22]

It is noteworthy that Sibelius' diary entries recording his sense of wonder on seeing migratory birds in flight are particularly frequent during the war years and coincide with the gestation of the Fifth Symphony. It is also significant that it was during the same years that his countryman Väinö Raitio composed both his only symphony (Op. 13), and also the fine tone poem *Joutsenet* ("The Swans"), an impressionistic and mysterious but also dramatic work that is substantially different from Sibelius' calm contemplativeness.

And it is this attitude to immersion in the secret, invisible workings of nature that constitutes the difference between Sibelius' Fifth and the music of another Finnish composer, Melartin, who used a Finnish folk song, the melody *Jo joutui armas aika* ("Here Comes the Good Weather"), in the opening movement of his Fourth "Summer Symphony" (1913–16), and in the *Andante* used, not the idealised image of swans in flight, but the more concrete chirping of a bird. In other words, Melartin is far closer to normality and the predictability of everyday life.

The Suspension of Time

The three last symphonies of Sibelius need to be interpreted either as strictly complementary or, preferably, as closely consequential. The well-known problems Sibelius had with pagination and size in the Fifth had to do with the need he felt to put things where they belonged: "Spent the evening with the [Fifth] symphony. The disposition of the themes: with all its mystery and fascination this is the important thing. It is as if God the Father had thrown down mosaic pieces from the floor of the heavens and asked me to put them back as they were." He had similar problems when he came to compose his Seventh (although he wrote to Carpelan that it would be in three movements).[23] These problems were caused by his seeking to reconcile the temporal performance of the music with an attempt to suspend time. James Hepokoski quite rightly connects that metaphor of heaven's mosaic with the thematic arrangement of all three symphonies and of *Tapiola* (at that time not yet programmed):

> By the spring of 1915 Sibelius' essential problem had become to sort out the themes and, ultimately, to permit them to refract and develop into the

[22] Jean Sibelius' letter to Axel Carpelan, May 20, 1918; Dahlström, *Jean Sibelius Dagbok*, 422.

[23] Dahlström, *Jean Sibelius Dagbok*, 423.

> four major works of the next twelve years: the Fifth, Sixth, and Seventh Symphonies, and the tone poem *Tapiola*, all of which, consequently, may be heard as sharing a deep kinship.[24]

At the beginning of the Fifth's finale we are clearly swept up in the hectic race of time, of life, and it is the "swan theme" that makes it possible for us to emerge victorious: "I have seen cranes every day; they sailed southwards with full music. Once again I have been their humble student. Their cries are the threads of my life. They pull me ever closer to heaven."[25] What in fact did the "student" Sibelius learn from the cranes? He learned that it is necessary to surmount time and its seasonal periodicity. This answer comes directly from comparing this symphony with the ones that followed, as both the Sixth and the Seventh also attempt to suspend time. It is no coincidence that the finale of the Fifth is the last movement of a symphony by Sibelius with a well-rounded, plastic theme; afterwards, he rarely achieved the same melodic inventiveness. In the Sixth, Sibelius clearly intended to adopt a thematic shaping at a level close to zero, constituted mainly by a conjunct melodic motion that could not be outlined in relief. In the Seventh, "the trombone theme" consists of neutral intervals of a perfect octave, fifth, and fourth. The *Tapiola* motto is also a simple sequence of joined degrees, almost Gregorian in derivation.

After the Fifth, Sibelius slowly overcame the constant fear of impending death and running out of time that had frequently haunted him during the war years. The beauty of nature, which he had long absorbed, is therefore no longer perceived as "becoming" but rather as "being." From this point on, his *Alleingefühl* ("Sense of loneliness"), which he often wrote about in his diary, was no longer perceived as being painful. The Fifth is therefore a "peace symphony" as it opened the way to the abstraction of Sibelius' late works. It is the opposite of Swedish composer Kurt Atterberg's Fifth (*Sinfonia funèbre*, 1917–22), which plumbs the depths of existential and creative crisis. Sibelius' willing disposition emerges for example in a letter he wrote to Aino in 1909: "Life is short and, when it has been at its best, it has consisted of work and strain."[26] Taking this basic optimism into account is essential for understanding

---

[24] James Hepokoski, *Sibelius. Symphony No. 5* (Cambridge: Cambridge University Press, 1993), 32–3.

[25] Diary September 10, 1916; Dahlström, *Jean Sibelius Dagbok*, 252.

[26] Jean Sibelius' letter May 18, 1909 from Berlin to Aino Sibelius; in *Syysilta. Aino ja Jean Sibeliuksen kirjeenvaihtoa 1905–1931*, ed. SuviSirkku Talas (Helsinki: Suomalaisen Kirjallisuuden Seura, 2007), 158; in orig. language: "Mutta elämä on lyhyt och när det varit som bäst har det arbete och möda varit."

Sibelius' longing for sublimation. To him, life always seemed short because composing was of such vital importance. After his Fifth, however, Sibelius was no longer in a hurry. The Sixth and Seventh Symphonies and *Tapiola* give only the illusion of tempo variation; they are the implementation of the advice Sibelius would later give a friend:

> Since I am much older than you and have more experience, allow me to give you some good advice: try to withdraw from the time; start to study the *Divina Commedia*, Milton and other authors of the past. In this way you will achieve—I can affirm it with certainty—extraordinary peace and plasticity in your style and in your life.[27]

Appendix

Around Sibelius' Fifth			
Type	*Year*	*Composer*	*Symphony*
Uncommitted	1913–15	W. Peterson-Berger	No. 3 ("Same Ätnam")
	1914–17	O. Lindberg	Op. 16
	1914–16	K. Szymanowski	No. 3 ("Song of the Night")
	1916–18	R. Langgaard	No. 3, No. 4 and No. 5
	1916	Y. Sköld	No. 1
	1918–19	V. Raitio	Op. 13
		H. Alfvén	No. 4 ("Från havsbandet")
Patriotic	1914–18	K. Atterberg	No. 3 ("Västkustbilder") and No. 4 ("Sinfonia piccola")
	1916–18	V. d'Indy	No. 3 ("De bello gallico")
	1917	C. Dopper	No. 7 ("Zuidersee")
	1917	H. Huber	No. 7 ("Schweizerische")
	1919	T. Rangström	No. 2 ("Mitt land")
	1919	H. Villa-Lobos	No. 3 ("The War"), No. 4 ("The Victory") and No. 5 ("The Peace")

[27] Tammaro, *Sibelius*, 443. Date and recipient not specified.

Meditative	1914	H. Suter	Op. 17
	1916	G. Enescu	No. 3
	1917	S. Lyapunov	No. 2
	1917–19	N. Y. Myaskovsky	No. 4 and No. 5
	1917–22	K. Atterberg	No. 5 ("Sinfonia funèbre")
	1918–19	E. N. von Reznicek	No. 3 and No. 4
	1918–19	B. M. Lyatoshynsky	No. 1
	1919–20	M. Vermeulen	No. 2 ("Prélude à la nouvelle journée")
	1920-22	R. Vaughan Williams	No. 3 ("Pastoral")
In memoriam	1916–18	L. Madetoja	No. 2
	1919	M. Emmanuel	No. 1
Playful	1916	P. Hindemith	"Lustige Sinfonietta"
	1916	F. Schreker	*Kammersymphonie*
	1917	S. Prokofiev	No. 1 ("Classic")
Eschatological	1914–19	Ch. Tournemire	No. 5, No. 6 and No. 7 ("Les Dances de la Vie")
	from 1910	C. Ives	No. 4 and *Universe Symphony* (unf.)
	1919	L. Glass	No. 5 ("Svastika")
Vitalistic	1913–16	E. Melartin	N. 4 ("Kesäsinfonia") and No. 5 ("Sinfonia brevis")
	1914–15	C. Nielsen	No. 4 ("Det Uudslukkelige")
	1915	R. Strauss	*Alpensymphonie*
	1916	F. Weingartner	No. 4
	1917–18	D. Milhaud	*Chamber Symphonies* No 1 ("Le Printemps") and No. 2 ("Pastorale")
	1917–18	N. Berg	No. 3 ("Makter")
	1918	P. Büttner	No. 4

SIBELIUS' EIGHTH SYMPHONY—FACT AND FICTION

ILKKA ORAMO

In a letter to Mrs Olga Bratt, Wilhelm Stenhammar's sister-in-law, dated December 20, 1926, Sibelius revealed that he was currently working on "a new thing for orchestra." This communication has been read as his first reference to the Eighth Symphony.[1] Over the following years, similar references to "new works" or "my work" occur intermittently in his letters. The word "symphony" does not appear until it pops up in a letter to Olin Downes on January 19, 1931: "However I think that there will quite soon be a new Symphony ready for printing—this information strictly private: only for you."[2]

Here Sibelius gives an estimate, although imprecise, of the symphony's appearance. Similar forecasts ("soon," "this season," "next season," etc.) recur in his answers to Koussevitzky's frequent inquiries after he had promised the Symphony's American première to the Boston Symphony Orchestra and its chief conductor.[3] Stronger still is the promise he gave Koussevitzky on October 26, 1932: "either I will send you the handwritten score in December or the printed material a couple of months later." Typically, an apology followed: "impossible this season ..."[4]

The only reliable fact about the materialisation of the Eighth Symphony—or a part of it (most likely the first movement)—is the letter accompanying an invoice from Sibelius' trusted copyist, Paul Voigt, dated September 4, 1933. "Most Honoured Maestro, I hereby deliver the completed work and hope that you, Herr Professor, will be satisfied with the result." On the reverse side of the letter, Sibelius had drafted a reply in

---

[1] Erik Tawaststjerna, "Sibelius' Eighth Symphony—an Insoluble Mystery. Part I," *Finnish Music Quarterly* 1–2 (1985): 65.
[2] Glenda Dawn Goss, *Jean Sibelius and Olin Downes: Music, Friendship, Criticism* (Boston: Northeastern University Press, 1995), 194.
[3] Tawaststjerna, "Sibelius's Eighth Symphony," 93.
[4] Ibid., 96–7.

German: "My best thanks. Please do not bind the copy yet. Title: Sinfonia 8. At the end: fermata. The Largo continues without a break. The whole piece will be roughly eight times as long as this."[5]

The rest is second-hand information. That Sibelius and his wife Aino (and their daughter Margareta) had either taken to the copyist or fetched from him a thick bunch of manuscripts, as Aino told Tawaststjerna after her husband's death,[6] does not add to our knowledge of the symphony's status. Moreover, we do not know for sure if Sibelius burnt the score sometime in the 1940s. For this reason, I think, Fabian Dahlström has given the Eighth Symphony an entry (JS 190) in his catalogue and classified it as "verschollen" (missing).[7]

New hopes of finding or rescuing the work arose when Sibelius' sketches from the family archives were deposited in the National Library and made available to scholars in 1982. According to the most optimistic scholarly view, the symphony could be reconstructed from the sketches.[8] A more down-to-earth opinion, however, holds that only a few of them can be credibly related to the work.[9] Of these late fragments, three have been recorded by John Storgårds and the BBC Philharmonic.[10]

The fundamental question is: why didn't Sibelius finish the Eighth Symphony and, if he did, why did he destroy it—if he did? A credible answer would help to understand, if not fully explain, the so-called "Silence of Järvenpää."

One of the first attempts to respond to the question is an article by conductor Simon Parmet from 1957. He regards Sibelius' silence during the last 30 years of his life as a result of his opposition to modern trends in the music of the 1920s and 30s and his faltering self-confidence in the face of an allegedly hostile world opinion that celebrated such modern trends.

---

[5] "Besten Dank. Bitte noch nicht einbinden. Ausgezeichnet geschrieben. Titel: Sinfonia n 8. Schluss: Fermate. Largo sofort anschliessen. Das ganze wird ungefähr achtmal dieses." Quoted in Tawaststjerna, "Sibelius' Eighth Symphony," 99–100.

[6] Ibid.

[7] Fabian Dahlström, *Sibelius Werkverzeichnis* (Wiesbaden, Leipzig and Paris: Breitkopf & Härtel, 2003), 624.

[8] Nors S. Josephson, "On Some Apparent Sketches for Sibelius's Eighth Symphony," *Archiv für Musikwissenschaft* 61 (1) (2004): 54–67.

[9] Timo Virtanen, "Palapeli ilman kuvaa: Jean Sibeliuksen myöhäiset luonnokset ja kahdeksas sinfonia" ["A Jigsaw Puzzle Without a Picture. Jean Sibelius Late Sketches and the Eighth Symphony"], *Musiikki* 41 (3–4) (2011): 103–30.

[10] Chandos CHAN 10809 (3) (2014).

"Sibelius had no other reason than his hypersensitivity either to doubt himself or to distrust his time."[11] Other explanations relate to his health, lifestyle, and mental condition: impaired eyesight, shaking hands, excessive reliance on alcohol, sense of loneliness (which he called his *Alleingefühl*) and inhibitive self-criticism probably all contributed to his alienation and loss of creative spirit. But this is hardly the whole truth.

Sibelius' long-lasting and terminal silence is all but unparalleled in music. Whereas Rossini's almost 40-year silence between two creative periods was "worldly and cosmopolitan," Sibelius' was "more austere, self-punishing and site-specific," as Julian Barnes has noted.[12] It is no wonder, therefore, that not only critics and scholars of Sibelius' life and works but also writers of fiction have shown an interest in it: fiction begins where facts cease.

To date, there are at least two plays, one opera, one novel, three short stories, and a comic strip that deal with the subject. I shall first present the fictional stories and their writers in a few words and introduce the content of the stories, and then assess their contribution to the discussion about the silence and the Eighth Symphony that it consumed.

The oldest of the fictional stories considered here is from Lars Gustafsson's *Det sällsamma djuret från norr* ("The Strange Animal from the North"),[13] a collection of short stories modelled after the archetype of the genre, Boccaccio's *The Decameron*. Lars Gustafsson is a Swedish writer and former philosophy professor. In 2015, he was awarded the Thomas Mann Prize of Hansestadt Lübeck and the Bavarian Academy of Fine Arts. He died in April 2016.

In the collection's framing tale, an old solar wind spaceship, Pascal II, is heading toward a remote solar system sometime during the 40th millennium. Eight Space Lords, subdivisions of the First Lord's (an AI) complex mental structure, are gathered in the officers' mess and tell each other stories for entertainment during the long journey.

The story told by the Sixth Lord is about Jean Sibelius' night. In early spring 1948, Sibelius is sitting at an open window in Villa Ainola, waiting

[11] Simon Parmet, "Den åttonde symfonins gåta," in *Con amore. Essäer om musik och mästare* (Helsingfors: Söderström & C:o, 1960), 123–36. First printing in *Nya Argus* 17/18 (1957).
[12] Julian Barnes, "Where Sibelius Fell Silent," *Intelligent life* (*The Economist*) (January/February 2012).
[13] Lars Gustafsson, "(Jean Sibelius natt)." *Det sällsamma djuret från norr* (Stockholm: Bra böcker, 1989), 159–67.

to hear the year's first cranes: "Their voices are my life's guidelines." Instead, he hears a strange noise from beneath. Leaning forward in his chair, he sees a young girl climbing the wall, her blue eyes looking at him pensively. He stretches his arms to help her inside and is surprised by her lightness. He thinks that he has fallen asleep and that the girl is his dream. He nevertheless begins a conversation with her, first wanting to know who she is. In a flirtatious manner she gives Mélisande as her name, but is reluctant to explain her provenance. Sibelius infers that she must be an American music student and thinks that, since she had come such a long way, he must answer some of her questions as a matter of courtesy. He offers to explain the trumpet theme at the end of the Fifth Symphony, but the girl says she has no problem with that: the theme is the same as in the "Scene with Cranes" from *Kuolema* (Death) and identical to the cello part at the beginning of the Eighth Symphony.

Now, Sibelius is even more convinced that he is dreaming, since there is no Eighth Symphony by Jean Sibelius. But he also becomes curious to know what else the girl could tell him about it. At his request, she begins describing the events in the score and humming the symphony's motifs. "Very strange, Mélisande, that I should dream you," Sibelius says. "You seem to know something about me that I don't. Or is it my subconscious that haunts me?" Mélisande suggests that more likely she is dreaming him, for it is always the logically stronger system that describes the logically weaker one. Confused, Sibelius once more asks: "Who would you be then, little girl?" And again Mélisande refuses to answer, saying that then Sibelius would only be unhappy about not having asked her more. Finally, she identifies herself as Sibelius' Eighth Symphony and says that she thought he had the right to see her once. Then the white curtain flutters, and she is gone. Sibelius survives the night but remains melancholy until his death.

Of another kind is a novel of almost five hundred pages, *Winter Fire*,[14] by the American novelist and historian William R. Trotter, who also wrote a book about Finland's Winter War.[15]

Winter Fire is a thriller. The events take place during the Finno-Russian Continuation War of 1941–4. After Nazi Germany attacked the

[14] William R. Trotter, *Winter Fire: A Novel of Music and War* (New York: Carroll and Graf, 1993); in Finnish: *Talven tuli*, trans. Eva Siikarla (Porvoo and Helsinki: Werner Söderström Osakeyhtiö, 1993).

[15] William R. Trotter, *A Frozen Hell: The Russo-Finnish Winter War of 1939/40* (Chapell Hill, North Carolina: Algonquin books of Chapel Hill, 1991).

Soviet Union in June 1941, Finland joined the war to regain the lands relinquished to the enemy by the Moscow Peace Treaty on March 13, 1940. As the Finns were not entirely trustworthy as allies, a German officer was ordered to investigate their loyalties and secure them for the Nazi cause. This officer is Captain Erich Ziegler, a conductor in civilian life who to some extent resembles the real-life conductor Helmuth Thierfelder. Following a rather weird turn of the plot Ziegler gets into contact with Sibelius, who lives in an isolated wartime safe house called Tapiola somewhere in central Finland, guarded by the military. This arrangement was made for the composer's safety since he was considered a "national treasure," and therefore a possible target for the Soviets.

Sibelius invites the German to dinner. During the conversation, Ziegler brings up a sensitive subject, asking questions about the Eighth Symphony. Sibelius becomes angry at his insolence and leaves the room. In the depths of the house a door slams. Aino Sibelius tries to explain her husband's vehement reaction, pointing out the burden that the world's expectations had placed on him. "He agonized over it, for fear that, when it is released, it will disappoint those who have made so much of it."

In spite of this incident, Ziegler, as a musician, manages to develop a trusting relationship with the elderly composer, who finally consents to play him the Eighth Symphony on the condition that he doesn't tell anyone that he has heard it. Ziegler agrees, and Sibelius plays him the work on the piano. Ziegler is impressed, noticing that the Eighth has grown organically from the composer's previous works: "The transformational techniques of *Tapiola* were raised here to heights of power, expressiveness, and formal logic beyond even that work's level of attainment."

However, as Sibelius stubbornly refuses to release the Symphony for public performance and insists that it will never leave Tapiola, Ziegler decides to save it for future generations and takes the manuscript by force, threatening the composer with his Luger. After the signing of the armistice between Finland and the Soviet Union in September 1944, he joins the German troops retreating from Finnish Lapland towards Norway, which is still under German occupation. Finnish troops chase the fleeing Germans, and open fire after catching sight of them in the distance. Bullets hit Captain Ziegler's leather dispatch case dangling over his shoulder, and leaves of paper, "fluttering like dove's wings," settle on the surface of a bog in Finnish Lapland. Ziegler desperately tries to retrieve them, but suction and the weight of his body carry most of the papers with him down into the bog. The Finnish commander is curious to see "what kind of document was valuable enough to be worth the risk of such a monstrous death. Something, surely, that Finnish intelligence would be interested in." He catches a few sodden pages but sees at a glance that there is, "nothing whatever of military value on them—only a few lines of barely legible music."

The extensive narrative also includes other elements: nature mysticism, animism, and shamanism (in the spirit of the poem from *Tapiola*'s printed score) that explain both the character of the symphony and the fate of its manuscript. Some scenes verge on the bizarre and the grotesque: in one of them, Sibelius, "cursing the Russians in at least two languages," starts shooting at enemy bombers flying overhead with an old Tsarist rifle. There are several subplots, one of which is an inevitable love affair between the German officer and Sibelius' housemaid "Kyllik[k]I," while another deals with the Glocken/Glockenspiel controversy in the finale of the Fourth Symphony, which Ziegler resolves by commissioning unique bells, specially conceived for the few bars in this piece, from an old Jewish artisan in Berlin whom Furtwängler had recommended. The bells produce "a cold and inhuman sound of the wind stroking the ice."

The *Kahdeksas sinfonia* ("The Eighth Symphony") by the Finnish playwright and Jungian analyst Harri Virtanen was staged at the Turku City Theatre in 1994 and adapted for radio the following year. In 2001, he wrote another play on the subject, *Puhtaaksikirjoittaja* (*The Copyist*), for TV.

In *Kahdeksas sinfonia*, Virtanen examines Sibelius' controversial character: his relationship with his wife, whose destiny is to take care of the garden and household; his friendships with contemporaries such as Robert Kajanus and Akseli Gallen-Kallela; his addiction to alcohol; and his relationship with money, sexuality, creativity, and nature. There is no unity of time and place. Themes emerge as if in a dream. Sibelius is anxious about his Eighth Symphony but reassures himself: "Es wird schon kommen." ("It will though be finished.") Finally, he succeeds, and his mood changes: "Das Zwingende is away. The giant struggle is over! The silence is over! I'm sober, and I don't feel anguished anymore. Nature is like … look out of the window! I don't drink any more … I don't have to … Look at those trees …" From this moment, life in Ainola becomes happy and the world will eventually have the Eighth Symphony—an imagined alternative solution.

The later play *The Copyist* is about dishonesty and theft. The model for the title character Hugo Autere, a cellist at the Helsinki Philharmonic, is Sibelius' trusted copyist Paul Voigt, who had been a second violinist in the same orchestra. Everything else is pure fiction. Autere not only makes a fair copy of the manuscript that Sibelius had brought to him but harbours his own secret compositional ambitions, and steals material for a Prelude for Orchestra. On Friday February 26, 1944 he conducts his Prelude in the Great Hall of the University. Sibelius attends the concert. An air-raid alarm interrupts the performance and a bomb hits the building, which then catches fire.[16] In the midst of the turmoil, Sibelius faces the composer and says: "I'm sorry, but this composition of yours doesn't work. Normally I wouldn't say this. But to release you I want to say it now." Musicians carry instruments out of the burning hall. A stage manager saves the score of the Prelude and turns it over to the composer who throws it into the flames. Sibelius watches the burning building from the Senate Square and says: "My music doesn't belong to this world."

The best known of these fictional accounts is probably Julian Barnes' "The Silence," from a collection of eleven short stories about aging, lateness, and death.[17] The title of the story is identical to that of the last chapter in Erik Tawaststjerna's biography,[18] and its contents are mostly from the same source, transformed into the composer's stream of consciousness. Sibelius' name is not mentioned. Readers ignorant of his life and music may wonder who the elderly composer might be. Single initials refer to three other persons, making their identification even more difficult: A. stands for Aino, K. for Koussevitzky, and N. for Carl Nielsen, with whom Sibelius disagreed about the respective importance of Mozart and Beethoven. The "French critic" who quoted Gounod saying, "Only God composes in C major" is Jean Chantavoine.

The name *The Lemon Table* stems from Sibelius' diary note on February 17, 1925, quoted in English by Tawaststjerna: "The lemon table at the *Kämp*! The lemon is the emblem of death with the Chinese. And in one of her poems, Anna-Maria Lenngren [a Finnish poet] writes, 'buried with a lemon in his hand.' That is a blessing!"[19]

---

[16] In real life a bomb did hit the main building of the university that day and the hall was destroyed, but there was no concert. The day before, however, a performance of Beethoven's Eighth Symphony had to be interrupted because of an air raid.

[17] Julian Barnes, *The Lemon Table* (London: Jonathan Cape; New York: Alfred A. Knopf, 2004).

[18] Erik Tawaststjerna, *Sibelius*. Vol. III, 1914–1957, ed. and trans. Robert Layton. (Faber & Faber: London, 1997), 318.

[19] Ibid., 257.

A wide range of themes Sibelius deals with in his diaries and correspondence are touched upon, including his disagreement with Mahler about the essence of the symphony, "Mr Stravinsky" blaming him for poor craftsmanship, the letter Aino wrote to him after he had conducted while drunk in Gothenburg, alcohol as the most faithful and understanding companion, Otto Andersson's working out of his family tree that made him feel ill, the Freudian theory of art as sublimation of suppressed desires, the infinite wretchedness of the artist's lot and the dreadfulness of old age: "Things don't go as quickly as they used to, and self-criticism grows to impossible proportions." Time to call for a lemon.

The only musico-dramatic work in our collection of fictions is *Zugvögel* ("Migratory Birds"), "a symphonic drama" in four scenes and an epilogue by the German composer and conductor Mathias Husmann, staged in Stralsund in 2009. The composer got the idea for his libretto, according to an interview,[20] from Kari Kilpeläinen's article on the Eighth Symphony.[21]

In the first scene, on May 10, 1927, Aino Sibelius' name day, her brothers Arvid, Armas, and Eero Järnefelt, all artists, discuss the Eighth Symphony with Sibelius. Armas, the conductor (and composer), says: "A modern work of art, whether it is a symphony or something else, must reflect the technical standard of its time." The sentence is an anachronism, a projection of Adorno's later claim that Sibelius "has not merely lagged completely behind the technical standard of the times," but "also fails to live up to his own standards ..."[22] Sibelius' anxiety grows. He throws everyone out and starts writing his Eighth Symphony, but develops an acute psychosis and, haunted by voices, tries to escape from the nightmare of his fantasy.

The second scene takes place on June 24, 1933, Janne's name day. Eero, the painter, brings news from Germany: In the country of Goethe and Kant, they now burn books in public. The *Reichstag* has been set on fire, and the Parliament itself has been abolished. What is worse, Jews are persecuted, deported, and gathered in concentration camps. "And I should be composing," says Sibelius.

---

[20] *Helsingin Sanomat*, March 7, 2009.

[21] Kari Kilpeläinen, "Sibelius Eighth. What Happened to it?" *Finnish Music Quarterly* 11 (4) (1995): 30–5.

[22] Theodor W Adorno, "Gloss on Sibelius," trans. Susan H. Gillespie, in *Jean Sibelius and His World*, ed. Daniel M. Grimley (Princeton and Oxford: Princeton University Press, 2011 [1938]), 334.

In the third scene, on November 30, 1939, the first day of the Russo-Finnish Winter War, Sibelius works through the mail with his secretary Santeri Levas and becomes irritated by impertinent questions. He fetches glasses and a bottle of whisky. Both get drunk. Sibelius climbs a table and starts dancing the third movement of his Symphony while conducting at the same time. The first bombs fall on Helsinki, and a glow of fire enlightens the horizon.

The fourth scene takes place on December 8, 1945, Sibelius' eightieth birthday. The guests are gone. Sibelius begins a monologue and falls asleep. Unexpected guests, casualties of war, come through the wall. They demand the Eighth Symphony. As Sibelius refuses, they compose a macabre war symphony using his head and hands. Sibelius sees two "migratory birds" heading to Hiroshima and Nagasaki. He dedicates his Symphony to the victims of fascism and war and burns the score.

"Kadonnut sinfonia" ("The Lost Symphony") is a short story by Miina Supinen in a collection of eight short stories on Sibelius by Finnish writers.[23] Of the same name is a comic strip by the writer and drawer Kari Korhonen, well known for his *Donald Duck* and *Angry Birds* cartoons.[24] Both fall under the notion of the *picaresque*, a genre of satiric prose fiction depicting the adventures of a deceitful and unreliable person.

In the former, Pertti Minkkinen, a musician and outpatient at a psychiatric clinic, presents a composition of his own as Sibelius' Eighth Symphony. He invites his doctor to the sensational première while pretending that he suspects a fraud. He describes Sibelius as a tired old alcoholic who had destroyed all his notes after desperately trying to achieve something valuable. "Finally, he burnt what he had managed to get on paper."

Dr. Kaarna has no words to describe the symphony. Somehow, it was more than just music. It ran over to the other senses, a synaesthetic experience. The performance was enthusiastically acclaimed in the press. It was the cultural highlight of the autumn, the year, and the decade, according to some. People came from all over the world to hear it. The symphony was more modern than Sibelius' previous works, a logical end

---

[23] Miina Supinen, "Kadonnut sinfonia" ["The Lost Symphony"], in *Sanasinfonia: novelleja Sibeliuksesta* [*Symphony in Words: Short Stories on Sibelius*], eds. Päivi Haanpää and Marika Riikonen (Hämeenlinna: Karisto, 2015), 74–88.

[24] Kari Korhonen, *Kadonnut sinfonia* [*The Lost Symphony*] (Helsinki: Sanoma Osakeyhtiö, 2011).

point of his experiments. New research projects were discussed at the Academy of Finland. Sibelius' biography needed to be rewritten.

"I knew, though, that the disclosure of the fraud was only a matter of time," Dr. Kaarna thought to himself. And so it was, as it became a police matter. "If it is not Sibelius' work, I don't know whose it is," said the music centre director when questioned by the police. But he knew, as did Dr. Kaarna. Afterwards, when seen on the streets of Helsinki, there was joy and determination in Minkkinen's figure, some music in his step.

In Kari Korhonen's comic strip, two representatives of the Arts Council from the city of Ankkalinna (Duckburg) come to see Scrooge McDuck, the rich banker, asking for his help. The jubilee year of the legendary composer Sipulius is at hand, but the composer had mysteriously disappeared years before without finishing his Eighth Symphony. "We were just informed that he was in your service at that time. Is that correct?"

Scrooge reluctantly agrees and promises to help with the search, since, he claims, he had always been a great patron of the arts. He will entrust his best man, his nephew Donald, with the job. Along with his nephews, Huey, Dewey, and Louie, who just had been reading about Sipulius at school, Donald Duck embarks on the search. They first visit Sipulius's last-known address, a city apartment house, where his housekeeper Aino tells them about the difficulties he had with his last symphony. "Then, one day he just left," she said.

Huey asks whether she can remember any melodic fragments from the symphony he was working on. She can indeed. One of them was something like, "Ti-taa taa-ti taa-ti-taa taa-ti-taa." She advises the boys to go and see his friends at the Hotel Komp for more information. The friends can also hum some fragments of a melody, but they don't know much more. One of them suspects that he had travelled to Germany to see Dr. Schnitzel, the psychiatrist, whereas Aleksi, the painter, advises them to continue the search in Africa. While Donald Duck takes their advice and embarks on the journey, Huey, Dewey, and Louie look closer at the melodic fragments and detect Morse code hidden in them reading "Scrooge is a slave driver and miser." The enigma is solved, and the location of the manuscript revealed. The boys go to see Scrooge McDuck and threaten to make the insult public if he doesn't relinquish the score. Scrooge has no other choice than to fetch it from his safe. At last, the work can be performed.

Sipulius, identified at the première, explains: "I was in debt to Scrooge. He commissioned the symphony and put such pressure on me. But his compensation for my efforts was lousy. My spirit for creating music was gone. I haven't written a note since then."

In Simon Parmet's view, the "Silence of Järvenpää" was a consequence of Sibelius' opposition to the modern trends in the music of the 1920s and 30s, on the one hand, and his disintegrating self-confidence on the other. The fictions of Trotter, Virtanen, and Husmann strongly suggest that it wasn't only the musical but rather the political development in Europe, and the war as its consequence, which silenced Sibelius. The political turmoil in Germany after World War I, and especially the rise of Nazism and Fascism, brought about the unprecedented politicisation of music.[25] This development manifested itself, when it came to Sibelius, in the writings of Adorno, notably his "Gloss on Sibelius."[26] Expressions such as "Blood and Soil" and "cultural Bolshevism," which belong to the language Viktor Klemperer called the LTI, or the *lingua tertii imperii*,[27] reveal that Adorno applies to Sibelius the same strategy of discreditation that the Nazis used against what they called *entartete Musik*, namely the, "political denunciation of aesthetically undesirable works."[28] René Leibowitz adopted the same approach when he accused Bartók of bowing to the "spirit of compromise" after he rejected the technique of composing with twelve tones which he and Adorno deemed the only solution to the problems of chromatic polyphony.[29] In this view, tonal music is associated with Nazi-mindedness, and atonal music with anti-Nazism and anti-Fascism.[30]

---

[25] See Eckhard John, *Musikbolschewismus: Die Politisierung der Musik in Deutschland 1918–1938* (Stuttgart and Weimar: Verlag J. B. Metzler, 1994).

[26] Adorno, "Gloss on Sibelius." See Ruth-Maria Gleißner, *Der* unpolitische *Komponist als Politikum* [Europäische Hochschulschriften. Reihe 36: Musikwissenschaft] (Frankfurt am Main etc.; Peter Lang, 2002).

[27] Viktor Klemperer, *LTI: Notizbuch eines Philologen* (Stuttgart: Reclam, 2010).

[28] Eckhard John, "Bemerkungen zur vorgeblichen Vergewaltigung der Frau Musica," *Neue Zeitschrift für Musik* 156 (1) (1995): 15–18. Cf. Ilkka Oramo, "Zur Rezeption der Musik von Jean Sibelius (1865–1957) in der deutschen Fachliteratur seit 1945," *Zur Neuorientierung der finnisch-deutschen Kulturbeziehungen nach 1945* (Veröffentlichungen der AUE-Stiftung 11), ed. W. Bastman-Bühner (Helsinki: AUE-Stiftung, 2000).

[29] René Leibowitz, "Béla Bartók ou la possibilité du compromis dans la musique contemporaine," *Les Temps Modernes* 3 (25) (October 1947): 705–34.

[30] See Danielle Fosler-Lussier, *Music Divided: Bartók's Legacy in Cold War Culture* (California Studies in 20th-Century Music) (Berkeley, Los Angeles and London: University of California Press, 2007), 28–33.

It is unlikely, although not impossible, that Sibelius was made aware of Adorno's gloss. But even if he wasn't, this line of thought must have been familiar to him. He probably found himself in an insoluble moral conflict that prevented him from composing music, and this contributed to his decision to not release the Eighth Symphony. His diary notes from 1943 point in this direction. In the same year, on September 13, he also wrote his final diary note on the Eighth: "The Symphony is in my thoughts. Our critics here are beneath contempt. Only very few understand what I have done and want to do in the world of the symphony. The majority have no idea of what it is about."[31] What he had in mind with this comment is not entirely explicit. "What I have done" apparently refers to the fact that in writing the Seventh Symphony and the symphonic poem *Tapiola* he had not only reached the utmost limits of condensation in symphonic thinking but also solved the problem of how to unite the generic tradition of symphonic music that split in two in the 1850s. This is what he felt the critics did not understand. "What I want to do" is harder to construe. It seems to suggest that he was still trying to figure out an idea of how to proceed from this point, the *telos* of decades of tightening the "profound logic" that he considered the essence of the symphony.[32] One option could have been an attempt to reconcile the two main streams of twentieth century music, the progressive and the moderate,[33] to achieve something comparable to Bartók's late works. For it was Bartók whom he—in a conversation with Yehudi Menuhin in the early 1950s—pointed out as the greatest composer of the twentieth century.[34] In this attempt, if it was indeed what he was after (or whatever it might have been), he ultimately failed.

A more creditable explanation for the failure than that offered in the fictions of Trotter, Virtanen, and Husmann would be to hard imagine. Mark McKenna, however, finds in Julian Barnes' story another truth: "Barnes knew intuitively what many others had failed to flesh out. The

---

[31] Jean Sibelius, *Dagbok 1909–1944* (Skrifter utgivna av Svenska Litteratursällskapet i Finland 681), ed. Fabian Dahlström (Helsingfors: Svenska Litteratursällskapet i Finland; Stockholm: Atlantis, 2005), 335. Quoted in English in Tawaststjerna, *Sibelius*. Vol. III, 327.

[32] See Lionel Pike, *Beethoven, Sibelius and the "Profound Logic": Studies in Symphonic Analysis* (University of London: The Athlone Press, 1978).

[33] See Nicholas Cook and Anthony Pople, "Introduction: Trajectories of twentieth-century music," in *The Cambridge History of Twentieth-Century Music* (Cambridge: Cambridge University Press, 2004), 1–17.

[34] Yehudi Menuhin, *Unfinished Journey* (London: Futura Publications, 1978), 432.

silence of Sibelius is the din of his beatification … Silence was, in fact, the only logical response Sibelius could make to his deification by the Finnish state. The story of his final years is a graphic illustration of the dangers of too close a connection between art and nationalism."[35] Although it is not quite clear what exactly in Barnes' story supports this argument, it completes the picture of an anguished old composer enclosed in a suffocating loneliness by domestic adoration, both official and public.

Lars Gustafsson's science fiction story suggests that Sibelius will still be known and remembered in the distant future. When it comes to the Eighth Symphony, the little girl who pays him a visit from another dimension makes it clear that it was only a dream. But whose dream? Sibelius' dream or the dream of others, of all those who have been burning to hear it? The two examples of *picaresque* about the lost symphony finally mock those who are eager to pursue the vain search for its remains, as if it were the Holy Grail of Finnish music.

[35] Mark McKenna, "Who Stopped the Music: How Jean Sibelius Ran Out of Notes," *The Monthly* 84 (November 2012).

2. Reception in Britain, France, and Germany

INSTITUTIONAL REGULATION AND PARISIAN PERCEPTIONS OF SIBELIUS, 1924–1931: THE SCHNÉEVOIGTS AND THE ASSOCIATION FRANÇAISE D'EXPANSION ET D'ÉCHANGES ARTISTIQUES

HELENA TYRVÄINEN

Examining some particular traits of French cultural life can lead to a better understanding of Sibelius' difficult position in France during his lifetime.[1] The French post-Revolution self-image of a champion of the rights of oppressed peoples, the established position of Paris as a cosmopolitan cultural capital, and a national concern for restoring the country's international prestige after its defeat in the Franco-Prussian war (1870–1)

---

[1] The article is part of my research project "Finland and France: Musical relations, cosmopolitanism, and national culture, 1880–1940," currently supported by the Wihuri Foundation. Previously, I have analyzed Sibelius' relations with France for example in Helena Tyrväinen, "Suomalaiset Pariisin maailmannäyttelyiden 1889 ja 1900 musiikkiohjelmissa" ["Finns in the Music Programmes of the Paris 1889 and 1900 World Fairs"], *Musiikkitiede* 1–2 (1994): 22–74; "Sibelius at the Paris Universal Exposition of 1900," *Sibelius Forum. Proceedings from the Second International Jean Sibelius Conference, Helsinki November 25–29, 1995*, eds. Veijo Murtomäki, Kari Kilpeläinen and Risto Väisänen (Helsinki: Sibelius Academy, Department of Composition and Music Theory, 1998), 114–28; "'La nature de primitif affiné qui le caractérise': La musique du Nord à Paris et la construction de l'altérité nordique," *Le prisme du Nord. Pays du Nord, France, Allemagne (1750–1920)*, ed. Michel Espagne (Tusson: du Lérot, 2006), 103–30; "'National,' 'archaïque,' 'nordique,' 'modal:' le 'Grieg finlandais' [Sibelius] se présente à Paris," Actes du Colloque International Jean Sibelius: Modalité, langage, esthétique, Paris, 5–7 novembre 2007, *Musurgia* XV 1–3 (2008): 119–140; "'*La nature de primitif affiné qui le caractérise*:' Sibelius' music in Paris and the construction of the Nordic 'Other'," in *Sibelius in the Old and New World. Aspects of his Music, Its Interpretation, and Reception*, eds. Timothy L. Jackson, Veijo Murtomäki, Colin Davis, and Timo Virtanen (Frankfurt am Main: Peter Lang, 2010), 401–17.

are all factors that added special importance to music's national reference in the French imagination, even where foreign composers were concerned. The relevance of the institutional regulation in Paris can be explained by the fact that in 1899 Aino Ackté—the Finnish star soprano of the Paris Opéra—following a patriotic plea by her compatriot Karl Fredrik Wasenius (known as a critic under his pseudonym Bis), failed to have Sibelius' *King Christian II* Suite included in the programmes of the Colonne concerts.[2] Only one year later, the Finnish composer experienced extraordinary success in the Parisian press following the concerts of the Helsinki Philharmonic Society Orchestra; significantly, the *King Christian II* music was among the successful works. But in 1900, the forum was the Paris Universal Exposition, hence the institution *par excellence* where France was expected to attend to the national expressions of other countries.[3] There, Sibelius was introduced to the world in Karl Flodin's words as "the master and flag-bearer of the young Finnish composers."[4] The universal expositions more generally contributed to the breakthrough in the nineteenth century of the ideals of "national character" and "national style." Of all universal expositions, those organised in Paris gave a privileged place to the arts.[5]

While important personal relations between Finnish and French persons diminished with the decades (I am thinking in particular of the loss of such an influential mediator as the Finnish painter Albert Edelfelt [1854–1905]), the importance of the institutions increased. This article will explore how

---

[2] Aino Ackté, *Muistojeni kirja* (Helsinki: Otava, 1925), 108. Cf. Pentti Savolainen and Matti Vainio (eds.), *Aino Ackté: Elämänkaari kirjeiden valossa* (Helsinki: WSOY, 2002), 101.

[3] In my sense: "Institutions are 'stable, valued, recurring patterns of behavior.' As structures or mechanisms of social order, they govern the behaviour of a set of individuals within a given community. Institutions are identified with a social purpose, transcending individuals and intentions by mediating the rules that govern living behavior." ("Institution." *Wikipedia*). In this article I intend to analyse the consequences of the French governmental initiative through only one important institution, the AFEEA.

[4] Karl Flodin, *La musique en Finlande* (Paris, 1900), 10, and Tyrväinen, "Sibelius at the Paris Universal Exposition of 1900," 120; for the political background to the Finnish representation in 1900 see also Kerstin Smeds, *Helsingfors—Paris: Finland på världsutställningarna 1851–1900* (Helsingfors: Svenska litteratursällskapet i Finland & Finska Historiska Samfundet, 1996), 277–9, 328–45.

[5] It was in the context of the Paris 1867 Universal Exposition that the nations were first asked to build their pavilions in a national style. See Smeds, *Helsingfors—Paris*, 45–7, 49, 96, 159.

the activity of L'Association Française d'Expansion et d'Échanges Artistiques (The French Alliance of Artistic Expansion and Exchange) might have influenced Sibelius' reputation in post-World War I France. The AFEEA was founded in Paris in 1922 in the nationalist climate of ideas following World War I, with the purpose of extending France's artistic influence in the world. It built on wartime activities, more particularly those run by the Service de décentralisation artistique which, following the initiative of pianist Alfred Cortot and the model of the national enemy Germany, engaged French artists in propaganda work. At the onset of peace, the French Ministry of Public Education (*Ministère de l'Instruction Publique et des Beaux-Arts*) chose to retain this useful unit, now renamed Service d'études d'action artistique à l'étranger. *Le Figaro's* music critic Robert Brussel was appointed as its director. When extending governmental endeavours into the realm of international artistic relations, the AFEEA joined the public and the private initiative alongside patronage. As French international institutional relations concerning the arts were subordinated to the French foreign ministry under an 1810 decree, the founding of the AFEEA took place under the protection of the French ministries of Foreign Affairs and of Public Education.[6] As a consequence of this twofold allegiance, information on the AFEEA today must be searched for in two different places. The Ministry of Public Education archive concerning the AFEEA (Service d'études) is held in the music department of the Bibliothèque nationale de France under the title Fonds Montpensier.[7] There is also ample documentation on this organisation (Service des Œuvres) in the archive of the French Ministry of Foreign Affairs. Both archives (Service d'études and Service des Œuvres) contain many traces of the AFEEA's cooperation with several Finnish musicians.

Bernard Piniau has remarked that the operative model of the AFEEA's founders leaned largely on principles that the French Third Republic had adopted in the period 1880–1910 amid the unsettling and inglorious circumstances following the Franco-Prussian war. With the aim being the restoration of France's international prestige, the great international encounters of the past within the industrial realm, such as the universal expositions, were among the models that were adopted.[8] By February 1924

---

[6] Bernard Piniau in collaboration with Ramon Tio Bellido, *L'action artistique de la France dans le monde: Histoire de l'Association Française d'Action Artistique (AFAA) de 1922 à nos jours* (Paris: L'Harmattan, 1998), 13, 21–2, 27–34, 69.

[7] Parts of the Fonds Montpensier's concert programmes are to be consulted under "Programmes" in the music department of the Bibliothèque nationale de France. See note 9.

[8] Piniau, *L'action artistique de la France*, 23–6, 45, 60.

the organisation had already engaged 250 foreign correspondents, established an archive and files concerning artistic issues, and produced 150,000 biographical and bibliographical folders as well as 100,000 repertories of press items written in fourteen languages.[9] While the Parisian Universal Expositions invited the world's artists to gather in the French capital, the AFEEA aimed at extending its authority by spreading French art and culture outside its borders.[10] However, the organisation also helped foreign musicians gain a foothold in France.[11]

The AFEEA and the Finnish Musicians

What do the archives reveal about the AFEEA's dealings with foreign music people, and what were Sibelius' chances of profiting from it? Placed in boxes related to specific countries and folders bearing the names of individual musicians or music ensembles, the Fonds Montpensier preserves, along with other documents, duplicated press forms related to each. These AFEEA forms mainly apply to one Paris concert at the time, but one form may also contain information about several events when a single musician has played many concerts during a short period. Annotated by hand are the musician's name, the concert hall concerned, and the date. In addition, these duplicated forms contain the names of many Parisian journals. Next to them, the names of the critics who wrote about the event are marked by hand. I conclude from this material that the organisation in one way or another controlled the musicians' relations with the local press. While the AFEEA did in fact introduce the creative aspect of music from other countries to France, this seems to have been of relatively little

---

9 Bibliothèque nationale de France, Paris, Département de la Musique. Programmes. Associations. Association Française d'Expansion et d'Échanges Artistiques. Association Française d'Expansion et d'Échanges Artistiques, Réception en l'honneur des musiciens suisses 21 février 1914, programme.

10 I have analysed the AFEEA's activities concerning Finland in a paper entitled "Journalist and Diplomat Wentzel Hagelstam: Cosmopolitan Builder of Independent Finland's Musical Life and Agent of France's Artistic Expansion," at the conference "Confronting the National in the Musical Past," Helsinki, Musiikkitalo, May 21, 2014.

11 Piniau, *L'action artistique de la France*, 23, 57; for a brief introduction to the AFEEA's (and later AFAA's) activities in the musical domain, see Danièle Pistone, "La musique come ambassadrice? L'Association française d'action artistique (1922–2006): bilans et enjeux," *Relations internationales*, revue trimestrielle d'histoire 156 (hiver 2013) "Musique et relations internationales II" (Nanterre: PUF, 2014), 21–35.

concern to the association.[12] Among Finnish composers, the organisation only supported one. Its cooperation with Sibelius' composition pupil—the author of the notorious *Sibelius: A Close-Up*—Bengt von Törne (known in France under his Gallicised name Benoît de Törne), in connection with a concert dedicated to his works in Salle Gaveau on May 29, 1927, was probably facilitated by his brother, Per Olof von Törne, Professor of Nordic History at the Åbo Akademi in Turku and a correspondent of the AFEEA.[13] There is no press form directly concerning Sibelius. Among foreign musicians, the main support was given to performers.

---

[12] However, the AFEEA organised a concert of Danish music in Paris (with works by Carl Nielsen, Peder Gram, Rued Langgaard, Peter Lange-Müller, Gustav Helsted, Hakon Børresen, Ludolf Nielsen, Louis Glass, Fini Henriques, Knudåge Riisager, Peter Heise, and Paul Schierbeck) in cooperation with Danish music societies Dansk Tonekunstnerforening and Unge Tonkunstneres Selskab, and another one dedicated exclusively to Nielsen's works. It also invited Armas Järnefelt, Sibelius' brother-in-law, principal conductor of the Swedish Royal Opera and a Swedish citizen since 1909, to conduct a concert of Swedish music in Paris on June 21, 1924 (with works by Kurt Atterberg, Natanael Berg, Wilhelm Stenhammar, Ture Rangström, and Hugo Alfvén). René Brancour, "Concert de musique danoise," *Le Ménestrel* 48 (1923): 504; Henri de Curzon, "Concert symphonique: Œuvres de Carl Nielsen," *Le Ménestrel* (October 29, 1926): 457; Pierre de Lapommeraye, "Concerts suédois," *Le Ménestrel* (June 27, 1924): 290–1.

[13] This concert, in which the composer conducted his own works (*Invocation*, *Poème*, excerpts from *La Basilisse*, and Symphony in F sharp minor), is the only one for which Fonds Montpensier conserves a press form. The Montpensier archive also contains several press clippings indicating von Törne's activity in France as a composer. In 1926 he organised a concert of his works in the Université Alexandre Merceteau in Paris (December 6) and another one in 1928 in the Salle Gaveau (April 25), on which occasion he conducted an orchestra of 80 in a performance of his symphony. On October 27, 1927 he conducted his *Fantaisie héroïque* in the hall of the Conservatoire and on September 19, 1932 gave a piano recital of his works in the private hall of Mme Œdenkowen. *Invocation* was performed at the Monte Carlo Opera on March 28, 1928. An undated press clipping from 1927 (*Hufvudstadsbladet*) in Fonds Montpensier states that Bengt von Törne had studied music in Paris for four years. Bibliothèque nationale de France. Département de la Musique. Fonds Montpensier. Compositeurs. Benoît de Törne. See also *Hufvudstadsbladet* July 3 and November 18, 1927, April 26 and 27, 1928, and *Comœdia* 1932, "Un récital des œuvres de Benoît de Torne" (May 19). The convoluted administration and the interdependence of the French ministries are revealed by the correspondence from 1926 concerning the invitation of Per Olof von Törne to be an AFEEA correspondent in matters concerning musical and theatre life in Turku. In order to find a suitable person, the director of the AFEEA first asked for the opinion of the French Ambassador to Finland Maurice de Coppet. De Coppet sent his proposition to director of the AFEEA Robert Brussel

The archives testify to the cooperation between the AFEEA and many Finnish performing musicians who gave concerts in Paris between 1924 and 1931, such as: violinist Kerttu Wanne; pianists Sigrid Sundgren-Schnéevoigt, Ernst Linko, Orest Bodalew, and Kerttu Bernhard; singers Greta von Haartman, Helge Lindberg, Aino Ackté, and Gertrud Alfthan; the Viborg Chamber Orchestra; and conductor Georg Schnéevoigt. Several of these musicians even performed Sibelius' works. Violinist Kerttu Wanne played *Souvenir* and Mazurka in the concert hall of the École normale de musique (on March 12, 1930). Of the singers, Aino Ackté sang "La jeune fille revint du rendez-vous" in the University of the Sorbonne Amphithéâtre Richelieu (*Flickan kom ifrån sin älsklings möte* in the original Swedish, March 6, 1928), Gertrud Alfthan also sang some Sibelius in the Amphithéâtre Richelieu (February 1929), Helge Lindberg *Säv, säv, susa* in the Maison Gaveau (February 3, 1925), and Greta von Haartman *Den första kyssen* and *Svarta rosor* in the Maison Gaveau (May 31, 1928).[14]

From the group of Finnish musicians who cooperated with the AFEEA and even executed Sibelius' works in Paris, the Swedish-speaking married couple Georg and Sigrid Schnéevoigt stands out. Both were among the

---

and a copy of his letter to the Service des Œuvres in the French foreign ministry (March 31). Brussel thanked de Coppet for the suggestion and expressed his intention to turn to von Törne (April 16). An official of the French Ministry of Public Education inquired via a representative of the Service des Œuvres if the nominated correspondent will be approved by the Ministry of Foreign Affairs (April 19). A representative of the Service des Œuvres informed Robert Brussel that there was no obstacle to the invitation (April 30). Archives du Ministère des Affaires étrangères, Paris. Archives diplomatiques. MN 417QO SEA 16/O VIII/2. Service des Œuvres françaises à l'étranger. Section littéraire et artistique Estonie, Finlande, Lettonie et Lithuanie 1923/1930.

[14] This information about the performances of Sibelius' works only concerns those concerts of Finnish musicians for which a press form exists in the Fonds Montpensier. Basically, the same people may have performed his music in other concerts in Paris. Ernst Linko played Bach, Beethoven, Mozart, Schumann, and Chopin in the Salle des Agriculteurs (January 28, 1928), and Kerttu Bernhard played Bach, Brahms, Chopin, Debussy, and Madetoja's "The Garden of Death" (*Kuoleman puutarha*) in the Salle Majestic (January 22, 1929). The Chamber Orchestra of the Viborg Conservatory played Bach, Scarlatti, Locatelli, Telemann, Paul Juon, Melartin, Kuula, and Ranta under the direction of Boris Sirob in the École Normale de Musique (May 10, 1932). Fonds Montpensier. Finlande. Artistes lyriques, Virtuoses, Villes (sauf Helsinki); *Hufvudstadsbladet*, "Finländsk musik i Paris" (February 12, 1929); Jean Messager, "Les récitals de la quinzaine," *Comœdia* (January 29, 1929); Maurice Imbert, "Concerts et récitals: Musique finlandaise," *Journal des Débats* (May 16, 1932).

most internationally successful Finns within their respective professional groups. A pupil at the Helsinki Music Institute, Sigrid Sundgren (1878–1953) had, at the age of 14, William Dayas, a former pupil of Liszt, for a piano teacher. Two years later she continued her studies in Berlin with Ferruccio Busoni, who introduced her to the Berlin public by organising a concert for her when she was 18.[15] At the age of 20 she married her compatriot, the cellist and future conductor Georg Schnéevoigt. Sigrid Sundgren-Schnéevoigt was an experienced pianist with an international reputation when, in 1923 at the latest, she started to play concerts in Paris. In 1927 she settled there permanently.[16] At the same time, Georg Schnéevoigt (1872–1947) had long been enjoying European-wide renown as a skilful, hypnotically energetic orchestral conductor. A rival of the nationally authoritative Robert Kajanus, conductor of the Helsinki Philharmonic, Schnéevoigt had gained his laurels mainly outside Finland. He could include in his curriculum vitae the directorship of the Munich Kaim orchestra (from 1903), the founding of the Riga symphony orchestra in 1909, success as an orchestra builder in the service of the Stockholm Concert Society from 1914, responsibility of the Christiania (Oslo) Concert Society orchestra from 1919, and appearances as guest conductor with a great number of European orchestras, for example the Berlin Philharmonic. He had left the Stockholm Concert Society in 1924 and the same year accepted a position as *Generalmusikdirektor* in Düsseldorf. He became the musical director of the Los Angeles Philharmonic Orchestra in 1927.[17] His name appeared in the French press many years before his Paris debut.[18]

In his opening Paris concert in December 1924, Schnéevoigt conducted the first French performance of Sibelius' Second Symphony, a work he adored[19]. Until then, only two performances of a Sibelius symphony had

---

[15] Margit Rahkonen, "Piano-playing Pulsating with Life," *Finnish Music Quarterly* 1 (2010): 30–3.

[16] Elsa von Born, "Professor Schnéevoigt hemma," *Astra* (February 12, 1927). Tip (pseudonym) "Hos Sigrid Schnéevoigt i Paris," *Veckans Krönika* (November 30, 1929).

[17] Vesa Sirén, *Suomalaiset kapellimestarit Sibeliuksesta Saloseen, Kajanuksesta Franckiin* (Helsinki: Otava, 2010), 85–90, 205–214. A German translation of Sirén's book will be published in March 2017 titled *Finnlands Dirigenten. Von Sibelius und Schnéevoigt bis Saraste und Salonen*, trans. Roman Schatz and Benjamin Schweitzer, ed. Felicia Englman (Scoventa Verlag).

[18] Concerning Schnéevoigt's successes in Spain, Holland, Norway (Christiania), and Sweden (Stockholm), see *Le Ménestrel*, March 18, 1921, September 30, 1921, May 27, 1921, and January 5, 1923.

[19] Sirén, *Suomalaiset kapellimestarit Sibeliuksesta Saloseen*, 213, 223, 224, 248.

taken place in France, both of them under the direction of Kajanus: the First Symphony during the Universal Exposition of 1900, and the Third Symphony together with works by other Finnish composers on May 13, 1920 in a concert of the Pasdeloup orchestra, partly financed by the Finnish government. For some reason, there are no press forms in the Fonds Montpensier for the Schnéevoigts' first Paris concerts.

Georg Schnéevoigt's Paris debut with Sibelius' Second Symphony

On Monday evening, December 15, 1924, Schnéevoigt conducted a programme consisting of Sibelius' Second Symphony, Mozart's D minor Piano Concerto, K. 466, and Beethoven's "Emperor" Concerto, Op. 73, with the renowned US pianist Eleanor Spencer as a soloist, and another favourite work of his, Ravel's *La Valse*, in the Conservatoire concert hall. The printed programme states that the orchestra consisted of 80 members of the Société des Concerts du Conservatoire orchestra. The concert was not organised by the Société des Concerts but by the A. Dandelot & Fils concert agency "in accordance with Mme L[ola] Bossan."[20] It would not be possible to interpret the position of all foreign AFEEA associates in the light of the AFEEA's dealings with Georg Schnéevoigt. Judging from the materials of the Fonds Montpensier, he was by far the most highly appreciated Finnish musician among those who performed in Paris. From the Schnéevoigt file a network of actors emerges, consisting of the conductor himself, Mme Lola Bossan, the AFEEA and its director Robert Brussel, and the body of Parisian music critics. Schnéevoigt is generally best remembered as an interpreter of German music. True, his repertoire included such masterworks of contemporary French music as Debussy's *Nocturnes* and Ravel's *La Valse* and *Daphnis et Chloë*.[21] Also true, the French press noted an all-French programme with works by Berlioz, Saint-Saëns, Dukas, Chausson, and Ravel which he conducted in Stockholm in 1922.[22] Yet, in the correspondence preceding his Paris visit and later, in the

---

[20] Concert programme of Schnéevoigt's Paris debut concert. Bibliothèque nationale de France. Département de la Musique. Fonds Montpensier. Finlande. Virtuoses. Georg Schnéevoigt.

[21] Sirén, *Suomalaiset kapellimestarit Sibeliuksesta Saloseen*, 85, 187, 220, 229, 232. From Debussy's *Nocturnes*, at least the movement *Fêtes* was part of Schnéevoigt's repertoire: he conducted it in Helsinki in February 1927. "Georg Schnéevoigt," *Svenska Dagbladet* (February 9, 1927).

[22] See *Le Ménestrel* (January 5, 1923).

French press accounts of his concert, his services to the new French music assume constrained proportions. This emphasis appears tendentious.

On December 4, 1924, Lola Bossan wrote to Brussel, referring (with reference to his letter of July 31) to his promise to provide her with information. She was organising a concert for a Finnish conductor and anticipated a positive reaction from the Parisian press and public. This was justified, she claimed, since the musician in question, though unknown in Paris, had been a determined propagator of French music and French musicians, and had already been awarded membership of the Légion d'Honneur for these services. Bossan even reported her intention to gather French composers around Schnéevoigt. The aim was to have their works played in the numerous concerts given by the conductor abroad. Bossan invited Brussel to the concert and on behalf of her client asked for organisational assistance.

On December 10, Brussel wrote (in German) to Schnéevoigt at his Düsseldorf *Cäcilienallée* address, thanking him for a letter he had received dated November 30. He expressed his delight at the Finn's upcoming concert in Paris and asserted his intention to invite the best Parisian critics to write about the event. He asked Schnéevoigt to oblige the concert agency by providing him with additional information. The same day, Brussel wrote to Bossan telling her that he had received her letter of December 4. He added that he had even received a letter from Schnéevoigt. He would be happy to come to the concert and intended to draw the attention of his colleagues from the "great Parisian press" to it. He wished to know for which critics a seat would be reserved, but he also expressed his concern at the composition of the programme, for two piano concertos were included. From the viewpoint of the press, he said, it would have been more opportune to introduce nothing but new, unknown orchestral compositions.

Letter of Robert Brussel to Music Critics.
Fonds Montpensier, Finlande, Département de la musique, Bibliothèque nationale de France.

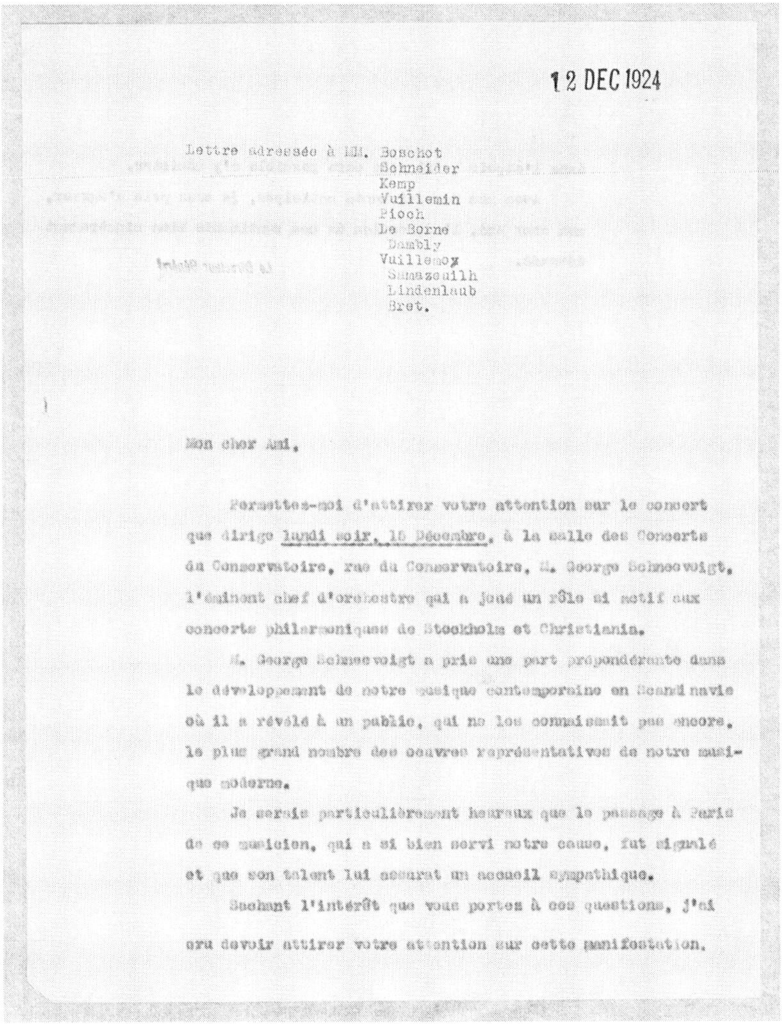

12 DEC 1924

Lettre adressée à MM. Boschot
Schneider
Kemp
Vuillemin
Pioch
Le Borne
Dambly
Vuillemoz
Samazeuilh
Lindenlaub
Bret.

Mon cher Ami,

Permettez-moi d'attirer votre attention sur le concert que dirige lundi soir, 15 Décembre, à la salle des Concerts du Conservatoire, rue du Conservatoire, M. George Schneevoigt, l'éminent chef d'orchestre qui a joué un rôle si actif aux concerts philarmoniques de Stockholm et Christiania.

M. George Schneevoigt a pris une part prépondérante dans le développement de notre musique contemporaine en Scandinavie où il a révélé à un public, qui ne les connaissait pas encore, le plus grand nombre des oeuvres représentatives de notre musique moderne.

Je serais particulièrement heureux que le passage à Paris de ce musicien, qui a si bien servi notre cause, fut signalé et que son talent lui assurat un accueil sympathique.

Sachant l'intérêt que vous portez à ces questions, j'ai cru devoir attirer votre attention sur cette manifestation.

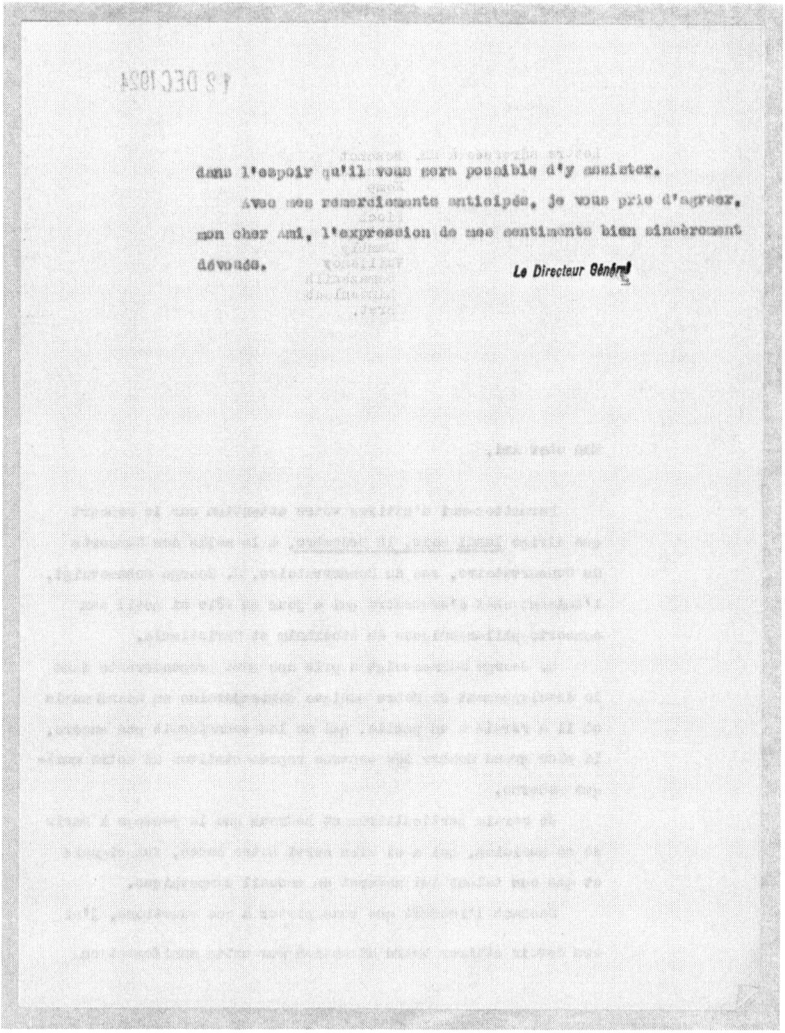

dans l'espoir qu'il vous sera possible d'y assister.

Avec mes remerciements anticipés, je vous prie d'agréer, mon cher ami, l'expression de mes sentiments bien sincèrement dévoués.

Le Directeur Général

On December 12, Brussel addressed a letter to eleven Parisian critics telling them about a concert to take place on December 15 in the hall of the Conservatoire. This was sent to Adolphe Boschot, Louis Schneider, Robert Kemp, Louis Vuillemin, Georges Pioch, Fernand Le Borne, Paul Dambly, Émile Vuillermoz, Gustave Samazeuilh, Théodore Lindenlaub, and Gustave Bret. The conductor Georg Schnéevoigt, he said, played an active role in concerts in Stockholm and Christiania. In accordance with Bossan's view, he stated, this conductor adopted a leading position in the promotion of contemporary French music in Scandinavia, to whose audiences he introduced modern French music more than anybody else. Brussel pleaded:

> I would be particularly happy if the passage to Paris of this musician who has so well served our cause were announced, and if his talent would assure him a sympathetic reception. Knowing your interest in these matters I have considered it my duty to turn your attention to this event, hoping that you will be able to attend.[23]

Due to Brussel's leading position in the AFEEA and his close relations with French colleagues among the Parisian music critics, this letter is powerful evidence. The letter exposes the extraordinary interest, specific to 1920s' Paris, in what is new and unprecedented. Apart from that, Schnéevoigt's usefulness to French music appears important. There is no mention in Brussel's letter of either Schnéevoigt's nationality or of Sibelius.

If the AFEEA propaganda had been successful, this would have been evident in the press accounts of the Brussel circle. Judging by a small sample of writings, this seems indeed to be the case. Unlike what happened during the 1900 Universal Exposition, the positive artistic value of a foreigner was no longer considered in terms of their national roots. In Brussel's own appraisal in *Le Figaro*, Schnéevoigt's services to modern French music, his Finnish origins and, belatedly, his Swedish residency are brought up, while his current position in Germany is bypassed. In the contemporary French context in which Classicism was valued, the shrouded reserve regarding Sibelius' symphony would have appeared markedly. Brussel writes: "He is a magnificent conductor, full of authority and passionate accents, meticulous too, and has the most powerful feeling for rhythm. He conducted in the hall of the Conservatoire Ravel's *La Valse*, of which he made a dazzling tableau, and Sibelius' Symphony in D, in which he excels and which suits particularly well his vehement temperament."[24] The review in *L'Excelsior* by Émile Vuillermoz

---

[23] "Je serais particulièrement heureux que le passage à Paris de ce musicien, qui a si bien servi notre cause, fut signalé et que son talent lui assurat un accueil sympathique. Sachant l'intérêt que vous portez à ces questions, j'ai cru devoir attirer votre attention sur cette manifestation, dans l'espoir qu'il vous sera possible d'y assister." Robert Brussel, a letter to French critics dated December 12, 1924. Fonds Montpensier. Finlande. Virtuoses. Georg Schnéevoigt.

[24] "C'est un chef magnifique, plein d'autorité et d'accent passionné, soigneux aussi et ayant du rythme le sentiment le plus fort. Il a conduit à la salle du Conservatoire, la *Valse* de Ravel, dont il a fait un tableau éblouissant, et la *Symphonie* en *ré* de

(composer, writer on music and, alongside Ravel, a former member of the cultural group *apaches* and a founder of the Société Musicale Indépendante), notes that Schnéevoigt is Finnish, has founded a philharmonic orchestra in Christiania, and is a professed propagandist of French music. Vuillermoz writes that Ravel's *La Valse* was animated with taste, and that Schnéevoigt's conducting was extravagant, but did not neglect the scores' nuances. The critic praises the piano soloist Eleanor Spencer for her interpretations of Mozart and Beethoven, but does not say a word about Sibelius.[25]

Sibelius did not go unnoticed by Louis Schneider, writing in French for *Le Gaulois* and in English for the *New York Herald*. According to *Le Gaulois*, the Second Symphony was entirely at the feet of German thought, contained commonplaces, and was pompous in style. He wrote that Schnéevoigt had worked for a long time in Stockholm and had promoted French music, and commented that the Finn was in turn a remarkable conductor whose baton technique was excellent. He showed all the nuances to his musicians without losing sight of the larger movement. The rhythms of *La Valse* were splendid, and even the piano soloist was good.[26]

In English, Schneider wrote:

> I only half relished the 2nd Symphony of Sibelius, in D major, where the classical influence is modified by modern German tendencies with their abuse of incidental phrasing, repetitions and a leaning to a pompous style. But the execution of this selection was quite remarkable.[27]

Thus, the composer was bad and the conductor good. I shall come back to this later.

It would be difficult not to regard Schnéevoigt's choice of work as a mistake. He seems to have relied excessively on the appeal of his favourite symphony without paying heed to the context. In a first performance during the 1920s, many Parisian critics expected to hear the voice of their own time—the first French performance of Sibelius' Second Symphony took place two decades too late. Knowing that, according to Schnéevoigt, the poetic content of this work was about the Finnish struggle for national

---

Sibelius, où il excelle, et qui convient si bien à son tempérament véhément." Brussel, "Les concerts," *Le Figaro* (December 22, 1924).

[25] An unsigned press clipping from *L'Excelsior*, dated December 25, 1924. Fonds Montpensier, the Georg Schnéevoigt file.

[26] Louis Schneider, "Les Concerts," *Le Gaulois* (December 25, 1924), 5–6.

[27] *New York Herald* 1924 (December 17), "Music in Paris by Louis Schneider," press clipping in the Georg Schnéevoigt file of Fonds Montpensier.

independence,[28] we may also ask if a subtler exponent could have generated a more positive response from the Parisians. Was not Schneider's experience of "pompousness" in the symphony a consequence of Schnéevoigt's well-known and often-criticised manner of accentuating contrasts excessively?

On January 5, 1925, Robert Brussel addressed a warm letter to Schnéevoigt in German, regretting not having had the opportunity to meet the conductor personally.[29] Later, Georg Schnéevoigt returned to the French capital for concerts at the helm of the Pasdeloup orchestra (February 28, 1925), the Orchestre Philharmonique de Paris (December 2, 1925, January 5, 1927) and the Orchestre Symphonique de Paris (November 17, 1929).[30] With the exception of the 1927 concert, the Fonds Montpensier preserves the press forms concerning these events. Sibelius' music was only included in the 1929 concert. As he had done at the moment of his 1924 Paris première, Schnéevoigt chose even here not to introduce the Finnish composer's more recent orientation; far from it, he gave Parisians an opportunity to hear the First Symphony once more, already familiar from the 1900 Universal Exposition.[31]

---

[28] Sirén, *Suomalaiset kapellimestarit Sibeliuksesta Saloseen*, 123.

[29] Robert Brussel to Georg Schnéevoigt in a letter dated January 5, 1925. The Georg Schnéevoigt file of Fonds Montpensier.

[30] On February 28, 1925 in a concert by the Pasdeloup orchestra, Schnéevoigt's programme consisted of Beethoven's Third Symphony, Mendelssohn's Violin Concerto in E minor with Zino Frencescatti as a soloist, Strauss' *Don Juan*, vocal numbers (Rachmaninov *À mon champs bien aimé*; Louis Aubert, *Le vaincu*; and Mussorgsky, *Hopak*, with Alice Derlange), and Wagner's Prelude to *Tannhäuser*. In two concerts by the Orchestre Philharmonique de France, he conducted Tchaikovsky's *Symphonie pathétique*, Ravel's *La Valse*, the Finale of Alfano's *Danse de Sakuntala*, songs of Richard Strauss (on December 2, 1925), Wagner's Prelude to *Die Meistersinger*, Beethoven's First Symphony, orchestral numbers from Vittorio-Gnecchi's scenic works, and a "cello concerto by Boccherini" (on January 5, 1927). (*Le Figaro* 1925 [March 1], *Petit Journal* 1925 [December 11], *Le Ménestrel* 1927 No. 1.) In his monumental study of Finnish conductors, Vesa Sirén only devotes two non-specific mentions to Georg Schnéevoigt's French career. Sirén, *Suomalaiset kapellimestarit Sibeliuksesta Saloseen*, 216, 221.

[31] The constraints of this publication do not allow me to discuss the reactions of the press. In addition to Sibelius' First Symphony, Georg Schnéevoigt performed on November 17, 1929 in the Salle Pleyel Weber's Overture to *Freischütz*, Haydn's Symphony No. 13, and Mendelssohn's Concerto for Violin and Orchestra No. 1 with Zino Frencescatti as a solist (*Comœdia* 1929 [November 24], *Écho de Paris* 1929 [November 18]).

Cosmopolitan Finnish Musicians in Post-World War I Paris

The earliest information about Sigrid Sundgren-Schnéevoigt's concert activity in Paris dates from 1923, but there are no traces from that time of cooperation with the AFEEA.[32] On April 10 she shared, modestly, a concert with three other musicians in the Salle Gaveau. Her programme consisted of a Rondino (possibly Op. 68 No. 2?) and a Valse (Op. 34?) by Sibelius, Selim Palmgren's "Nuit de Mai" (*Toukokuun yö*, Op. 27 No. 4) and Prélude (Op. 45 No. 1?), three Chopin pieces, and, together with Mr A. Lévi, Rachmaninov's Cello Sonata in G minor.[33] During the period 1926–31 she played several recitals in this concert hall, of which the AFEEA press forms from 1927–31 are conserved in the Fonds Montpensier. From Sibelius' catalogue, she performed the E major Sonatina, Op. 67, on January 19, 1927, the Valse, Op. 34, and the C sharp minor Rondino Op. 68 on May 7, 1928. No Sibelius was programmed in the 1929 recitals (October 14, October 25, November 13) or those in 1931 (June 10), but his Valse was again included in her share of a marathon concert by several musicians organised on February 19, 1933 by the newspaper *Le Journal*. The pianist proved to have been somewhat more faithful to her compatriot Palmgren, who was a family friend, than she was to Sibelius.[34] In 1927, she played "Chant d'oiseau" (*Fågelsång* Op. 17 No. 19), "Mer" (*Havet* Op. 17 No. 12), and Étude; in 1928, Prélude, Op. 45 No. 1; in 1931, *Valse impromptu*, Op. 34; and in 1933 (19 February), *Valse-impromptu* and *Étude de concert.*[35]

---

[32] This conclusion is based on information in the Sigrid Schnéevoigt scrapbook in Brages Pressarkiv, Helsinki, and the Sigrid Sundgren-Schnéevoigt file in the Fonds Montpensier.

[33] *Le Figaro* 1923 (April 10); *La Semaine à Paris* 1923 (April 6), 34.

[34] Kimmo Korhonen, *Selim Palmgren: Elämä musiikissa* (Helsinki: WSOY, 2009), 514–15, 581–9.

[35] Concert program of March 5, 1926 in Fonds Montpensier; *Guide du Concert* 1927–1929, 1931; *Le Journal* (February 17, 1933).

Programme of Sigrid Schnéevoigt's 1927 Concert
Fonds Montpensier, Finlande, Département de la musique, Bibliothèque nationale de France.

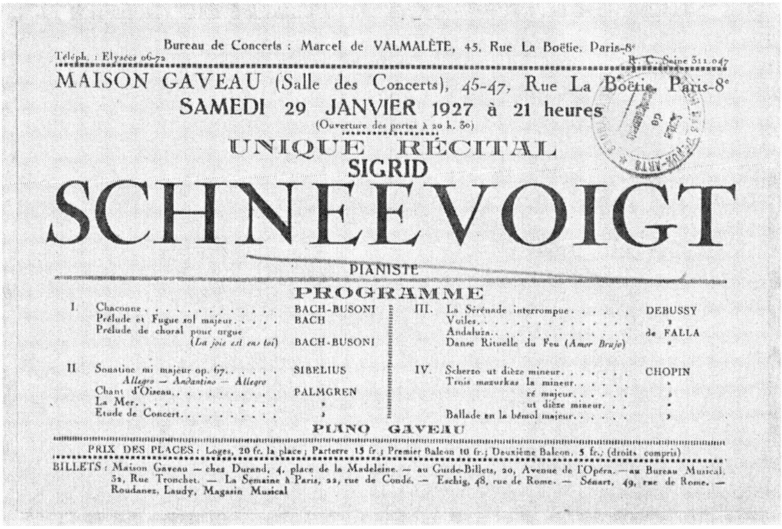
Bureau de Concerts : Marcel de VALMALÈTE, 45, Rue La Boëtie, Paris-8e
Téléph. : Elysées 06-72 R. C. Seine 311.047

MAISON GAVEAU (Salle des Concerts), 45-47, Rue La Boëtie, Paris-8e
SAMEDI 29 JANVIER 1927 à 21 heures
(Ouverture des portes à 20 h. 30)

UNIQUE RÉCITAL
SIGRID
SCHNEEVOIGT
PIANISTE

PROGRAMME

I. Chaconne . . . . BACH-BUSONI
Prélude et Fugue sol majeur . . . . . BACH
Prélude de choral pour orgue (*La joie est en toi*) BACH-BUSONI

II Sonatine mi majeur op. 67 . . . . . SIBELIUS
Allegro — Andantino — Allegro
Chant d'Oiseau . . . . PALMGREN
La Mer . . . . »
Etude de Concert . . . . »

III. La Sérénade interrompue . . . . . DEBUSSY
Voiles . . . . »
Andaluza . . . . de FALLA
Danse Rituelle du Feu (*Amor Brujo*) »

IV. Scherzo ut dièze mineur . . . . . . CHOPIN
Trois mazurkas la mineur . . . . . »
ré majeur . . . . . »
ut dièze mineur . . . »
Ballade en la bémol majeur . . . . . »

PIANO GAVEAU

PRIX DES PLACES : Loges, 20 fr. la place ; Parterre 15 fr. ; Premier Balcon 10 fr. ; Deuxième Balcon, 5 fr. ; (droits compris)

BILLETS : Maison Gaveau — chez Durand, 4, place de la Madeleine. — au Guide-Billets, 20, Avenue de l'Opéra. — au Bureau Musical, 32, Rue Tronchet. — La Semaine à Paris, 22, rue de Condé. — Eschig, 48, rue de Rome. — Sénart, 49, rue de Rome. — Roudanez, Laudy, Magasin Musical

It would be hard to presume any other reason for Sigrid Schnéevoigt's dropping Sibelius' works from her Paris programmes except for the modest response they evoked. The review from 1927 of Robert Brussel's friend Pierre Leroi in his capacity as critic for *Le Gaulois* is symptomatic:

> From the pianists we heard this week it is appropriate to praise Mme Sigrid Schnéevoigt highly. It is in the great works of Bach in particular that this beautiful artist appeared in her full measure, for she did not exclusively show very solid technical qualities, but was even capable of restoring to these pages their complete sublimity and architectural greatness. She presented works of Sibelius and Palmgren, works of poetic sentiment and drawn from popular sources, and a successful selection of pieces of Debussy, de Falla and Chopin, these with a mindful and delicate care, embellished by a reserve of the best of tastes.[36]

[36] "Parmi les pianistes que nous avons entendu cette semaine, il convient de louer hautement Mme Sigrid Schnéevoigt. C'est surtout dans les grandes œuvres de Bach que cette belle artiste donna toute sa mesure, car elle fit montre non seulement des qualités techiques d'une grande fermeté, mais elle sut restituer à ces pages toute leur sublimité et leur grandeur architecturale. Des œuvres de Sibelius et Palmgren, d'un sentiment poétique puisé aux sources populaires, et un choix heureux de

According to Stan Goléstan, writing for *Le Figaro* in 1928, the pianist's "style and technique were perfect" in her compatriots' works.[37]

Such seemingly polite but stereotypically small remarks on the "poetic sentiment" and "popular sources" of Sibelius' and Palmgren's compositions were due to a not insignificant extent to the great number of piano recitals in the metropolis. In Paris, Sigrid Sundgren-Schnéevoigt performed in an extremely competitive environment, and any mentions of performers were generally brief. It happened that Arthur Rubinstein played an all-Chopin evening in the Gaveau hall just a couple of weeks before she did the same. In the resulting comparisons between musicians, Sigrid Schnéevoigt was praised for her solid technique, her mastery of large-scale forms, and for a strength considered to be unusual for a woman, while her sensitivity and spontaneity left something to be desired.[38]

As a performing artist, Sigrid Schnéevoigt obviously suffered less than Finnish composers from the limited French interest in Finnish music. Her technique was solid, and her European repertoire was versatile. In addition to works by the great German composers (Bach and arrangements of his works, Beethoven, Schumann, and Brahms) and the romantic masters of the piano (Chopin and Liszt), she played from the contemporary French (Saint-Saëns, Ravel, Debussy, Migot, Rhené-Baton), Spanish (de Falla, Albéniz, Infante), and Russian (Rachmaninov, Scriabin) repertoires. The three recitals with three different programmes she gave in Salle Gaveau within one month in the autumn of 1929 are strong evidence of her sovereignty. She had opportunities to perform as the soloist of an orchestra (Grieg Concerto in Théâtre des Champs-Élysées with the Pasdeloup orchestra and conductor Rhené-Baton on October 14, 1928, and Saint-Saëns's Second Piano Concerto in the hall of the newspaper *Le Journal* with an orchestra conducted by Henri Tomasi on February 17, 1933) and to make recordings.[39] She, like her husband, was a true cosmopolitan.

---

pièces de Debussy, de Falla et Chopin fut présenté par elle avec des soins attentifs et délicats, paré d'une réserve du meilleur goût." Pierre Leroi, "Concerts et virtuoses," *Le Gaulois* (February 6, 1927), 4.

[37] Stan Goléstan, "Séances musicales," *Le Figaro* (May 20, 1928), 4.

[38] Pierre Leroi, "Concerts et virtuoses," *Le Gaulois* (May 13, 1928); Jean Messager, "Concerts et recitals de la semaine," *Comœdia* (May 15, 1928); George Mussy, "Concerts et recitals," *Le Figaro* (October 28, 1929); Mussy, "Concerts et recitals," *Le Figaro* (November 2, 1929); Jean-André Messager, "Récitals et concerts," *Comœdia* (November 1, 1929); Messager, "Récitals et concerts," *Comœdia* (November 23, 1929).

[39] *Le Journal* (February 17, 1933). Sigrid Schnéevoigt's recordings made in Paris in 1931 (Albéniz's *Castilla* and *Granada* from *Suite española* Op. 47, and

Many of the AFEEA's methods and operations remain to be clarified. Since musicological research has so far dealt little with its 1922–31 period,[40] conclusions concerning its influence should be cautious. Clearly, the top-down strategy reaching from the French government to the grassroots of musical life, and the standpoint which Jann Pasler accurately called "music as public utility,"[41] are worth noting. However, the AFEEA's network does not stand out distinctly from its social background. We have seen that Robert Brussel led Parisian public opinion, but his activities and views are themselves symptomatic of the French climate of ideas. The identity question, which at the time of the 1900 Universal Exposition stimulated French curiosity about the cultural expressions of other nations, appears to be reduced to a politically motivated rivalry concerning international leadership. We find the world of music polarised: Parisian critics were keen to distinguish a commitment to the archetypal enemy, Germany, within romantic expression. Many of these music critics were themselves composers, and the French-classical ideal was widely accepted in this circle. Georges Migot's 1922 article on Sibelius is exceptional.[42]

In December 1924, even critics who were not contacted by Robert Brussel could discuss the Second Symphony in terms used by those who did receive his letter. This may be a consequence of the publicity material: the printed programme of Schnéevoigt's concert mentions his services to French music and his distinction of being an Officer of the Légion d'Honneur. Thus, Pierre de Lapommeraye in *Le Ménestrel* calls Schnéevoigt a great conductor who had toured just about everywhere with the exception of France. Sibelius' symphony, he thinks, is ultra-romantic, often pompous, has commonplace motifs and heavy orchestration, while Mr Schnéevoigt could extract from it "unexpected effects that sustained

Chopin's Valse in B flat, Op. 64 No. 1 and Études Op. 25 Nos. 1 and 9) can be consulted on the webpage of the Finnish national library (https://viola.linneanet.fi).

[40] For AFEEA's activities in the field of music education, see Marie Duchêne-Thégarid, "Les élèves musiciens étrangers en France dans l'entre-deux-guerres," *Littératures et musiques dans la mondialisation, XXe-XXIe siècles*, dir. Anaïs Fléchet & Marie-Françoise Lévy (Paris: Publications de la Sorbonne, 2015), 45–56.

[41] Jann Pasler, *Composing the Citizen: Music as Public Utility in Third Republic France* (Berkeley, Los Angeles, London: University of California Press, 2009).

[42] Georges Migot, "Jean Sibelius," *La Revue musicale* No. 5 (March 1, 1922), 256–61. See also Tyrväinen, "'La nature de primitif affiné qui le caractérise'," 103–30; Tyrväinen, *Sibelius in the Old and New World*, 401–17.

the interest."[43] Gustave Doret in *Le Courrier Musical* calls Schnéevoigt "a great Finnish conductor." However, to his mind, concision is not among the qualities of Sibelius' symphony, exposing too obviously the influence of Wagner. He finds the orchestration too rich.[44]

Considering the politicised media strategies and Sibelius' invisibility on the Parisian scene, it would be difficult to suggest which of his works might have guaranteed him success in 1920s' Paris. It is the performing musicians with their cosmopolitan repertoires who profited the most from the cooperation with the AFEEA. Mentions of the Schnéevoigts in the French press often brought up, besides their country of origin, their former residencies and international careers. Indeed, it would be arbitrary to draw a direct comparison between their nationality and the substance of their art, considering especially that the couple lived abroad for years without ever setting foot on Finnish soil—their "exile" was over with Georg Schnéevoigt's appointment in 1932 as the conductor of the Helsinki Philharmonic Orchestra as successor to Kajanus.[45] Beneath the surface of more or less genuine interest from the French side, the danger of schematism was hidden. The AFEEA's archive was an abundant data source, but without fresh supplies a certain backwardness emerged.[46] I wonder, for instance, why a programme note in the Fonds Montpensier from 1928 of the Finnish soprano Greta von Haartman (who even performed Sibelius' songs) leans on ideas of Finnish music written for the 1900 Trocadéro Finnish concerts.[47] Sibelius too was a cosmopolitan, but his reputation in France extended the national image that was forged at the moment of the 1900 Universal Exposition.

Of all artistic disciplines, music was a privileged field of activity during the AFEEA's early phase. The association's strategies changed together with the organisational reform of the early 1930s; the impact of musicians and of international cooperation diminished. Renamed the Association Française d'Action Artistique in 1936, it directed its activities outside its

---

[43] Pierre de Lapommeray, "Concert Schnéevoigt—Eleanor Spencer," *Le Ménestrel* No. 4625 (December 19, 1924), 536.

[44] D., G. [Gustave Doret], "Eleanor Spencer et Georg Schnéevoigt," *Le Courrier Musical* 1 (1925).

[45] Von Born, "Professor Schnéevoigt hemma"; Tip, "Hos Sigrid Schnéevoigt i Paris"; *Hufvudstadsbladet* (March 23, 1930). "Sigrid Schnéevoigt till Helsingfors," cf. Sirén, *Suomalaiset kapellimestarit Sibeliuksesta Saloseen*, 226.

[46] See Piniau, *L'action artistique de la France*, 30.

[47] An unsigned programme note entitled "La musique finlandaise" in Greta von Haartman's concert programme of May 31, 1928, including *Den första kyssen* and *Svarta rosor*, Fonds Montpensier. Finlande. Artistes lyriques. G. von Haartman.

borders.[48] This would be the reason why, from the early 1930s onwards, press forms in Fonds Montpensier concerning Finnish musicians ceased to exist. It is only logical to conclude that this evolution led to the decrease of Sibelius' visibility in France.

[48] Piniau, *L'action artistique de la France*, 23–4, 37–46, 54–7.

"THE COMPANY YOU KEEP": RECIPIENTS OF HONORARY DOCTORATES FROM THE 1936 HEIDELBERG CELEBRATION—SIBELIUS AND THOSE HONOURED ALONGSIDE HIM

TIMOTHY L. JACKSON

Who were the recipients of honorary doctorates lined up behind Jean Sibelius to receive a highly controversial honorary degree from Heidelberg in 1936? Who were these awardees who were willing to cross the picket line of the international boycott of the 1936 Heidelberg Celebration? Given the rigorous process for nominating, vetting, and accepting doctorates from this Nazi "academic Olympics," it is clear that the person in question had to have done something the Nazis deemed quite significant in favour of the regime. All of the recipients were legitimately men of considerable talent and accomplishment. In some cases, however, it has proven difficult to discover the rationale for their nomination because these people themselves, their academic institutions, and their biographers were eager—post-war—to expunge this Nazi connection from their biographies.

The recipients can be divided into four general categories. The first comprises awardees who were "hard-core" fascists or racists, men whose pro-Nazism cannot be disputed; the second awardees who were more "soft-core" in their pro-Nazism, men who were willing to be sympathetic and to "cut the Nazis considerable slack"; the small third category comprises awardees for whom no evidence showing a pro-Nazi, pro-fascist, anti-Semitic orientation could be found, but with no guarantee that it does not exist somewhere; and a fourth category where the Nazis clearly misjudged the political orientation of the awardee; in one case, that of Bosch-Gimpera, they even rescinded the degree. Here, because of space constraints, I shall provide a few details about the awardees. At the end of my discussion, I will suggest that Sibelius belongs to the second category.

Sibelius' apologists point out that the honorary doctorate from Heidelberg was only one foreign honour among the many that he received during his long life; however, his acceptance of this particular doctorate at this particular time is qualitatively different. We must consider the figure against the ground; in other words, Sibelius' acceptance of the honorary doctorate in the ideological context of the time. Receiving an honorary doctorate from Heidelberg in 1936 was a political-cultural act of tremendous significance because it crossed "the picket line" of a widely publicised international boycott of this particular event, Goebbels' Nazi "academic Olympics" of 1936. For all of the many non-Nazi awards Sibelius accepted, there was no controversy, no picket line to be crossed, no international boycott to be ignored. But regarding the Heidelberg event in 1936, not only was the matter debated at length in most of the major newspapers of the time throughout the world—even Nazi papers—but in America a whole book was devoted to the subject and distributed to every university in the country. Of the 43 honourees receiving doctorates, Sibelius was by far the most prominent, and for this reason the Nazi propagandists placed his name *first* on the published lists of awardees at least in some German newspapers.

Against those who argue that Sibelius kept his distance physically—and therefore mentally—from the Nazis, it should be pointed out that it was unnecessary for Sibelius to go personally to Heidelberg to achieve the requisite propaganda effect of his decision to accept the award. Of the 43 awardees, a mere 13 actually attended the award ceremony; the remaining 30 all received their honorary doctorates *ex post factum* in in their home countries (as did Sibelius). The main point for the Nazis was that the names of those accepting the honorary doctorate should be widely publicised, and that Sibelius' name should always top the list.

For potential foreign participants like Sibelius, the crucial issue regarding the celebration of Heidelberg's 550th Anniversary was whether to offer the imprimatur of international support, whether at a personal or institutional level, to the fundamental changes brought about by the Nazi regime to the German universities. The issues at stake cut to the very heart of the scientific-academic enterprise. These fundamental matters included: (1) the nature of scientific truth; (2) the independence of the university from politics; (3) the university as a sanctum for the objective, disinterested pursuit of truth; and (4) for such research to form the basis for international cooperation in all fields, especially the sciences.

Professional ethics were at stake as well. Should a substantial body of professors, who were performing their requisite duties honourably and dutifully and who enjoyed great distinction in their respective fields, be expelled en masse from their positions on the basis of their Jewish ethnicity and/or possible anti-Nazi political orientation? Should international associations, learned societies, and vetted scientific journals countenance mass expulsions for these reasons? Through the Heidelberg celebration, and especially through the granting of honorary doctorates to international luminaries, the Nazis sought to legitimize the radical changes they had wrought in the German universities, not just at Heidelberg, but throughout German academe, changes that all but erased the boundaries between politics and university and destroyed scientific method as the objective, universal, unprejudiced search for valid inferences concerning the nature of the world. Thus, for foreign honoraries and invitees, again both individuals and institutions, the issue became whether or not to boycott the Heidelberg ceremony and the honours to be proffered there.

On December 19, 1936, Thomas Mann received a letter from a Dean at the Rheinische Friedrich-Wilhelms-Universität Bonn informing him that the university had *rescinded* his honorary doctorate. In responding, Mann referred to the honorary doctorate that he had recently received, along with Albert Einstein, on June 21, 1935, from Harvard University:

> I cannot refrain from explaining to you the grounds upon which it was conferred. My diploma contains a sentence which, translated from the Latin, runs as follows: "… we the President and Fellows with the approval of the honourable Board of Overseers of the University in solemn session have designated and appointed as honorary Doctor of Letters Thomas Mann, famous author, who has interpreted life to many of our fellow citizens and together with a very few contemporaries sustains the high dignity of German culture; and we have granted to him all the rights and privileges appertaining to this degree."
>
> In such terms, so curiously contradictory to the current German view, do free and enlightened men across the ocean think of me.[1]

In a tit-for-tat from Nazified Heidelberg to Harvard, the Nazi Minister of Education Bernhard Rust (1883–1945) needed a commensurate *eminence*

---

[1] Thomas Mann, *An Exchange of Letters, with a Foreword by J. B. Priestly* (Stanford, Connecticut: The Overbrook Press, 1938), published in an edition of 350 copies, on the occasion of a dinner given by the Yale Library Associates in honour of Thomas Mann, Thursday, February 24, 1938. For a detailed discussion of the rescinding of Thomas Mann's honorary doctorate see Paul Egon Hübinger, Thomas Mann, *Die Universität Bonn und die Zeitgeschichte. Drei Kapitel Deutscher Vergangenheit aus dem Leben des Dichters 1905–1955* (München, Wien: R. Oldenbourg Verlag, 1974).

gris to the anti-Nazis Einstein and Mann, and he found him in Jean Sibelius.

As soon as the Nazis assumed power in early 1933, Minister Rust purged the universities of Jews, liberals, pacifists, leftists, and anti-Nazis, while Nazis and their sympathisers assumed all administrative positions. At Heidelberg, on July 8, 1933, the Senate "elected" Wilhelm Groh, an undistinguished Nazi jurist, rector (I place "elected" in quotation marks because the election was not done by secret ballot). Across German universities and technical institutes, over a thousand professors were fired, including Einstein. At Heidelberg, one quarter of the entire faculty was removed from office. In his speech at the 550th Anniversary of the University of Heidelberg in June 1936, the Nazi Propaganda Minister Joseph Goebbels failed to make any mention of his two most influential professors at that university, namely his own dissertation supervisor Friedrich Gundolf (1880–1931) and Max Freiherr von Waldberg (1858–1938), since both were Jewish.[2] The works of Gundolf and Waldberg were proscribed, and Waldberg was forced to retire in 1933. Thus, Heidelberg, the oldest university in Germany, was quickly Nazified.

In an important 2004 study of honorary doctorates granted by universities in Nazi Germany, Ingo Bach observed that their bestowal was transformed from an *academic* into a *political* act, namely into a means of retaining the support of influential foreigners for the Nazi cause.[3] It was deemed essential by the regime that those awarded honorary doctorates be Nazi sympathizers, and to ensure that this always would be the case, a multi-stage vetting process was implemented that involved the university administration, the Education Ministry, the Foreign Office, and the Party Chancellory. This vetting system was designed to ensure that there was no awardee who was either "unpolitical" or hostile to the National Socialism.

The intensive vetting process put in place meant that the final list of 43 honoraries for doctorates associated with Heidelberg's 550th Anniversary Celebration would be different from the initial nominations by the deans of the various faculties. Since music fell under the aegis of the philosophy faculty, one would have expected Hans Güntert, the dean of that faculty, to have put forward Sibelius' name. But, a careful examination of the

---

[2] Max Freiherr von Waldberg (1858–1938) was a professor of modern literature. Goebbels wrote his dissertation *Wilhelm von Schütz als Dramatiker. Ein Beitrag zur Geschichte des Dramas der Romantischen Schule* (1922) under Waldberg.

[3] Ingo Bach, "Verleihung und Aberkennung des Titels 'Doktor Ehrenhalber' als Spiegel nationalsozialistischer Hochschulpolitik," in *Die Universität Greifswald und die deutsche Hochschullandschaft im 19. und 20. Jahrhundert*, ed. Werner Buchholz (Wiesbaden: Franz Steiner Verlag, 2004).

documents reveals that this was not the case; rather, nominations also emanated from sources outside the university, namely the Education Ministry and the Foreign Office. Furthermore, some of the names originally proposed by the Heidelberg deans and faculty members were dropped as they were investigated by the university administration, the Education Ministry, and the Foreign Office.

From Olli Lehto's biography, we learn that Rolf Nevanlinna was knowledgeable about Sibelius' music to the point of being able to critique well-known conductors with regard to their interpretations. Such was Nevanlinna's knowledge of music in general, and Sibelius' work in particular, that he was asked to serve as Chairman of the Board of Directors of the Sibelius Academy from 1941–5. During the same period, Nevanlinna became Rector of the University of Helsinki, and Chair of the Finnish SS Committee. As a mathematician with an intensely pro-Nazi perspective of his own, Nevanlinna could step into the shoes of his German-Jewish mathematical colleagues with alacrity, all the time justifying his actions as "saving" German science and culture.

In his memoirs, Nevanlinna himself writes about the war years, distancing himself from Sibelius during the war: "I would have loved to visit Ainola, but I did not have the necessary courage to disturb Sibelius."[4] However, Lehto implies that there *was* personal contact between Nevanlinna and Sibelius when he writes, "Of all of the people whom he [Nevanlinna] met, only Sibelius exercised a similar effect to Mannerheim upon him;" however, I have not been able to ascertain when, where, and in what context(s) Nevanlinna encountered Sibelius.[5] Additionally, Lehto confirms that Nevanlinna was friends with two of Sibelius' daughters who were his contemporaries, Katarina and Margareta, and their respective spouses, conductor Jussi Jalas and banker Eero Ilves.[6] Thus, Nevanlinna was well placed to learn of and vouch for the pro-Nazi orientation of Sibelius and his family in the mid-1930s.

Let us return now to the period in question, namely 1935–6. Like Sibelius, Nevanlinna was nominated to receive an honorary doctorate from Heidelberg. Again, the nomination came about in a curious and unexpected way. One would assume that Nevanlinna would have been nominated by someone in the department of mathematics. But further investigation in the Heidelberg University Archives led to a surprising

---

[4] Rolf Nevanlinna, *Muisteltua* (Helsinki: Otava, 1976), 135 (his Memoirs in Finnish). I am grateful to Veijo Murtomäki for this information.

[5] Lehto, 148: "Von den Personen, denen Nevanlinna begegnete, übte außer Mannerheim nur Sibelius eine ähnliche Wirkung."

[6] Private communication with Olli Lehto.

discovery: Nevanlinna was proposed for the honorary doctorate not by any member of the Heidelberg faculty; instead, the nomination emanated from the Reich Education Ministry in Berlin from one Prof. Rudolf Mentzel, then the "Referent" or "expert official" in charge of the natural sciences at the universities and personnel issues within their faculties. The Nazis had gutted the faculty of the Göttingen Institute for Mathematics; there was now a dearth of competent "Aryan" mathematicians to fill all of the chairs vacated by Jewish, liberal, and left-leaning professors. By September 6, 1935, Nevanlinna had received an official invitation to join the Mathematics Institute in Göttingen. Without any qualms as to why the position had become open, Nevanlinna immediately responded enthusiastically.

As early as November 1935, Mentzel began checking Nevanlinna for "political reliability." Interestingly, Mentzel did not contact the Foreign Office directly, but rather wrote to Rudolf Hess, the "Deputy Führer," requesting an investigation in Finland of Nevanlinna. Perhaps Mentzel took this course in order to expedite the process. Just over a month later, Mentzel received a response from a bureaucrat named Helms in Hess' office to the effect that such an investigation had been made in Finland by "the responsible Party organs" and had yielded a highly favourable report.

On January 30, 1936, Nevanlinna received an invitation from Mentzel to come to Berlin to discuss his move to Göttingen in person at the ministry. Another indication of the Education Ministry as the source of the Nevanlinna nomination is its "lateness": Nevanlinna's name was later added to the list in Heidelberg because the source was external to the university. Since we now know that the nomination of Nevanlinna originated in the Education Ministry, and that Mentzel was trying to recruit Nevanlinna, it is highly probable that the source of Nevanlinna's nomination was, in fact, Mentzel himself.

It is noteworthy that few nominations actually survived the rigorous vetting process. The first Finns to be nominated *internally* by the Heidelberg University faculties were Pentti Eskola (1883–1964), named Extraordinary Professor in 1924 and Ordinary Professor of Geology in 1928 at the University of Helsinki, a position he held until 1953, and Gustaf Komppa (1867–1949), Professor of Chemistry at the Helsinki University of Technology. It is unclear who nominated Eskola; Komppa was nominated by Heidelberg chemist Karl Freudenberg (1886–1983), who stressed his "racial fitness," noting that, "in his scientific existence, Komppa is rooted completely in *Deutschtum* … By appearances, Komppa is of Finnish blood. His children also appear to be. I consider it most unlikely that he has Jewish elements."[7] Komppa was retained on the list, attended the ceremony in person to receive his honorary doctorate, and stayed with Freudenberg during the celebration. He also officially represented the University of Turku. Thus, before Sibelius and Nevanlinna were even nominated, the two Finns proposed for honorary doctorates were Eskola and Komppa. Antti Tulenheimo (1879–1952) was also nominated internally by Karl Engisch, Dean of the Heidelberg Faculty of Law. Engisch was careful to check whether Tulenheimo was "friendly" towards Nazi Germany, soliciting information from the Academy for German Law. In their confidential report, which Engisch then forwarded to Rector Groh, Tulenheimo is mentioned as belonging to the right-wing Kokoomus Party and described as a "Freund des Dritten Reiches" ["friend of the Third Reich"], a euphemism for being pro-Nazi. Engisch's letter nominating Tulenheimo is dated February 19, 1936, thus post-dating the nominations of Sibelius and Nevanlinna. The university protocols contain a memo dated February 20, showing that Rector Groh sought even further confirmation of Tulenheimo's pro-Nazi sympathies, since he immediately spoke with [presumably by telephone] Paulus von Stolzmann in the Foreign Office about Tulenheimo, and asked him to undertake further investigation. As late as April 17, Dr. med. Johann Achelis (1898–1963) nominated Yrjö Reenpää (1894–1976), Professor of Physiology at Helsinki University (1927–62). The nomination letter is significant in that it once again discloses the role of the German embassy in Helsinki in checking the "German friendliness" of potential recipients of honorary doctorates. According to Veijo Murtomäki, Reenpää "was one of the most actively pro-German, perhaps even pro-Nazi Finnish scholars; he and his students worked in Germany and had good contacts there. He obviously knew to some extent about the cruelties of the German medical sciences and their experiments."[8] However, in spite of this careful vetting, on April

---

[7] Steven B. Remy, *The Heidelberg Myth. The Nazification and Denazification of a German University* (Cambridge MA.: Harvard University Press, 2002), 63. Freudenberg served as Professor of Chemistry and Director of the Heidelberg Institute of Chemistry from 1926–56. During the Nazi period, Freudenberg seems to have kept his nose clean to the point that, after the war, he was allowed by the Americans to participate in the rebuilding of the university.

[8] Veijo Murtomäki, private communication. Murtomäki adds that, "In his memoires, *Ajateltua ja koettua* ['My thoughts and experiences'], he hardly 'remembers' his German contacts and activities. He praises the loyalty and friendship of Nevanlinna. However, he mentions his visits to Germany in 1942 and 1943 to the Research Center of the German Air Forces and the lectures he gave at

20 Rector Groh wrote back to Achelis declining Reenpää, saying that there were already enough Finns on the list. My hypothesis is that Eskola had to be dropped when Sibelius and Nevanlinna were proposed by an external, higher-level authority, namely Mentzel at the Education Ministry.

Who was Prof. Dr. med. Johannes Stein?

Sibelius was officially nominated by Prof. Dr. med. Johannes Stein, Vice-Rector at Heidelberg. Who was Stein? With no connection to music, why did Stein nominate Sibelius? A pastor's son, Stein began studying theology and philosophy in Bonn. Returning from World War 1, Stein decided to study medicine. On May 1, 1933, Stein enlisted in the SS and rose up the ranks steadily. On October 1, 1933, Rector Groh named his own "Chancellery," including Stein as Chancellor. When Groh moved to Berlin in 1939 to work under Mentzel in the Education Ministry, Stein gave a speech at the farewell ceremony. In December 1940, Stein was nominated to the Reichsuniversität in Strassbourg, where he was appointed the director of the medical clinic and dean of the medical faculty. To this Wolfgang Eckart, the expert on Heidelberg University during the Nazi period, added about Stein:

> Regarding Stein there is a lot to say. He was indeed one of the most perfidious Nazi ideologists in Heidelberg at this time. He had close connections to the *SS*, the *Sicherheitsdienst* etc. and I am sure he had best connections to Berlin and—which may very well be—to Goebbels' Ministry of Reich-Propaganda as well as to the cultural department of the Reich Foreign Office. Goebbels himself had been promoted to a Dr. phil. in German studies (*Germanistik*) in Heidelberg. As far as I know, Stein was not involved in *Euthanasie* personally, but of course, as a faculty colleague, he collegially knew Carl Schneider, the fanatic Heidelberg NS-professor, initiator of the local children-"euthanasia" and leading "euthanasia"-reviewer in Berlin, very well. In 1941 Stein went to the *Reichs-University* of Strassburg. Attached to Strassburg was the concentration camp Natzweiler where Auschwitz and other prisoners were subjected to killing experiments. There is no doubt that Stein, although again not personally involved, knew about every detail carried out mostly by former Heidelberg medical scholars. There is no doubt that Stein was the leading figure in Heidelberg's as well as Strassburg's National Socialist snake pit.[9]

---

some universities. He mentions also that in 1942 there was still great confidence in the positive outcome of the war, although in 1943 he had some doubts about it."

[9] Private communication.

Let us consider Stein's nominations of Sibelius and the Swiss medical doctor Naegeli for honorary doctorates on February 12, 1936. A letter from Groh dated February 14, 1936, makes it clear that the rector was taken by surprise by Stein's two nominations, which arrived almost a month after the due date. In the case of Sibelius, Groh was "on board" "as long as no objections are raised by the Foreign Office." In other words, the Foreign Office would still have to confirm Stein's claim of Sibelius' pro-Nazi orientation. However, Groh complained that Naegeli might not be reliably pro-Nazi.

From everything that we have learned about Stein, it is clear that he was an extremely canny political operator and ideologue who would not have committed himself to nominating either Sibelius or Naegeli unless he was absolutely certain of their pro-Nazi credentials surviving intense scrutiny. It would have been simply too dangerous for him to have submitted these late nominations if he was unsure of the pro-Nazi orientation of his nominees; to have nominated either Sibelius or Naegeli without *insider assurance* of their pro-Nazi orientation would have been too risky; therefore, it is likely that Stein himself had received confirmation from unimpeachably reliable sources that both Naegeli and Sibelius were politically "trustworthy."

From Naegeli's personnel file in the Zurich University Archives, we discover that he lectured in Nazi Germany after the medical profession had become thoroughly Nazified. Further inquiries to a young Swiss scholar writing his dissertation on the connection between Swiss and Nazi medicine confirmed that Naegeli was indeed "deutschfreundlich" in the sense of being intensely pro-Nazi:

> In the sources I studied, it became clear that the Nazis considered Prof Naegeli a pro-German ally. For example, he was in contact with Ernst Rüdin and Otmar von Verschuer, two of the leading racial hygienists in Nazi Germany … It was clear that Naegeli was "deutschfreundlich." He was not only sympathetic towards German eugenic politics but he also was an anti-Semite.[10]

My point is this: Stein really did his "homework" about the pro-Nazi attitude of Sibelius and Naegeli. Through contacts in his own field of medicine, Stein made sure that Naegeli was pro-Nazi. In the case of Sibelius, Stein relied on Mentzel, his patron in the Berlin Education Ministry, who in turn was informed about Sibelius by Nevanlinna and pro-Nazi organizations in Finland. The formulation of Stein's nomination

[10] Letter from Pascal Germann, April 4, 2015.

letter for Sibelius suggests that a person knowledgeable about music in general and Sibelius in particular dictated its contents, namely Nevanlinna.

The Controversy: To Accept or Not Accept the Heidelberg Invitation, That is the Question

As a consequence of the mass firings and ongoing reports of the perversion of science and learning at German universities, on February 2, 1936 Dr. Hensley Henson (Dunelm), the Bishop of Durham, wrote a letter to the *Times of London* calling for a boycott of the Heidelberg event by all British universities and learned societies. He wrote:

> The appearance of British representatives at the Heidelberg celebration, and the presenting by them of congratulatory addresses, could not but be understood everywhere as a public and deliberate condonation of the intolerance which has emptied the German universities of many of their most eminent teachers, and which is filling Europe with victims of cynical and heartless oppression.

The Bishop's call for a boycott initiated a flurry of impassioned correspondence in the pages of *The Times* among some of the most distinguished members of British academic and cultural circles. This debate was deemed so important for consideration by American universities and colleges invited by Heidelberg that it was immediately published in book form by Viking Press in early 1936 with the title *Heidelberg and the Universities of America*, with a foreword by eminent Americans.

Seeing which way the wind was blowing, on March 2, 1936, Rector Groh decided to retract Heidelberg's invitation to all British universities.[11] The Canadian universities, following their British counterparts, observed an almost total boycott of Heidelberg. In South Africa, the English-oriented universities participated in the boycott; however, the two

---

[11] *The New York Times* reported on March 3: "The Nazi government struck back at the Universities of Oxford, Cambridge, and Birmingham today when the rector of Heidelberg University formally withdrew its invitations to all British universities or academies to send delegates to the ceremonies marking the 550th anniversary of the university's foundation. This effort to save face had, as a matter of fact, become inevitable after the two leading British universities declined and it became evident that other British institutions could be expected to follow suit. The step was taken after representatives of the Nazi Minister of Culture [more precisely, Education], Dr. Bernhard Rust, spent the weekend consulting with the rector and his associates."

predominantly Afrikaner universities did send envoys, namely Stellenbosch and Pretoria. Stefanus Francois Naude Gie (1884–1945) attended the Heidelberg celebration in a dual capacity, both as a Stellenbosch faculty member and the ambassador of the Union of South Africa to Berlin, a position he held from 1934–44. To be awarded the position of Ambassador to Germany, Gie was active in the National Party and also in the racist *Broederbond.* Hitler attracted a significant number of Afrikaner Nationalists, and the Afrikaner *Broederbond* numbered pro-Nazis among its ranks. Gie wrote: "It was especially their work, *their upholding of the white man's honour*, their courage, patience and sense of freedom which gave us a South Africa where we can be happy, free and prosperous."[12] As with the professors from small colleges in America, the racist notions of the Nazis, who despised blacks almost as much as Jews, must not have seemed too distant to scholars like Gie.

The French universities, like the British, boycotted Heidelberg, and the French and British flags were not raised as part of the festivities; nevertheless, according to the list of acceptances, two Frenchmen did attend, namely the politician Louis-Germain Martin (1872–1948), listed as the representative for the Institut de France, and the medievalist Mario Roques (1875–1961), described as the representative of the Académie des Inscriptions et Belles-Lettres, one of the five academies comprising the Institut de France. Elected as a member of the Académie des Sciences Morales et Politiques in 1927, Martin served as finance minister in various French governments from 1930–5. Noteworthy in the present context as an indication of Martin's pro-Nazi, anti-Semitic sentiments is that, under the German occupation of France (1940–4), Martin was a member of the Vichy Conseil National. During that period, Martin worked closely with the collaborationist Pierre Laval (1883–1945) who, in 1942, gave permission to the Gestapo to hunt down Resistance members in unoccupied France, sent skilled labourers to Germany in exchange for the return of prisoners of war, and was responsible on the French side for the deportation of Jews to Auschwitz. While Laval was tried and executed by firing squad, Martin escaped prosecution.

Why did the presidents of Harvard, Yale, Cornell, and Columbia overrule the majority of their faculties and students and send official representatives? Were they unaware of the book burnings of 1933? Had

[12] Quoted from Ciraj Rassool and Leslie Witz, "The 1952 Jan Van Reibeeck Tercentenary Festival: Constructing and Contesting Public National History in South Africa," *Journal of African History* 34 (1993): 450, which cites Stephanus Francois Naude Gie, *Geskiendenis van Suid-Afrika* (Stellenbosch, 1940), iii (my emphasis).

they forgotten that these book burnings also included some of the most important American volumes alongside German books, which were characterised by Sinclair Lewis, America's only Nobel Prize winner for literature, as "the noblest books produced by Germany in the last twenty years ... the [American] authors should feel nothing save satisfaction at receiving this unintentional tribute from an organized mob?"

The reasons were: (1) money, namely financial support for faculty and student exchange programs from both German-American and German sources; (2) pro-Nazi and pro-fascist professors and students congregated in their departments of German and Italian, and some other departments; (3) senior administrators who were themselves anti-Semitic, refusing to hire Jewish professors, whether "local" Jews or German-Jewish émigrés; and (4) some universities and colleges, especially those with Lutheran orientations, were sympathetic to certain aspects of Nazi ideology, especially the racist anti-Semitism of the so-called "German Christians."

The choice of representatives suggests that the administrations at some American universities collaborated with the Nazi authorities by sending envoys to Heidelberg who were pro-Nazi, or had shown signs of Nazi sympathies and anti-Semitism. In some cases, it has been especially difficult to track down the tell-tale signs of these individuals' Nazi leanings since this is not an aspect of their biographies that their institutions wish to advertise on their websites and in other resources today.

Harvard University selected as its representative George David Birkhoff (1884–1944), mathematician, Dean of the Faculty of Arts and Sciences and Perkins Professor of Mathematics, a professor with a reputation for anti-Semitism. Einstein and mathematician Norbert Wiener (1904–1964), among others, accused Birkhoff of advocating anti-Semitic hiring practices.

Yale University chose Hanns Oertel (1868–1952) as its delegate. Oertel was the teacher of Walther Wüst (1901–1993), who in 1941 became the rector of the University of Munich. It is noteworthy that Oertel's chair in Munich was taken over by Wüst with Oertel's support. By lending Wüst his backing in the succession, Oertel was promoting one of the most virulent Nazi ideologues, a man described in the *Völkischer Beobachter* as, "among the most loyal and dependable to the Führer"—a man who would soon become the head of Himmler's *Ahnenerbe*.[13]

Again, with Columbia's representative, we detect pro-Nazi leanings on the part of the professor selected. President Butler's choice fell upon

---

[13] See Heather Pringle, *The Master Plan: Himmler's Scholars and the Holocaust* (New York: Hyperion, 2006), 313, and footnote 92, p. 414.

Professor Arthur Frank Joseph Remy (1871–1954), Villard Professor of Germanic Philology, which "was also provocative" since Remy had appeared as a speaker with Germany's ambassador Hans Luther in December 1933 at a pro-Nazi rally.

At Cornell University, President Livingston Farrand—against vociferous objections from the student body and alumni—appointed James Bennett Nolan, a Cornell alumnus, Class of 1900, who was attending the Heidelberg ceremony anyway and offered to represent Cornell, as well as Albert W. Boesche, Professor of German, who was already in Germany.

So what was the position taken by the Scandinavian universities toward Heidelberg? In Norway, the University of Oslo rejected the invitation. With regard to the Swedish universities, an analogous situation to that with Vassar College in the United States obtained regarding some Swedish "representatives": most of the Swedes described as "representatives" by the Germans did *not* enjoy official sanction by their universities.

Stockholm declined the Heidelberg invitation. On March 12, 1936, the *Helsingin Sanomat* reported that, "the academic institutions of Sweden also will not send their delegates to Heidelberg," while on March 21 *The New York Times* specifically identified Stockholm as having refused the invitation from Heidelberg. Only Uppsala sent an official emissary in Lundborg, professor and head of the [Swedish] National Institute for Eugenics (1921–35) at Uppsala.[14] Strongly pro-Nazi, he probably held enough sway at Uppsala to compel official attendance at the Heidelberg event.

Fortunately for Rector Groh and Heidelberg, there was a change of Rector at Vienna to the pro-Nazi prehistorian Oswald Menghin (1888–1973); Menghin personally attended the Heidelberg celebration representing Vienna University. A racist anti-Semite, Menghin was a member of a secret society of Austrian Nazis (1919–26) where he became acquainted with Arthur Seyss-Inquart (hung at Nuremberg for crimes

[14] His books have titles like *Über Degeneration und degenerierte Geschlechter in Schweden* ["Concerning Degeneration and Degenerated Genetic Lines in Sweden"] (1901), *Vad kan göras för att höja den Svenska Folkhälsan och Förhindra Urartning?* ["What can be Done to Further Swedish Public Health and Prevent Degeneration?"] (1919), *The Racial Characters of the Swedish Nation* (1926), *Die Rassenmischung beim Menschen; mit gebührender Berücksichtigung analoger Verhältnisse bei Pflanzen und Tieren* ["Racial Mixture in Humans; with Appropriate Consideration to Analogous Relationships in Plants and Animals"] (1931), *The Race Biology of the Swedish Lapps* (1932), and *Västerlandet i Fara; Befolkningsfrågor i Biologisk och Rashygienisk Belysning* ["The West in Peril; Population Question Considered from a Biological and Racial Perspective"] (1934).

against humanity); after the Anschluss, Seyss-Inquart appointed him Education Minister in the so-called Anschluss Cabinet. In this position, he was responsible for purging Vienna University of approximately 40% of its faculty either as ethnic Jews and/or political undesirables. From 1938 on, in Austrian-Catholic circles, Menghin was branded a traitor; as a member of the Seyss-Inquart regime he was considered a war criminal.

The Propaganda Event: An Academic Nuremberg Rally

Goebbels and his Propaganda Ministry set up a special office in Heidelberg to orchestrate the festivities as a synthesis of the "Nuremberg Rally" with an "Academic Celebration;" no expense was spared to showcase the "New German" academe.

The celebration began on Saturday June 27, at 8 o'clock pm, with the festive raising of the flags of all the participating nations in front of the Old University by SS-uniformed men. Photos show two large pylons with flaming pyres erected in the square in front of the flags. At the Berlin book burning ceremony on March 11, 1933 Goebbels had declared: "The old goes up in flames, the new shall be fashioned from the flame in our hearts."[15] Pictures of Goebbels greeting some of the foreign academics were published in the German media. Monday June 29, 1936 began with a ceremonial procession of the delegates from German and foreign universities to the City Auditorium [*Stadthalle*]. A photograph shows that the delegates, led by Rector Groh, were preceded by four trumpeters in pseudo-Renaissance garb, followed by two beadles carrying Heidelberg University insignia. A crowd of between one and two hundred thousand onlookers lining the streets was held back by unbroken cordons of SA and SS men.

The ceremony for the public announcement of the honorary doctorates began at 9:30 am on Tuesday June 30 in the Stadthalle. The festivities were initiated with a performance of Max Reger's *Vaterländischer Ouvertüre*. Completed in September 1915, when Germany still felt optimistic about winning World War I, this brash, nationalistic fifteen-minute piece celebrates Germanness through quotations of *Das Deutschlandlied* ("Deutschland, Deutschland über alles"), *Die Wacht am Rhein* ("Es braust ein Ruf wie Donnerhall"), and the student song *Gelübde*

[15] *The New York Times*, May 11, 1933, "Nazi Book-Burning Fails to Stir Berlin. 40,000 Watch Students Fire Volumes in a Drizzle, but Show Little Enthusiasm. Some 'Fetes' Postponed. But 'Un-German' Literature is Consigned to the Flames in Most University Towns," by Frederick T. Birchall.

("Ich hab mich ergeben mit Herz und mit Hand")[16] that Brahms also employs in his *Academic Overture.* Then, the 13 of the 43 recipients of honorary doctorates present received their diplomas directly from Rector Groh. Stein, who had nominated Sibelius for the honorary doctorate, gave his address on "Medicine and the Public." The event concluded with a performance of Beethoven's Ninth Symphony conducted by Hermann Abendroth.

Let us now consider the recipients of honorary doctorates mentioned at the outset.

(1) "Hard-core" fascists and racists:

Sigurd Erixon, a "folkish" Swedish ethnologist sympathetic to Nazism.

Erwin Wittstock, German "folkish" author in Siebenbürgen.

Verner von Heidenstam in Oevralid, pro-Nazi Swedish poet; Heidenstam won the Nobel Prize for Literature in 1916 but ceased writing for the last thirty-five years of his life (somewhat like Sibelius). From 1933 until his death in 1940 he did indeed prove a true "friend of [Nazi] Germany." In April 1933, interviewed by the German newspaper *Der Tag*, he expressed unequivocal support for the Hitler's "seizure of power": "I knew that Germany's moment would come and great now is the nation's awakening." In 1935 he was visited by Hitler's deputy Rudolf Hess at his home in Övralid. Heidenstam was a prominent member of the "Reich Society of Sweden-Germany" founded in 1937 in Lund "to promote fair treatment of the New Germany on a purely Swedish basis, without the bias of a political party." Beginning in 1938, the organisation published a newsletter *Sverige-Tyskland* that was a Swedish propaganda instrument for the "New Germany." Heidenstam's funeral was used as a platform for pro-Nazi propaganda. Even though Heidenstam ceased writing in 1915, his pro-Nazism has posthumously cast a dark shadow over his name and writings.

Junjiro Takakusu (Japan), theorist of the militaristic, racist "new Nipponism." An internationally recognised Buddhist scholar, during this period he also became an exponent of the combination of the Buddhist

[16] This nationalistic piece was overplayed during the Nazi period; post-war, it completely vanished from the repertoire to the point that there is no modern recording of the orchestral version.

concept of selflessness with Japanese patriotism with strongly militaristic connotations, a facilitator of the *Kamikaze* mentality.

Erik Wellander, pro-Nazi Germanist at Stockholm University; Wellander's academic achievements and pro-Nazi sympathies made him an ideal candidate for an honorary doctorate. He vocally resented Sweden accepting refugee German-Jewish scholars. In addition, in 1935 he accepted the position of superintendent of a new German School in Stockholm initiated by Hitler's deputy Rudolf Hess. Upon his return to Sweden, Wellander authored a lengthy pro-Nazi article about the Heidelberg 550th Anniversary Celebration in the *Svenska Dagbladet*.

Gustavo Cordeiro Ramos, Portuguese philologist and Germanist, pro-Nazi university professor, minister of education in three military governments. In 1934, he published *Some Special Literary Aspects of Modern German Nationalism* in which he praised Nazi cultural politics, stating that:

> the National Socialist Movement, far from being an enemy of culture as it has been accused by its detractors, is based upon a solid body of doctrine; the renewal in the political field extends to the literary domain … The book is no longer conceived merely as the object for commercial exploitation but converted into a tool for developing high culture and morals as well.

In 1938, Ramos wrote the prologue to a German translation of speeches and other texts by the dictator Salazar, which included a preface by Goebbels in an edition sponsored by the Nazi authorities. In 1939 Ramos was received personally by Hitler, handing him a copy of *The Lusíadas* in German translation.

Luis Cabral de Moncada, a professor at the University of Coimbra, Portugal, was another Portuguese professor with Nazi sympathies, who stated: "Found a republic in Portugal … away from the hateful and odious Jewish spirit, the innate enemy of all nations, and far from … stupid modern Bolshevism, enemy of all values of the spirit and, thus, of all civilization and culture."

Gerhard May, German "folkish" theologian in Yugoslavia.

Hermann Lundborg (Uppsala), Swedish race researcher and hereditary biologist. A eugenicist, Lundborg played a major role in the enactment of laws for forced sterilisation in Sweden, which served as a model for similar measures in other countries. His ideas were enormously influential in Nazi Germany; Hitler's library (now in the Library of Congress) contains a signed copy of Lundborg's book.

Harry H. Laughlin, an American who received an honorary doctorate, like Sibelius, *in absentia*. He was the director of the Eugenics Record Office at Cold Spring Harbor. In the early 1920s he influenced American immigration policy against admitting Southern Europeans and Eastern European Jews, while arguing in favour of the compulsory sterilisation of people deemed hereditarily "unfit." In 1922, Laughlin sought to establish quotas for Jews studying at universities and colleges, drawing up an "Outline of a Plan for the Determination of Jewish Racial Quota-Fulfillments among Both Institutional and College Jews in the United States." However, by the 1930s Laughlin's work began to be discredited as bogus science. In 1935, a review panel convened by the Carnegie Institute, which had funded his research, concluded that it did not have scientific merit. When, in 1939, the Institute withdrew funding for the Eugenics Record Office, it was closed. Ironically, it was precisely when Laughlin's work was debunked that it served as the basis for the German Nuremberg Laws.

Otto Naegeli, pro-Nazi, anti-Semitic professor of medicine at Zurich.

Iris Ava, professor emeritus at the Imperial University in Tokyo, important functionary in the Nazified German-Japanese Society.

William May Garland, pro-Nazi member of the Olympic Committee responsible for preventing the American boycott of the 1936 Games.

Giovanni Novelli and Mariano D'Amelio, both Presidents of the Court of Appeal in Rome. Novelli was General Director of the notorious Institutions of Prevention and Penalty; Pietro de Francisci headed the Institute for Fascist Culture, Mussolini's pre-eminent "think tank," and was rector of the militarised University of Rome.

Matsukichi Koyama, President of Hosei University in Tokyo, promotor of Japanese militarism and imperialism. In 1934, Koyama was appointed the Rector of Hosei University, a post he retained until 1945. While Minister of Justice, Koyama had been opposed to Japan's war with China, which had brought him into conflict with the Minister of War Sadao Araki. But after becoming rector of Hosei, Koyama is reported to have repaired his relationship with Araki, and even invited him to visit the university. Araki, a charismatic supporter of totalitarianism, militarism, and expansionism, appears to have influenced Koyama. On March 3, 1934 Koyama allowed the publication of a photograph of himself in the *Wide World Magazine* holding a samurai sword with the caption "In much the same style as the billiard artist looks over his cue, Koyama, Japan's Minister of Justice, is shown here inspecting one of his fine collection of swords in his home in Tokyo." Since one of Araki's *bon mots* from this period is "the sword is our steel Bible!" one senses an ideological convergence.

Raimund von Klebelsberg, professor of geology and later rector at the University of Innsbruck, pro-Anschluss and anti-Semitic.

Bálint Hóman, professor of Hungarian history, Hungarian Minister of Religion and Education, member of the Arrow Cross regime and virulently anti-Semitic.

Wang Jingwei, former Prime Minister of the Republic of China, a politician who would become notorious as a pro-fascist "collaborator-traitor" who betrayed China to the Japanese.

Carlos Saavedra Lamas, Minister of the Foreign Office of the Republic of Argentina, eugenicist responsible for preventing Jewish emigration to Argentina in particular and South America in general.

Ramón S. Castillo Barrionuevo, Argentinian law professor, later minister of the interior, vice-president, and president in a fraudulently-elected right-wing government. Pro-German if not pro-Nazi orientation (although officially neutral).

(2) Rightists sympathetic to Nazism and fascism:

Mihail Arnaudov, Rector of the University of Sofia.

Kirsopp Lake, professor of Archaeology at Harvard. I was profoundly mystified as to why Lake, an eminent biblical scholar of British extraction who had emigrated to America to teach at Harvard, would have been selected by the Nazi authorities to be awarded a Heidelberg doctorate. However, considerable light is shed on this question by a letter Lake addressed to the editor of *The New York Times* on November 15, 1938. Just after *Kristallnacht*, Lake wrote:

> I have always been, and still am, a warm admirer of German scholarship and intellect. It has always seemed to me that the present German Government was called into existence by the injustice of the Versailles treaty, and nations which were responsible for that treaty cannot complain if Germany took the only means open to her for restoring the empire to its proper position. I thought that if Germans feel that Jews are undesirable inmates they have a right to turn them out of their country.

Until *Kristallnacht*, Lake had excused the Nazis and their policies, including their anti-Semitism, with the perceived injustice of the Versailles Treaty as justification. Now, after *Kristallnacht*, he did a sudden about-face: he repudiated the Nazi policies and urged that immigration to the United States be facilitated for the victims. He signed his letter as "Corresponding Member of the Prussian Academy," clearly hoping to send a strong message to the Nazi authorities.

Christoph Martin, medical doctor and German community organiser in Southern Chile sympathetic to Nazism.

Nikolaos Louveris, right-wing Greek minister of education.

Ferdinand Thun and Henry Janssen, German-American businessmen, major donors to Heidelberg, willing to overlook all criticism of the Nazis. Apparently, they also persisted against protests from their own families and "spiteful Jews," as was disclosed by Dean Carl Brinkmann of the Economics Faculty at Heidelberg in his nomination letter to Groh. Dated January 17, 1936, Brinkmann's nomination letter again points out the importance of the German Embassy and Foreign Office in verifying the Nazi sympathies of the nominees for honorary doctorates from Heidelberg; naturally, Brinkmann makes no mention of the support from American-Jewish donors for the New University Building, or of the opposition from ("Aryan") German-Americans like Carl Schurz's heirs to the continued (mis)use of his name by Thun and Janssen:

> The German-Americans Jansen [*sic*] and Thun (both born in Barmen) have been proposed for honorary doctorates as outstanding representatives of Germanness in America by the German Embassy in America, with which the Foreign Office concurs. Reich Education Minister [Rust], in a decision of October 31, 1935, has made this proposal his own. The services of the above-named to German science and culture are beyond dispute. They have continually expressed their strong interest in German cultural institutions through the donation of large sums, especially for the erection of the New University building in Heidelberg. They have held to their position in spite of

> resistance from their own families and in spite of hateful Jewish attacks. With their nomination for honorary doctorates that also can serve to honor their seventieth birthdays—which both men celebrate this year—the University of Heidelberg fulfills an honorable obligation.[17]

Lauwers-Rech notes that, in 1935, when pressed to break cultural relations with Germany, Thun declared that, "a positive, optimistic attitude of 'for[e]bearance, tolerance, friendship, recognition of what is good' toward Germany would improve the situation."[18] Thus, for their loyalty to the "New" Germany, both Thun and Janssen were awarded honorary doctorates at Heidelberg.

Chou Lou, Rector of the University of Canton, right wing and ardent anti-Communist.

Gustav Komppa, Finnish chemist also active in Nazi Germany. Like other Finnish pro-Nazi academics, Komppa seems to have sanitised his papers post-war. However, a surviving letter from the "Technical Office" of the Nazi Party Headquarters in the Brown House in Munich dated January 11, 1935 discloses that the Party was very interested in Komppa's technique

---

[17] "Die Deutsch-Amerikaner Jansen [*sic*] und Thun (beide in Barmen geboren) sind als hervoragende Vertreter des Deutschtums in Amerika von der Deutschen Botschaft in Amerika, der sich das Auswärtige Amt anschließt, zur Ehrenpromotion vorgeschlagen worden. Der Reichswissenschaftsminister [Rust] hat diesen Vorschlag durch Verfügung vom 31. Oktober 1935 zu eigen gemacht. Die Verdienste der Genannten für die deutsche Wissenschaft und Kultur stehen außer Zweifel. Immer wieder haben sie ihr warmes Interesse für die deutschen kulturellen Einrichtungen durch die Spende größerer Summen, insbesondere anlässlich der Errichtung des neuen Universitäts-Gebäude in Heidelberg bekundet. Sie haben an dieser Einstellung trotz Widerstandes in den eigenen Familien und trotz gehässiger jüdischer Angriffe festgehalten. Mit ihrer Ernennung zu Ehrendoktoren, die zugleich als Ehrung anlässlich des 70. Geburtstages erfolgen kann, den beide Herren in diesem Jahre feiern, erfüllt die Universität Heidelberg eine Ehrenpflicht." Remy writes (*The Heidelberg Myth*, 64): "Brinkmann did not consider Janssen and Thun prominent scholars, but he did think they were important conduits between Germany and the United States who had donated 'great sums' toward promoting 'German science and culture,' including donations for the construction of the new university building in Heidelberg. They had held to their positions, Brinkman added, 'despite opposition within their own families and spiteful Jewish attacks.'"

[18] Magda Lauwers-Rech, *Nazi Germany and the American Germanists. A Study of Periodicals 1930–1946* (New York, Washington DC/Baltimore, San Francisco, Bern, Frankfurt am Main, Berlin, Vienna, Paris: Peter Lang, 1995), 85–6.

for making oil out of peat. Also, in Komppa's correspondence with Freudenberg (who nominated him for the Heidelberg doctorate), Freudenberg mentions that he heard about Komppa's plans to visit Germany from a Heidelberg colleague Richard Kuhn rather than directly from Komppa himself. This fact suggests that Komppa also maintained a close professional relationship with Kuhn, who worked as an advisor and collaborator at I. G. Farben, the chemical conglomerate charged by the Nazis with making synthetic fuel and rubber for the German war machine. I suspect that in early 1936 Komppa responded positively to this request for information about his technique, and for this cooperation the party and then the Foreign Office were grateful. The "reward" for Komppa's expertise on such a vitally important issue could have been the 1936 honorary doctorate from Heidelberg. Indeed, Komppa must have remained important to the Nazis because in 1941 he was invited on an extended speaking tour of the Reich.

Otto von Franges, Croatian Yugoslav agriculturalist and government minister, friend of Walter Darré, the Nazi agriculture minister.

(3) Undetermined

Marinos Gerulanos (Greece), professor of surgery at the University of Athens.
Alfred Vogt, Professor of Opthomology, Zurich.

Reginald Aldworth Daly, Harvard geologist who maintained contacts in Nazi Germany but showed no indication of pro-Nazism.

(4) Mistakes

Léon Cardenal-Pujals, Professor of Surgery and Rector of the University of Madrid, who proved sympathetic to the left.

Bosch-Gimpera, archeologist of part-German ancestry, member of the leftist government in Spain. His honorary doctorate was withdrawn during the war.

Enrico Fermi, nuclear physicist who accepted his position at the University of Rome and honours from the fascist regime, but defected to the United States in 1938 after accepting the Nobel Prize when Mussolini adopted anti-Semitic policies that affected him personally.

Stefan Pienkowski or Penkovsky, Polish physicist, who, after the German invasion of 1939, declined a German offer to work on their atomic bomb project and instead became the head of the Underground University of Warsaw.

*

This information shows beyond any doubt that the great majority of men lined up behind Sibelius to receive honorary doctorates were correctly judged by the Nazis to reveal some kind of sympathy to Nazism, pro-fascism, or right-wing political orientation, racism, and/or anti-Semitism, in varied combinations. While Sibelius cannot be included in the "hard-core" first group, the totality of evidence lends credence to the hypothesis that Sibelius belongs to the second category of Nazi sympathisers.

On March 9, 1935, the Office of the League of Nations' High Commissioner for Refugees (Jewish and Other) Coming from Germany, published a 28 page report entitled *A Crisis in the University World*.[19] The mass firing of over six hundred professors (by that date) created a problem of international dimensions (the total number would exceed sixteen hundred). Given this crisis, the pro-Nazi intelligentsia around the world at that time had to be both myopic and deaf not to see and hear what was going on. My point here is to focus on the intelligentsia, not just in Finland but throughout the so-called civilized world: to take the attitude that "my most distinguished colleagues can be summarily dismissed and I can behave as if all is normal" requires studied aversion.

Let me conclude with reference to a painted indictment of such deliberate ignorance by Georg Grosz, created in 1942 in his New York exile, entitled *The Mighty One on a Little Outing Surprised by Two Poets.*

[19] *A Crisis in the University World* (London: Office of the High Commissioner for Refugers [Jewish and other] Coming from Germany, Sentinel House, Southampton Row, March 9, 1935).

Plate 1

George Grosz, A mighty one on a little outing surprised by two poets (1942), now at Hofstra University.

Plate 2

George Grosz, A mighty one on a little outing surprised by two poets (1942), detail.

The title is somewhat inaccurate, since the second figure on the right is clearly a musician, a composer, who is singing, accompanying himself on the lyre—a perverted Orpheus. The poet appears to be trying to write something in the *lingua tertii imperii*, as Viktor Klemperer famously described it in his brilliant exegesis of Nazi language (note the Swastika), while anxiously tugging at the hem of Hitler's coat. Is the fact that both "poets" are clearly elderly—note their wispy white hair—a reference to the famous artists and musicians like Sibelius and Richard Strauss who cooperated with the Nazis' propaganda efforts? To keep his geriatric "compliant artists" in line, "the Mighty One" carries a bullwhip behind his back. The "poets'" buttocks already bear the marks of his lash, and they fear being hit again. The figures are stuck in the snow of the Russian-Finnish winter; while the artists only have torn rags to shield themselves from the cold, Hitler, of course, is well protected by his thick warm greatcoat. Most remarkably, if one looks at the painting very closely, one notices that Grosz's "poets" wear elaborate *earplugs*, wooden blocks screwed onto their ears: "hear no evil, see no evil," i.e. they are deliberately made ignorant of what is really going on around them as they sing and write the praises of "the Mighty One."

THE FINALE OF SIBELIUS' SECOND SYMPHONY IN RECORDINGS

BENJAMIN T. HILGER

How Conductors Interpret *Poco a poco ravvivando il tempo*

In the late nineteenth century, the tempo design of music beyond the basic tempo indication of a musical piece came more and more into focus for Western European art music composers. Exemplary is Tchaikovsky's Sixth Symphony, where the main theme has to be played in tempo *Allegro non troppo*, and the second theme in tempo *Andante*. Of course, the tempo of musical performances has never been stable and was always subordinated to the vivid execution of the text. Therefore, slight tempo differences between the two main sections of a classical sonata form may have been common long before being explicitly written in the scores. This phenomenon, which is especially visible in Tchaikovsky's music, illustrates an attempt to intensify the musical expression with the help of a parameter which so far has been consistent, at least in the "theory" of musical scores.

In the music of Jean Sibelius, aspects of tempo design also came more and more into focus, but not in order to intensify musical expression. Obviously, Sibelius does not follow Tchaikovsky in his use of contrasting tempo expressions for the main subjects of a sonata form, as far as this traditional pattern in an academic sense can be applied to one of his works at all. Sibelius' concern focused instead on enabling different views of musical elements (his "tesserae" which God throws into the world)[1] and barely perceptible changes between formal sections. Therefore, he not only used different tempo denotations but explicitly marked gradual tempo changes.

---

[1] See Jean Sibelius' statement to Jalmari Finne, who talked about Sibelius's idea of music in his letter to Anna Sarlin, June 28, 1905; Finne's letter is located in the Finnish National Archive.

A notable example is the first movement of the Fifth Symphony. This work in its final version is a fusion of two originally independent movements—a slow movement in *Tempo molto moderato* and a fast, dance-like movement in tempo *Allegro moderato*—something that was to have significant consequences for the tempo design, as Sibelius' later published metronome markings show.[2] Beyond the written tempo indications in the score, the metronome markings indicate a gradual *accelerando* which culminates at the very end of the movement.[3]

In his book about the style of musical recordings in the first half of the twentieth century, Robert Philip states that Sibelius and his contemporaries:

> had detailed tempo changes in mind, but did not indicate them in the published scores. Since flexibility of tempo was a general practice of the time, these composers presumably took it for granted that their scores would be treated in the usual way by their contemporaries, without the need for elaborate instructions.[4]

This changes the focus from a musical work and the composer's intentions, towards the realisations by musical performers. Obviously, Sibelius had good reasons to clarify his ideas about tempo design beyond written tempo indications, to reflect some 20 years of performance practice since the premiere of his Fifth Symphony. How performers realised a symphonic movement in the history of musical recording, which is not necessarily identical to a live performance as intense reworkings in recording studios show, is the basis of a study by Bethany Lowe.[5] Investigating 43 recordings via tempo measurement, she carves out how conductors solved the tempo question in the Fifth Symphony's first movement. According to the assumption that "any type of tempo change can be used to mark a structural point … [which] may in certain cases be

---

[2] David Cherniavsky, "Sibelius' Tempo Corrections," *Music and Letters* 31 (1) (1950): 53–5; and earlier Jean Sibelius, *Metronombezeichnungen zu seinen Symphonien* (Leipzig: Breitkopf & Härtel, 1943).

[3] *Allegro moderato* beginning dotted minim equals 80, rising via 96 (b. 218), 104 (b. 372), 112 (b. 423), 126 (b. 447) to 138 (b. 507, *Presto*).

[4] Robert Philip, *Early Recordings and Musical Style: Changing Tastes in Instrumental Performance, 1900–1950* (Cambridge: Cambridge University Press, 1992), 14.

[5] Bethany Lowe, "Analysing Performances of Sibelius' Fifth Symphony: The 'One Movement or Two' Debate and the Plurality of the Music Object," *Music Analysis* 30 (2/3) (July/October 2011), 218–71.

interpreted as a structural boundary,"[6] she categorises types of tempo design[7] reflecting views about the formal structure of the movement. Herbert von Karajan transpires to be the inventor of a tempo design in 1953 which is classified as a "two movements" interpretation, and realizes the gradual *accelerando* that Sibelius indicated. Lowe plausibly connects her results about the new tempo outline with the analytical writing of Gerald Abraham[8] and the publication of the composer's metronome markings in 1943 and 1950.[9]

Analysis and Observations

Another movement with a long passage of obviously intended gradual tempo change is the final movement of Sibelius' Second Symphony. According to Cecil Gray, it is, "formally, and in every other sense as well … the simplest and most straightforward movement in the symphony, and the least in need of thematic analysis or explanation of any kind,"[10] an estimation which is certainly true with regard to the formal structure, which may be seen as a sonata-like scheme.[11] The movement starts with a characteristically rising three-note motif (part A1) which finally culminates in a fourth note (building the apotheosis of the symphony) and is "succeeded by several satellites."[12] One of these "satellites" is the delayed off-beat accent in the accompaniment which also grounds the following descending motif, starting in the woodwinds in b. 44 (part A2). Both parts are furthermore linked by the same tempo indication and are—despite motivic differences—two sides of one musical idea. This becomes clear when a third musical character enters stage *a tempo ma tranquillo*. Beginning in b. 66, wave-like minor scales in cello and viola constitute a

---

[6] Ibid., 225.

[7] Lowe differentiates four tempo outlines: "One-movement," "Two-movement," "Diagonal," and "Stepped" (ibid., 227f.). The stepped tempo outline in this study is solely connected with Russian conductors, a fact that is brought together with the results of José Antonio Bowen (footnote 27) concerning again the tempo relations in Tchaikovsky's Sixth Symphony (Lowe 2011, 254).

[8] Gerald Abraham, "The Symphonies," in *Sibelius: A Symposium*, ed. G. Abraham (London: Oxford University Press, 1952), 14–37.

[9] See footnote 2.

[10] Cecil Gray, *Sibelius. The Symphonies* (London: Oxford University Press, 1935), 25.

[11] The interpretation of this movement as sonata form follows the contrasting main characters of the music and the repetitive form of the musical surface, ignoring that the resulting development is all but a development in a classical sense.

[12] Gray, *Sibelius*, 25.

contrasting passage and carry the woodwind material (part B), which may be viewed as the second theme of a sonata form, an interpretation which is supported by the repetition of these sections.[13]

This endlessly prolongable passage (which is in fact almost doubled from 40 to 78 bars in the recapitulation) seems unstoppable on its own terms. Thus, another "satellite" of the three-note motif, the fanfare from b. 5, enters in b. 102, confusing and interrupting the wave-like scales and subsequently leading to a recitative-like *pizzicato* line in the lower strings under modulating chords in the high strings. The tempo changes to *Moderato assai* in b. 106 and is more and more reduced towards the indication *a tempo ma tranquillo* in b. 113 in performance. What follows is the lynchpin of the movement's musical process: a dialogue unfolds (part C), contrasting the orchestra's main instrumental sections (strings and woodwinds) and the movement's main motifs (the three-note motif from part A and the beginning of the *tranquillo* theme from part B with the retarding accent on the second beat). With the *tranquillo* theme's disappearance, the three-note motif seems to be the "winner" of this competition (see figure 1).

Figure 1. Symphony No. 2, movement 4, tempo and musical elements (part C and D)

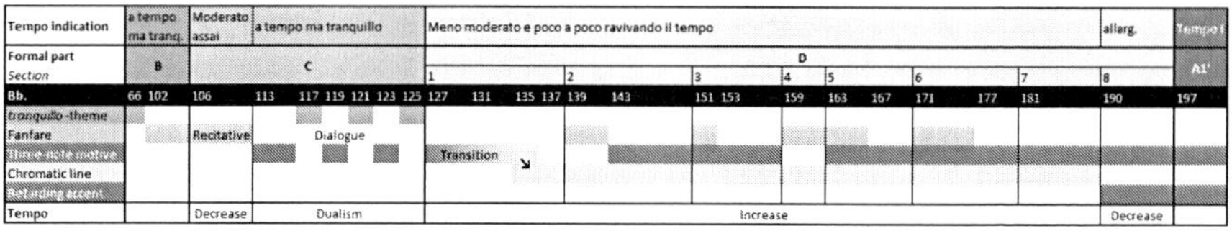

In the subsequent development passage (part D), more urgent motifs "are worked to a climax, culminating in the triumphant restatement of the first section of the movement."[14] This passage is marked *Meno moderato e poco a poco ravvivando il tempo* (regrettably without further metronome markings[15]), and is the focus of this investigation. It is divided into eight subsections. The first is characterised by the dissolution of the ascending three-note motifs' distinctive minims being gradually undermined by an increasing crotchet line. This conversion (it may be called liquidation of

[13] The recapitulation A1' begins in b. 197, A2' in b. 240, and the prolonged second theme section B' lasts from b. 262 to b. 339.

[14] Gray, *Sibelius*, 26.

[15] Sibelius gives minim equals 88 for the whole movement (Cherniavsky, "Sibelius' Tempo Corrections").

motif to motion) is supported by an intended increase of tempo which different performers approach quite differently. The resulting chromatic line grounds the musical process until section seven via instrumentation in the manner of a Shepard-scale, the acoustical equivalent to Escher's endless staircases. Sections two to six are marked by the beginning of the fanfare motif, section seven by the withdrawal from *fortissimo* to *mezzoforte* in combination with a reduced instrumentation, and section eight by the re-entrance of the retarding off-beat accent from A1 and A2 (figure).

These details influence the tempo design of performances: the motivic dialogue (part C) entails a dualistic tempo outline, the transition as well as the following sections (part D) show an intended increase of tempo, while the final section slows down towards the recapitulation. David Hurwitz's statement that this movement "poses a few really serious interpretive problems"[16] is especially true for these sections. He claims: "The first of these concerns tempo ... The key to a successful performance lies ... in catching the music's sense of flow, and making sure that the feeling of inevitable forward progress is never interrupted."[17] How conductors address this problem in terms of pacing events so that they are not simply a muddle of competing motifs but a striking process slanted towards the recapitulation is the interest of this study. Accordingto the demand for longitudinal cuts through the performance history,[18] an investigation was started to detect if similar changes are demonstrable for the Second Symphony's performance history, as was the case in Lowe's study of the Fifth Symphony.

Therefore, 91 recordings by 58 conductors over the decades since Robert Kajanus' first recorded performance in 1930 were analysed (for details see at the end of this text and footnote).[19] The 1930s include the complete known recordings by Kajanus, Koussevitzky, and two examples

---

[16] David Hurwitz, *Sibelius. The Orchestral Music. An Owner's Manual* (Unlocking the Masters Series, No. 12) (New Jersey: Amadeus Press, 2007), 87.

[17] Ibid.

[18] See Jürg Stenzl, "Herbert von Karajan (1908–1989) zwischen espressivo, neusachlicher und historischer Interpretation. 'Die Szene am Bach' aus Beethovens 6. Sinfonie," in *Herbert von Karajan (1908–1989). Der Dirigent im Lichte einer Geschichte der musikalischen Interpretation*, eds. Lars E. Laubhold and Jürg Stenzl (Salzburg: Pustet, 2008), 12.

[19] The recordings are listed with the year of origin, which in some cases differs a lot from the date of publication (for example in the case of Toscanini's early radio broadcast recordings). Owing to the number of various dates from recording to first publication to republication on CD this is partially not easy to verify, but was done as far as possible.

by Toscanini. In the 1940s, according to Guy Thomas' *The Symphonies of Sibelius on Record*,[20] only three recordings are missing here. According to the same source, the further decades are not complete, but cover at least a representative number of a minimum of ten recordings. To bring things up to date, live recordings from internet sources were also added.

A simple comparison of average durations in chosen periods of time shows what one might expect, bearing in mind the results of Robert Philip, "that the maximum tempos within movements are usually slower in post-war than in pre-war performances, so that the average tempo … has generally dropped"[21] and the duration increased correspondingly. The average duration of the final movement recorded between 1930 and 1959 amounts to 763 sec. (12'43") and increases to 846 sec. (14'06") in the following period from 1960 to 1979 (plus 10.9% respectively plus 83 sec.). This value is approximately stable in the subsequent time spans.[22]

Figure 2. Symphony No. 2, movement 4, duration

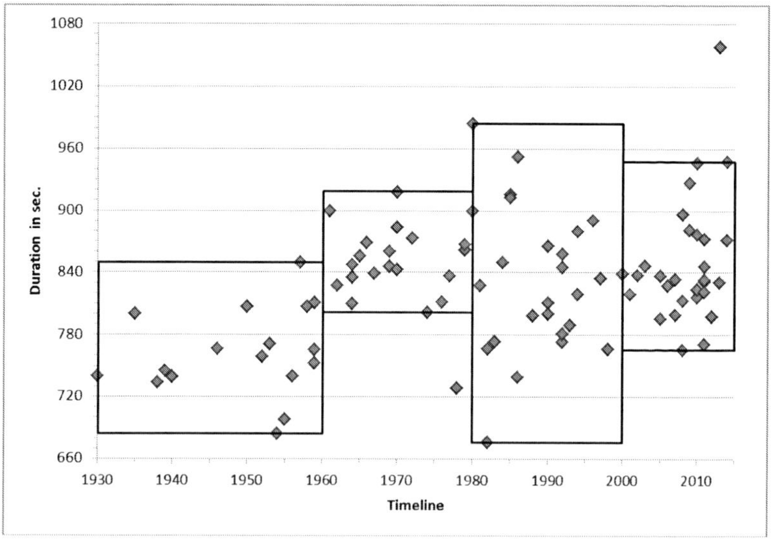

[20] Guy Thomas, *The Symphonies of Sibelius on Record: A Discography and Discussion*, reprinted with minor changes November 2012, 34–42.
[21] Philip, *Early Recordings and Musical Style*, 35.
[22] 1980–1999: 832 sec. (−1.6 %); since 2000: 850 sec. (+2.2 %). For movement one (average duration: 558, 595, 587, 604 sec.; increase: +6.6 %, −1.2 %, +2.8 %) and two (average duration: 788, 850, 859, 874 sec.; increase: +7.8 %, +1.0 %, +1.7 %) similar results appear. In movement three the change is below 20 sec.

The individual variety of durations is of course much more diverse (see figure 2) than suggested by average values. The span reaches from Beecham's 684 sec. (11'24")[23] to the duration of 1058 sec. (17'38"), reached in a live recording by Maazel[24] in 2013. Projected against this timeline, a characteristic distribution becomes visible: durations were clearly below 840 sec. (14') before 1960, and between 780 and 900 sec. (13–15') in the 1960s and 70s[25]; there was a huge variety of different durations in the 1980s, which was reduced in the 1990s, and a further spread of durations in recent years. This allows the recording history to be separated into the four time spans used here.

Investigation and Results

To gain deeper insights into the tempo design of recordings, more data than just generally measured time spans is needed. The required data collection was implemented with *Sonic Visualiser*,[26] a General Public License Software developed at the Centre for Digital Music at Queen Mary University of London. Via tapping a computer key, a so-called Time Instants Layer measures the durations between the taps which are placed at the onset of each bar. The collected time values are extracted to a text file, imported to a spreadsheet programme, converted to variable measurements such as durations of formal parts and metronome values (beats per minute or bpm) for selected passages or the whole piece, and finally visualised in graphs which are then interpreted.

This method of tempo measurement has been investigated and widely discussed, even in its vulnerability for errors. José Antonio Bowen states:

> When converted to a tempo measurement the accuracy was no greater than + or –3 beats per minute when measuring tempos in the 100 beats per

---

[23] Undercut only by Vladimir Fedoseyev's in 1982 with 676 sec. (11'16").

[24] Maazel's recordings cover a time span of almost 50 years: from 1964 (847 sec. = 14'07") via 1990 (865 sec. = 14'25") to late live recordings from 2009 (927 sec. = 15'27") and 2013 (1058 sec. = 17'38"). The very last recording uses massive and frequent tempo reductions, in the recapitulation even below the outstanding long-lasting recordings of Karajan (1980: 984 sec. = 16'24") and Kamu (918 sec. = 15'18"); (see figure 9).

[25] With the exception of Yuri Ahronovitch's recording in 1978 with 729 sec. (12'09").

[26] See Chris Cannam, Christian Landone, and Mark Sandler, "Sonic Visualiser: An Open Source Application for Viewing, Analysing, and Annotating Music Audio Files." *Proceedings of the ACM Multimedia 2010 International Conference.* http://www.sonicvisualiser.org/sv2010.pdf (February 27, 2016).

> minute range; i.e., 3% or 0.06 seconds per measurement. The error is not cumulative and the large changes in tempo on a multi-bar or phrase level are reflected accurately.[27]

Additionally, it is useful to mention that the accuracy of performances is subject to human error, especially (but not always the case) in early recordings, which occasionally require pragmatic decisions either to follow the melody or the accompaniment.

Data was generated on two different levels: firstly on the formal level measuring the duration of constituent sections, and secondly on the bar level between b. 106 and b. 272 (formal parts C, D, A1', A2', 11 bars in B'). Additionally, a few recordings were tapped completely. The measurement on bar level is of course a simplification in comparison with the measurement of every beat, but due to the error-vulnerability in high tempi[28] this method was chosen because its accuracy seemed sufficient for the current purposes.

Figure 3. Evolution of average tempo in formal parts

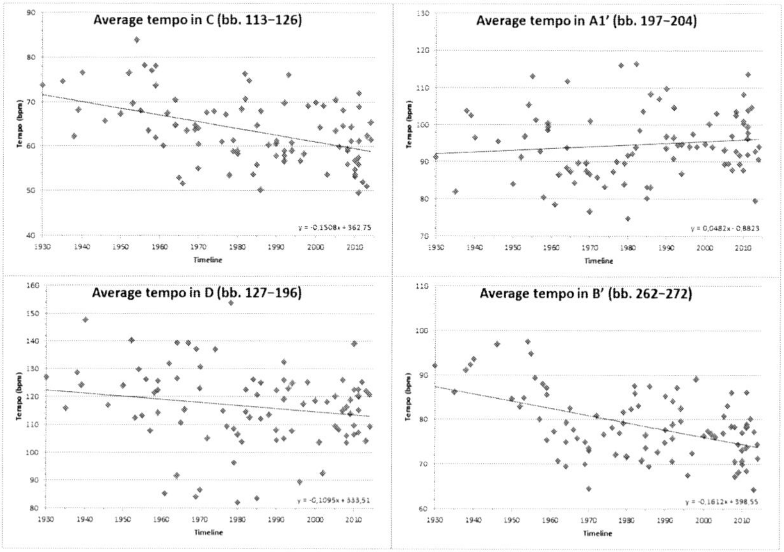

[27] José Antonio Bowen, "Tempo, Duration, and Flexibility: Techniques in the Analysis of Performance," *The Journal of Musicological Research* 16 (2) (1996): 130. This was also proved by several scientists, including Nicholas Cook.

[28] Barbirolli and Ahronovitch partially scratch the border of 160 bpm.

Although the duration of the Second Symphony's final movement on the whole has increased (as seen before), a detailed look at the formal sections gives another impression (see figure 3). The comparison of average tempo values reveals that the tempo clearly reduced in the dialogue passage (part C, bb. 113–126) from around 70 to around 60 bpm. This deceleration goes hand in hand with an increasingly emphasised character of the motivic dialogue, which rounds off the following passage. Accordingly, the tempo of the second theme (part B', at letter L, detected with the introductory eleven bb. 262–272) declined from over 80 bpm before 1960 to mostly below 80 bpm afterwards, whereas the tempo is slightly accelerated in the recapitulation (part A1', detected with the initiating eight bb. 197–204). The average tempo value also declined in the development (part D, bb. 127–196), but with regard to the massive variability of tempo in this passage (due to the tempo indication *poco a poco ravvivando il tempo*) this fact is of little significance.

For more detailed consideration, individual tempo maps are indispensable. They reveal a different formal integration of the motivic dialogue (bb. 113–126) which is interpreted as a conflict of different tempi (see figure 4): Kajanus increases the tempo from b. 113 onwards aside from slight tempo differences between the competing motifs and makes the following *ravvivando* appear as a consequence of the disappearance of the second theme motifs. Ahronovitch choses the opposite solution—slowing down until b. 126 in what seems to be a good preparation for his outstanding fast acceleration that follows. By far the most common solution (even if it is, of course, not always as clearly executed as in the examples) can be found in the recordings of Beecham and Rosbaud: here, the dialogue appears as an insertion between two formal parts, separated by a considerable reduction of tempo, both before and afterwards.

Figure 4. Tempo outline of motivic dialogue (bb. 106–138).

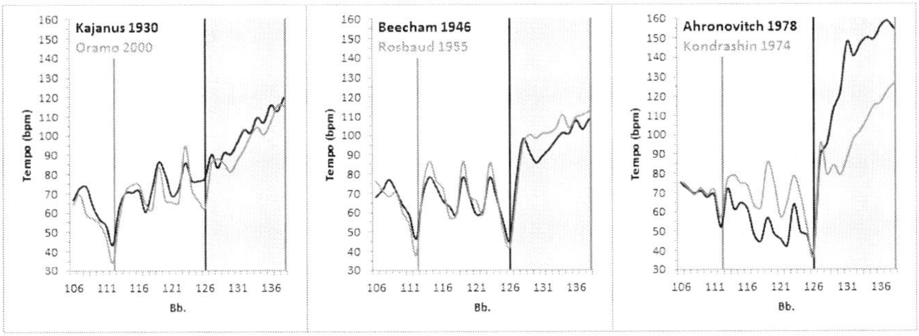

In early recordings some conductors exceed 130 bpm, while others do not but are at least above 110 bpm. A common feature in both outlines is that the strongest tempo increase occurs in section one. This changed from 1961 with Herbert von Karajan, who interprets *ravvivando il tempo* at a significantly lower rate and creates a constant (though in comparison with earlier recordings not very extensive) increase of tempo. This new outline is immediately "copied" by Maazel in 1964 (see figure 8).

The graph proves Karajan's legendary tempo control and reminds us of his words: "I can accept a wrong note from an orchestra, but when everything is getting faster or slower, that I cannot accept."[29] That his pupil Okko Kamu[30], winner of Karajan Conducting Competition, was the right choice for the completion of Deutsche Grammophon's Sibelius cycle becomes clear when comparing their smooth and narrow tempo maps for a longer passage with the rapid tempo changes of other conductors, which are much more the "normal" case (F): both remain below 100 bpm (see figure 9).

Another discovery concerns the outstanding maximum tempi of Simon Rattle in the later years of this survey.[31] The tempo map reveals that he combines a strong tempo increase in the first section with a constant but still strong tempo increase until section seven (see figure 10). This may reflect influences from one of the many recordings of Barbirolli[32] as well as from the recordings of Karajan. That solutions other than a long and gradual increase of tempo are possible is demonstrated by Leonard Bernstein's two late recordings (see figure 5). His tempo curve reaches a maximum in section four followed by a constant slowing down towards the recapitulation. Although unusual and probably against Sibelius' intentions[33] this cannot be an accident: firstly this pattern was established in 1985 and was repeated in 1986, secondly the peak in the middle of part D is connected with the section without the three-note motif as its turning point.

---

[29] Richard Osborne, *Conversations with Karajan* (Oxford: Oxford University Press, 1990), 96.

[30] Kamu's cycle of all symphonies (released September 2015) appeared after this investigation and could not be added any more.

[31] Unfortunately, the new recording (released October 2015) could not be included.

[32] Barbirolli's 1952 recording seems noticeably related to Rattle's 1984 recording regarding the slight reduction of tempo at the beginning of the *ravvivando* passage.

[33] One might remember the anecdote of Karajan blaming Bernstein for smashing his attempts at making Sibelius more popular; see Roger Vaughan, *Herbert von Karajan. Ein biographisches Porträt*, 2nd ed., trans. Hans-Ulrich Seebohm (Frankfurt am Main: Ullstein, 1986), 225.

Figure 5. Bernstein's tempo outline

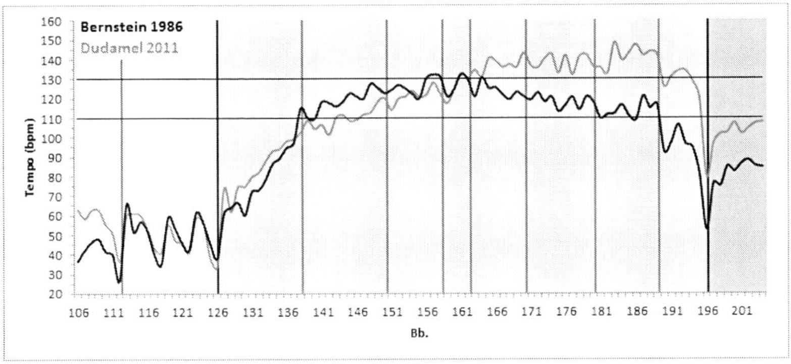

One last discovery concerns recordings which immediately follow each other at the beginning of the 1990s (see figure 11): Esa-Pekka Salonen (as well as Mariss Jansons) seems to reanimate the early tempo outline of Barbirolli, albeit at a lower tempo level, while Jukka-Pekka Saraste (just like Paavo Berglund) appears to follow the tempo outline of Kajanus. In the same manner Osmo Vänskä imitates Karajan's characteristic tempo design, which had become exemplary too.

In order to visualise performance trends beyond individual characteristics, the graphs were simplified by calculating average values for every section of part D. Projecting the results according to the four phases of performance history shows four noticeable different charts (see figure 6):

(1) 1930–1959: Closely combined graphs on a level above 100 bpm reached in section two
(2) 1960–1979: Extremely widespread graphs, several above 100 bpm, yet in section one, others entirely below 120 bpm
(3) 1980–1999: The mainstream starts below 130 bpm in section two, ending with tempi above 120 bpm in section seven
(4) Since 2000: Most recordings start between 100 and 120 bpm in section two and rise above 120 bpm in section seven

Figure 6. Average tempo per section (part C/D/A')

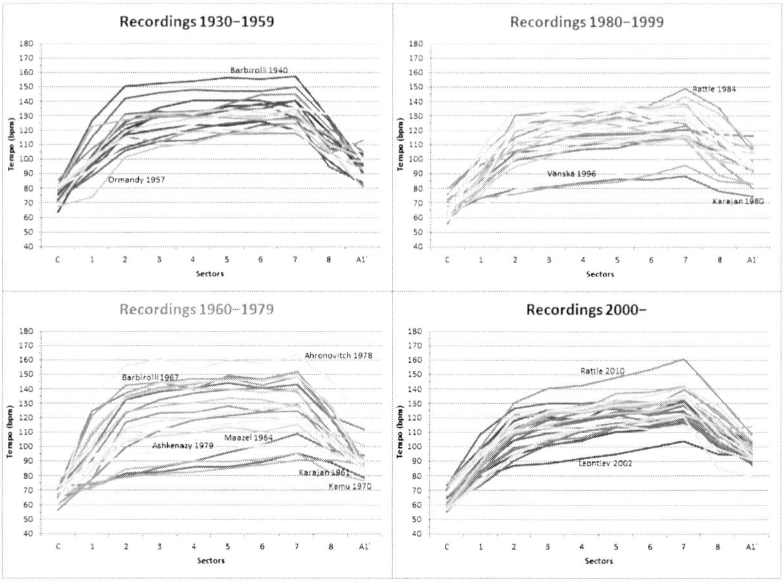

Figure 7. Average tempo per section and time phase of part D

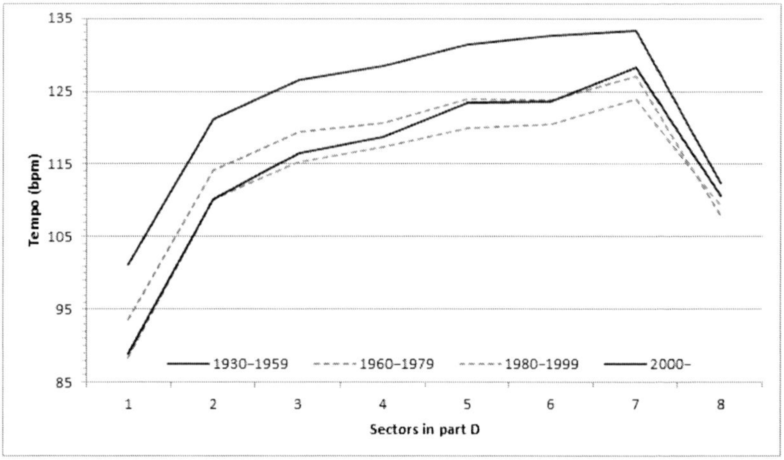

These graphs can be condensed to one average graph for each time phase (see figure 7). From this, two trends emerge: firstly, a general tempo decline from phase one to phase three; secondly, a reshaping of the tempo design towards a more intensively rising graph in phase four. The performance history therefore appears as a kind of transformation process, with the combination of two exemplified tempo designs tested in the meantime.

Conclusions

Summing up, one can find the following implementations of Sibelius' tempo indication *ravvivando poco a poco il tempo* in the early recordings. The "logarithmic" outline following Kajanus with decreasing acceleration, and the "abrupt-stable" outline with fast acceleration yet little or none after section one, following Barbirolli. Both outlines are characterised by a more-or-less enormous change of tempo. This differs from Karajan's tempo design which is composed of "linear" tempo acceleration within a much smaller range and on a much deeper level (see figure 8). This cannot prevail and is abandoned by a combination of a wide tempo range and continuous increase, as demonstrated by Rattle (see figure 10), and the rediscovery of old outlines (see figure 11).

It seems reasonable to bring Karajan's "new way" in correlation with changes of recording technique from gramophone to record and mono to stereo during the 1950s. The musical features of the investigated part of Sibelius' Second Symphony are strengthened towards the recapitulation through tempo increases, instrumentation increases, and volume increases, the last being the central aspect for Karajan. Therefore, an extraordinary reduction and a very gradual change of tempo are deployed in order to put the sound into focus, exploiting the newly established potential of stereo recordings.

By contrast, older recordings (and conductors who still worked during the 1960s) tend to focus more on the motivic process. The extreme acceleration of the first section is related to "tempo modifications" which include "not only slowing down for passages of great significance, but also speeding up to pass over passages requiring less emphasis."[34] This becomes visible here: early interpretations try to reach the motivic level as fast as possible, bridging the passage I called "liquidation of motif to motion." For this reason, in the early recordings the development seems to be development in a classical sense as a motivic "game" preceding the

---

[34] Philip, *Early Recordings and Musical Style*, 9.

recapitulation, while in Karajan's approach it is a phase of dynamic increase culminating in the recapitulation. Accordingly the features of early recordings, "the flexibility and flux of ... 'barely perceptible' internal tempo changes turn, in modern performances, into larger, 'structural' tempo shifts between sections."[35]

The later recordings seem to partially unite these divergent views and therefore may be considered as historically informed performances which prove that modern conductors are aware of the relevant performance history, and consciously update their interpretations accordingly.

Figure 8. Karajan's new tempo outline

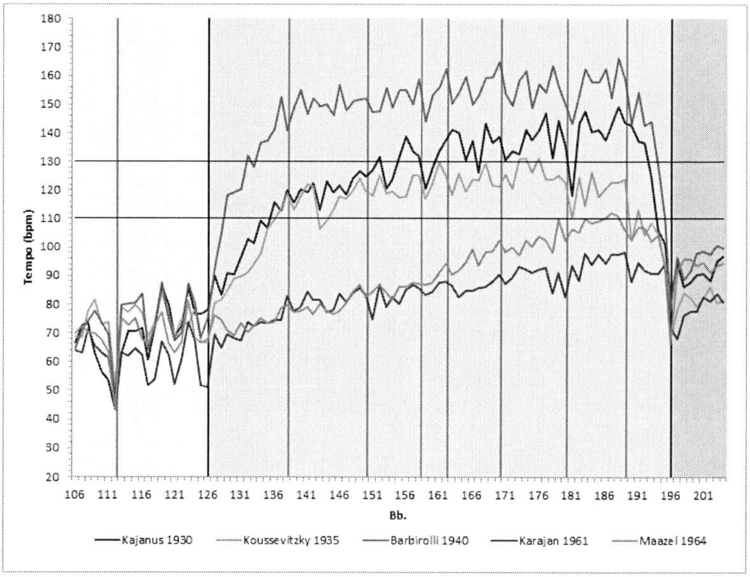

[35] Bowen, "Tempo, Duration, and Flexibility," 148.

Figure 9. Karajan and Kamu compared to other conductors

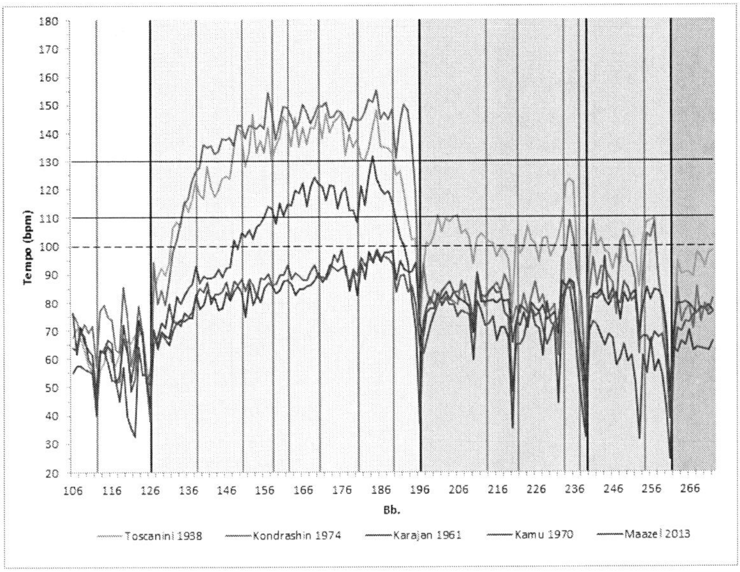

Figure 10. Rattle's role models

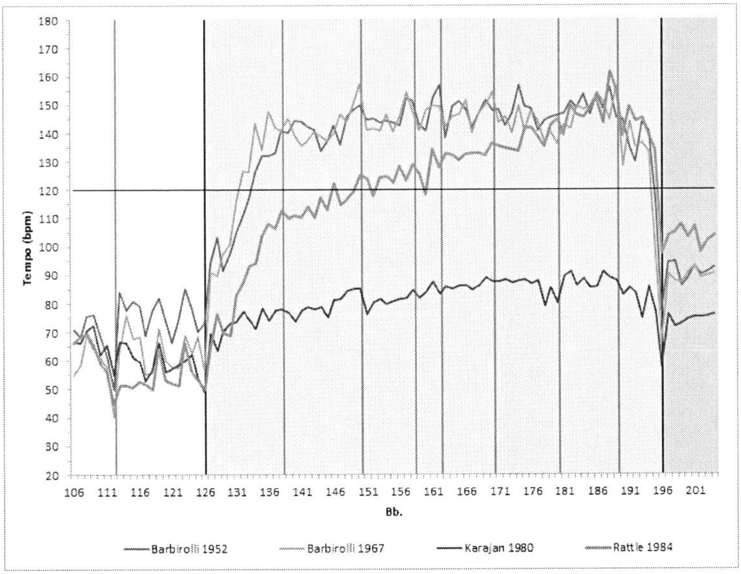

Figure 11. Revival of pre-1960 tempo outlines

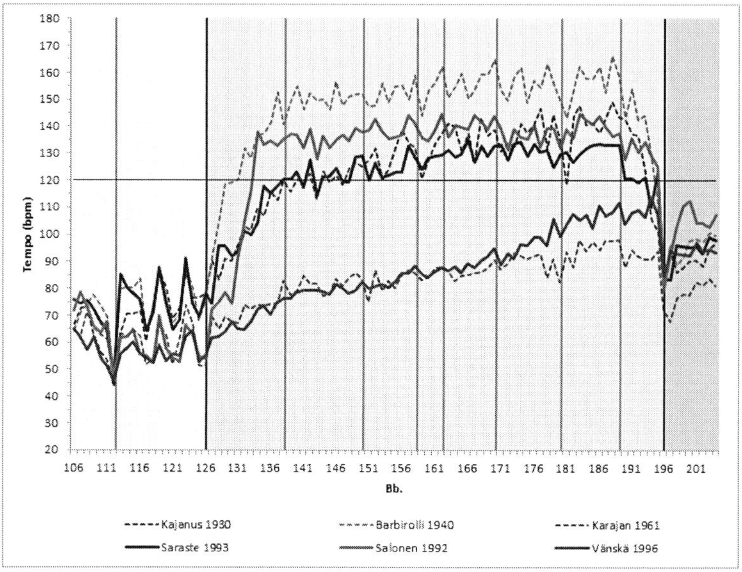

Table 1. Symphony No. 2, collected recordings[36]

Year	Conductor	Symphony Orchestra (SO)	Mvt. 4
1930	Kajanus, Robert	London SO	740"
1935	Koussevitzky, Serge	Boston SO	800"
1938	Toscanini, Arturo	BBC SO	733"
1939	Toscanini, Arturo	NBC SO	745"
1940	Barbirolli, John	New York Philharmonic	739"
1946	Beecham, Thomas	London Philharmonic Orchestra	766"
1950	Koussevitzky, Serge	Boston SO	807"
1952	Barbirolli, John	Hallé Orchester	759"
1953	Collins, Anthony	London SO	771"
1954	Beecham, Thomas	BBC SO	684"

[36] Five recordings: Barbirolli (1940, 1952, 1962, 1967, 1969); four recordings: Berglund (1976, 1986, 1998, 2005), Davis (1979, 1988, 1994, 2006), Maazel (1964, 1990, 2009, 2013); three recordings: Bernstein (1966, 1985, 1986), Jansons (1992, 2005, 2007), Salonen (1992, 2010, 2011), Segerstam (1992, 2003, 2014); two recordings: Thomas Beecham (1946, 1954), Blomstedt (1992, 2008), P. Järvi (2001, 2010), von Karajan (1961, 1980), Koussevitzky (1935, 1950), Ormandy (1957, 1972), Rattle (1984, 2010), Saraste (1993, 2007), Szell (1964, 1970), Tali (2011, 2014), Toscanini (1938, 1939), Vänskä (1996, 2011).

1955	Rosbaud, Hans	Südwestfunk-Orchester	698"
1956	Horenstein, Jascha	French National Radio Orchestra	740"
1957	Ormandy, Eugene	Philadelphia Orchestra	849"
1958	Sargent, Malcolm	BBC SO	807"
1959	Hannikainen, Tauno	Sinfonia of London	810"
1959	Monteux, Pierre	London SO	765"
1959	Paray, Paul	Detroit SO	753"
1961	Karajan, Herbert von	Philharmonia Orchestra	900"
1962	Barbirolli, John	Royal Philharmonic Orchestra	828"
1964	Maazel, Lorin	Wiener Philharmoniker	847"
1964	Stokowski, Leopold	BBC SO	810"
1964	Szell, George	Concertgebouw Orkest Amsterdam	835"
1965	Celibidache, Sergiu	Swedish Radio SO	856"
1966	Bernstein, Leonard	New York Philharmonic	868"
1967	Barbirolli, John	Hallé Orchester	839"
1969	Barbirolli, John	Kölner Rundfunk-Sinfonie Orchester	846"
1969	Rozhdestvensky, Gennady	Moscow Radio SO	860"
1970	Kamu, Okko	Berliner Philharmoniker	918"
1970	Sanderling, Kurt	Berliner Sinfonie Orchester	884"
1970	Szell, George	Cleveland Orchestra	843"
1972	Ormandy, Eugene	Philadelphia Orchestra	873"
1974	Kondrashin, Kirill	Orchestre National de l'ORTF	801"
1976	Berglund, Paavo	Bournemouth SO	811"
1977	Abravanel, Maurice	Utah SO	837"
1978	Ahronovitch, Yuri	Gürzenich-Orchester Köln	729"
1979	Ashkenazy, Vladimir	Philharmonia Orchestra	862"
1979	Davis, Colin	Boston SO	867"
1980	Atzmon, Moshe	Tokyo Metropolitan SO	900"
1980	Karajan, Herbert von	Berliner Philharmoniker	984"
1981	Lilje, Peeter	Estonian National SO	827"
1982	Fedoseyev, Vladimir	Tchaikovsky SO	676"
1982	Gibson, Alexander	Scottish National Orchestra	767"
1983	Järvi, Neeme	Gothenburg SO	773"
1984	Rattle, Simon	City of Birmingham SO	850"
1985	Bernstein, Leonard	Boston SO	916"
1985	Temirkanov, Yuri	State Academy SO of the UdSSR	912"
1986	Berglund, Paavo	Helsinki Philharmonic Orchestra	739"
1986	Bernstein, Leonard	Wiener Philharmoniker	952"
1988	Davis, Colin	Staatskapelle Dresden	798"
1990	Boughton, William	Royal Philharmonic Orchestra	811"
1990	Maazel, Lorin	Pittsburgh SO	865"
1990	Mehta, Zubin	New York Philharmonic	800"
1992	Blomstedt, Herbert	San Francisco Symphony	845"
1992	Jansons, Mariss	Oslo Philharmonic Orchestra	773"
1992	Salonen, Esa-Pekka	Swedish Radio SO	781"
1992	Segerstam, Leif	Danish National SO	858"

1993	Saraste, Jukka-Pekka	Finnish Radio SO	789"
1994	Davis, Colin	London SO	880"
1994	Mackerras, Charles	Royal Philharmonic Orchestra	819"
1996	Vänskä, Osmo	Lahti SO	891"
1997	Sakari, Petri	Iceland SO	834"
1998	Berglund, Paavo	Chamber Orchestra of Europe	767"
2000	Oramo, Sakari	City of Birmingham SO	839"
2001	Järvi, Paavo	Cincinnati SO	877"
2002	Leontiev, Roman	St. Petersburg SO Klassika	837"
2003	Segerstam, Leif	Helsinki Philharmonic Orchestra	847"
2005	Berglund, Paavo	London Philharmonic Orchestra	795"
2005	Jansons, Mariss	Royal Concertgebouw Orchestra	837"
2006	Davis, Colin	London SO	828"
2007	Jansons, Mariss	BR Sinfonieorchester	833"
2007	Saraste, Jukka-Pekka	Oslo Philharmonic Orchestra	799"
2008	Blomstedt, Herbert	NHK SO *(incomplete)*	-
2008	Inkinen, Pietari	New Zealand SO	813"
2009	Maazel, Lorin	New York Philharmonic	927"
2009	Nelsons, Andris	WDR Sinfonieorchester Köln	896"
2009	Tate, Jeffrey	L'Orchestre de la Suisse Romande	882"
2010	Gilbert, Kenneth	New York Philharmonic	946"
2010	Järvi, Paavo	Orchestre de Paris	819"
2010	Rattle, Simon	Berliner Philharmoniker	816"
2010	Salonen, Esa-Pekka	Wiener Philharmoniker	823"
2011	Dudamel, Gustavo	Gothenburg SO	832″
2011	Jensen, Eivind Gullberg	Danmark Radio SO	833"
2011	Salonen, Esa-Pekka	Chicago SO	821"
2011	Søndergård, Thomas	BBC National Orchestra of Wales	771"
2011	Tali, Anu	Nordic SO	846"
2011	Vänskä, Osmo	Minnesota Orchestra	872"
2012	Ticciati, Robin	Los Angeles Philharmonic	798"
2013	Maazel, Lorin	New York Philharmonic	1058"
2013	Storgårds, John	BBC Philharmonics	830"
2014	Segerstam, Leif	Orchestre National de France	947"
2014	Tali, Anu	Columbus SO	871"

DAHLHAUS' PARADIGM AND SIBELIUS RECEPTION

BARRY WIENER

Since the 1915 version of Sibelius' Fifth Symphony became available to scholars forty years ago, it has generally been perceived as an imperfect precursor of the 1919 revision. I propose instead that the 1915 version be viewed as a modernist work that displays a network of intertwined modal and sonic relationships. My approach to the symphony mediates between James Hepokoski's motivic analysis[1] and Ron Weidberg's sonic analysis.[2] It challenges Carl Dahlhaus' historiological model for the modernist "crisis" of composers born in the 1860s[3] and serves as a corrective to Hepokoski's more nuanced view of Sibelius' historical position.

Both Hepokoski and Tim Howell have pointed with disapproval to dissonant harmonies and disjunct textures in the 1915 version. Hepokoski characterises the statement of a "three-note *forte* trumpet entry," Db5–Ab4–G4, early in the last movement (mm. 198–211) as "disturbing,"[4] and

---

[1] See James Hepokoski, *Sibelius: Symphony No. 5* (Cambridge: Cambridge University Press, 1993); James Hepokoski, "Structural Tensions in Sibelius' Fifth Symphony: Circular Stasis, Linear Progress, and the Problem of 'Traditional' Form," in *Sibelius Forum*, eds. Veijo Murtomäki, Kari Kilpeläinen, and Risto Väisänen (Helsinki: Sibelius Academy, 1998), 213–36.

[2] Ron Weidberg, "Comparing the 1915 and 1919 Versions of Sibelius' Fifth Symphony: From Sonic Experimentalism to Functional Synthesis," in *Sibelius in the Old and New World: Aspects of His Music, Its Interpretation, and Reception,* eds. Timothy L. Jackson, Veijo Murtomäki, Colin Davis, and Timo Virtanen (Frankfurt am Main and New York: Peter Lang, 2010), 239–67; see also Ron Weidberg, "Sonic Design in Jean Sibelius' Orchestral Music," in *Sibelius Forum II*, eds. Matti Huttunen, Kari Kilpeläinen, and Veijo Murtomäki (Helsinki: Sibelius Academy, 2003), 216–26.

[3] See Carl Dahlhaus, *Nineteenth-Century Music*, trans. J. Bradford Robinson (Berkeley and Los Angeles: University of California Press, 1989), 335–6.

[4] "It should be added that anticipations of this 'Neapolitan theme' had also intruded, much more disturbingly, into earlier portions of the finale in urgent, held-note trumpet dissonances," Hepokoski, *Sibelius: Symphony No. 5*, 50.

quotes other commentators as expressing "puzzled disapproval, or even shock" at the "splashy intrusions."[5] Similarly, Howell criticises the "somewhat oddly-placed trombone interjections" near the end of the scherzo.[6] Howell perceives the 1915 version as a failed attempt to create a clear sense of harmonic progression[7] or continuity and directed motion.[8]

In contrast to Howell and Hepokoski, Ron Weidberg has focused on the distinctive sonic qualities of the 1915 version, suggesting that it embodies a musical logic based on entirely different presuppositions from those that underlie the 1919 version. According to Weidberg, "[I]n [the first version of the Fifth] we discover the culminating point of a unique constructivist sonic abstraction. The final version, on the other hand, although more elaborated in its sonic structures, signals Sibelius' return to functional harmonic processes."[9]

As Weidberg has noted, Sibelius abbreviated many sound blocks in the 1919 version, transforming them into music that displays clear developmental processes.[10] He also revised or deleted dissonant passages and episodes characterised by disjunct textures so that the symphony now appears to be a stylistically traditional work. He did not, however, modify the much-discussed chromatic episode in the first movement that I label as the "Ligeti-like" sound block (mm. 71–90 [1919], mm. 73–92 [1915]). Today, due to Sibelius' revisions, the episode stands out as an anomaly within the symphony as a whole. While some scholars claim that it exhibits avant-garde features, Eero Tarasti has noted that this point of view depends on removing a single passage from its stylistically more conservative context.[11]

My investigation takes the "Ligeti-like" sound block as its point of departure. An examination of the entire 1915 version of the symphony reveals that the episode is representative of many of the passages deleted

---

[5] Ibid.

[6] Tim Howell, "Two Versions of the Fifth Symphony: A Study in Compositional Process," in *Proceedings from the First International Sibelius Conference, August 1990*, ed. Eero Tarasti (Helsinki: Sibelius Academy, 1995), 74–87, esp. 85.

[7] Ibid., 83.

[8] Ibid., 84–5.

[9] Weidberg, "Comparing the 1915 and 1919 Versions of Sibelius' Fifth Symphony," 240.

[10] Ibid., 259.

[11] "Such a situation is not far from Ligeti's field technique. But Sibelius' predominantly 'static' field arises from a continuous, micro-organic process." Eero Tarasti, *Signs of Music: A Guide to Musical Semiotics* (Berlin & New York: Mouton de Gruyter, 2002), 97.

or revised in 1919. The 1915 version is not an example of stylistic retrenchment. It is, rather, a work that reflects Sibelius' interest in the avant-garde during the years preceding World War I. Sibelius' attitudes towards his contemporaries during the pre-war years underline his high modernist allegiances. He expressed admiration for Schoenberg's music,[12] but criticised the recent works of Richard Strauss: "Mr Sibelius told me two years ago that Richard Strauss had ceased to compose music worth while since he had been figuring it in terms of marks, francs and dollars."[13] Sibelius' remarks about Strauss recall his later condemnation of Stravinsky's eclecticism and serve as a refutation of the thesis that he was sympathetic to composers who repudiated modernism.[14]

In the 1915 version, Sibelius creates structural contrasts by employing all of the parameters of the musical discourse, including harmony, timbre, texture, register, and rhythm.[15] A central element of his musical design is the manipulation of sonic shapes, a process akin to motivic development. In the first movement, Sibelius presents two dramatic ascending modal progressions,[16] played by tremolo strings. They both begin in the bass, accompanying statements of the movement's second theme group (mm. 18–27, 59–70 [1915]) (see Exx. 1 and 2). The two progressions have similar trajectories. In mm. 18–24, the violas and cellos ascend an octave and a half; in mm. 59–68, almost two octaves, from G3 to Gb5.

---

[12] For a discussion of Sibelius' attitude to Schoenberg, see Tomi Mäkelä, *Sibelius*, trans. Steven Lindberg (Woodbridge: The Boydell Press, 2011), 251–5.

[13] Ivan Narodny, "The Socialization of Music," *Musical America* XXIV (7) (1916): 44. Sibelius' comments denigrating Strauss evidently referred to the 1912 version of *Ariadne auf Naxos* and, perhaps, to *Der Rosenkavalier* (1910).

[14] Hepokoski, *Sibelius: Symphony No. 5*, 7–9.

[15] "In [twentieth-century music] the parameters of dynamics, articulation, rhythm, and register are no longer just ornamental but become functional in the generation of musical structure and tonal progression. This forces the prospective analyst to look at music from completely different perspectives, regarding these musical parameters as integral and not incidental." Paolo Susanni and Elliott Antokoletz, *Music and Twentieth-Century Tonality: Harmonic Progression Based on Modality and the Interval Cycles* (New York: Routledge, 2012), 7.

[16] In the first of these passages, the top line of a series of triads, played by violas and cellos, outlines an eight-pitch collection consisting of two major tetrachords, separated by a half-step: C#–D#–E#–F#/G–A–B–C. The two underlying voices state the octatonic-II collection. For a definition of the octatonic collections, see Pieter C. van den Toorn, *The Music of Igor Stravinsky* (New Haven and London: Yale University Press, 1983), 50.

Example 1 Ascending modal bass progression, in Jean Sibelius, Symphony No. 5 (1915), I, mm. 18–19.

Example 2 Ascending modal bass progression, in Jean Sibelius, Symphony No. 5 (1915), I, mm. 61–62.

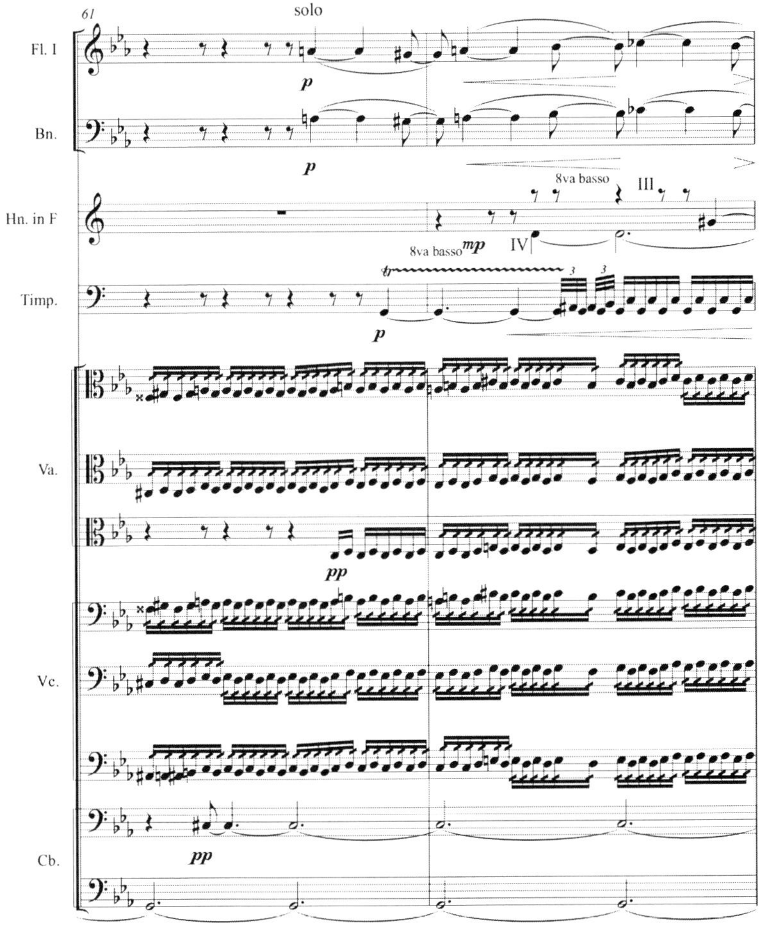

The progressions serve a semi-autonomous function within the musical narrative as distinctive sonic shapes. In the second movement, Sibelius presents another rising string progression, together with a variant of the first theme group, rather than the second (mm. 223–243) (see Ex. 3).

Example 3 Ascending modal bass progression, in Jean Sibelius, Symphony No. 5 (1915), II, mm. 223–226.

In addition to their shared motivic material and modal harmony, the textural and registral correspondences between the two first movement passages produce a formal parallelism that helps to define the movement's structure. When he revised the symphony, Sibelius modified both passages, altering the range of the strings and obscuring these similarities.[17]

The resemblances between the two passages highlight their differences. The measured tremolos of the first passage reiterate single pitches, while those of the second passage oscillate, often chromatically, between neighbour notes. This neighbour-note oscillation provides a link to the thoroughgoing chromaticism of the following "Ligeti-like" sound block. In these three passages, Sibelius progressively transforms comparable textures.

Sibelius underlines the similarities between the whirling tremolos of the second ascending bass progression and the patterns of the "Ligeti-like" sound block by creating a motivic correspondence between the two passages. At the beginning of the earlier passage, Flute I and Bassoon I state a motif (mm. 61–63) that anticipates the bassoon's chromatic figures in the "Ligeti-like" sound block (mm. 78ff.) (see Exx. 4a and b).

Examples 4a–c Chromatic motifs, in Jean Sibelius, Symphony No. 5 (1915), I.

4a Flute's chromatic motif, in Jean Sibelius, Symphony No. 5 (1915), I, mm. 61–63, flute only.

4b Bassoon's chromatic motif in the "Ligeti-like" sound block, in Jean Sibelius, Symphony No. 5 (1915), I, mm. 83–84, bassoon only.

[17] Compare mm. 18–27 [1915] with mm. 18–27 [1919]; mm. 59–70 [1915] with mm. 50–59 [1919]. See Weidberg, "Comparing the 1915 and 1919 Versions of Sibelius' Fifth Symphony," 250–1.

4c Chromatic motif immediately prior to the "Ligeti-like" sound block, in Jean Sibelius, Symphony No. 5 (1919), I, mm. 68–70, Horns I and III only, concert pitch.

In 1919, Sibelius followed the restatement of the second theme group with a dramatic tonic restatement of the "closing" theme (I, mm. 62–68 [1919]),[18] which is accompanied by forceful orchestral chords that break up the continuity of the musical texture between the two passages with whirling string patterns (I, mm. 50–61 and 71–90 [1919]). In the 1915 version, the two passages are divided only by a brief diatonic chord progression (I, mm. 71–73 [1915]), a momentary pause in the musical narrative.

Sibelius' interpolated restatement of the "closing" theme in the 1919 version makes it difficult for the listener to hear the relationship between the two passages, while reinforcing the extended formal parallels between Hepokoski's rotations one and two.[19] After the restatement of the "closing" theme, Sibelius compensates for his revision of the original narrative structure by inserting a motif, played by the horns, that both recalls the "anticipatory" chromatic motif[20] and serves as a bridge to the beginning of the "Ligeti-like" sound block (I, mm. 68–70 [1919]) (see Ex. 4c). The horn figure's significance as a link between the two episodes suggests their pairing within the musical structure. My reading of the first movement's form contrasts with Hepokoski's division of these two passages between rotations two and three.[21]

In the symphony's 1915 version, Sibelius not only employs sonic shapes to delineate the form, but creates a harmonic continuum between diatonicism, modality, and chromaticism as well. Together with this technique, he often presents modal or chromatic variants of originally diatonic ideas, a technique comparable to procedures that Bartók

---

[18] Compare I, mm. 28–34 with I, mm. 62–68 [1919].

[19] I, mm. 3–35 (rotation one); mm. 36–71 (rotation two) [1919]. See Hepokoski, *Sibelius: Symphony No. 5*, 63–6.

[20] Stated in octaves by flutes and bassoons in mm. 52–54 of the 1919 version.

[21] Hepokoski, *Sibelius: Symphony No. 5*, 65–7.

employed in the following decades.[22] The progression from the first theme group's diatonicism to the modal chromaticism of the ascending string patterns and the tonal ambiguity of the "Ligeti-like" sound block in the first movement suggests that at least one aspect of Sibelius' original formal plan was a "modulation" between diatonic, modal, and chromatic regions. In this reading, the fully chromatic "Ligeti-like" sound block serves as the structural pivot of the movement, followed by a brief return to diatonicism via modal chromaticism in its concluding measures. Discussing the 1919 version of the Fifth Symphony, Arnold Whittall has described the first movement's harmonic language in similar terms, portraying it as "polarised between stabilising and destabilising impulses, the former 'in dialogue' with the latter."[23] Elliott Antokoletz has likewise described the harmonic structure of Sibelius' Fourth Symphony as dependent on the interaction of diatonic and modal pitch sets.[24]

Sibelius employs similar harmonic strategies in the second movement of the 1915 version. He again progresses gradually from diatonicism to chromaticism, which he employs most notably in the movement's penultimate episode. In mm. 93–108, Sibelius transforms the opening diatonic motif of the movement into its modal variant, a looping tritone figure.[25] Beginning in m. 232, he combines a whirling modal bass progression (see Ex. 3) with the looping tritone figure, now stated in octaves by the clarinets (II, mm. 232–243 [1915]; I, mm. 283–294 [1919]).[26] In the following measures, Sibelius presents a chromatic variant of an originally diatonic idea. The half-step oscillation between first inversion triads (II, mm. 246–262 [1915]; I, mm. 298–321 [1919]) recalls

---

[22] For a discussion of Sibelius-Bartók parallels see Nors S. Josephson, "Sibelius and Modern Music," in *Sibelius in the Old and New World*, 125–38, esp. 129–30.

[23] See Arnold Whittall, "The Later Symphonies," in *The Cambridge Companion to Sibelius*, ed. Daniel M. Grimley (Cambridge: Cambridge University Press, 2004), 49–65, esp. 56.

[24] Elliott Antokoletz, "The Musical Language of the Fourth Symphony," in *Sibelius Studies*, eds. Timothy L. Jackson and Veijo Murtomäki (Cambridge: Cambridge University Press, 2001), 296–321.

[25] Sibelius retained this passage in 1919 (I, mm. 142–157 [1919]).

[26] G5/G4–G4/G3–C#5/C#4–G5/G4 etc. The tritone oscillation from G–C# is emblematic of larger structural processes at work in the symphony's 1915 version. The first ascending bass progression (I, mm. 18–27) begins with a C#^{6} triad (E#2/G#2/C#3), resolving to G in m. 24. As Hepokoski points out, the entire passage is centred firmly on a G^6 triad in the 1919 version; see Hepokoski, *Sibelius: Symphony No. 5*, 63.

the whole-step oscillation between inverted seventh chords at the beginning of the first and second movements (see Exx. 5a and 5b).[27]

Example 5a Diatonic oscillation between seventh chords, in Jean Sibelius, Symphony No. 5 (1915), I, mm. 1–2, piano reduction.

Example 5b Chromatic oscillation between triads, in Jean Sibelius, Symphony No. 5 (1915), II, mm. 251–258, piano reduction.

[27] Hepokoski notes the harmonic parallel between the two passages, but not the contrast between diatonic and chromatic versions of the same chord pattern. See Hepokoski, "Structural Tensions in Sibelius' Fifth Symphony," 221–2.

The oscillating chords lead to a sound block (II, mm. 300–380 [1915]) that includes chromatic winding, descending stepwise patterns and ascending diatonic scalar patterns. Both ideas are presented in counterpoint with ascending and descending arpeggiated triads, played by the strings. The ascending scalar patterns parallel the winds' earlier chains of rising thirds (II, mm. 113–124, 141–160 [1915]). The winding stepwise figures recall the chromatic lines of the "Ligeti-like" sound block, again underlining the motivic, textural, and harmonic parallels between the first and second movements (see Ex. 6).

Example 6 Descending chromatic patterns, in Jean Sibelius, Symphony No. 5 (1915), II, mm. 309–317, Flute I and Bassoon I only (cf. Ex. 4b).

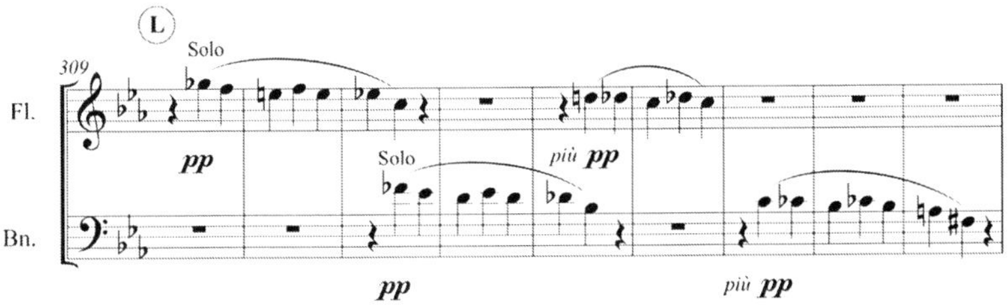

In the 1919 revision, Sibelius modified both the form and function of this sound block. He balanced the descending chromatic patterns more evenly with ascending scalar patterns (I, mm. 364–486 [1919]). In addition, he underlined the origins of the arpeggiated triads that serve as a counterpoint to the chromatic patterns, inserting the motif from which they are derived into the musical narrative.[28] The alterations change the character of the music, so that the chromatic patterns become only one among several equally prominent ideas in the sound block, although they gradually grow in importance as the music approaches a climax.

In 1919, Sibelius altered the narrative structure of the second (now first) movement's final sound block as well. He eliminated crosscutting interpolations that he had previously employed for dramatic effect as harbingers of the movement's conclusion. In the 1915 version, these brief, forceful interjections by the timpani and trombones alternate with the winds' modal theme,[29] creating a mosaic effect (II, mm. 421–422, 425–

[28] Compare I, mm. 372–405 with I, mm. 258–274 [1919].

[29] The theme has the ambitus, Bb–Bb, and resolves to Eb, characteristics of the plagal form of the Eb major scale.

426 [1915]) (see Ex. 7). They evoke Stravinsky's use of crosscutting in *Petrushka* (1911) and *The Rite of Spring* (1912), for example, in the "Russian Dance" (*Petrushka*, mm. 113–119) and the "Ritual of Abduction" (*The Rite of Spring*, rehearsal nos. 46–47).

Example 7 Stravinskian cross-cutting, in Jean Sibelius, Symphony No. 5 (1915), II, mm. 421–427.

In the interpolations, the trombones state the three-note figure, Bb–Eb–F, which Sibelius immediately incorporates into the musical narrative as the movement's closing motivic idea. By eliminating his use of crosscutting in the 1919 version of the Fifth Symphony, Sibelius removed a significant marker of the work's ideological affinity with the high modernism of his younger contemporaries. At the same time, he inserted waves of arpeggiated tonic triads near the end of the movement (I, mm. 555–570 [1919]) in order to strengthen its tonal structure.

The last movement of the 1915 version of the Fifth Symphony divides into two halves. The end of each part is signalled by Sibelius' presentation of the chromatic variant of the swan hymn. The movement is marked by Sibelius' introduction of ideas that disrupt the musical narrative harmonically, rhythmically, and texturally. He later modifies these ideas and inserts them into the symphony's master narrative.

The first intrusion into the texture of the last movement is the brief dissonant motif played by the trumpets, Db5–Ab4–G4 (IV, mm. 198–211), which Sibelius later deleted from the score. Only the first two pitches, Db–Ab, actually create dissonance with the dominant C major harmony of the passage. Sibelius delays the resolution to G, however, lessening its significance. Sibelius later presents additional motifs that are dissonant relative to the surrounding texture.[30] These ideas were retained in the symphony's 1919 version.[31]

Measures 392–546 comprise an extended three-part sound block, which I label as the "tripartite sound block." In part I, Sibelius states the swan hymn; in part II, the swan hymn with its counter-theme. In part III, Sibelius states the chromatic variant of the swan hymn. Sibelius shortened the first two parts of the sound block in 1919 and deleted the final, most stylistically radical portion in its entirety.

In the 1915 version, the subdivided strings alternate in playing *jeté* sixteenth-note patterns throughout the sound block. In the final part, the first violins, violas, and cellos alternate with the second violins, which play in every third measure (IV, mm. 463–542). When he revised the symphony in 1919, Sibelius simplified the sound block's orchestration, making it more practical for performance. He modified the string patterns, so that they alternate between the rapid *jeté* figures and up-bow eighths. He also eliminated the hocket-like exchanges between the string parts (III, mm. 360–406).

---

[30] IV, mm. 275–281, 296–299, 304–307 [1915].
[31] III, mm. 243–249, 264–267, 272–275 [1919].

In the final part of the tripartite sound block, Sibelius adds weak-beat contrabass sustained notes to the patterns played by the other strings. The contrabasses oscillate between Db2 and Ab2, producing a harmonically abrasive and rhythmically jagged effect. The strings then present the initial statement of the swan hymn's chromatic variant. Accented half-note oboe dyads double the strings when they play the highest notes of the arching swan hymn. Despite their *piano* dynamic, the oboe dyads serve as timbrally sharp intrusions into the string texture, perhaps in imitation of the sound of honking birds (IV, mm. 494–542) (see Ex. 8a).

Example 8a First statement of swan hymn's chromatic variant, in Jean Sibelius, Symphony No. 5 (1915), IV, mm. 499–507.

The oboe dyads conclude with a string of seven Bb4/Bb5 octaves that produce the effect of periodic electronic beeps or flashing lights (IV, mm. 524–542). The passage as a whole may be the most deliberately "avant-garde" music that Sibelius ever wrote. Sibelius' diary provides evidence that he considered the chromatic variant of the swan hymn to be a naturalistic, even abrasive, portrait of the sound of the swans. In the diary, Sibelius compared the swan call to both the trumpet and sarrusophone. He wrote out the chromatic variant of the swan hymn (see Ex. 8b) and linked it to the sound of trumpets: "Fifth Symphony's final theme: legato in the trumpets!!"[32]

Example 8b Sketch of swan hymn's chromatic variant.[33]

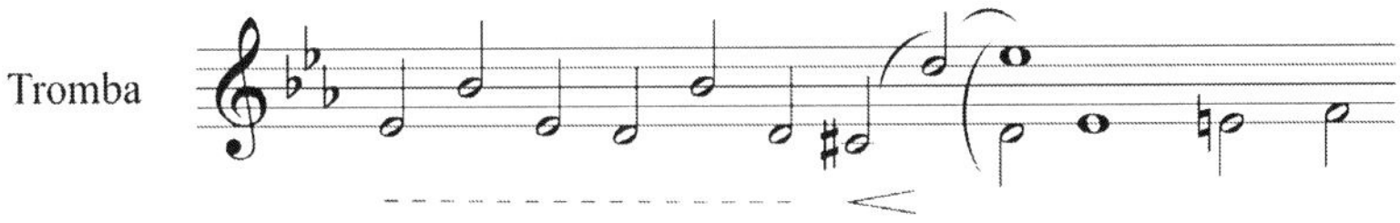

Before Sibelius presents the oboe dyads, the flutes state the motivic fragment, Ab–Bb (IV, mm. 478–483), derived from the swan hymn's counter-theme (IV, mm. 463–470). The oboes' subsequent honking repeated Bb octaves can therefore be perceived, not only as part of the swan hymn's chromatic variant, but also as a further reduction of its counter-theme to the single pc, Bb (see Exx. 9a–c).

Examples 9a–c Motivic reduction in Jean Sibelius, Symphony No. 5 (1915), IV.

Example 9a Swan hymn's counter-theme, in mm. 463–470, flute only.

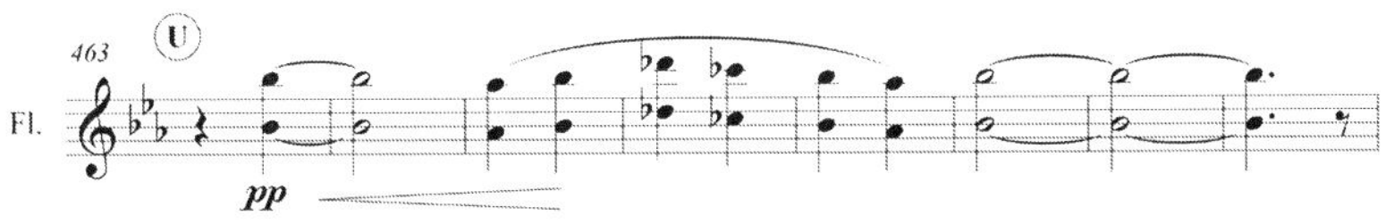

[32] "V Sinfonins [op. 82/1915] finaltema: bindningen i trumpeten!!" Jean Sibelius, *Dagbok, 1909–1944*, ed. Fabian Dahlström (Helsingfors: Svenska litteratursällskapet i Finland, 2005), diary entry from April 21, 1915, 225. See also Erik Tawaststjerna, *Sibelius, Vol. III: 1914–1957*, trans. and ed. Robert Layton (London: Faber & Faber, 1997), 23; Hepokoski, *Sibelius: Symphony No. 5*, 36.
[33] See Jean Sibelius, *Dagbok*, 225.

Example 9b Motivic fragment, Ab–Bb, derived from swan hymn's counter-theme, in mm. 478–483, flute only.

Example 9c Intersection of swan hymn's chromatic variant and its counter-theme in the repeated Bbs, in mm. 523–530, oboe only.

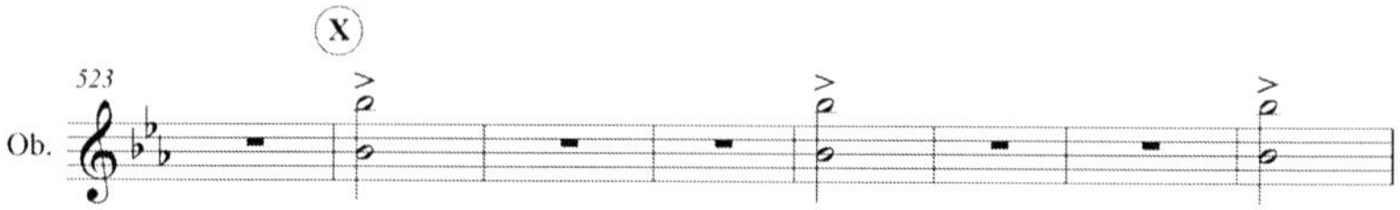

Later in the movement, the winds and brass reintroduce the swan hymn's chromatic variant, recalling the last segment of the tripartite sound block and creating large-scale formal symmetry. Like other motivic and thematic reworkings, this restatement integrates previously disruptive ideas into the movement's master narrative. Sibelius adapts the swan hymn's chromatic variant to the flowing rhythms and smoothly ordered textures of its primary, diatonic version. He employs the chromatic variant to reinforce both the final drive to the tonic and the swan hymn's apotheosis at the work's conclusion. The winds play accented weak-beat dyads that double the highest notes of the chromatic variant (mm. 622–627, 642–647). Sibelius emphasises the wind dyads by their *forte* dynamics, creating a parallel to the honking oboe dyads of the tripartite sound block.

Sibelius' excision of the initial statement of the swan hymn's chromatic variant in the 1919 version of the symphony unbalances the movement's original formal plan. In addition, his alteration of the counter-theme to stress the arrival at the tonic in the lyrical *Largamente assai* (mm. 429–436) prompts the listener to question the narrative significance of chromaticism in the symphony's final pages. It is consequently difficult for the listener today to grasp the full import of the careful balance between diatonicism and chromaticism within the symphony's structure as originally conceived. In the 1915 version of the Fifth Symphony, the "teleological goal" of the finale is the unification of all of the disparate elements of the music—tonal, modal and chromatic, consonant and dissonant, smoothly ordered and disruptive—at the very end of the work.

When Sibelius revised the symphony, he rewrote the *Andante mosso*, creating contrasts of texture and tempo, and altering the movement's form.

In the 1915 version, the movement is the simplest and most stylistically conservative in the symphony. Nevertheless, its structure is dependent on compositional strategies characteristic of the rest of the work. For example, Sibelius divides the movement into two halves by presenting sequential statements of a harmonically and timbrally jarring ascending modal progression (III, mm. 68–75 [1915]).

In the 1919 version, the climax of the movement occurs instead at the *ritenuto al tempo primo* that leads to the concluding section (II, m. 154 [1919]). Sibelius handled this transition so that it resembles an analogous passage in the third movement of Mahler's Fourth Symphony, the sudden transition from *Allegro molto* to *Andante subito* (rehearsal no. 11).

Sibelius' alterations strengthened already perceptible stylistic allusions to the Mahler movement. Both movements are in variation form, begin with music that is elegiac in character, and give prominence to pizzicato strings. They also share a common key, G major, as well as common harmonies, in particular the prominent use of the G major tonic triad with added sixth, E, by Mahler in mm. 3–4, and by Sibelius, notably in mm. 157–163.

In this essay, I have demonstrated that Sibelius employed compositional techniques akin to those of Bartók and Stravinsky in the 1915 version of his Fifth Symphony. He created networks of sound blocks, modulated between diatonicism and chromaticism, and used sonic shapes in a manner equivalent to motifs. In addition, he employed textural disruption as a formal device. When Sibelius revised the symphony, he removed many of the "markers" that refer to high modernism in the outer movements. He simultaneously revised and expanded the slow movement in such a way as to reinforce its parallels with the slow movement of Mahler's Fourth Symphony, notably the dramatic return to *tempo primo* near the end of the movement. He also attempted to reinforce motivic and tonal relationships throughout the work. Sibelius' emphasis on traditional tonal relationships in the 1919 version is not completely compatible with the underlying diatonic–chromatic continuum that he had created in 1915.

Sibelius did not simply refine his original conception when he revised the Fifth Symphony. Rather, he carefully repositioned the piece ideologically so that it would be perceived as a return to the "early modernism" of his most popular compositions, rather than a further step along the path of high modernist exploration that his Fourth Symphony seemed to presage. Nevertheless, the work retains many of its avant-garde characteristics, and has become the subject of controversy due to its stylistic ambiguities.

To summarise, the compositional history of the Fifth Symphony shows Sibelius to be an avant-gardist who was, however, ambivalent about his compositional path.

3. Sibelius and Musical Life in Finland

Why Kajanus Went to St Petersburg

Martti Laitinen

In this article I will first describe what is known about the competition that took place in 1896 and 1897 when Jean Sibelius, Robert Kajanus, and Ilmari Krohn applied for the position of music teacher at a university in Helsinki. Subsequently, I shall attempt to give an explanation, based on historical documents, for the notorious trip Kajanus made to St Petersburg when he submitted a formal complaint about the process. At the end of the article I will contemplate what this ultimately means.

The most prestigious position a musician could hold in the late nineteenth-century Grand Duchy of Finland was that of the music teacher at the Imperial Alexander University—presently called the University of Helsinki. Academic life had featured music since the founding of the university in Turku in 1640, and a fixed post was established in 1747. The first six teachers were Carl Petter Lenning, Johan Petter Lenning, Johan Torenberg, Carl Wilhelm Salgé, the so-called father of Finnish music Fredrik Pacius, and, from 1871, the organist Richard Faltin.[1] The teacher was obliged to: (1) conduct the Academic Orchestra for two hours a week; (2) teach music theory or history likewise for two hours a week; (3) compose music for the academic festivities; and (4) be responsible for the instruments and sheet music owned by the university.[2] For these modest services, the annual salary of 3,600 Finnish marks was rather generous,[3] equivalent to approximately € 17,000 in present-day currency.[4]

---

[1] Matti Vainio, *"Nouskaa aatteet!" Robert Kajanus. Elämä ja taide* (Helsinki: Werner Söderström, 2002), 327; Matti Vainio, "Helsingin yliopiston musiikinopettajan virantäytön vaiheet 1896–1897 ja Robert Kajanuksen näyteluento," *Musiikki* 37 (1) (2007): 43–55, especially 43–4; Einari Marvia, "Ylioppilaskunnan Soittajien vuosisataiset perinteet," *Ylioppilaskunnan Soittajat 1926–1986: 60-vuotisjuhlakirja* (Helsinki: Ylioppilaskunnan Soittajat, 1986), 9–34.

[2] Valfrid Vasenius, *Författningar och beslut rörande Kejserliga Alexanders-Universitetet i Finland från och med den 1 oktober 1852 till utgången af år 1887* (Helsingfors: Valfrid Vasenius, 1889), 29, 45, 57.

[3] Vainio, "Helsingin yliopiston musiikinopettajan virantäytön vaiheet 1896–1897," 44.

[4] "Rahanarvonkerroin 1860–2006," http://tilastokeskus.fi/til/eki/2006/eki_2006_2007-01-17_tau_001.html; "Liitetaulukko 5. Kuluttajahintaindeksi 2005=100";

When Faltin retired in 1896 and the position became vacant, three candidates emerged:

- Ilmari Krohn, aged 28; organist, Candidate of Philosophy (i.e. Master of Arts before a promotion ceremony) and doctoral student
- Jean Sibelius, aged 30; musician and former law student at the University
- Robert Kajanus, aged 39; conductor who had left school at the age of 18[5]

Even though Krohn was academically better qualified than the other candidates, he was outranked by them in other fields that proved to be more important: by Sibelius as a composer and by Kajanus as a conductor. Composition was the decisive factor in the race.[6] In summary, the contest principally became one between Sibelius and Kajanus, who had both deputised for the post previously. Sibelius became by far the most popular candidate in the newspapers.[7] He probably applied for the post chiefly for the salary, whereas Kajanus was interested in the prestige that came with the position. Both of them had their mothers as the principal motivators behind the scenes.[8]

In Autumn 1896 a committee was established by the University Consistory in order to evaluate the candidates. Alongside Faltin, two professors were nominated as members: the mathematician Edvard Rudolf Neovius and the physicist August Fredrik Sundell.[9] They were non-musicians but not uninterested in music: Neovius was the inspector of the Academic Orchestra[10] whereas Sundell was a member of the board of the Helsinki Music Society, the organisation behind the Helsinki Music Institute (the present-day Sibelius Academy, University of the Arts

---

http://tilastokeskus.fi/til/khi/2014/01/khi_2014_01_2014-02-19_tau_005_fi.html.

[5] The applications are stored at the Central Archives of the University of Helsinki (hereafter referred to as CAUH), Archive of the Chancellor's Office II, Act 9/1897, Fa 63.

[6] Vainio, *"Nouskaa aatteet!"*, 327.

[7] See e.g. Juhani Aho, "Helsingfors-bref," *Åbo Underrättelser*, December 1, 1896; Anonymous, "Musikläraretjänsten vid universitetet," *Nya Pressen*, January 9, 1897; Tuomas (i.e. Juhani Aho), "Kirje Helsingistä," *Päivälehti*, January 10, 1897.

[8] Vainio, "Helsingin yliopiston musiikinopettajan virantäytön vaiheet 1896–1897," 45.

[9] Consistory minutes, September 12, 1896. CAUH, Consistory Archive, minutes 1896, Ca 70. All dates in this article are given in accordance with the Gregorian calendar, which was observed within the Grand Duchy of Finland but not in St Petersburg.

[10] Ibid.

Helsinki).[11] Each candidate was asked to give a lecture on music theory or history.[12] The lectures responded to the national imperatives of the day quite diversely. Kajanus spoke about Bernhard Henrik Crusell as a Finnish composer,[13] whereas Sibelius offered his thoughts concerning the influence folk music could have on composition.[14] Krohn's lecture was the best in academic terms, and he was the only one to speak in Finnish rather than Swedish,[15] but his topic had nothing whatsoever to do with Finland—it was about Robert Schumann as a music critic.[16]

Neither Kajanus nor Sibelius gave their compositions to the committee for evaluation as had been requested. Their works were deemed so well-known that Faltin's word was sufficient. Since the other members of the committee were amateurs, it seems that Faltin alone decided what the committee reported to the Consistory in January 1897. The report was a eulogy in praise of Sibelius, whom the committee recommended for the post. Kajanus was named as the *proxime* and Krohn as the third candidate. The committee explicitly recommended that Sibelius should be offered a firm financial position in order to be able to compose.[17] This was one of the arguments on which Kajanus later based his complaint.

After some consideration, on March 3, 1897 the Consistory nominated the candidates in the same order with an overwhelming majority of 25.

---

[11] Peter Holmberg, "Sundell, August Fredrik (1843–1924)," *Kansallisbiografia* (Helsinki: Suomalaisen Kirjallisuuden Seura, 2002), http://www.kansallisbiografia.fi/kb/artikkeli/6437.

[12] Anonymous, "Yliopisto," *Päivälehti*, September 13, 1896.

[13] Robert Kajanus, "Bernhard Henrik Crusell," Finnish trans. Matti Vainio. *Musiikki* 37 (1) (2007): 56–62.

[14] Jean Sibelius, "Några synpunkter beträffande folkmusiken – Joitakin näkökohtia kansanmusiikista," trans. Ilkka Oramo, *Musiikki* 10 (2) (1980): 86–105; "Some Viewpoints Concerning Folk Music and Its Influence on Musical Arts," trans. Margareta Martin with an introduction by Daniel M. Grimley, in *Jean Sibelius and his World*, ed. Daniel M. Grimley (Princeton: Princeton University Press, 2011), 315–25.

[15] Committee report January 23, 1897. Appendix B of the Consistory minutes January 30, 1897. CAUH, Consistory Archive, minutes 1897, Ca 71.

[16] Ilmari Krohn, "Robert Schumannin merkitys arwostelijana," *Uusi Suometar*, December 2, 1896 and December 4, 1896. Also published in Ilmari Krohn, *Sävelten alalta; Kirjoituksia ja mietelmiä* (Helsinki: Otava, 1899), 1–26; Anonymous, "Yliopiston musiikinopettajawirkaa," *Suomalainen Wirallinen Lehti,* November 12, 1896; see also Vainio, "Helsingin yliopiston musiikinopettajan virantäytön vaiheet 1896–1897," 45.

[17] Committee report January 23, 1897.

Only three professors voted in favour of placing Kajanus above Sibelius.[18] Two months later, the Acting Vice-Chancellor Thiodolf Rein submitted the nomination to the Chancellor, who was a military official—Russian-Finnish minister-secretary Woldemar von Daehn—based in St Petersburg.[19] He had the final say on the appointment.[20]

What happened next is sometimes presented as follows: Kajanus filed an official complaint first to the Consistory. Failing that, he tried to influence the Acting Vice-Chancellor and finally filed his complaint to the Chancellor.[21] However, the whole process in fact began in May 1897 when Kajanus made a trip to St Petersburg and left the only complaint of which we are aware with the Chancellor's office.[22] There is very little documentation concerning the trip; for the purposes of this article, however, I presume that Kajanus did indeed travel to St Petersburg in person. At the very least, the assumption is supported by a rumour that I will now describe.

Making a complaint was no radical act in itself, and according to the statutes of the university, complaints were to be filed to the Chancellor.[23] But why did Kajanus not simply mail the document (or use a messenger) instead of travelling himself? According to a story that became popular among Sibelius' close friends and was also espoused by Krohn, Kajanus went to St Petersburg in order to influence the Chancellor through his friends in the hierarchy.[24]

Generally, historians have not found this claim credible, and practical and political reasons have been presented for Kajanus' subsequent

---

[18] Consistory minutes January 30, February 13, and March 3, 1897. CAUH, Consistory Archive, minutes 1897, Ca 71. Kajanus' defendants were the education theorist Waldemar Ruin, the historian Johan Richard Danielson-Kalmari, and, above all, the economist and legal scholar Joel Napoleon Lang (ibid.). See also Vainio, "Helsingin yliopiston musiikinopettajan virantäytön vaiheet 1896–1897," 47–8.

[19] Rein to von Daehn May 5, 1897. CAUH, Archive of the Chancellor's Office II, Act 9/1897, Fa 63.

[20] Vasenius, *Författningar och beslut*, 6.

[21] See e.g. Vainio, *"Nouskaa aatteet!"*, 336–7, 623; Vainio, "Helsingin yliopiston musiikinopettajan virantäytön vaiheet 1896–1897," 48–9, 52–3.

[22] Kajanus' complaint, dated May 1, 1897. CAUH, Archive of the Chancellor's Office II, Act 9/1897, Fa 63. Kajanus was extremely critical towards Sibelius in the complaint. See Vainio, *"Nouskaa aatteet!"*, 333–4.

[23] Vasenius, *Författningar och beslut*, 51; see also Rein to von Daehn May 5, 1897 and Erik Tawaststjerna, *Jean Sibelius II* (Helsinki: Otava, 1967), 109.

[24] Tawaststjerna, *Jean Sibelius II*, 109; Vainio, *"Nouskaa aatteet!"*, 336–7; Glenda Dawn Goss, *Sibelius: A Composer's Life and the Awakening of Finland* (Chicago and London: University of Chicago Press, 2009), 227–9.

success.[25] However, the incident affected the interpersonal relations between the applicants, and no other reason for Kajanus' personal intervention has been advanced. In what follows I will try to offer an explanation. If it does not make Kajanus entirely innocent, it does at least exclude the aforementioned claim.

According to §220 of the contemporary university statutes, a formal complaint could have been filed within 60 days from the nomination (not counting the same day).[26] Since the candidates were nominated on March 3, 1897, the appeal period began on March 4 and expired on May 2. Kajanus' complaint is a thorough text of 11 pages, and his signature is dated Helsinki, May 1. This was a Saturday, and Kajanus' orchestra in fact had a concert the same evening.[27] At the top right corner of the first page of the complaint, its arrival in St Petersburg was registered two days later, on Monday May 3 (or, according to the Julian calendar, April 21) at 11 am.

Kajanus was therefore already late by the time he finished the text. His concert began on Saturday at 7.30 pm, and after the rather lengthy programme[28] it was too late to catch the night train at 8.15 pm. The next train departed from Helsinki on Sunday morning and arrived in St Petersburg at almost midnight.[29] When Kajanus left his complaint with the Chancellor's office, it was already the 61st day after the nomination.

In my Master's thesis I postulated that there are two reasons why Kajanus made the trip. One of them is that he accidentally thought that there were only 60 days in the two-month period from March 3 to May 3. In this case, he could have made the trip simply to ensure that the letter would have arrived at the office by Monday May 3. Postal trains from Helsinki to St Petersburg did run on Sundays,[30] but it would have been risky to post the letter on Sunday morning and expect that it would be delivered by Monday.

The other option is that Kajanus did understand the situation and hoped that the complaint would be received without trouble when delivered in

---

[25] Tawaststjerna, *Jean Sibelius II*, 108–9; Vainio, *"Nouskaa aatteet!"*, 336–7; Vainio, "Helsingin yliopiston musiikinopettajan virantäytön vaiheet 1896–1897," 53.
[26] Vasenius, *Författningar och beslut*, 51.
[27] Robert Kajanus, "Filharmoonillinen Seura," *Päivälehti*, May 1, 1897.
[28] "Filharmoniska sällskapet," *Program-Bladet*, April 30, 1897.
[29] *Aikataulu N:o 53 junille 13 (1) p:stä Lokakuuta 1896*. Suomen Valtionrautatiet: Helsinki.
[30] For this information I am indebted to Soile Siltala and the Finnish Postal Museum.

person. In any case, the trip was worth making. Kajanus' complaint was received and deemed in a routine-like manner to have arrived in time.[31]

Why did Kajanus act so late? The best explanation I have come up with is that perhaps he regarded making a complaint as the very last option. In a letter dated March 17, Agnes Kajanus had urged her son to advance his cause by influencing "old man Rhein," i.e. the Acting Vice-Chancellor, behind the scenes.[32] This seems to have been a useless piece of advice since Rein had no discretion on the matter; his simple duty was to function as a messenger between the Consistory and the Chancellor.[33] However, Kajanus may have thought otherwise, especially since the matter remained in Helsinki for a considerably long period. Even though the Consistory had already decided upon the nomination on March 3, Rein received it on his desk much later on April 29.[34] This is why he forwarded the matter to the Chancellor as late as May 5 (i.e. after the two-month appeal period).[35] If Kajanus followed his mother's advice, that would be compatible with his resorting to a formal complaint only at the last moment—or, in fact, later.

What happened after this is largely well known. The Chancellor, von Daehn, asked for a statement on the matter from Rein,[36] who requested one from the Consistory,[37] which in turn asked for one from the committee and another from Sibelius.[38] Even though Sibelius declined to provide a statement,[39] the committee did vehemently defend its view on the matter,[40]

---

[31] Von Daehn to Rein July 29, 1897. CAUH, Vice-Chancellor's Archive, received letters 1897, Ea 51. There was no recourse for this decision (Vasenius, *Författningar och beslut*, 51).

[32] Vainio, "Helsingin yliopiston musiikinopettajan virantäytön vaiheet 1896–1897," 52.

[33] Vasenius, *Författningar och beslut*, 50–1.

[34] Edvard Hjelt to Rein, March 3, 1897 (arrived on April 29, 1897). CAUH, Vice-Chancellor's Archive, received letters 1897, Ea 51.

[35] Rein to von Daehn, May 5, 1897. CAUH, Archive of the Chancellor's Office II, Act 9/1897, Fa 63.

[36] Von Daehn to Rein, May 8, 1897. CAUH, Vice-Chancellor's Archive, received letters 1897, Ea 51.

[37] Rein to the Consistory, May 11, 1897. CAUH, Consistory archive, received letters 1897, Eb 48.

[38] Consistory minutes, May 13, 1897. CAUH, Consistory Archive, minutes 1897, Ca 71. Only those members of the committee present in Helsinki were requested to give a statement (ibid., see footnote 40).

[39] Consistory minutes, June 2, 1897. CAUH, Consistory Archive, minutes 1897, Ca 71.

and Kajanus gained only one new supporter in the Consistory.[41] The Acting Vice-Chancellor replied to the Chancellor in July that there was no reason to change the nomination.[42] However, von Daehn unexpectedly lifted Kajanus above Sibelius and appointed him as the new music teacher.[43]

In summary, Kajanus gained little from the incident; in addition to suffering the reputational damage, he quickly became unmotivated by the job. In time, the Academic Orchestra withered away and it was finally disbanded by the few remaining players in 1926, only two years before his retirement.[44] One of the students who was given the task of informing Kajanus about the decisions was Ilmari Krohn's youngest son.[45]

At the same time, it is hardly likely that either Krohn or Sibelius could have done any better. They in turn progressed much further in their own respective fields—Sibelius as a composer and Krohn as the future professor of musicology—so Kajanus' gain was perhaps not their loss at the end of the day.

After Kajanus, the position of music teacher was occupied by the composers Leevi Madetoja, Eino Roiha, and Eino Linnala,[46] and subsequently converted into the post of lecturer in musicology.[47] This post, which predominantly remained focused on music theory, history, and composition, was then held by Erkki Salmenhaara, Kalevi Aho,[48] and

---

[40] Committee statement May 28, 1897. Appendix A to Consistory minutes June 2, 1897. The statement is signed by Neovius and Sundell who were vehemently critical towards Kajanus (ibid.). For more see Vainio, *"Nouskaa aatteet!"*, 335.

[41] Consistory minutes, June 12, 1897. CAUH, Consistory Archive, minutes 1897, Ca 71. The new supporter was the literary scholar Carl Gustaf Estlander (ibid.).

[42] Rein to von Daehn, July 10, 1897. CAUH, Archive of the Chancellor's Office II, Act 9/1897, Fa 63.

[43] Appendix to the letter from von Daehn to Rein, July 29, 1897. There was no recourse for this decision (Vasenius, *Författningar och beslut*, 51).

[44] Tiina Talvitie (ed.), *Ystävyyden rapsodia. Ylioppilaskunnan Soittajat 80 vuotta* (Helsinki: Ylioppilaskunnan Soittajat, 2008), 28.

[45] Taneli Kuusisto, *Musiikkimme eilispäivää* (Helsinki–Porvoo: Werner Söderström, 1965), 161–2.

[46] "Helsingin yliopiston opettaja- ja virkamiesluettelo 1918–2000," http://www.helsinki.fi/keskusarkisto/virkamiehet/voimistelulaitos/yliopistonvoimistelulaitosharjmest.htm.

[47] Vainio, "Helsingin yliopiston musiikinopettajan virantäytön vaiheet 1896–1897," 43.

[48] "Helsingin yliopiston opettaja- ja virkamiesluettelo 1918–2000."

finally Harri Vuori and Harri Suilamo. On April 28, 2016, the University of Helsinki announced the abolition of its oldest music-related office.[49]

Regarding Kajanus' complaint and his trip to St Petersburg, there is one more interesting possibility that I will mention here.

If we look closely at the first page of Kajanus' complaint, we can notice something written in pencil under the headline and erased afterwards. It says, in Swedish, "60 days (§220) after 3 March 1897" and "N 25."

"§220" refers to the statute quoted above. "N 25" refers to the request for comment which von Daehn had sent to Rein because of the complaint. But why did someone write that Kajanus' complaint was filed within 60 days after the nomination? The following remarks can be made:

(1) The handwriting is probably not Kajanus' own—in fact, it bears more resemblance to the date at the top of the page, written by an office clerk.
(2) If these words were written by an official working in the Chancellor's office, the act was exceptional. Phrases like this were not normally written on official documents at all. Besides, all remarks were written with ink— certainly not in pencil, let alone erased afterwards.
(3) In any case, the words express something that is not true. There is always the possibility that the writer simply calculated wrong. But why would they have written the words on the document, even in pencil? It seems possible at least that someone in the office knew that Kajanus was late, and that they wanted somebody else to think that he was not.

If the scenario I have presented here is true, it opens up new possibilities: Kajanus probably did go to St Petersburg personally in order to advance his cause, but with the objective that his overdue complaint simply would be accepted. Given that this is correct, it is not my task to judge whether the act was substantially dishonest or not. However, if the whole trip can be explained in this way, there is probably no reason to speculate whether Kajanus influenced the process behind the scenes after filing the complaint. This would also explain why he did not give reasons

49 "Säästökuuri vei Helsingin yliopistosta musiikinopettajan tehtävän—rahat riittivät 400 vuotta," http://yle.fi/uutiset/saastokuuri_vei_helsingin_yliopistosta _musiikinopettajan_tehtavan__rahat_riittivat_400_vuotta/8847786.

for his trip afterwards. Additionally, it might shed new light on his other notorious trip to St Petersburg in 1911.[50]

In conclusion, it seems probable that Kajanus handled his calendar somewhat creatively and ended up being accused of something much more grave. Such small misunderstandings can break great friendships.

---

[50] Yrjö Suomalainen, *Robert Kajanus. Hänen elämänsä ja toimintansa* (Helsinki: Otava, 1952), 156–63.

First page of Kajanus' complaint. Central Archives of the University of Helsinki, Archive of the Chancellor's Office II, Act 9/1897, Fa 63.
Text at the top right corner, written in ink: *ank. d 21 april/3 mars kl. 11 p. fm. 1897.* [= arrived on 21 April/3 March 1897 at 11 AM.]
Text below the headline, written with a pencil and erased: *60 dagar (§ 220) efr. den 3 mars, 1897. N 25.* [= 60 days (§ 220) after 3 March 1897. Number 25.]

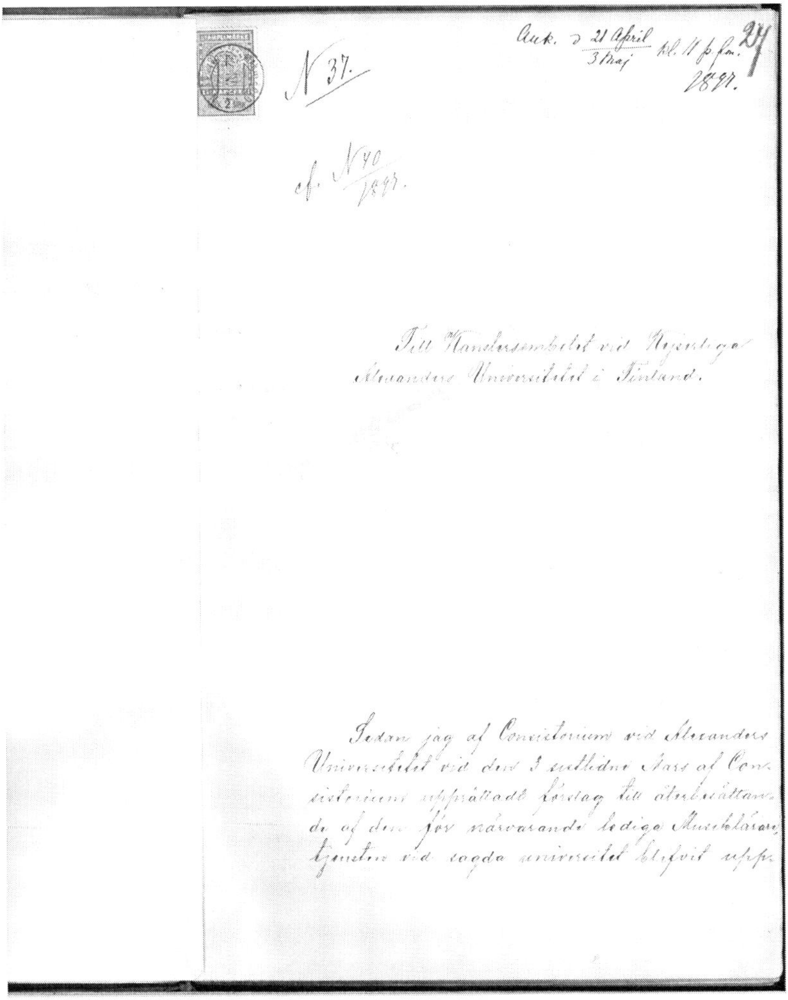
Ank. d 21 April / 3 Maj kl. 11 f.fm. 1897.
N 37.
cf. N 70/1897.

Till Kanslersembetet vid Kejserliga Alexanders Universitetet i Finland.

Sedan jag af Consistorium vid Alexanders Universitetet vid den 3 sistlidne Mars af Consistorium uppråttadt förslag till återbesättande af den för närvarande lediga Musiklärare tjensten vid sagda universitet blifvit upp-

SIBELIUS AS POPULAR COMPOSER: MUSIC BY SIBELIUS IN KAJANUS' POPULAR CONCERTS

VESA KURKELA AND OLLI HEIKKINEN

Objective

This article highlights the position of Sibelius in the repertoire of Robert Kajanus' popular concerts between 1891 and 1919. During the years under discussion, the Helsinki Philharmonic Society's Orchestra[1] played popular concerts two to four times a week. With an average of 80 performances in a season, popular concerts formed by far the most important venue for orchestral music in Helsinki. These popular concerts were held almost ten times more frequently than the standard symphony concerts, which differed at least in programming and atmosphere. With the aid of a varied and mixed programme, Kajanus' popular concerts provided Helsinki audiences with a remarkably wide assortment of orchestral music. From 1891 onwards, Sibelius' music, along with that of Wagner, Tchaikovsky, and some contemporary Nordic and French composers, belonged to the most anticipated and longed-for repertoire in Kajanus' popular concerts. Compared to the other favoured composers, Sibelius had a big advantage: he was a Finn, and his music was suitable for various national achievements.

In what follows our main question is: what was the popular-concert repertoire that contributed towards Sibelius being the most loved and distinguished indigenous composer in Finland before the Great War? The shortlist of the most-often-played works by Sibelius is easily defined and quickly presented and, as such, requires little analysis. So our objective includes further questions:

---

[1] Robert Kajanus (1856–1933) founded the orchestra in 1882 and was its principal conductor until his death. In 1914, the orchestra became a municipal institution with the name Helsinki Philharmonic Orchestra (*Helsingin kaupunginorkesteri*).

(1) Why did Sibelius become such an important composer in the popular concerts?
(2) Are there any features that can be identified as typical of the works by Sibelius frequently played in popular concerts?
(3) Was popular Sibelius somewhat different from the Sibelius of the more serious concerts?
(4) What was the impact of Kajanus' popular concerts on Sibelius' early career, on his later career—and on his career in general?

Popular Concert?

Kajanus' popular concerts (*populär konsert* in Swedish, *helppotajuinen konsertti* in Finnish) were informal concerts modelled after promenade concerts in the European metropolises. Philippe Musard, Louis-Antoine Jullien, Joseph Lanner, and Joseph Strauss conducted their orchestras in parks and restaurants in Paris, London, and Vienna to accompany the social life of the upper- and middle-class audiences.[2] Closer models for the popular concerts in Helsinki are to be found in Tivoli, Copenhagen, Berns Salon in Stockholm, and Ozerki, a summer resort close to St Petersburg. In Helsinki, the tradition of organising popular concerts is traceable to the 1860s when the recently founded Theatre Orchestra under the batons of Filip von Schantz and August Meissner regularly held musical *soirées* with varied programmes.

In addition to providing entertainment, popular concerts aimed at cultivating the taste of the audiences to appreciate the masterpieces of music. These concerts followed most of the aesthetic ideals of more "serious" symphony concerts, and some of the repertoire was even identical, but in general was easier to understand. In a way, they resembled popular lectures, plentiful at the end of the nineteenth century, in which subject matters of genteel order were divertingly explained to non-expert audiences without using difficult language. As a matter of fact, the Finnish epithet for the concerts, *helppotajuinen*, means exactly that: easy to understand. This cultural layer between "highbrow" and "lowbrow" has often been called "middlebrow."[3]

Beginning in 1882, from the first week of October to the first of May, Kajanus' orchestra annually played popular concerts, first twice and later

---

[2] Derek B. Scott, *Sounds of the Metropolis. The 19th-Century Popular Music Revolution in London, New York, Paris, and Vienna* (Oxford: Oxford University Press, 2008).
[3] See Joan Shelley Rubin, *The Making of Middlebrow Culture* (Chapel Hill: The University of North Carolina Press, 1992).

three and even four times a week. The most active period was the 1901–2 season with 103 popular concerts. After this peak, the number of these concerts slowly decreased. However, in the 1910s popular concerts still belonged to the annual repertoire of the orchestra: in the 1910–11 season the number of concerts was 50, but in 1913–14 it was only 24. Kajanus' last series of popular concerts was held in 1919, by which time the orchestra was called the Helsinki Philharmonic Orchestra.[4]

The venue was usually Seurahuone ("Society House"), the oldest and for a long time the most distinguished entertainment centre in Helsinki, with a hotel, various restaurants, and a large concert hall under one roof. In addition to hotel guests, the concert audience was comprised mainly of the so-called new middle classes: university teachers and students, schoolteachers, artists, functionaries, businessmen, and their families. The popular concerts formed the economic backbone of the orchestra, and audiences regularly crowded into the concert venue.

A comparison of Kajanus' popular concerts with the repertoire of his serious series demonstrates that the musical differences were smaller than one might imagine. Orchestral works typical of symphony concerts, such as overtures, concertos, and orchestral suites, also appeared on popular concert programmes. In addition, popular concerts notably included minor and lighter works, like concert waltzes, orchestral medleys (or potpourris) from operas and operettas, ballet and other incidental music, patriotic marches, and so on. The biggest difference between the popular and the symphony concerts was that—with a few exceptions—no complete symphonies were played in the popular concerts; it was possible to perform individual symphony movements, but this occurred quite seldom. Furthermore, compared to symphony concerts, popular concerts included canonised classics less often, favoured contemporary music, and presented the newest and most eagerly awaited trends in French, Scandinavian, and Russian music.[5] Based on the content of the programmes, Kajanus' popular concerts should be called "miscellaneous concerts."[6] The programme was highly mixed and constantly shifting from one atmosphere to another, according to a certain pattern. The roots of this

---

[4] Helsingin musiikkilautakunta Ua4, Ua5, Helsinki City Archives.

[5] For a more detailed description of Kajanus's popular programs, see Vesa Kurkela, "Seriously Popular. Deconstructing Popular Orchestral Repertoire in Late-19th-Century Helsinki," in *Critical Music Historiography: Probing Canons, Ideologies and Institutions*, eds. Vesa Kurkela and Markus Mantere (Surrey and Burlington: Ashgate, 2015), 123–38.

[6] William Weber, *The Great Transformation of Musical Taste. Concert Programming from Haydn to Brahms* (Cambridge: Cambridge University Press, 2008), 13–18.

form go back to the eighteenth century, when all concerts consisted of mixed programmes of great variety. This old concert form was familiar to all habitués, who expected the changing moods.

The popular-concert atmosphere was also familiar to the popular concert-goers. From the perspective of the audience, popular concerts differed from the more serious ones in terms of general atmosphere, which stressed a relaxed and wealthy lifestyle and were the opposite of a serious and intense concert situation. The listeners sat at small tables, eating and drinking as they listened to the music, while an army of waiters dressed in tailcoats ran around the great concert hall, including between the tables, serving the audience.

Popular concerts were highly appreciated by local music critics and regularly mentioned in their reviews.[7] Accordingly, Kajanus seems to have carefully kept his popular repertoire "varied but never worthless."[8] This actually meant that the repertoire was clearly more elegant and less grotesque than that of the *varieté* shows and the then extremely popular *Damenkapellen* (women's orchestras), which Kajanus saw as being a serious competitor to his popular evenings.[9] The conductor clearly strove to keep all his concerts part of the art world and high culture, and thus on the good side of art music criticism. However, in the practical programme planning Kajanus had to take into account the actual musical taste of his restaurant audiences. The end result was a musical programme that followed middlebrow artistic principles, containing a suitable combination of both high- and low-cultural elements.

Popular Top Ten

According to the local press, music by Sibelius was played for the first time in Helsinki popular concerts on April 28, 1891 when two of his orchestral works, Overture in E major and *Balettscen*, were performed in a new concert venue: Brandkårshuset/Palokunnantalo. In the following years, Sibelius' music was regularly played in popular concerts, although the frequency of performances was quite moderate. During the 1893–4

[7] For the public image of the popular concerts in the Helsinki press, see Vesa Kurkela, "Jalostavaa huvittelua. Robert Kajanuksen helppotajuiset konsertit sivistämisprojektina," *Etnomusikologian vuosikirja* (2015): 56–73.

[8] Einari Marvia and Matti Vainio, *Helsingin Kaupunginorkesteri 1882–1982* (Porvoo, Helsinki and Juva: WSOY, 1993), 228.

[9] For instance, in the orchestra's 1895–6 annual report, Kajanus accused the variety shows in the Societetshuset of having a "low artistic level." Papers of the Helsingin Filharmooninen Seura, Helsinki City Archives (Ca, minutes of annual meetings).

season, for instance, Sibelius' music was performed 11 times, and every second piece of music was from the *Karelia* Suite.

The actual breakthrough for Sibelius' popularity in popular concerts came at the turn of the century. In the 1900–1 season, Sibelius' music was played 31 times, and in 1905–6 a record-breaking 45 times in 28 concerts. Sibelius maintained his position in the repertoire until 1912 when performances suddenly dropped by half.

Figure 1. Music by Sibelius in Kajanus's popular concerts, 1891–1918.

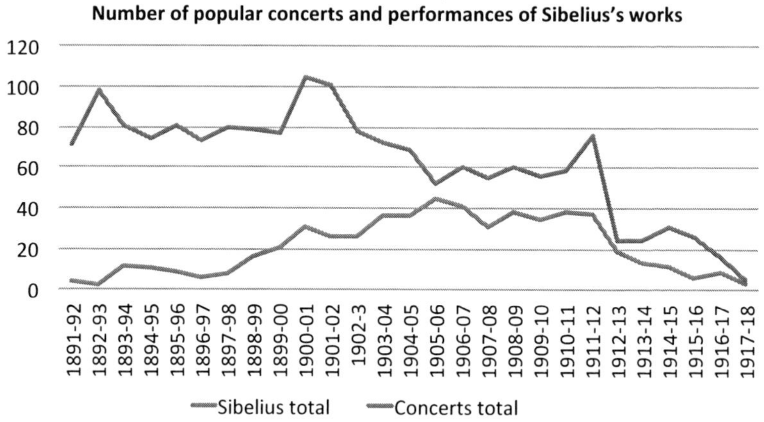

However, at the same time, the popular concerts diminished by two-thirds. The reason for this was the so-called "Orchestra War," which was going on in Helsinki at the time. As a result of administrative decisions, Helsinki then had two symphony orchestras, one led by Kajanus, and the other, city-funded, led by Georg Schnéevoigt. Competition was hard, and concerts were held at the same time and very often with the same type of programme.[10] One way to beat the competitor was to play as much Finnish music as possible, which may explain the slightly lesser drop in performances of Sibelius' works compared to the overall drop in popular concerts.

But what were the works performed? Table 1 shows the ten most frequently performed works by Sibelius in the Helsinki popular concerts. The table contains information for the period 1891–1919 from 394 popular concerts with music by Sibelius. The number of different works is 67 and the number of single performances totals 587.

[10] Marvia and Vainio, *Helsingin Kaupunginorkesteri*, 302–13.

Table 1. Sibelius Top Ten in Helsinki popular concerts 1891–1919.

Title	Number of performances (NOP)	
1. Karelia Music	111	
Entire suite	55	
Alla marcia	21	
Intermezzo	17	
Karelia Overture	15	
Ballade	3	
2. King Christian II	85	
Entire suite	27	
Elegia	27	
Musette	17	
Other movements	14	
3. Spring Song	59	
4. Finlandia	48	
5. En saga	44	
6. The Swan of Tuonela	42	
7. Valse triste	36	
8. Lemminkäinen's Return	21	
		Total NOP: 587
9. Pan and Echo	20	
		Number of concerts: 394
10. Pelléas & Mélisande	19 (all movements 12)	
		Number of titles: 67

Table 2. Sibelius Top Ten in "significant" concerts 1891–1919 according to Nils-Eric Ringbom (1932, pp. 93–114).

Title	NOP
1. Symphony No. 2	16
2. Lemminkäinen Suite	12
3. Symphony No. 1	11
4. Symphony No. 3	8
4. Symphony No. 4	8
6. Pohjola's Daughter	7
7. The Ferryman's Bride	6
7. Finlandia	6
7. Violin Concerto	6
7. The Oceanides	6
7. Symphony No. 5	6

Music suitable for national resistance and patriotic feelings is easily noticeable on the list. Of the most frequently performed, the "number one" Sibelius work is the *Karelia* Suite, and number two is the *King Christian II* Suite. These works had strong connotations to the past of the nation—invented or real—thus expressing national values almost automatically. It is necessary to add that both suites had other qualities contributing to their popularity: they are skilfully composed music for amusement; and, thus, they are ideal material for popular concert repertoire. In addition, there are many other important works on the list that quite early on became musical symbols of Finnishness and Finnish nature, for example *Finlandia*, *The Swan of Tuonela*, and *En saga*.

There is still another reason for the high number of performances of the above-mentioned works: they were all composed in the 1890s, and so by the end of the popular-concert era they all had been available for inclusion in the repertoire for at least 20 years. In the 1900–1 season, the most-often performed works were the "Karelia Music" (eight times, including performances of single movements as well as the whole suite) and *King Christian II* (eight times), which from its inception in 1898 was a steady favourite. *Spring Song* (1895) came third (six times), and *Finlandia*, which premiered the previous summer, was placed fourth (performed five times).

If we examine the 1911–12 season, the last one before the "Orchestra War," things are slightly different. Out of the 37 performances, the "Karelia Music" is still the favourite (performed seven times). *King Christian II* was played three times, as was the quite recently composed

The Dryad (1910). Other works composed in the twentieth century that did not quite make the overall top-ten list were *Pohjola's Daughter* (1906, 15 performances all in all) and the theatre-music suites *Belshazzar's Feast* (1907, 13 times) and *Pelléas et Mélisande* (1905, 12 times). If the popular concerts had been continued after 1919, the top ten list would surely have been different.

A short comparison of Sibelius in popular concerts versus in the "significant"[11] concert repertoire shows that, first, the significant concerts had considerably less music by Sibelius and, secondly, the two types generally included quite different works. Only two works, the *Lemminkäinen* Suite and *Finlandia*, belong to the top ten lists of both. The number two piece in the prominent-concert list, *Lemminkäinen* Suite, was also played in the popular concerts, but never in its entirety: only its two shortest movements, *The Swan of Tuonela* and *Lemminkäinen's Return*, were performed, although these were heard frequently.

It is self-evident that a lot of well-known music by Sibelius is not mentioned in the popular concert top ten list. First, choral music is totally missing, since choirs did not belong to the popular concerts' artistic arsenal. So, the most patriotic repertoire, real protest songs by Sibelius like *Song of the Athenians*, did not belong to the popular-concert repertoire. Furthermore, there were many important works by Sibelius that were presented in popular concerts from time to time, but not as frequently as the works on the top ten list. For example, the final movements of the First and Second Symphonies were performed once, and the Violin Concerto was played in popular concerts several times, even more often than in the symphony concerts.

Patriotic Demand

In late-nineteenth century Helsinki it was an old habit to organise popular concerts with patriotic content on certain anniversaries like the Flora Day (the traditional spring festival of the university students on May 13), the day of the national poet Runeberg (February 5), and the commemoration day of Fredrik Pacius, the "Father of Finnish music," as this German-born musician is often called (January 8). However, the need for patriotic

[11] Nils-Eric Ringbom, *Helsingin orkesteri 1882–1932* (Helsinki: Helsingin orkesteriyhdistys, 1932), 93–114; the term refers mainly to symphonic concerts but the concert list compiled by Ringbom also contains some other concerts that were, according to the author, "significant," i.e. worth mentioning in the orchestra's history.

concerts considerably increased at the end of the 1890s when the imperial Tsarist government launched a severe policy of Russification.

During this "first period of oppression," as the years between 1899–1905 are called in the national histories of Finland, public concerts were one of the few possibilities to express nationalist resistance and patriotic feelings. Preventive censorship hampered conventional ways of expressing political opinions in the press and other printed media, and quite soon the Tsarist authorities also forbade organising all kinds of national meetings, including big national festivals.[12] Popular concerts were above all entertaining evenings and targeted at the narrow circles of the educated classes. From the perspective of censorship authorities these concerts seemed innocent and harmless, and Kajanus could quite safely increase the number of patriotic and uplifting works in his concert programmes. Clearly, there was a real social demand for national music in the repertoire of popular concerts.

During these years we find two kinds of popular concerts organised by the Helsinki Philharmonic Society: (1) conventional concerts for amusement, and (2) concerts with patriotic content. The latter concerts were not held often, but bigger press coverage increased their importance in public life. Sibelius' music was suitable for and played in both types of concerts. The programme sheet from the concert on January 20, 1900 (see Figure 2) shows how easily Sibelius' music was combined with international popular repertoire; in this case, the *Alla marcia* from the *Karelia* Suite found a place among the works of popular composers like Johann Strauss II, Massenet, Adam, and Grieg.

---

[12] Tuomo Polvinen, *Imperial Borderland: Bobrikov and the Attempted Russification of Finland, 1898–1904* (London: C. Hurst & Co. Publishers, 1995), 192–9, 234–8; for the role of patriotic music festivals in Finland, see Saijaleena Rantanen, "Laulu- ja soittojuhlat suomalaisen kansakunnan rakentajina 1800-luvun lopulla," *Musiikki* 3–4 (2013): 61, 80–1.

Figure 2. Typical popular concert program of Kajanus's orchestra, January 20, 1900.

Filharmoniska Sällskapet.

Program

till

44:de

Populära Konserten

Lördagen den 20 Januari 1900.

1. Ouverture till „Nürnbergerdokkan" . . . . Adam.
2. Seid umschlungen Millionen, vals Strauss.
3. Prélude ur „Tovelille" . . . Hamarik.
4. Alla marcia . . . . Sibelius.

Paus.

5. Ouverture till op. „Le Roi de Lahore" . . . . Massenet.
6. a) Serenade melancolique för violin Tschaikowsky
   b) Polonaise (A dur) för violin Wieniawski.
   (hr Oscar Braun)
7. Fyra sinfoniska danser . . . Grieg.
   Allegro moderato. Allegretto grazioso. Allegro giocoso. Allegro molto.

Paus.

8. Fantasi ur op. „Zigenarbaron". Strauss.
9. Romance ur op. „Trumpetaren från Säkkingen" . . . . . . Nessler.
   (hr Th. Nordin.)
10. Mosella marsch . . . . Sitt.

Konserten äger rum i

Societetshuset.

As can be seen on the programme of the concert on February 15, 1900 (Figure 3), the patriotic concerts provided a good opportunity not only for Sibelius, but also for other domestic composers to have their new music performed for Helsinki audiences. In addition, the older heroes of national music, Fredrik Pacius and Filip von Schantz, had an almost permanent position in the repertoire. Actually, purely indigenous content in the patriotic concerts seems to have been more a rule than an exception. The focus on "compatriots" stressed the importance of new and old Finnish music for the national identity.

Figure 3. Patriotic popular concert program of Kajanus's orchestra, February 15, 1900.

Filharmoniska Sällskapet.

Program

till

54:de

Populära Konserten

Torsdagen den 15 Februari 1900.

1. Wasa marsch . . . . Collan.
2. Polska . . . . Schantz.
3. Adagietto för stråkork. . . . Kajanus.
4. Suomalaisia kansanlauluja . . . Pahlman.

Paus.

5. Lyrisk-Ouverture . . . . Järnefelt.
6. Romans för trumpet . . . . Flodin.
(hr Emile Trognée)
7. Suite ur „Kung Kristian". . . . Sibelius.
Nocturno. Elegie. Musette.
Serenade. Ballade.

Paus.

8. Soldatgossen } . . Pacius.
9. Suomis sång för stråkork. }
10. Björneborgarnes marsch . . . — — —

Konserten äger rum i

Societetshuset.

In the patriotic concerts Sibelius was given a special position. His music considerably improved the nationalist atmosphere, as the following press report by the composer and music critic Oskar Merikanto illustrates:

> The series of popular concerts began yesterday at the Society House. The concert venue of this first concert was full of an audience with a highly excited spirit ... Since the programme was wholly indigenous, the festive spirit increased with every number and went into orbit in the Sibelius section. Several numbers were claimed to be repeated, such as Järnefelt's jolly *Prélude*, Kajanus' sorrowful, gentle Lullaby from the *Summer Reminiscence* Suite, Sibelius' masterful *Finlandia* and his brisk Intermezzo from the *Karelia* Suite.[13]

It is noteworthy that Sibelius himself participated in many popular concerts and his presence was usually mentioned in press reviews.[14] Sibelius was also invited to conduct his own music, as on New Year's Day 1904 when the second set of the popular concert was dedicated to his music. The orchestra, under the baton of the composer, played *Spring Song*, *The Swan of Tuonela*, and the finale of the First Symphony, and the performance and the composer "were greeted and rewarded with the strongest displays of high-spirited enjoyment by the audience." The concert finished, before the final march, with *Finlandia*[15]—a convention that, according to programme data, seems to have evolved quite soon into a tradition for all kinds of patriotic concert.

Impact and Benefit

In conclusion, there is good reason to consider how a great number of performances in Kajanus' popular concerts benefited Sibelius' artistic career. First of all, these concerts considerably aided Sibelius in making a breakthrough as the top composer in Finland. His orchestral music became well known, first locally in Helsinki, and quite soon nationally as well. Music by Sibelius not only belonged to the repertoire of the Helsinki Philharmonic Society orchestra, but many other municipal orchestras in Finland performed it—both in their popular and symphony concerts. For example, in the autumn of 1900 in Viborg a local journalist made a news report on the popular concerts by a local orchestra. He was pleased with the great number of Sibelius' pieces on the concert programme and wished that as many works as possible could be heard in the future during the coming seasons.[16]

---

[13] *Päivälehti*, October 2, 1903.
[14] E.g. *Uusi Suometar*, May 1, 1892; *Hufvustadsbladet*, February 5, 1902; *Uusi Suometar*, April 30, 1902; *Päivälehti*, April 30, 1902.
[15] *Uusi Suometar*, January 3, 1904 (Evert Katila).
[16] *Wiipurin Sanomat*, October 5, 1900.

In Helsinki, most of the popular concerts were regularly reviewed in four local newspapers, *Hufvudstadsbladet*, *Uusi Suometar*, *Päivälehti–Helsingin Sanomat*, and *Nya Pressen*. Reviews were normally quite short compared to the press coverage of the standard symphony concerts. However, even in the shortest popular concert reviews, Sibelius was almost always mentioned if Finnish music was part of the programming.

During the years of Russification and political oppression, popular concerts with patriotic programmes brought Sibelius' music to a blaze of national publicity. The patriotic concerts were often described with more detailed reviews, and in these reports Sibelius soon became a real national hero.

The list of the most-often performed works by Sibelius makes one wonder if the canon of his orchestral music was already formed at the turn of the twentieth century or, at least, before the Great War. Of course, many central works were yet to be composed, but by about 1910 the core of the most popular repertoire by Sibelius was already born, and actively performed. This early canon also consisted of the very same works that paved the way for further popular use of Sibelius' music in various cultural environments and institutions: radio and television broadcasting, cinema, schools, and popular education. It was exactly this music—along with the symphonies—that generated the long-lasting public image of Sibelius as a *national* Finnish composer.

As Erik Tawaststjerna[17] has pointed out, Sibelius himself was not necessarily overjoyed about the popularity of his patriotic "protest music" that attracted wide audiences and inspired public opinion. Perhaps Sibelius thought that this kind of national publicity might easily overshadow the fame of his more sophisticated and precious orchestral works, thus deflating his public image as a cosmopolitan symphonic composer. Surely this was not the first time in music history that a composer's intentions and ambitions conflicted with the taste and desire of his audiences. However, it seems likely that in his later career Sibelius more voluntarily assumed the role of the national composer. After becoming world-famous with his symphonic works, patriotic Finnishness no longer conflicted with Sibelius' artistic image. Finally, as Veijo Murtomäki remarks,[18] in his later years Sibelius seems to have been willing to do PR work for Finland as a famous Finnish citizen, although mostly disputing the national interpretations of his music.

---

[17] Erik Tawaststjerna, *Jean Sibelius 2* (Helsinki: Otava, 1989 [1967]), 20–1, 138–9.
[18] Veijo Murtomäki, *Jean Sibelius ja isänmaa* (Helsinki: Tammi, 2007).

JEAN SIBELIUS' MUSIC IN FINNISH PROPAGANDA FILMS DURING WORLD WAR II

KAARINA KILPIÖ

This article offers a look at the use of Sibelius' music in Finnish war propaganda films from World War II. My study of music and sound in Finnish non-fiction film is in its early phase, and the use of Sibelius' music in war propaganda has been one of the first cases I have focused on. I began by asking the following general question: what is it that the Finnish propaganda makers have wished to convey when combining certain music with various non-musical elements?

The premise of the project is that the so-called functional music perspective can be worthwhile, as is also the case with Sibelius's music. This approach is affected by my own past as a researcher of music in advertising contexts, the history of functional background music products, and different (mainly historical) uses of music in everyday life.

It was typical for most belligerent countries during World War II to construct propaganda messages using the full capacities of audio-visual media, i.e. moving image and sound. The 86 publicly shown Finnish propaganda newsreels made during the war were called Surveys of the Armed Forces. These films had two principal aims: evoking goodwill outside Finland and upholding patriotism and trust in victory locally. Every Finnish cinema showed the newsreels, and newspapers estimated "tens of millions" readers around the world.[1] No one has so far studied the sonic expression of these films and the auditory way they portrayed not only the Finnish nation, but its cultural icon, the only widely-known composer of the young republic.

All music used in Finnish audio-visual productions naturally had to be licensed in the 1940s. The Finnish Composers' Copyright Society Teosto, formed in 1928, administered and protected the composers' rights when it

[1] Jari Sedergren and Ilkka Kippola, *Dokumentin ytimessä: suomalaisen dokumentti- ja lyhytelokuvan historia 1904–1944* [*In the Heart of the Documentary: the History of Finnish Documentary and Short Film, 1904–1944*] (Helsinki: Finnish Literature Society, 2009), 362.

came to licensing the use of their music in films. These archived Teosto reports also exist for propaganda material. The documents provide us with a good view on the sonic material used in the propaganda films. Thus, it is possible to conduct a study of Sibelius' "reception" and interpretation among the makers of propaganda in war-time Finland.

My methods are: (1) constructing a statistical understanding (using mainly Teosto documents) of the music that has been included in war propaganda film soundtracks; (2) close reading of the films, available on the internet via the National Audiovisual Institute database Elonet[2]; and (3) an analysis of the musical context and the overall positioning of the films in the soundscape and cinematic expression of their time. The first part, archival work with copyright documents, has only recently begun, and I have an initial understanding of the combining work that needs to be done with different sources. In this text are selected examples of the second and third parts.

Sound on these newsreels was almost exclusively added in the film production. The few exceptions to this are sequences from indoor events, where sound could be recorded with minimal technical problems. For the purposes of analysis, I shall view the soundtracks as constructed of three elements. The foreground element—when present never drowned out or interfered with by other sonic elements—is a read commentary from written and carefully inspected manuscripts. These were always products of teamwork and passed through the censoring authorities within the Armed Forces organisation. The two non-verbal sonic elements were sound effects (possibly partly from the Finnish broadcasting company Yleisradio, but also staged and taped material) and music. As far as I can tell at this point, no commissioned music or exclusive performances have been used in the propaganda newsreels. Every musical sound comes from recordings; these are commercial recordings or, in some cases, possibly Yleisradio tapes.

What is mainly heard on the soundtracks is Finnish composers' music: classical orchestra repertoire and so-called "lighter repertoire." Instances of lighter orchestral music from European composers are also featured. Standard repertoire composers such as Beethoven, Wagner, Liszt, and J. S. Bach are not used. The soundtracks include "smaller" names, perhaps familiar to some at the time from light concerts, a tradition that had faded in Finland since the beginning of the twentieth century. Symphonic repertoire, however, was not something necessarily familiar to all viewers in the movie theatres. Orchestral concerts were mainly attended by the

[2] http://www.elonet.fi/fi/elokuvat/suomalaiset-elokuvat.

middle and upper classes, and the movie theatre audience consisted of a wider spectrum of the population than the concerts did.

Finnish films—fiction, documentary, and educational—had featured Sibelius' music since the beginning of the local film industry. Before World War II, filmmakers usually selected the composer's incidental or choral works. In the war propaganda films, Sibelius' works were utilised extensively.[3] During wartime, not only incidental works but also his symphonies became regular material on the propaganda soundtracks. A licentiate work on the newsreels calculated that 49% of the music on the sample films was by Jean Sibelius, with the remaining 51% by all the other composers.[4]

Why, then, are the soundtracks so predominantly Sibelius-infused? At the time of writing, I have not yet gathered enough detailed information on the musical backgrounds of the Finnish propaganda team members' personal musical preferences or possible governmental guidelines concerning propaganda messages. Hence, the overall picture will probably become more nuanced through archival work in the future. For now, four main reasons for favouring Sibelius on the propaganda soundtracks emerge.

Firstly, the Karelian district and *runo* singing associated with the area were widely seen as important inspirations for Sibelius, at least for several of the composer's early and middle career works. The composer himself had somewhat distanced himself from the nationalistic movement by the 1940s. The propaganda makers did not see this as a hindrance to utilising his reputation as one of the heroic Karelianistic cultural figures.[5] This was

---

[3] Kaarina Kilpiö, "Patriotic soundtracks," *Finnish Music Quarterly* 1–2 (2015): 26–7, http://www.fmq.fi/2015/04/patriotic-soundtracks.

[4] Pirkko-Liisa Nieminen, *Puolustusvoimien uutiskatsaukset—suomalaista elokuvaa ja propagandaa jatkosodan aikana* [*The Surveys of the Armed Forces: Finnish Film and Propaganda during the Continuation War*] (Licentiate work, Finnish history. University of Jyväskylä, 1989), 233.

[5] On Karelianism and *runo* singing in building the public figure of Sibelius, see: Veijo Murtomäki, "Sibelius: Composer and Patriot," in *Sibelius Forum II: Proceedings from the Third International Jean Sibelius Conference, Helsinki, 7–10 December 2000*, eds. Matti Huttunen, Kari Kilpeläinen, and Veijo Murtomäki (Helsinki: Sibelius Academy, Department of Composition and Music Theory 2003), 328–37; Tina Karina Ramnarine, "An Encounter with the Other: Sibelius, Folk Music and Nationalism," in *Sibelius Forum: Proceedings from the Second International Jean Sibelius Conference, Helsinki, 25–29 November 1995* (Helsinki: Sibelius Academy, Department of Composition and Music Theory1998), 166–73; Philip Donner and Juhani Similä, "Jean Sibelius—The Idol," *Musiikin Suunta* [Finnish Ethnomusicologial Society Journal] special issue "Myths and Idols in Music," 1985), 66–79.

well-matched with the verbal content of the propaganda, constantly underlining the folklore of Karelia as the origin of Finnish national culture. The acts of war between Finland and the Soviet Union were taking place predominantly in Karelia, in the region where the *runo* tradition had been alive the longest.

Secondly, as mentioned previously, it was one of the main tasks of war propaganda to awaken foreign sympathy for the small nation at war with its neighbour. The national cultural hero was extremely useful for this purpose. Though his fame was by no means uncontroversial, Sibelius was by the 1940s acknowledged in many parts of the world as a major cultural figure, especially in Great Britain and the United States.[6] Thus he could be portrayed as a product of a culture emphasising its distinctly European nature, that was perhaps small in size but nevertheless great in thought.

Thirdly, the Finnish propaganda newsreel had been created using the German *Wochenschaus* as models. This archetype used music and sound extensively. Among the main musical categories used by the German propaganda machinery were orchestral classics. This meant choosing for the soundtrack large symphonic sounds by composers who were racially not dubious and "*völkisch*" in their composing.[7] The foremost of these composers in Germany was Wagner; in Finland there was not a single composer who could compete with Sibelius' significance in this respect.

The fourth reason in my list still lacks final proof, but it seems that Sibelius granted permission to the Defence Force to use all of his work in the war efforts for no charge. Since no document of money transactions via Teosto has been discovered—and the sums would have been substantial—it appears that there was an agreement. Making sure composers got remuneration for the use of their music was the reason Teosto existed, and since it is evident from archival documents that they did have all the information about the use of the composer's work in the films, it is my conclusion that the use of Sibelius' music in newsreels was free of charge. This motive for using Sibelius should naturally not be underestimated, but it is hardly the most important, let alone the only one: as stated above, slightly over a half of the music on the newsreels was nevertheless from other composers besides Sibelius.

---

[6] Elina Melgin, *Propagandaa vai julkisuusdiplomatiaa? Taide ja kulttuuri Suomen maakuvan viestinnässä 1937–52* [*Propaganda or Public Diplomacy? Finnish Art and Culture in Communicating the National Image 1937–52*] (Helsinki: Historiallisia tutkimuksia Helsingin yliopistosta XXXVI, 2014), 54.

[7] Catherine Chamblee, "The Juxtaposition of Visual and Musical Elements in Nazi Films (1933–1945)," *Music Research Forum* 18 (2003): 2–28.

Going to the movies was very popular in 1940s' and 1950s' Finland, more so than ever before or after those decades.[8] In the early 1940s, many of the viewers came to the theatres in order to escape the wearing circumstances of life during wartime. They wished to watch entertaining films and forget the prolonged stress and anxiety. Every Finnish movie theatre showed the Armed Forces' surveys as "starters," so it is reasonable to conclude they had an effect on people's moods and also constituted a shared media experience.

In what follows, I shall present the initial results from my viewings and analysis. They highlight some characteristics of the uses that Sibelius' music was put into in Finnish war propaganda films.

As mentioned above, the propaganda makers used not only the composer's incidental music but also his symphonies, and this was exceptional. In other Finnish non-fiction films of the era, it was rare to hear his symphonies on the soundtracks. In fiction films, they were not used at all. This may or may not have been due to Sibelius' policy on licensing; no records exist on those requests of filmmakers to use the composer's music that were denied. My interpretation is, from analysing the audio-visual expression in the films, that associating Sibelius' symphonies so closely with the armed forces had much to do with the evocative power of the symphony orchestra sound. The sound (at that time) was connected with larger spaces and audiences. As stated earlier, the composer's symphonies were neither sonically nor repertoire-wise necessarily familiar to all the cinemagoers. Also, via bombastic symphonic sound, the cause of fighting is portrayed as greater than the individuals (meaning both the soldiers on screen and the viewers in the movie theatre).

My first example, from August 1941,[9] shows Finnish forces victorious in the Aunus region in Karelia, taking back territories lost to the Soviet Union in the Winter War. In a noisy section of warfare sounds, the troops have made rapid progress and prepared artillery, with *Night Ride and Sunrise* prominent on the soundtrack. When the firing starts, music gives way to the sounds of artillery and machine gun fire. I focus on the part of the film following this combat scene. The section starts with a shot of fallen enemies lying on the forest floor and continues to follow the brisk progress of Finnish soldiers and Karelian villagers returning to their

---

[8] Jaakko Keto, *Elokuvalippujen kysyntä ja siihen vaikuttaneet tekijät Suomessa 1915–1972* [*The Demand of Movie Tickets and Factors Affecting it in Finland 1915–1972*] (Helsinki: Acta Academiae oeconomicae Helsingiensis. Series A; 10, 1974), 64.

[9] *Survey of the Armed Forces 6 / Suomalaiset etenevät Aunuksessa* [*Finns Advancing in Aunus*] (August 1941). http://www.elonet.fi/fi/elokuva/638068.

homes. During these takes, Sibelius' Third Symphony gathers speed. The devastation of the dead Soviet soldiers—who, the commentary assures us, "got what they asked for"—is combined with the sturdy theme of the first bars, played by double basses and cellos. When additional elements appear in the music, the visual narrative has already moved on, to the "irresistible push of our vanguard, the light bicycle units" crossing a bridge and entering a Karelian village. The fallen men are thus portrayed as a prerequisite of "life returning" to the area, as this section of the film is musically built on the "quiet rows" of their bodies.

The optimistic and victorious tone of the autumn 1941 newsreels is verbalised in their associated commentaries through words like "unwavering," "accurate," and "precise." These commentaries are repeatedly paired with certain passages from Jean Sibelius' symphonies. The Second, Third, and Fifth Symphonies are most recurrent in this phase of the war. The passages used are mainly in medium to fast tempos, clearly with energising aims. The Third Symphony is the one most frequently used in films featuring the munitions industry, armaments, and the strength of the home front. This may have partly resulted from the notable role of rhythmic elements in the symphony's first movement: the word *eteenpäin* (onwards) is repeated in these propaganda films.

The influence of Sibelius' music on nationalist rhetoric has certainly been both direct and indirect. By direct influence I am referring to the fact that Finns (as well as nationals in several other countries) viewed and heard the propaganda films during the war in local movie theatres, and associated the music with the spoken content and the images. As I stated earlier, the distribution of the propaganda films was extensive in Finland and also in Europe and the United States. But there are also indirect influences, and I am going to briefly analyse an example of them.

Among the last propaganda newsreels made in Finland is number 84 (1944),[10] in which music is foregrounded exceptionally. I will juxtapose this newsreel with the most iconic Finnish war fiction film, *The Unknown Soldier* (1955).[11] The latter is hugely significant to the Finnish way of commemorating the country's fight for retaining its independence. As

---

[10] *Survey of the Armed Forces 84 / Torjuntataistelut Kannaksella, evakuointia* [*Defensive Battle in Kannas Area, Evacuation*] (July 1944). http://www.elonet.fi/fi/elokuva/611630.

[11] *Tuntematon sotilas* [*The Unknown Soldier*], dir. Edvin Laine, screenplay Juha Nevalainen, eds. Armas Vallasvuo and Osmo Harkimo, sound Kurt Vilja, Taisto Lindegren, Yrjö Saari and Kaarlo Nissilä; running time 181 min (prod. Oy Suomen Filmiteollisuus, 1955). The opening and closing scenes are viewable at https://www.youtube.com/watch?v=dRvHsbrkJws.

John Sundholm states, the film has, especially during the first decades of its existence, "not only become the narrative of the Continuation War, but of War and Independence," and its "meaning and the experience of the narrative were ritualised in connection with the recurring broadcasts of the film on TV."[12]

These two films start nearly identically. Without visuals, there would be almost no difference: the sound in both cases is the beginning of *Finlandia* (although the recordings differ slightly in tempo and sound). The music is combined with first a dark screen,[13] then a summer sky,[14] and then pictures of a procession of weary Finns on their way from the front. On the newsreel, these Finns are evacuees; in the fiction film, they are fatigued soldiers carrying a fallen comrade and supplies, and stretchering two wounded soldiers. The dark screen very powerfully directs the viewer's attention to the sonic information. Peter Sundholm characterises the opening as mood-setting for the whole film: he interprets the result as the viewer being "manipulated in emotional and physical terms before the first picture emerges and the rationality of the eye takes over."[15] Susanna Välimäki also sees a strong connection being built between the film and the music here: in her words, the cinematic work is, "in a manner of speaking, born from inside *Finlandia*."[16]

It is hard to see the similarity of these two audio-visual constructions as a coincidence. From Vesa Sirén's writing, we further learn that *The Unknown Soldier* was not originally meant to include *Finlandia* at all: the director Edvin Laine was talked into using it by the writer Väinö Linna.[17] The writer's role thus emerges as very interesting. It is likely impossible to

[12] Peter Sundholm, "'The Unknown Soldier,' Film as a Founding Trauma and National Monument," in *Collective Traumas: Memories of War and Conflict in 20th-century Europe*, "Multiple Europes" 38, eds. Conny Mithander, John Sundholm, and Maria Holmgren Troy (Peter Lang: Brussels, 2007), 137.

[13] The newsreel additionally features the logo present in all of the surveys, as well as the number of the survey (84), before the black screen changes to the summer sky.

[14] The sky is grey and white on black and white film, but clearly points to the colours of the national flag: blue and white. The lilacs against the sky of the propaganda newsreel opening also refer to an older propaganda film about the beginning of the Continuation War in midsummer 1941, *When the Lilacs are Blooming 1941*, http://www.elonet.fi/fi/elokuva/743684.

[15] Sundholm, "'The Unknown Soldier'," 132.

[16] Susanna Välimäki, *Miten sota soi? Sotaelokuva, ääni ja musiikki* [*War Films, Sound and Music*] (Tampereen yliopistopaino, Tampere, 2008), 84.

[17] Vesa Sirén, "Poliittinen & politisoitu. Kenen joukosta säveltäjä lopulta löysi itsensä?" [*Political & Politicized. On Whose Side did the Composer find Himself Eventually?*] *HS Teema* 6 (2014), *Jean Sibeliuksen juhlavuosi*, 32.

find out precisely how Linna, his work, and his conceptions of presenting war audio-visually may have been influenced by propaganda newsreels. But the case of persuading the tough-minded, dynamic director to use *Finlandia* this way raises curiosity, to say the least.

Linna served on the front in the Syväri area in the Continuation War from 1942 to 1943, and started his writing career during this time. In 1954 he wrote the novel originally titled *Sotaromaani* [*War Novel*], of which the film *The Unknown Soldier* is an adaptation. The novel's tone, however, is "contradictory, ironic, and disillusioned,"[18] containing messages that can be (and were) interpreted as pacifist. Thus, its narrative is significantly less idealistic and nationalistic than the screen adaptation's, which was premiered only one year after the publication of the book. The role of *Finlandia* in constructing the idealistic essence of the film adaptation is not to be underestimated. We may never know whether Väinö Linna actually got the idea for the opening scene from the propaganda newsreel he had watched a decade before. But it is also worth asking whether he felt it necessary to ensure the use of a musical work oozing with national significance in the opening. His novel had been criticised vehemently for portraying the Finnish soldier as a "grumbler," and thus undermining the image of him as unquestioningly patriotic.[19]

The endings of these two films are strikingly different, although both again employ *Finlandia* in the final sections of their soundtracks. The closing of *The Unknown Soldier* brings *Finlandia* back as a hymn, gently hummed by a male choir. Peace has come, and the soldiers climb up from the trenches, hesitating at first, and then in a more relaxed manner. Scenes follow of soldiers relaxing (with some speech over the music), and the camera pans to the surroundings, revealing first a torn and horribly disfigured landscape and homes bombed to ruins. These are followed by a shot of a healed pine forest with gentle sunshine sifting through the branches, and finally *Finlandia*'s hymn part closes with the screen going black once more. As Susanna Välimäki has charaterised the ending: "out of war and historical trauma, a bearable narrative is built … and a new dawn for Finland follows."[20]

---

[18] Sundholm, "'The Unknown Soldier'," 123.

[19] Elina Martikainen, *Kirjoitettu sota. Sotadiskursseja suomalaisessa kaunokirjallisuudessa (1917–1995)* [*Discourses on War in Finnish Literature*]. (University of Tampere: Tampere, 2013), 49, 188–9, 251–2, https://uta32-kk.lib.helsinki.fi/bitstream/handle/10024/94690/978-951-44-9283-9.pdf?sequence=1.

[20] Välimäki, *Miten sota soi?*, 86.

Survey number 84, of course, has no such option: no dawn was in sight. The final soundscape in this film is the total opposite, with *Finlandia* being practically drowned out by the din of heavy artillery that is also the visual focus of the ending. In the newsreels, riding roughshod over the national composer's work and foregrounding the sounds of war are not unheard of, but also in no way typical. My interpretation in this case is that the propaganda makers wished to point towards the importance of perseverance and boost the viewers' morale. More importantly, they also emphatically had to rule out the possibility of giving in and negotiating peace (although—or because—the voices demanding the government consider peace negotiations had grown stronger in Finland by 1944).

In the case of the propaganda newsreel, the relationship of the screen events is indexical to begin with: the viewer is expected to watch the images as records of non-staged events. Then again, mixing documentary shots with staged sections has moved the way of experiencing the fiction unfolding on screen towards an indexical reception in *The Unknown Soldier* as well. The Finnish ritualistic way of viewing the film and its being broadcast every Independence Day on Finnish TV have gradually consolidated its position: it has become the correct interpretation and the collective memory of the trauma of war. The film has been one of the most important uses of *Finlandia*, also significant in the sense that it meant that the work had "crossed ideological boundaries"[21]: it was no longer associated with White Finland only.

To conclude: there is no doubt that Sibelius's music was one of the most important defining elements of the Finnish war propaganda soundtracks in the 1940s. The influence of this collective media experience has also extended to later media contents in a powerful way. This was expressed in a striking way in a letter to the newspaper *Helsingin Sanomat* discussing whether a new version of *The Unknown Soldier* was needed: "even Sibelius' *Finlandia* now appears to have been composed for that movie"[22] (referring specifically to the adaptation of 1955). This indicates that there may be in some cases a blending together of worlds of experience: the cinematic, musical, and (partly) the historical experience

---

[21] Hannu Salmi, "Jean Sibelius and Finnish Culture—the Changing Significance of *Finlandia*," in *Sibelius 150: Lahti Sibelius Festival*, eds. Teemu Kirjonen, Taina Räty, and Hannele Eklund (Sinfonia Lahti: Lahti, 2015), 18. https://www.academia.edu/16750619/Jean_Sibelius_and_Finnish_Culture_the_changing_significance_of_Finlandia_Jean_Sibelius_ja_suomalainen_kulttuuri_Finlandian_muuttuvat_merkitykset.

[22] Sundholm, "'The Unknown Soldier'," 133.

of the nation's fight for retaining its independence have become one and the same.

According to this early stage analysis, the roles of music in the propaganda films are mainly the following. Music creates, maintains, and communicates to the viewer the intended mood of the film. In this function, the music sometimes bypasses both the visuals and the rest of the soundtrack (the spoken message and the sound effects). I hope to be able to return to this fascinating characteristic in later research. Music is also employed to transform chaos, violence, and hardship into meaningful action. One of the recurring instances of this kind is emphasising the vigorous role of the Finnish forces even when the film material—or, indeed, the war events at that time—did not convey an active image. Via the national composer's music, the propaganda makers were able to underline the noble cause of fighting. This is particularly noticeable when Sibelius' symphonies are combined with the propaganda images. Through the use of large orchestral sounds and the implied social act of a large number of musicians/citizens working together, the idea of a shared endeavour is constructed musically. In the propaganda messages, it was important to be able to communicate and locate the activity of fighting and persevering beyond individuals, on and off screen, and to inject historical significance into the fight and the sacrifice.

In the case of Sibelius, and particularly his symphonies, the propaganda films also succeeded in establishing recognisable tropes. These include associations of efficiency, perseverance, home-front motivation, gentleness, and nature scenes as inspiration for the patriotic zeal. I suspect several of these proved temporary, for several reasons. Using Sibelius' works in audio-visual media presumably narrowed after the Continuation War ended and the need for war propaganda ceased to exist. The ceded territory in Karelia became a politically sensitive issue, which meant a change in the ways of communication concerning the area, previously the home of over 11% of the Finnish population. Also, cinematic expression changed significantly during the following decades. New ways of combining sound and image were favoured by professionals in making functional communication, e.g. advertising and civic educational films. It seems, however, that whenever archival material about wartime events is used in later filmmaking or user-generated media, on YouTube for example, certain tropes prevail. Their repetition also adds a fresh layer of extra-musical meaning to the music used each time, be it by Jean Sibelius or other composers.

II

Aesthetics and Style

There are Several Ways of Setting It—Sibelius as a Reader

Gustav Djupsjöbacka

In the majority of cases, the starting point for an art song composer was a pre-existing poem. The reverse situation, creating text to pre-existing music, is also possible of course, but occurs much less often. But if poetry is born out of music, as poets say, which one came first: the word or the music? The chicken or the egg? Maybe they were born out of the same entity and, now separated, have a nostalgic desire for reunion? The melding together of words and music in art song is what semiotics calls, "an interjunction of two independent sign systems [which] creates a third, song."[1] In poetry, the writer, by playing with, combining, and confronting words, conveys something different, deeper, and vaster than the actual semantic information these words normally provide. When, as readers, we refer to reading "between the lines," this is what we actually do: out of simple words we re-establish and recreate a universe. Poetic language is fundamentally different from everyday language, and resists a precise or a univocal effect; what occurs instead is the opposite: suggestion is the essence of poetry. As Paul Verlaine put it: "Rien de plus cher que la chanson grise/ Ou l'Indécis au Précis se joint."[2]

Thanks to this rich symbolism, different readers approach the same poem and, according to their individual backgrounds and experience, concentrate on different aspects and find individual resonances. In this sense, the composer, when moved by a poem, is just one reader among others. Their reading of the poem ignites their creative fantasy going inside the sign system of music, in thematic-harmonic terms, and through the musical result of these choices emerges their interpretation of the poem. In an essay entitled "Über das Verstehen von Kunst durch Kunst," Hans Heinrich Eggebrecht wrote that:

---

[1] Kofi Agawu, "The Challenge of Semiotics," in *Rethinking Music*, eds. Nicholas Cook and Mark Everist (Oxford: Oxford University Press, 2001), 157.

[2] Paul Verlaine, "Art poétique," in *Jadis et naguère, Choix des poésies* (Paris: Léon Vanier, 1961 [1882]).

> der Hörer vollzieht nach, wie der Komponist das Gedicht kompositorisch aufgefasst hat, in welcher bestimmten Art und Weise hier Kunst durch Kunst verstanden wurde. Das Hören eines Liedes wird wird zum Verstehen eines Verstehens.[3]

The composer interprets the piece of art—the poem—by creating another piece of art—music—and these exist side-by-side, or inside each other. In this way, art song in the Schubertian sense, where vocal melody, poetry, and piano accompaniment are integrated, should really be regarded as a *Gesamtkunstwerk*. The physical expression of singer and pianist adds even further dimensions to the entity, but this aspect is beyond the scope of the present article.

When synchronised in art song, the degree of independence between these art forms becomes interesting. As Kofi Agawu suggests, "it allows us to specify ways in which words and music enhance, contradict or remain indifferent to each other."[4] Music does not describe. It never carries denotational meaning in a verbal sense; rather, it is "sonically moving forms" (*tönend bewegte Formen*), as Eduard Hanslick terms it. Even if we don't regard music as a language per se, we might still find some parallel phenomena: musical procedures that support poetic ones (or contradict them!). Whether the music is merely a supplement, only modestly underlining the poem without disturbing it, or a strongly independent statement, even challenging the poem, it nevertheless guides and directs our experience of the poem.

In this simultaneous co-existence, music's sensual character, when compared with the written, spoken, or recited word, still tends to assume the leading role in the melting pot of poetry and music. Robert Schumann wrote: "Das Gedicht soll dem Sänger wie eine Braut im Arm liegen, frei, glücklich und ganz."[5]

---

[3] Hans H. Eggebrecht, "Vertontes Gedicht. Über das Verstehen von Kunst durch Kunst," in *Dichtung und Musik*, ed. Günter Schnitzler (Stuttgart: Klett-Cotta-Verlag, 1979), 36. "The listener fulfils how the composer has grasped the poem as a composition, in which specific way art is here being understood through art. Listening to an art song becomes an understanding of an understanding." Translation by this writer.

[4] Kofi Agawu, "Theory and Practice in the Analysis of the Nineteenth-Century 'Lied'," *Music Analysis* 11 (1) (1992): 3–36.

[5] The poem should feel to the singer like a bride lying in his arms, free, happy, and completely. Robert Schumann, "Lied und Gesang," *Neue Zeitschrift für Musik*, Band V 44 (November 29, 1836).

If there is a contradiction between poetry and music, music tends to be stronger. This is what Suzanne K. Langer calls "assimilation."[6] The non-verbal quality of the music seems to get "under our skin" and even eliminates the poem. In Schumann's words: "The poem must be crushed and have its juices expressed like an orange; it must wear the music like a wreath, or yield to it like a bride."[7]

If we are used to hearing a poem sung it might sometimes be rather difficult to isolate it as such from the music, and this is bound to blur and disturb the poetic content itself, and may even rob it of its identity. If, however, we are accustomed to reading or listening to a poem we don't necessarily want to have our perception of it challenged or disturbed by music. Not every poet is delighted to have their poetic lines crushed to juice by music that is dominant. That is probably why Goethe, a well-trained reader, familiar with hearing his poems recited, did not necessarily appreciate the songs of the young Schubert (including *Gretchen am Spinnrad* and *Erlkönig*), sent to him by Schubert's friend Josef Edler von Spaun in Vienna a few years after their publication. It's plausible that the poetic order and the carefully elaborated rhythm of his texts in these songs were disturbed by the song's strange harmonies or the hammering octaves in the piano part.[8]

An art song is born from a reading—but the composer does not necessarily read or experience the poem in the same way throughout their lifetime. If they are exploring their potential, returning to the same poem in several versions, does our respect for their "final intentions" make the earlier stages of the process less valuable? Are the late, stripped-back versions of Liszt's Petrarch sonnets better at catching the essence of the poems than the grandiose, luxuriant ones of 20 years before? Studying different versions of the same poem by a composer, whether slightly or radically different, may challenge and deepen our reading of the poem as well as offer a better understanding of the characteristic disposition of the composer-reader. Schubert set Goethe's *Nur wer die Sehnsucht kennt* six times during a period of 11 years, every time highlighting different aspects, obviously never being fully satisfied.

---

[6] Susanne K. Langer, "The Principle of Assimilation," in *Feeling and Form* (New York: Charles Scribner's Sons, 1953), 152.

[7] Quoted in Eric Sams, *The Songs of Robert Schumann* (London: Faber and Faber, 1975), 3–4.

[8] Fischer-Dieskau suggests that Goethe either gave the songs to Zelter, his musical counsellor, or he simply didn't have a competent pianist available; see Dietrich Fischer-Dieskau, *Auf den Spuren der Schubert-Lieder* (Wiesbaden: F.A. Brockhaus, 1972), 82.

Sibelius also set a number of the same poems several times, indicating that the texts could be read and set in different ways. Those completed alternative versions, where the differences are significant and the works factually separate creations, were not published during his lifetime. In the *Jean Sibelius Works* edition, however, there are now alternatives of two published songs: *Säv, säv, susa* was set twice in 1900, one published as Op. 36 No. 4, while the other version was a sketch, only later identified as a setting of the same text by Fröding in Robert Keane's doctoral dissertation *The Complete Solo-Songs of Jean Sibelius* (1993).[9] *Vänskapens blomma* was set twice in 1909, as Op. 57 No. 7, and in a version that remained in manuscript. A third case, *Den första kyssen*, was published as Op. 37 No. 1 in 1900, but the alternative version was left as an unfinished sketch, which I completed for a production at YLE in the 1990s. For the complete BIS recording, Folke Gräsbeck has made a slightly different completion.[10] Neither of these two sketches has been published. In all these three cases, the two versions significantly differ from each other: they have different identities and should be regarded as separate works. The complete BIS recording also includes fragments of *Höstkväll* and *Arioso* in alternative versions, neither of which was completed. Alongside these, there are several other cases with only minor differences—mainly technical rather than conceptual—from the final ones, reflecting different stages of a compositional process. Four of these, *Soluppgång*, *Hymn to Thaïs*, *Kullervo's Lament*, and *Solitude*, are now published in the critical edition, as a few others are only described or referred to in the critical commentary. The poem "Skogsrået" ("The Wood Nymph") by Viktor Rydberg seems to have occupied Sibelius' mind over a long period. The first version was the song for solo voice and piano, and was set in 1888–9. There are three other versions (a tone poem for orchestra, a version for narrator, piano, two horns and strings, and a solo piece for piano), based on the same poem and musical material, exploring the word-music relation on a more abstract level (1893–5).

The first line of a poem might ignite a composer's imagination, and the general character of the music might then be adequate without catching every aspect of the poem. In his 1912 essay "The Relation to the Text," Arnold Schoenberg dealt with the reading of a poem, writing that he was ashamed of not having any idea of the content of the poems of the Schubert songs that he knew so well:

---

[9] See the critical commentary in *Jean Sibelius Works*, Serie VIII, vol. 4, (Wiesbaden: Breitkopf & Härtel, 2005), and Robert Keane, *The Complete Solo-Songs of Jean Sibelius* (PhD thesis, University of London, 1993).

[10] *Den första kyssen* JS 57, in *The Sibelius Edition*, Songs Vol. 7 (2008), disc 1.

> But when I had read the poems it became clear to me that I had gained absolutely nothing for the understanding of the songs thereby … On the contrary, it appeared that, without knowing the poem I had grasped the content, the real content, perhaps even more profoundly than if I had clung to the surface of the mere thoughts expressed in words.

And he continues about his own songs:

> inspired by the first words of the text I had composed many of my songs straight through without troubling myself in the slightest about the continuation of the poetic events, without even grasping them in the ecstasy of composing, and that only days later I thought of looking back just to see what was the real poetic content of my song.[11]

Schoenberg's conclusion is that he couldn't have done any greater service to the poet than letting himself be guided by his first impression, as the poetic content in its entity already exists complete in a germ. It is easily possible to disagree with this opinion. The first line is not necessarily representative of the atmosphere and content of the whole poem. We shouldn't deny the importance of the instinct and the idea of the poem embedded in the germ. There are numerous examples of compositions, though, where inspired first lines have led to musical solutions that completely overrun the spirit of the text. Let us consider this with an example from Sibelius' production: the early "Hjärtats morgon" ("Morning of the heart") Op. 13 No. 3. Here, the difference between the two sign systems makes this song difficult to handle for the performer. The Runeberg poem starts in the imperfect tense by describing the previous dark periods in the life of the poet before the appearance of love takes place in the present tense. The opening lines are:

> Darkness filled my soul
> And my poor heart was chill
> Until a kindly angel
> Lit the love in it.
> See how the sun, after the night
> Beaming, marches through the firmament
> The mist lifts, sea and land
> Lie haloed.

---

[11] Arnold Schoenberg, "The Relationship to the Text," in *Style and Idea. Selected Writings by Arnold Schoenberg*, ed. Leonard Stein (London & Boston: Faber and Faber, 1975), 144.

The overall musical form is ABAB'A. Sibelius begins the song in a driving, almost tumultuous way with repeated chords in the low register of the piano in B minor, easily associated with the darkness and coldness of the soul. For the second verse—the dawn and the emergent love—Sibelius modulates to B major. After the third verse, again in the tonic, the fourth verse (B') turns into the third-related E flat major, and the enthusiasm is expressed in a brilliant and high vocal eruption above heavy chords in the piano. In order to secure a sense of architectural balance, Sibelius now finishes as he started, in a stormy drive, almost despairing, of B minor. The music does not convey any change in the life of the poet: the dark character returns, and the piano's brutal minor chords have the last word. The music completely eliminates (assimilates) the poem here. One might argue that there is some ambiguity in the poem, namely the question left hanging in the last verse where the poet asks *why* he had to live through such heavy moments before the transformation occurred. In this *Sturm und Drang* song, however, it seems as though nothing has changed. The roaring music does not differentiate between the two different tenses of the poem. It seems that the young Sibelius, like Schoenberg, was carried away by the poem's opening line.[12]

A classical example, where intensive emotional expression in the music overruns a critical or ironic attitude in the poem, is the fourth song, "Wenn ich in deine Augen seh," of Schumann's *Dichterliebe* Op. 48. The poet describes the joys of the beloved's nearness, building up a feeling of intimacy and sincerity, but in a typical Heinesque manner the poem's last line abruptly destroys it. When the beloved declares "I love you" the poet cries bitterly "Doch wenn du sprichst 'Ich liebe dich,' so muss ich weinen bitterlich." This sudden reversal suggests that the declaration of love is a lie. Schumann's ardent, sweet, and empathic postlude dwells on and strengthens this declaration of love, rather than distancing itself from it. It is difficult not to see Schumann thus missing Heine's irony.[13] If the sweet music really was intended as an ironic inversion, this would indicate a sudden change in the musical identification from Dichter-view to beloved-view.

Different composers reading and setting the same poem give us another way of comparing variant readings of the text. Let us now pair three songs by three composers to settings by Sibelius of the same words. Most of Sibelius' songs are set to poems in Swedish, and accordingly most of the composers with the same text choices are to be found in

[12] The song was written in Vienna during a period when the young lovers had to endure the separation preceding their wedding in June 1892.

[13] Schumann, too, was composing in a love fever during his *Liedjahr* 1840.

Scandinavia, principally in Finland and Sweden. My first example is the well-known "Långsamt som kvällsskyn" ("As slowly as the evening sky"), a popular poem by Karl August Tavaststjerna (1860–98), published in 1884 in his collection *För morgonbris*. This poem, often read even at funerals, recalls the poet's memories from a summer evening (in the Finnish archipelago):

> As slowly as the evening sky drains of purple,
> above the glittering expanses of the bay,
> As gently as the breeze is lulled to sleep
> farther away than the eye can see
> As distantly as the echo that dies away
> after the last, lingering note of the island-girl's song.
> Will I forget you who once brought purple, spring breezes and music to my life.[14]

There is an early setting of this text from 1888 by Baron Reinhold Felix von Willebrand (1858–1935), a unique personality: lawyer, political representative of the gentry in the diet, magazine editor, amateur composer, gymnastics enthusiast, and activist in many different sports organisations. As a lawyer he was for some time a colleague of Sibelius' future father-in-law, Alexander Järnefelt, who was governor in Vaasa at the time of Aino's and Janne's wedding. In Aino's letters to Janne in Vienna there are several opinions of the baron.[15] Willebrand's song soon became immensely popular at weddings and funerals. In the records of the National Library in Helsinki there are notions of 124 sound documents, records, and discs of this simple song, which have been printed in 33 editions and collections. It is scarcely possible that back in Finland Sibelius could have been ignorant of this song. Written by an amateur composer for domestic music making, Willebrand's romance would have been to Goethe's taste. As in a simple song by Zelter or Reichardt, nothing disturbs the natural declamation of the singer in the middle register. The beautiful melody over the sweet syncopation in the piano part gives a pleasant, harmless character to the song. The poem as well as the music are repeated and at the end the melody is intensified by an extra leap a third upwards. No wonder this *Biedermeier* song became so popular.

---

[14] The poem translations are by Jeremy Parsons, in *Jean Sibelius Complete Songs* (2004 [1984]), Decca 476 1725.

[15] The baron was also leader of the Finnish sport delegation (!) to the Olympic Games in 1908 and 1912. For more details on his versatile activities, see an article in *Biografiskt lexikon för Finland*, www.blf.fi/artikel.php?id=3690.

When Sibelius set the poem in 1910, he completely broke with this conventional serenade, choosing to reveal the text's languor in the introduction. Above slow arpeggios on an organ point E, the hesitant dissonances almost seem to tear the soul apart, thus reminding us of an almost expressionistic dimension. These completely tonal but unresolved, almost emancipated dissonances, stretching the borders of tonality, have become a Sibelian trade mark from the idiom of the symphonies. The text declamation in slow triplets, often polyrhythmically free above a barely recognisable static harmonic progression, creates the ambiguous feeling of an unstable mindset, and of suppressed memories reaching the surface of the conscious mind. With its chain of linked images, the poem points towards its final line, but Sibelius creates a break with the pedal-point harmony, introducing a single "dividing" seventh, D. He continues with a growing, almost pathological yearning with quiet sighs in the piano part, turning it into a huge *crescendo* on heavy chords with a vocal high point (on g2) at the words "du som gav purpur" ("you who gave purple"). This strong climax, in a register hardly existent elsewhere in the song, reveals a pain light-years away from the salon atmosphere of Willebrand's setting. The vocal melody itself ends on a dissonance, c, and leaves the final cadence in E major to the piano. The powerful evocation of longing in this song is closely related to the songs in Op. 50 (*Sehnsucht*, *Aus banger Brust*) and Op. 57 (*Jag är ett träd*), as well as Op. 61 (*Fåfäng önskan*). In *Längtan heter min arvedel*, Op. 86 No. 2 the longing is reduced to a more intimate, chanson-like idiom.

My second example is "Sommarnatten" ("Summer Night"), a poem by Johan Ludvig Runeberg (1804–77), originally published in his collection *Dikter* in 1830.

Out on the peaceful forest lake
I sat the whole summer night
unthinkingly casting snares from my boat
into the billowy hordes
But a thrush sang on the shore
as if his soul were rapt away
until half-indignantly I said:
"Better for you to lay your beak
under your wing and save for the day
your notes and warbling"
But the intrepid bird was heard to reply:
"It were better for you to lay your rod aside.
If you looked about you at land and lake
perhaps you too would sing at night."
And I lifted my eyes

> Bright was the earth and bright the heavens
> and from the wave, the shore and the sky
> my girl came into my mind.
> And, as the bird in the grove had predicted
> I sang this song there and then.

The poet's fishing is disturbed by a loudly singing thrush, which brings him to realise the beauty of the surrounding nature. In Runeberg's poems the connection between pantheism and love is an often reoccurring theme. The Swedish composer Ture Rangström (1884–1947), one of his country's great song composers, published a set of 15 Runeberg poems in his cycle *Idyll* in 1917. Rangström knew the possibilities of the human voice particularly well, as he had studied singing himself. He was also an excellent writer with fine literary taste, even writing the poems to some of his songs himself.[16] "Sommarnatten" is among his best-known songs. With slow, undulating harmonies over a pedal and a syllabic, narrating melody in F sharp minor, Rangström creates the impression of a serene and beautiful lake on a summer night. The bird suddenly announces its presence in bar 11 with a signal (with passing resemblances to the motif in the middle section of another bird song, Grieg's *En svane*, Op. 25 No. 2). Through obstinate repeats it opens up the dialogue: the poet expresses his irritation in a *parlando*-like melody, now in double speed. The bird's message – open your eyes to the beauty of nature – is delivered in the first genuinely expressive melody, a descending cantilena in the parallel major key, A major. The poet's reflections appear in an intensified syllabic melody above the undulating F sharp minor harmony of the opening, now faster and gradually aiming a third higher. The conclusion is a synthesis—nature joins the poet to love and inspiration. In musical terms, the poet adapts the cantilena of the bird, thus identifying himself with the nature-love constellation. The piano concludes with a capricious twist, with perhaps a little nod from the victorious bird on the branch. The musical conception of this song hence rather closely follows the form and the text of the poem with its suggestions of serene peace, irritation, and the bird's message by means of static pedal points, a recitativo-like dialogue, the bird signal motif, and the cantilena as its basic elements.

Sibelius' *Sommarnatten* Op. 90 No. 5 was written in 1917, the same year as Rangström's song. He uses more homogeneous melodic material without letting the dramaturgy guide him as carefully as Rangström.

---

[16] The poems of the ten songs of the *Havets sånger* cycle are by the composer. For more information on Rangström, see www.gehrmans.se/en/composers/rangström_ture.

Sibelius' summer lake is significantly more vital, with swelling piano arpeggios in E flat major across a wide register, rather than the serene surface of the poem. The opening sweeping melody in broad strokes functions repeatedly as an indicator for the narrator, poet, and bird. The bird's presence is here announced only in the form of small accents in the high register as part of the static harmony in the piano part. The irritated reaction of the poet now appears in the same melody as the narrator's opening. For the bird's answer, Sibelius again recycles the melody of the opening, now modulating into the mediant key, G flat major, the piano part remaining in its static "bird-signal" mode. For the conclusion—the poet's insight into nature's beauty—Sibelius now leaves the arpeggios and creates a short but powerful incantation over broad majestic V7 chords in E flat minor. This monumental moment is suddenly interrupted by a small *parlando*-like stretto, making the connection to the beloved in the twinkle of an eye. The melody from the opening returns, now again in E flat major, and brings the song to a swift close. From the very beginning, Sibelius stresses the basic unity of the two roles, bird and poet, in broad lines. For purposes of contrast he uses the modulation to third-related keys and major-minor variants, and puts aside the personal, individual, and emotional reactions of the poet. The most dramatic part of this song is the poet's praising of nature. The sudden contrast in the connection to love contains an element of wry humour, whereas in Rangström's version the bird gets the last word.

My third example is the gorgeous Runeberg poem "Norden" ("The North") from the collection of the same name of 1830. It describes the changing of the seasons, and the eternal migration of the swans. Also here, Runeberg's connection between pantheistic feeling and idealisation of the beauty of nature is obvious:

> The leaves fall,
> the lakes freeze over—
> Migrating swans,
> sail, o sail
> sadly southward
> in search of food,
> thoughts tending homeward,
> plough other seas,
> yearning for ours.
> Then a pair of eyes
> will look up from
> the palmtree's shade and say:
> "Pining swans, what enchantment is it
> that the North holds?

When a southerner
feels longings,
those longings seek a heaven."[17]

This poem was set in 1906 by the Swedish composer Harald Fryklöf (1882–1919), mainly known for his sacred music for organ and choir. Fryklöf's production is limited, as he died at the age of only 37.[18] His setting of "Norden" is not a mainstream song like Rangström's "Sommernatten." It nevertheless shows us one that Runeberg's poems broadly inspired Swedish composers around the turn of the century. The beginning of Fryklöf's setting is a gloomy and static unison melody between singer and pianist in a somewhat B-A-C-H character, rather in sympathy with the falling autumn leaves and the freezing lakes. (It is also reminiscent of the ghostly beginning of Schubert's *Der Doppelgänger*: "Still ist die Nacht.") Through ascending fourths the melody then intensifies the sadness of the migrating swans. Fryklöf observes the change in the narrative position ("Then a pair of eyes") by gradually introducing thirds in the empty chords, at the same time also adding further expressivity and warmth in the vocal melody. Wider intervals strengthen the emotion and the climax is reached in the very last bars on the word "himmel" ("heaven"), a dramatic outburst of considerable dimensions in an otherwise rather timid atmosphere. The vocal line does not challenge but rather carefully follows the dramaturgy and declamation of the text. In most bars, the piano part simply supports the vocal line's *espressivo* without any clearly independent or complementary motifs. As in Sibelius' *Långsamt som kvällsskyn*, the change in general musical atmosphere between the modest beginning and the emotionally powerful end is huge, leaving us with a powerful echo.

Sibelius' *Norden*, Op. 90 No. 1, from 1917 is one of his most glorious songs. The large-scale form is AA'. The gloomy atmosphere at the beginning is created by a pentatonic, almost arabesque melody above syncopated chords on the piano, all within an octave with unresolved leading tones (which could also be interpreted as bitonal). As the melody develops, climbing ever higher, it simultaneously strengthens the yearning dissonances in relation to the ever-continuing, syncopated harmonies on

---

[17] The swan symbol repeatedly occurs in Runeberg's poems. Best known is "Svanen," with the swan seen both as a symbol of fidelity and as a symbol of the beauty of Finnish nature.

[18] He also set another Runeberg poem, also set by Sibelius, namely "Se'n har jag ej frågat mera." For more information on Fryklöf see *Svenskt biografiskt lexicon* at http://sok.riksarkivet.se/sbl/artikel/14524.

the piano, which all remain within the compass of an octave. In the second half (synchronised with the above-mentioned change in the poem), the melody of the voice part is repeated slightly varied, bringing the same but continually growing, unresolved and aching dissonances to greater expressive effect. As the destination and focus of the swans' longing become more explicit, the tonal development in the syncopated harmonies moves in a diatonic direction. While the vocal melody ends in the middle of a cadence, on the dominant, the piano texture takes the song to a full Wagnerian cadence.

The combination of constant inner movement with a rhythmic as well as a harmonic drive in the syncopated chords brings cohesion to the structure, never losing its sense of direction. The serene, ornamental quality of the opening melody turns into an intensively expressive vocal line, again stretching the borders of tonal magnetism. In this way the swans' longing gains obvious connotations for the reader-listener, thus conveying the basic (presumed) intention of the poet. Instead of creating a powerful climax, focusing on one expressive word, Sibelius again uses the unresolved dissonances and syncopated chords to create a vigorous drive, which takes the song to a full and satisfying ending. The composer's habit of generating abrupt endings, usually leaving the completion of the *Gestalt* to the listener,[19] is here replaced by a short postlude with a full-stop cadence. A masterpiece of economy and architecture, this song is in constant movement, testing the borders of dissonance, making full use of its scanty material.

---

[19] See, for example, *Den första kyssen*, Op. 37 No. 1; *Flickan kom ifrån sin älsklings möte*, Op. 37 No. 5; *Sehnsucht*, Op. 50 No. 2; or *Rosenlied*, Op. 50 No. 6.

THE REPRESENTATION OF EMOTIONS IN THE SONGS *VÅREN FLYKTAR HASTIGT* AND *SVARTA ROSOR*

SANNA IITTI

On Finnishness and Sibelius' compositions

A critic for the journal *Nya Pressen* claimed that a genuinely Finnish undertone characterised the songs of Jean Sibelius which had been performed at the Helsinki Music Institute on October 19, 1891.[1] It is indeed commonly thought that Jean Sibelius' songs and orchestral music capture something vital about the quality of Finnishness; I do not question this belief in reflecting on the nature of Finnish emotional life in the light of Sibelius' two songs *Våren flyktar hastigt* ("Spring Passes Swiftly"), Op. 13 No. 4, and *Svarta rosor* ("Black Roses"), Op. 36 No. 1. The fact is that that life, as regarded in the light of these songs, seems quite gloomy.

In his edited volume *Suomalaisia säveltäjiä*, Erkki Salmenhaara dates *Våren flyktar hastigt*, the fourth of the Op. 13 songs, to the year 1890, but does not indicate where the song came into being.[2] Sibelius studied composition in Vienna in 1890–91 with Robert Fuchs and Karl Goldmark. He wrote to his fiancée Aino Järnefelt from the city at the beginning of November 1890 that he had written a few songs for soprano, and that the poems' texts were by Johan Ludvig Runeberg. He stated that Runeberg's poems were more real than anything else he had read thus far.[3]

Sibelius criticised his own music and the works-in-progress, noting to Aino in a letter dated November 22, 1890 that he had abandoned all composition based on Runeberg's poems except the songs *Hjertats*

1 *Nya Pressen,* October 20, 1891.
2 *Suomalaisia säveltäjiä*, ed. Erkki Salmenhaara (Keuruu: Otava, 1994), 495.
3 *Sydämen aamu. Aino Järnefeltin ja Jean Sibeliuksen kihlausajan kirjeitä*, ed. SuviSirkku Talas (Suomalaisen kirjallisuuden seuran toimituksia 821) (Jyväskylä: Suomalaisen kirjallisuuden seura, 2001), 27.

morgon ("The Heart's Morning") and *Likhet* ("Resemblance").[4] One wonders whether *Våren flyktar hastigt* belonged among these abandoned songs. In Fabian Dahlström's work list in the *New Grove Dictionary of Music and Musicians*, *Våren flyktar hastigt* is nonetheless dated 1891, and none of the Op. 13 songs are listed under 1890.[5] According to Andrew Barnett, *Våren flyktar hastigt* was composed during Spring 1891[6] and Karl Ekman claims that the song was written in Vienna.[7] Sibelius also related in that letter that, besides music, he only thought about Aino, feeling fortunate about her affection and their engagement.[8] Three of Op. 13's seven songs were written during Sibelius' honeymoon in Lieksa in the summer of 1892: *Under strandens granar* ("Underneath the Firs along the Beach"), *Kyssens hopp* ("The Kiss's Hope"), and *Till Frigga* ("To Frigga").[9]

In my view, Op. 13 No. 4 illustrates Sibelius' developing response while residing in cosmopolitan Vienna to the issue of national identity. This meant coming to terms with what was particularly Finnish as compared to other Nordic mentalities, such as the Norwegianness represented by composers such as Grieg.

Runeberg's text had appeared in his 1830 collection *Idyll och Epigram* ("Idylls and Epigrams"). According to Huldén, the collection's principal subjects include heartache and lovesickness. The poems' form is often that of a monologue. Furthermore, in speaking about love, Runeberg often puts the words into a girl's mouth.[10]

Gestures as a Means of Emotions' Representation

I propose that gestures are the means for the representation of emotions in selected songs by Sibelius. Regarding gestures, I make a general distinction between socially performative and libidinal gestures. My general definition of gestures is that in vocal music these comprise

---

[4] Ibid., 58.

[5] Fabian Dahlstöm, "Sibelius: worklist," *New Grove Dictionary of Music and Musicians*, vol. 23, 2nd ed., ed. Stanley Sadie, Executive Editor John Tyrrell (London: Macmillan, 2001), 343.

[6] Andrew Barnett, *Sibelius* (Great Britain: Yale University Press, 2007), 64.

[7] Karl Ekman, *Jean Sibelius ja hänen elämäntyönsä*, 4th ed. (Keuruu: Otava, 1956), 131.

[8] *Sydämen aamu*, 57.

[9] Ekman, *Jean Sibelius ja hänen elämäntyönsä*, 131.

[10] Lars Huldén, "Esipuhe," in Johan Ludvig Runeberg, *Runoja II–III*, trans. Tarmo Manelius (DDR: Sahlgrenin kustannusliike Oy, 1989), 10.

particularly expressive musical moments. What is more, gestures construct gender by a performative manner, or produce structures allusive to the libido. These are often motivated by the text, which in such cases often involves a content suggestive of desire. The gestures are traceable by the study of performance practice indications or dynamic markings: these often provide clues, which stand out as more expressive than the rest of a musical texture. But it is noteworthy that the libido is always manifested either freely or alternatively can be suppressed in various ways.

Sibelius' songs present examples of both types. In *Våren flyktar hastigt*, Op. 13 No. 4, we encounter young lovers whose libido unfolds freely in a spontaneous manner. In this song, the girl first complains of the transience of spring and summer. She states "Snart, I sköna kinder, skolen I förvissna och ej knoppas mera" ("Soon, fair cheeks,/ You will fade,/ And bud no more"). The notion of one's cheeks fading is a metaphor for unwelcome ageing.

After the repetition of the song's short prelude in bb. 23–26, it is the boy's turn to speak. He consoles and encourages the girl. Moreover, he is more optimistic than her, noting that spring may swiftly pass happily just as cheeks, too, can fade. This suggests that the boy has faith in their ability to survive. As he reflects on the changing seasons, his attitude is strengthened by defiance. He claims that spring's memories warm up autumn's days. Moreover, he notes that summer's harvest will last throughout wintertime. Issues such as self-sufficiency stand out as important points in Runeberg's poem. The boy is willing to seize the moment and live for the here and now. He is not afraid of all things' fading. His final lines articulate his libidinal desire and yearning, as he declares: "Let us now just devote ourselves to loving./ Let us now just kiss."

The phrase "Let us now just devote ourselves to loving" constitutes a so-called libidinal gesture, as I have proposed above. This gesture is motivated by the poem's content, and stands out from the rest of the texture as a grandiose, operatic gesture. The phrase is particularly expressive and serves as a culmination of the preceding progression, with the long G followed by the descent via F to C in bb. 40–43.

In Op. 13 No. 4 the libido breaks free spontaneously, because the boy is sure of himself and has a great deal of belief in the future. He expresses his desire for love as a straightforward command: "let us now devote ourselves to loving."

The Danish vocalist Sigrid Wolff performed three songs by Sibelius to Runeberg's poems in October 1894 in Copenhagen. Sibelius' Finnish style was not especially warmly received: Charles Kjerulf wrote in the newspaper *Politiken*, particularly with regard to *Under strandens granar*, that the songs were clumsy and tasteless, and lacked any natural grace. But the overview was nevertheless positive, since Kjerulf observed that *Jägargossen* ("The Hunter's Lad") displayed a "fine and original line, and a particularly beautiful atmosphere in the two final stanzas." According to Kjerulf, Sibelius was a talented composer.[11]

Symbolism in *Svarta rosor*, Op. 36 No. 1

Let us now turn to *Svarta rosor*, Op. 36 No. 1. This song was written to a poem by the Swedish poet and painter Ernst Josephson. With respect to the song's symbolism, one infers that roses are the symbol of romantic love. Indeed, black roses are the poem's central metaphor. This particular colour, black, leads one to suspect that disappointment in love is the reason for the speaker's sorrow, since black is the colour of mourning. The flowers of the rose tree that grows within the speaker's heart are as red as blood and as white as death, it is related. White as the colour of death alludes to love's death, or that of the beloved. The libido is thus denied, being suppressed by the overpowering sense of mourning.

The song involves a dialogue: the first speaker addresses a second by asking why he or she is sad, when they are usually happy. The second speaker replies that they are no happier when the first considers them to be joyful.

The phrases that stand out gesturally are distinguished by the change of tempo: a switch to *Lento* in bb. 10 and 20, and to *Largamente* in b. 32. In the first two cases, the phrase is followed by a return to the original *commodo*-tempo, whereas the phrase that starts *Largamente* leads to the song's ending. All these phrases have the text "for sorrow's roses are as black as night." This gloomy remark is in practice a declaration of the libido's death.

Harmut Krones observes that the harmony of b. 10 works in the manner of a Neapolitan chord. It seems motivated by the poem's death symbolism, induced by the image of black roses. What is more, this device originates in Sibelius' employment of a Viennese harmonic convention; accordingly, Krones describes the song as one that employs a Schubertian manner.[12]

---

[11] Erik Tawastjerna, *Jean Sibelius*, vol. 2, 2nd ed. (Keuruu: Otava, 1989 [1967]), 53; *Nya Pressen*, October 28, 1894.

[12] Hartmut Krones, "Traditionelle 'Wiener' Semantik im Liedschaffen von Jean Sibelius," *Jean Sibelius und Wien*, ed. Hartmut Krones (Wiener Schriften zur

The two *Lento* gestures stand out owing to the accentuated keyboard part, which is marked *pianissimo*, and also by the cessation of the semiquaver pattern which has hitherto been predominant. But the gesture which comprises the song's final phrase is characterised by a *fortissimo* dynamic level and by heavy chords in the accompaniment: the observation about black roses is now being shouted aloud and constitutes the song's climax.

One can determine the impact of Symbolism in Josephson's poem about black roses. Besides being an artist, Josephson was also a poet, and *Svarta rosor* had appeared in the 1880s as part of a collection under the same title. Sibelius' setting of the poem dates from the year 1899, and came into being at the time of heavy political oppression by Russia. According to Andrew Barnett, "This setting of words by the poet Ernst Josephson was sketched in Helsinki in April [of 1899] but seems to have been completed in Kerava a few months later."[13] Sibelius restates the poem faithfully in the song: Josephson's text is not altered in any way.

Nordic Emotional Life in the Light of Opp. 13 No. 4 and 36 No. 1

As it is regarded in the light of both Op. 13 No. 4 and Op. 36 No. 1 that Nordic emotional life seems quite gloomy. The girl in Op. 13 No. 4 perhaps fears the loss of her beauty or her youth, whereas the second speaker in Op. 36 No. 1 is in a deep depression. Sadness prevails in both cases. *Svarta rosor* presents a tragic character, whose yearning for love has been repressed. The speaker's loved one is either absent or dead.

Cecil Gray felt that with Sibelius' music, "the North becomes fully articulate for the first time in the history of music." He even believed that "such things as 'Kullervo' and 'En saga' … could not possibly have been written by a composer of any southern race."[14] Although these comments are nothing more than myth making, one may nevertheless reflect on the qualities in these songs that suggest the North's musical articulation. The qualities in Op. 13 No. 4 one might claim to be Finnish, or more generally Nordic, entail simplicity as well as transparency and lightness, a spirit that prevails in the song's ending on the phrase "låt oss nu blott kyssas." This

Stilkunde und Aufführungspraxis, Sonderband 4) (Wien, Köln, Weimar: Böhlau-Verlag, 2003), 153.

[13] Barnett, *Sibelius*, 127.

[14] Cecil Gray, *Sibelius* (London: Oxford University Press and Humphrey Milford, 1931), 181–2.

phrase may constitute yet another libidinal gesture, although it is less emphasised than the preceding phrase "låt oss nu blott älska." But the reference to kissing or erotic love bestows a libidinal status upon the phrase.

Gustav Djupsjöbacka observes that literature had been an important source of inspiration for Sibelius ever since his early youth. Moreover, Johan Ludvig Runeberg became for Sibelius what Goethe had become for Schubert: an inspirational source that liberated his creativity. But Sibelius nevertheless claimed, "I am not a literary composer. In my opinion, music starts where the words end ... My songs may be performed without words. They are not as dependent of the poem as the songs of some other composers."[15]

Djupsjöbacka continues by pointing out that he believes that Sibelius intended the boy's operatic outburst ("let us now love") at the end of *Våren flyktar hastigt* to be a parodic rather than a sincere declaration of love.[16] However, there is no need to understand this phrase as a parody: although the gesture may seem somewhat exaggerated, it makes sense when considered as an outburst of the libido.

Cecil Gray noted that songs represent an important side of Sibelius' creative activity, but that these are curiously uneven: "within each opus number admirable examples are found side by side with others markedly inferior."[17] *Svarta rosor* at least belongs among Sibelius' finest and best-loved songs, and those of Op. 13 are all genuinely original and attractive.

Sibelius' own love life perhaps provides a point of comparison for his song composition. At the end of 1890 he lived in Vienna and was devoted to his fiancée Aino Järnefelt. Having read Juhani Aho's novel *Yksin* ("Alone"), in which she is described, he claimed that he wanted to challenge Aho to a duel. He wrote that he was determined to meet Aho with a brace of pistols and allow fate to decide which of them would be the lucky one, since Aho was also in love with Aino. Sibelius nonetheless realised that Aino might regard such behaviour as foolish.[18]

Sibelius' letters during his engagement period suggest that he attempted to ensure Aino's love for him at all costs, and that he felt that

---

[15] Cited in Gustav Djupsjöbacka, "Sibelius and his Poets," *Sibelius in the Old and New World. Aspects of His Music, Its Interpretation and Reception*, eds. Timothy L. Jackson, Veijo Murtomäki, Colin Davis, and Timo Virtanen (Interdisziplinäre Studien zur Musik, eds. Tomi Mäkelä and Tobias R. Klein, vol. 6) (Frankfurt am Main: Peter Lang, 2010), 16.

[16] Ibid.

[17] Gray, *Sibelius*, 119.

[18] *Sydämen aamu* , 113.

their marriage would be beneficial for his career. Accordingly, Sibelius was jealous of Aho, realising that Aho was a skilled artist whom Finland needed.[19]

Sibelius' vivid imagination enabled him to describe varying emotions through his song composition. The figure of one's beloved remains distant throughout Op. 13 and appears most concretely through the dialogue presented by Op. 13 No. 4. Sibelius' sensitivity to poetry is equally apparent in *Svarta rosor*, a song which testifies to his dramatic abilities. The prominent visual imagery of the song—black as the colour of mourning, white as the colour of death, and red as the colour of blood—amounts to a form of symbolism, which builds on one's knowing that red roses are the symbol of romantic love. Karl Ekman speaks of this song's barely suppressed passion.[20] The fact that red alludes to blood instead of red roses and romantic love motivates the song's sense of an internal struggle. The final outburst, "Ty sorgen har nattsvarta rosor" ("For sorrow has night-black roses") concludes the song brilliantly, aptly transmitting a sense of tragedy.

Why, then, should one pay attention to musical gestures in dealing with Sibelius' songs? I propose that this would render new insights in the composer's songs that employ a declamatory style. The study of gestures would open up a new perspective upon these songs alongside the scrutiny of motivic work.

---

[19] Ibid., 114.

[20] Ekman, *Jean Sibelius ja hänen elämäntyönsä*, 186.

SIBELIUS AND SYMBOLIST PAINTINGS

TUIJA WICKLUND

When we talk about the impacts and impulses Sibelius received from the outside, we tend to talk about other composers' music. I would like to point out some visual impacts instead.

In addition to music, Sibelius was always very interested in visual arts and sculpture. As a boy, he made an effort to combine music and sculpture into a new form of art, as he later mentioned to his fiancée Aino Järnefelt in a letter. Unfortunately, he did not explain this experiment any further and his wording reveals that Aino already knew about his idea. No other mentions have currently been found, so it seems we will never know what this combination was about. Sibelius' experiment did not succeed and eventually he chose music as his means of artistic expression. In Sibelius' writings, not many sculptures are mentioned, but many painters —many of which were his close friends—and paintings are. In the following, I will study the encounter with one of the painters in particular whom Sibelius got to know quite early in his career and who undoubtedly affected him, namely the symbolist painter Arnold Böcklin.

The Swiss painter Arnold Böcklin was born in Basel in 1927 (see Fig. 1). He studied at the Düsseldorf Academy and was first associated with the Düsseldorf School of landscape painting. He continued his studies in Antwerp, Brussels, and Paris, and, in addition, lived in various other cities including Rome, Munich, Basel, and Florence.

Böcklin's main interest was painting, but he also carved stone masks.[1] In addition, he was keenly interested in flying, and believed it would be possible for human beings to fly like birds. He studied the matter thoroughly in the 1880s and made several attempts himself: some of these attempts were sketched by his son Carlo. Böcklin went as far as to draw plans for a flying machine working under manual power, and he presented

[1] See the onlinecollection at sammlungonline.kunstmuseumbasel.ch/eMuseumPlus.

them to the German Association for the Promotion of Aeronautics in 1887.[2]

At the end of the nineteenth century, symbolism was a new and fashionable trend in Europe. The symbolists took subjects from dreams, mysticism, myths and legends, and the human subconscious. These ideas and topics were freely mixed and moulded. Symbolists sought to enhance their expression by simplifying forms and colours, and highlighting contours.

Böcklin was highly esteemed, and regarded as the leading symbolist painter. In 1897, Max Lehrs wrote: "The 15th [century] gave us *Leonardo*, the 16th *Albrecht Dürer*, the 17th the great *Rembrandt*. In the 18th century it is difficult to find an equivalent name, —while the 19th gave us *Arnold Böcklin*."[3] Böcklin was also appreciated in Sweden, where he had been elected a member of the Academy of Arts in 1891. *Die Toteninsel* (*The Isle of the Dead*) is the work through which Böcklin is perhaps best known (see Fig. 2). He made five versions of the work, painted between 1880 and 1886.

Böcklin's paintings inspired several late-Romantic composers. Felix Weingartner, whom Sibelius also knew, composed a symphonic poem *Das Gefilde der Seligen* in 1894–6, titled after Böcklin's painting. Hans Huber's Second Symphony, dating from 1900, was entitled *Böcklin-Sinfonie*. Four composers wrote a symphonic poem entitled *Die Toteninsel*: Andreas Hallén in 1899, Sergei Rachmaninov and Heinrich Schulz-Beuthen in 1909, and Prince Joachim of Prussia in 1913. Rachmaninov was also inspired by Böcklin's painting *Die Heimkehr* when writing his Prelude in B minor in 1910 (Op. 32 No. 10). In 1913, Max Reger composed a set of Four Tone Poems after Böcklin (*Der geigende Eremit*, *Im Spiel der Wellen*, *Toteninsel*, and *Bacchanale*). Furthermore, in 1904 Otto Weisert designed an Art Nouveau typeface and named it "Arnold Böcklin" in his honour.

---

[2] See Ferdinand Runkel and Carlo Böcklin (eds.), *Neben meiner Kunst. Flugstudien, Briefe und Persönliches von und über Arnold Böcklin* (Berlin: Vita, Deutsches Verlagshaus, 1909).

[3] "Das fünfzehnte schenkte uns einen Lionardo, das sechzehnte Albrecht Dürer, das siebzehnte den grossen Rembrandt. Für das achtzehnte sind wir schon in Verlegenheit, einen Namen von ebenbürtigem Klange zu nennen, —und das neunzehnte gab uns Arnold Böcklin." Cited in Salme Sarajas-Korte, *Suomen varhaissymbolismi ja sen lähteet: Tutkielma Suomen maalaustaiteesta 1891–1895* (Helsinki: Otava, 1966), 297. Originally in Max Lehrs, *Arnold Böcklin. Ein Leitfaden zum Verständnis seiner Kunst* (München, 1897), 14–15.

Fig. 1. Arnold Böcklin, *Selbstbildnis mit fiedelndem Tod* (detail), 75 × 61 cm, oil on canvas (1872), Alte Nationalgalerie, Staatliche Museen zu Berlin. Photo Tuija Wicklund.

Fig. 2. Arnold Böcklin, *Toteninsel*, 80.7 × 150 cm, oil on panel (1886), Museum der bildenden Künste, Leipzig. Photo Tuija Wicklund.

Symbolism in Finland

Symbolism was known to Finns as well; it landed in Finland at the turn of the 1890s and flourished particularly during that decade. The first symbolist paintings were displayed in the exhibition of Suomen Taiteilijat (Artists in Finland) in 1891 (for example, "Self-portrait" and "Portrait of a Breton Lady" by Magnus Enckell [1870–1925]). In November the writer Kasimir Leino gave a lecture on symbolism, which was also discussed in newspaper reviews of the art exhibitions in Helsinki. Leino's lecture was also published. He wrote:

> The symbolists do not seek feelings but rather atmospheres, states of mind. To feel, to want, to act is of minor value; the moods created by the nerve system are everything. Therefore, they do not want to give life and make visible the object they are describing; it is said only to hinder the getting to the right state of mind. In the first place, one must try to win the readers by suggestion … What is art going to become like in the future is hard to say. But we can be sure that it really will take into account the symbolists' demands of spirituality and signification.[4]

The first Finnish symbolist paintings are considered to be *Tuonelan matkalla* ("On the Way to Tuonela," dating from as early as 1888; see Fig. 3) and *Mäntykoski* (1892) by Axel Gallén (1865–1931), as well as his *Satu* (or "Sibelius as the composer of En saga") (see Fig. 4). In 1894 he also painted *Tuonelan virta* ("The River of Tuonela"), *Symposion*, *Conceptio artis*, and *Ad astra*.[5] Gallén had acquainted himself with symbolism while studying in Paris in 1884–9 and was a key figure in introducing it to Finland. Other Finnish artists who painted symbolist works include

---

[4] See Sarajas-Korte (1966, 7–9). Leino's lecture was published in *Valvoja* (1892), 25–41; his focus is on literature. "Symbolistit eivät etsi tunteita, vaan tunnelmia, mielialoja. Tunteminen, tahtominen, toiminta on vähäarvoista; hermoston synnyttämät mielialat ovat kaikki. Tämän vuoksi ei tahdokaan saada eläväksi ja kaikille näkyväksi sitä, mitä kuvataan; se vain muka estää joutumasta oikeaan mielentilaan. Etupäässä täytyy koettaa suggestioonin avulla voittaa lukijat … Minkälaiseksi tulevaisuuden taide on muodostuva, sitä lienee vaikea sanoa. Vaan että se todella on ottava huomioon symbolistein vaatimukset henkisyydestä ja sisällyksestä, siitä voitanee olla varmat."

[5] Interestingly, Gallén painted two works at Mäntykoski rapids, which are reminiscent of Böcklin. *Mäntykoski* itself is a vertical depiction of the rapids, falling from a cliff with five golden strings. The other painting portrays Gallén's wife standing on the left side of the waterfall. See *Mäntykoski* at www.wikiart.org/en/akseli-gallen-kallela/m-ntykoski-waterfall-1893. Gallén's other paintings can be seen at http://kokoelmat.fng.fi/app?lang=en&si.

Magnus Enckell, Väinö Blomstedt, Hugo Simberg, Pekka Halonen, and Eero Järnefelt, as well as Oscar Parviainen later on, all known to Sibelius personally.

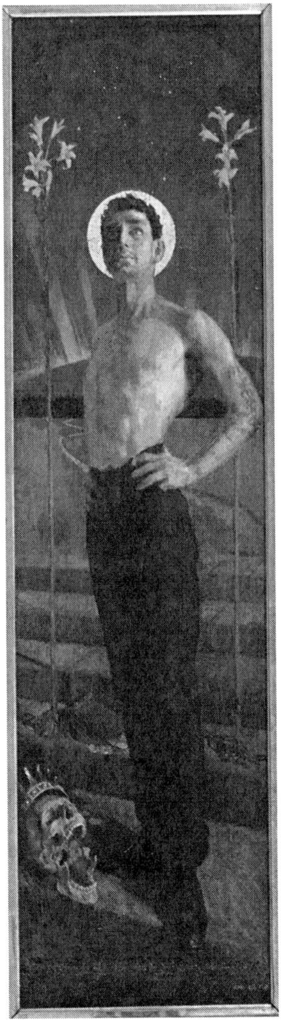

Fig. 3. Axel Gallén, *Tuonelan matkalla*, 138 × 39.5 cm, oil on canvas, (1888–94), Gösta Serlachiuksen taidesäätiö, Mänttä. Photo Studio Koivunen / Jussi Koivunen (2016).

Fig. 4. Axel Gallén, *Satu* (*Sibelius Sadun säveltäjänä*), 21.5 × 29 and 32 × 16.5 cm, watercolour on paper (1894), Ainolasäätiö. Photo Tuija Wicklund.

Sibelius and Symbolism

As mentioned above, Sibelius was interested in the visual arts and had close friends in those circles. His enthusiasm was perhaps partly due to the fact that he was also a synaesthetic; that is, he saw sounds as colours and heard colours as sounds. He eagerly visited art galleries during his trips abroad, the first time while studying in Berlin in 1889–90 and Vienna in 1890–1. There he surely acquainted himself with the then-fashionable symbolism, which probably appealed to him with its mysterious subjects drawn from myths and nature: topics that enthralled him throughout his life.

In Berlin, Böcklin's *Meeresbrandung* (*The Breakers*, see Fig. 5), *Ackerfluren im Vorfrühling* (*Farmland in Early Spring*), *Der geigende Eremit* (*Hermit Playing the Violin*), and *Diana von Faunen belauscht* (*Sleeping Diana Watched by Two Fauns*) were exhibited at the art museum. Obviously, Sibelius may have seen other paintings too, but no documents indicate whether this was the case. Sibelius also visited Leipzig for a week in 1889–90 with his friends the pianist Ferruccio Busoni (1866–1924) and author Adolf Paul (1863–1943), where he may have visited the art museum and seen Böcklin's *Frühlingshymne* (*Spring Hymn*, see Fig. 6) and another version of *Die Toteninsel*.

From Vienna, Sibelius wrote to Aino, recording that he had visited the museum and seen among other things a painting *Lautenschlägerin* (*The Female Lutenist*, 1882) by Friedrich von Kaulbach. Sibelius liked the painting because the "girl with black hair and eyebrows with languishing eyes and mouth" reminded him of Aino.[6] Also in Vienna, Böcklin's *Meeresidylle* (*Sea Idyll*) was among the paintings on display.

Although Böcklin is often mentioned in connection with Sibelius, the only time Sibelius himself spoke about Böcklin was in 1892 while composing *En saga*. In a letter to Adolf Paul he wrote: "I have been thinking about Böcklin's paintings. He paints too clear air, too white swans, too blue sea, and so forth."[7] The reference to swans is revealing because Böcklin has swans in only two paintings: *Die Gefilde der Seligen* (*The Elysian Fields*, 1878) and the ten-years-older *Lebensinsel* (*Island of Life*, 1888). Although titled independently, these are sister works. *Die Gefilde der Seligen* has been in the Nationalgalerie Berlin ever since its completion, and therefore it is certain that Sibelius saw it during his stay in 1889–90. The painting is quite large (1.7 × 2.5 metres) and it is easy to understand the impact it made. The painting disappeared in 1945 and has not yet been found, but the later work, *Lebensinsel* (see Fig. 7), was purchased by the Kunstmuseum Basel from a private owner.[8]

Sibelius' brother-in-law, the painter Eero Järnefelt, saw an art exhibition in Berlin in late 1894, and wrote that "*Die Gefilde* is quite excellent. Particularly the landscape with its colouring gives the painting a splendid appeal." He described Böcklin's art as containing "such healthy worldliness, which celebrates the magnificence of nature. It includes healthy optimism, which today is so rare … He [Böcklin] has got that joy

---

[6] Sibelius to Aino on October 29, 1890 (National Archives, Sibelius Family Archive, box 94): "mustatukkainen ja mustakulmainen neito, jolla on kaihoisat silmät ja—suu."

[7] Sibelius to Paul on December 10, 1892 (National Library of Finland, Coll. 206.62.1): "Jag har tänkt på Böcklins taflor. Han målar ju den för klar luft, för hvita svanar, för blått haf med m." For more details about *En saga* (*Satu*) see Tuija Wicklund, *Jean Sibelius's* En saga *and Its Two Versions: Genesis, Reception, Edition, and Form* (Helsinki: Unigrafia, 2014).

[8] For details on Böcklin's paintings see Rolf Andree, *Arnold Böcklin: Die Gemälde*. Mit Beiträgen von Alfred Berner, Giorgio de Chirico, Hans Holenweg, Hermann Kühn, Winfried Ranke, und Georg Schmidt (München: Prestel-Verlag, 1977).

of life and humour and above all, he is not 'grave'."[9] Eero also wrote to his mother and sent greetings to Sibelius: "tell Janne that now for the first time I have seen Böcklin and am completely stupefied and besotted. It is something you only see in dreams."[10]

Axel Gallén, inspired by Sibelius' symphonic poem *En saga*, painted an aquarelle *Satu* (or *Sibelius as the Composer of En saga*, see Fig. 4).[11] Both the portrait and the landscape appeared in an exhibition in the spring of 1894 in Helsinki. According to critics, the portrait of Sibelius was "one of the very best items in the exhibition," and successfully depicted Sibelius deep in thought. The landscape, said to depict Sibelius' thoughts, caused confusion. Viewers found it on the one hand odd and even amusing, and on the other quite agreeable: "This mishmash, however, gives a splendid, beautifully coloured area, and thereby affects [the viewer] very pleasantly."[12] Gallén may have discussed *En saga* and the programmatic ideas behind it with Sibelius; after all, they spent time in conversations with other artists interested in symbolism at that point. However, no currently known document indicates whether Sibelius drew an analogy

---

[9] According to Ludwig Wennervirta, *Eero Järnefelt ja hänen aikansa 1836–1937* (Helsinki: Otava, 1950), 198, 200. "Die Gefielde pitää aivan mainiona. Hän sanoo että varsinkin maisema ja sen väritys antaa sille "erinomaisen viehätyksen … Tuollaista tervettä maailmallisuutta, joka jubileeraa luonnon ihanuutta. Siinä on tervettä optimismia, joka on nykyään niin harvinaista … Hänessä on elämäniloa ja huumoria ja ennen kaikkea hän ei ole 'grave'."

[10] Eero to Elisabeth Järnefelt in November 1894 (NA, Järnefelt Family Archive): "sano Jannelle, että minä ensi kertaa nyt olen nähnyt Böcklini'ä ja olen aivan lyöty ja ihastunut. Se on semmosta, jota vaan unissaan näkee."

[11] The painting was also mentioned in 1935 when the early version of *En saga* resurfaced and was performed again (*Helsingin Sanomat* of April 15, 1935). The portrait is quite similar to the one that appears later in 1894 in the *Symposion* painting. As Nina Kokkinen, "Taiteilija vihittynä mestarina," in *Ota sielusi täyteen! Tutkimuksellisia polkuja Akseli Gallen-Kallelan taiteeseen*, ed. Gallen-Kallelan Museo, (Porvoo: Bookwell, 2011), 46–59, has suggested, Gallén's painting could be seen in the light of theosophy, according to which people should aim to develop their senses and reach for more spiritual knowledge (divine wisdom), which masters or prophets are capable of achieving. Interestingly, only a master is able to see a salamander, which is ascribed an affinity with (elemental) fire and is also connected with creativity and inspiration. The transcendental landscape in Gallén's painting (with the salamander, among other things) depicts something that can only be seen by such a master—in this case Sibelius.

[12] "ett af utställningens allra förnämligaste nummer" pseudonym F. [Karl Flodin] in *Hufvudstadsbladet* of May 6, 1894; "tämä sekasotku antaa kumminkin erinomaisen kaunisvärisen pinta-alan ja vaikuttaa semmoisena hyvin miellyttävästi," A. J. [Armas Järnefelt] in *Uusi Suometar*, April 29, 1894.

between the painting and his music.[13] (As a note I might add that at least the colour red sounded as C major to Sibelius, corresponding to the main key C in the early version of *En saga*.) Gallén gave the painting to Sibelius who kept it hanging on his wall; presently, it rests in the library at Ainola.

Sibelius mentioned Böcklin in connection with *En saga* to some of his friends, but he may have even mentioned it publicly. At least the critic Erik Furuhjelm mentioned Böcklin's art in a magazine article in 1905: "That the composition as early as its first performance captured listeners' minds is due in the first place to the emotional intensity related to Böcklin's art … the scenes that 'En saga' unfolds before the imagination are blood-red, feverishly hot."[14] Of course, this description may have been influenced by Gallén's painting, which was exhibited in 1894 only one year after the premiere of *En saga*.

[13] Janne Gallen-Kallela-Sirén, *Minä palaan jalanjäljilleni: Akseli Gallen-Kallelan elämä ja taide* (Helsinki: Otava, 2001), 198, writes that Sibelius, "however, did not find the landscape a suitable symbol for his own *En saga*" ("ei kuitenkaan pitänyt maisemaa sopivana vertauskuvana omalle *Sadulleen*").

[14] Erik Furuhjelm, "Sibelius' tondikt 'En saga'. Musikalisk analys." *Finsk musikrevy*, Vol. 1 (1905), 13–17. "Att tonverket dock redan vid sitt första utförande fjättrade åhörarnes sinnen beror väl i främsta rummet på den med Böcklins konst besläktade känslointensiteten … Blodröda, feberheta äro de scener, som i 'En saga' upprullas för fantasin."

Fig. 5. Arnold Böcklin, *Meeresbrandung*, 121 × 82 cm, oil on panel (1879), Alte Nationalgalerie, Staatliche Museen zu Berlin. Photo Tuija Wicklund.

Fig. 6. Arnold Böcklin, *Frühlingshymne*, 125 × 97 cm, oil on panel (1888), Museum der bildenden Künste, Leipzig. Photo Tuija Wicklund.

Fig. 7. Arnold Böcklin, *Lebensinsel*, 93 × 140 cm, oil on panel (1888), Kunstmuseum Basel. Photo Kunstmuseum Basel / Martin P. Bühler.

In summer 1894, Sibelius travelled to Bayreuth and Munich. On the way he wrote to Aino, recording that, "I am so happy to be able to see paintings in Munich and especially those by [Franz von] Stuck, whose paintings Erik [Eero Järnefelt] has as pictures."[15] He visited the annual international art exhibitions with his brother-in-law Armas Järnefelt, who also reported on the exhibitions in three articles in a Finnish newspaper. Two exhibitions were held: "The other, big one, is older, from which the other one has only recently separated. The latter is called 'Secession'."[16] All in all, the exhibitions included about two thousand items, of which about 1,200 were oil paintings. In his newspaper articles, Armas listed some of the works. These include those whose painters were famous and possibly known in Finland too, and on the other hand those he himself felt attracted to. They saw Böcklin's paintings, including at least an unspecified self-

[15] Sibelius to Aino, July 23, 1894 (NA, SFA, box 94): "Iloitsen niin saada nähdä Munchenissa tauluja ja erittäin ne Stuck'in joista Erikillä on kuvat."

[16] *Uusi Suometar*, September 13, 1894: "Toinen, suuri, on wanhempi, josta toinen wasta tuonnoin on eronnut, muodostaen jonkunlaisen oppositsioonin edelliselle. Jälkimmäinen on nimeltään 'Secession'." For the other articles dated October 4 and 15, 1894 see http://digi.kansalliskirjasto.fi/sanomalehti/search?language=en.

portrait, *Triton und Nereide* (*Triton and the Naiads*), *Teutonenkampf* (*Teuton's Fight*), *Kreuzabnahme* (*The Deposition from the Cross*, see Fig. 8), *Schlafende Diana von Faunen belauscht* (see Fig. 9), *Nymphe von Waldteufel überrascht* (*Nymph Surprised by a Wood Devil*), and *Willa am Meer* (*Villa by the Sea*). Also, one work by Stuck appeared in Munich (see Fig. 10, *The Sin*).

Sibelius was enthusiastic and reported to Aino: "It is very nice to see all the paintings here. The collections are huge. The other arts affect me more than other composers' music."[17] Later, he added: "I have been looking at the paintings and been excited, I have criticised and thanked. We have debated with Armas. That's very good."[18]

After returning from Munich, Sibelius described at least one other Böcklin painting to Magnus Enckell, who was to leave for Italy in October 1894. After seeing the painting himself, Enckell wrote to their mutual friend Yrjö Hirn: "Boecklin; it really was something I did not expect. His 'Vita somnium breve' was exactly the way Sibelius described Boecklin to me. It was a joy, but it rather makes a melancholy impression"[19] (see Fig. 11).

---

[17] Sibelius to Aino on July 28, 1894 (NA, SFA, box 94): "Hyvin hauska on katsella tauluja täällä. Täällä on suuria kokoelmia. Minuun vaikuttavat muut taiteet enemmän kun muitten musiikki."

[18] Sibelius to Aino on August 17, 1894 (NA, SFA, box 94): "Tauluja olen ollut katsomassa ja olen ollut innoissani, haukkunut ja kiitellyt. Olemme Armaan kanssa väitelleet. Se on hyvin hyvä."

[19] A letter to Yrjö Hirn, dated October 28, 1894 in Milan (NLF, Coll. 75.89): "Boecklin; det var verkligen något som jag ej väntat mig. Hans 'vita somnium breve' det var alldeles så som Sibelius beskrifvit Boecklin för mig. Det var glädje men som snarare verkar melankoli." Enckell also describes the meeting with Sibelius in a letter to his mother on October 5, 1894 (NLF, Coll. 471).

Fig. 8. Arnold Böcklin, *Kreuzabnahme*, 164 × 250 cm, tempera on panel (1879), Alte Nationalgalerie, Staatliche Museen zu Berlin. Photo Tuija Wicklund.

Fig. 9. Arnold Böcklin, *Schlafende Diana von Faunen belauscht*, 77 × 105 cm, oil on canvas (1877), Düsseldorf, Stiftung Museum Kunstpalast. Photo bpk / Lutz Braun.

Fig. 10. Franz von Stuck, *Die Sünde*, 95.5 × 59.5 cm, oil on canvas (1893), Neue Pinakothek, München. Photo Tuija Wicklund.

One further "meeting," so-to-speak, between Sibelius and Böcklin was documented in Aino's letter. When Sibelius travelled to Italy with his family in January 1901 they stopped in Basel. Aino described their stay in a letter to his brother Kasper:

> We first travelled through Germany to Basel. We stayed there for a while and it was very interesting. The style there is very much Swiss. All the buildings in an old style. In the evening, we saw a torchlight procession organised by students to honour the memory of the just deceased Böcklin. We also saw many paintings by Böcklin in the museum. You see, he was born in Basel.[20]

At least these paintings were in Basel at that time: *Vita somnium breve*, *Der heilige Hein* (*The Sacred Grove*, see Fig. 12), *Selbstbildnis*, *Kentaurenkampf* (*Battle of the Centaurs*), *Odysseus und Kalypso*, *Medusa*, *Das Spiel der Nereïden* (*Naiads at Play*, see Fig. 13), and *Tannen im Schnee* (*Fir Trees in Snow*). The collection includes many more, as is currently at over 120 items.

Before closing, I would like to discuss one more picture, a drawing related to Sibelius (see Fig. 14). The moonlight landscape with symbolist traits was first mentioned by Harold E. Johnson in 1959.[21] He describes it as "a pencil drawing (about 1887) to accompany a quartet." The G minor Quartet is for violin, cello, piano, and harmonium; in the worklist it appears as JS 158.

Copies of the parts and the drawing appear in the Sibelius Museum. When the copies were made at the turn of the 1960s, John Rosas attached a note saying that Sibelius composed the quartet "in his boyhood" for Israel Sucksdorff, "Uncle Isu," to whom the work was also dedicated.[22] It was played at the Sucksdorff's in Loviisa. Johnson's dating "about 1887" is probably quite accurate, because Sibelius had already begun his composition studies and visited Loviisa early in that year. It cannot date from much later because Uncle Isu died in March 1888.

---

[20] Böcklin died on January 16, 1901. Aino to Kasper on February 14, 1901 from Rapallo, Italy (NA, SFA, box 117). "Matkustimme ensin läpi Saksan Baseliin. Siellä vähän viivyimme, ja oli se hyvin intressantia. Siellä on tyyli jo hyvin schweitziläinen. Kaikki rakennukset vanhan aikuiset. Näimme siellä illalla soihtukulkueen, jonka ylioppilaat olivat panneet toimeen vasta kuolleen Böcklinin kunniaksi. Myöskin näimme siellä museossa monta Böcklinin taulua. Hän oli näet Baselista syntyisin."

[21] Harold E. Johnson, *Jean Sibelius* (New York: Knopf, 1959).

[22] "Komposition är skriven i pojkår." Sibelius Museum Collection.

In 1979 a law firm contacted the Sibelius Museum asking for a cost estimation of the original manuscript, which had gone missing (it remains lost). In this letter the drawing was said to originate from Sibelius' hand, but is described as a felt-tip pen drawing. Johnson's mention of pencil is more plausible, or else it might even be a charcoal sketch. Thus, there are discrepancies between the different sources, which is understandable while the latest letter is about fourth- or fifth-hand information.

The question that remains is: is this drawing really by Sibelius, or by someone else and only attached to the autograph? I am not convinced that Sibelius is the artist. This drawing does not appear on the music pages, but is a separate leaf, for some reason attached to the music, and is unsigned. Moreover, the drawing suggests an experienced hand and artistic talent. If Sibelius had been that good, we surely would know more his drawings. The style in Sibelius' drawings (mostly in manuscripts) is, however, quite different. Fig. 15 shows an undated drawing definitely by Sibelius. Judging from the subject—mermaids and other creatures lurking in the waves as well as the *Kalevala*-based figure in the sky with kantele—it could date from the 1890s.

I suspect that the 1887 illustration was drawn by someone in Loviisa. Perhaps the drawing already existed and Sibelius found it suitable for depicting his composition. Or maybe someone drew it based on Sibelius' composition or was inspired by it. The matter remains unclear at the moment.

Be that as it may, it is clear that the visual arts and particularly symbolism fascinated Sibelius and inspired his vivid imagination. These impulses surely affected his music during the 1890s, in works like *En saga*, *Skogsrået*, *Lemminkäinen in Tuonela*, and the *Swan of Tuonela*. Other *Kalevala*-based works can also be seen in a symbolist light. Even after the turn of the century, although the number of abstract pieces including symphonies and other genre-based works increased, Sibelius continued to compose works that drew upon symbolist subjects. These include, for example, *Malinconia* in 1900, the music to Arvid Järnefelt's symbolist play *Death* in 1903, as well as *The Dryad*, *Luonnotar*, *The Bard*, and *The Oceanides* in the 1910s ending with *Tapiola*, to name only a few. Although the impact seems clear, tracing the effects in the music is another thing.

Fig. 11. Arnold Böcklin, *Vita somnium breve* [*Das Leben ein kurzer Traum*], 180 × 114.5 cm, oil on panel, 1888, Kunstmuseum Basel. Photo Kunstmuseum Basel / Martin P. Bühler.

Fig. 12. Arnold Böcklin, *Der Heilige Hein*, 105 × 150 cm, oil on canvas (1882), Kunstmuseum Basel. Photo bpk / Lutz Braun.

Fig. 13. Arnold Böcklin, *Das Spiel der Nereïden*, 151 × 176.5 cm, oil on canvas (1886), Kunstmuseum, Basel. Photo bpk / Herrmann Buresch.

Fig. 14. Jean Sibelius (attributed), drawing, pencil (1887), Sibelius Museum (copy).

Fig. 15. Jean Sibelius, drawing, 31.5 × 34.5 cm, pencil on paper, undated, The National Library of Finland, Sibelius Family Archive, box 1.

SIBELIUS AND SCHOENBERG

RON WEIDBERG

Having been denounced for being conservative by Second Viennese School apostles Theodor Adorno[1] and René Leibowitz[2], and known for stating with irony that Schoenberg's best achievement was Alban Berg,[3] it may not be promising to affiliate Jean Sibelius with the music of Arnold Schoenberg, in either ideological or textual terms. Tomi Mäkelä, who was probably the first to address the topic directly,[4] remarked that, "Today, every comparison between them seems absurd." In fact, Sibelius did express a combination of admiration and reservation towards Schoenberg a number of times, attended performances of his music, and evidently gained access to some of his scores as early as 1914. Most of Sibelius' significant statements regarding Schoenberg occurred during the period of 1912–14, while he himself created some of his most innovative and audacious scores, among them *The Bard*, *Luonnotar*, and both versions of *The Oceanides*. Regretfully, the question of correlation between Sibelius and Schoenberg is, in essence, one-sided, reflecting Sibelius' dialogue with contemporary modernism in general, while Schoenberg evidently listed Sibelius, as late as in 1947, among the nineteenth-century popular

---

[1] Theodor W. Adorno, "Glosse über Sibelius," in *Jean Sibelius and his World*, ed. Daniel M. Grimley (Princeton and Oxford: Princeton University Press, 2011), 333–7.
[2] René Leibowitz, *Sibelius, le plus mauvais compositeur du monde* (Liège: Aux Editions Dynamo 1951).
[3] In Santeri Levas, *Jean Sibelius, a Personal Portrait*, trans. Percy M. Young (London: J.M. Dent & Sons, 1972), 74; also in Glenda Dawn Goss (ed.), *The Sibelius Companion* (Westport, Connecticut and London: Greenwood Press, 1996), 228.
[4] Tomi Mäkelä, *Jean Sibelius*, trans. Steven Lindberg (Woodbridge: The Boydell Press, 2012), 250–6.
[5] Leonard Stein (ed.), *Style and Idea, Selected Writings of Arnold Schoenberg*, trans. Leo Black (Belmont Music Publishers, 1975), 162.

national romantic composers, reflecting no real interest in the advanced features of the Finnish composer.[5]

Although Sibelius' "modernity" has currently become a much-discussed topic among scholars, there is a tendency to emphasise his idiosyncratic modernity as well as his impact, mainly on late twentieth century trends such as spectralism and minimalism. Less has been discussed about Sibelius' interrelationship with his contemporary avant-garde music, notably the Second Viennese School. Such interrelations can be discussed by means of historical and cultural studies, as well as through the comparative study of selected scores, in light of the following observations:

- Both Sibelius and Schoenberg were, for a certain time, under the spell of Richard Wagner's chromatic harmony and sonic structures as well as his written ideas on new music and drama
- The emergence of a new approach to Sibelius' historic and cultural position as a prominent representative of the "Nordic breakthrough,"[6] alongside such eminent figures as August Strindberg and Edvard Munch. According to this approach, Sibelius' settings to proto expressionist Swedish and Fenno-Swedish poetry[7] and his intensive preoccupation with symbolist and experimental theatre at the beginning of the twentieth century[8] paved the way for all the great symphonic achievements of his later major works from 1906 onwards. New Nordic literature and art had

[5] Leonard Stein (ed.), *Style and Idea, Selected Writings of Arnold Schoenberg*, trans. Leo Black (Belmont Music Publishers, 1975), 162.

[6] According to Georg Brandes' 1883 concept of "the modern breakthrough;" see Arnold Weinstein, *Northern Arts, the Breakthrough of Scandinavian Literature and Art, from Ibsen to Bergman* (Princeton: Princeton University Press, 2008), p. 1.

[7] Including Bertel Gripenberg's *Teodora* (1908) and ten of Ernst Josephson's poems (1899, 1908, 1909). Victor Rydberg's settings of 1903 will be discussed below.

[8] Including Gripenberg's translation to Maeterlinck's *Pelléas and Mélisande* (1905), Hjalmar Procopé's orientalistic *Belshazzar's Feast* (1906), August Strindberg's *Swanwhite* (1908), and Mikael Lybeck's expressionistic play *The Lizard* (1909). See Glenda Dawn Goss, *Sibelius, a Composer's Life and the Awakening of* Finland (Chicago and London: The University of Chicago Press, 2009), 308–9; one may add to this list Arvid Järnefelt's Finnish play *Kuolema* (1904), which was much in awe of August Strindberg's *A Dream Play*. See Erik Tawaststjerna, *Sibelius, Volume II: 1904–1914*, ed. and trans. Robert Layton (London: Faber and Faber, 1986), 288, as well as Edvard Munch's *Death and the Maiden*, see Mäkelä, *Jean Sibelius*, 111.

a crucial role in the emergence of expressionist art in German-speaking Europe, in which Schoenberg was a legitimate voice, both as a visual artist and as a composer

- Since both composers have been associated with expressionism, it is natural that their works would share, at least partially, some musical features, such as melodic and tone organisation, sonority and form. In terms of melodic and harmonic concepts, Schoenberg's gradual path towards atonality is well known. It might be surprising how frequently Sibelius adopted suspended tonality and chromatic strategies, which are related to the post-romantic Germanic tradition and the early stages of the Second Viennese School
- Sibelius' modernism and its relation to the Second Viennese School are manifested most successfully within the parameter of sonority. From the beginning of his professional career Sibelius strived for a new sonic language, establishing sonority as a primary parameter to be compared with Schoenberg's concept of *Klangfarbenmelodie*. Mäkelä's call for a comparative study of both creators in this respect[9] will be challenged in this essay
- Schoenberg's concept of *developing variation* correlates with Sibelius' *profound logic*, a term suggested by him to Mahler in 1907 while discussing the essence of the symphony[10]

Both Sibelius and Schoenberg outlived the first half of the twentieth century, yet their artistic activity interlocked for only 16 years between 1899 and 1915. In 1915, Schoenberg entered into a period of what was, essentially, a creative silence. Only in 1923 did he re-emerge with his new method of composition with 12 tones. By that time, Sibelius was completing his last great orchestral works. He later withdrew into his own creative silence, which lasted for the rest of his life. This would have made any discussion comparing Sibelius' and later Schoenberg developments, notably serial composition, quite impractical. Our discussion focuses, therefore, on Schoenberg's "first and second" periods. Obviously, these were the periods of most radical revolution in the history of music and the arts, including atonality, cubism, expressionism, and abstract painting. Precisely at that time, Sibelius freed himself of strict national idioms and turned to the Pan-Nordic and Central European currents of his time. For

[9] Mäkelä, *Jean Sibelius*, 210.
[10] Tawaststjerna, *Sibelius, Volume II*, 76.

both composers, the year 1915 marked a point of stylistic climax and the end of an era.[11]

The history of the artistic development of both creators during that period reveals parallels as well as contrasts. The year 1899 can be considered Schoenberg's starting point as a mature composer creating *Verklärte Nacht*, while Sibelius acquired his position as a Hegelian "great man" in Finnish society,[12] as expressed most clearly by *Finlandia* (*Suomi herää* in its early version). Curiously, both works, different as they are from each other, drew their inspiration from Richard Wagner.[13] That year also marked the beginning of a transition in exploration and style for both composers towards a greater individualism and abstraction.

In 1905, Schonberg composed his Quartet, Op. 7, which premiered only in 1907 in Vienna, while in 1908 he created the Quartet, Op. 10, which is recognised as his breakthrough from extended tonality into free atonality and the "emancipation of the dissonance." The same years were also crucial for Sibelius' transition of style, as he adopted some new concepts of tonality while crystallising his original concept of sonority. Not unlike Schoenberg's Op. 10 Quartet, Sibelius performed his own dramatic stylistic transition in the course of works such as *Pohjola's Daughter* and the Third Symphony.

The year 1912 can be considered the peak of Schoenberg's experimentation with free atonality, with his innovative *Sprechstimme* as well as his crucial participation in the *Blaue Reiter Almanach*. At that time, Sibelius reached the peak of his modernistic breakthrough, shockingly expressed in the Fourth Symphony and later, as stated above, *The Bard, Luonnotar*, *The Oceanides*, and the gloomy and dissonant 1915 version of the Fifth Symphony. In 1912, Sibelius was offered a professorship in Vienna's *Akademie für Musik und darstellende Kunst*, which he rejected.[14] It is interesting to note that the same person who offered Sibelius the position was also a loyal supporter of Schoenberg during his difficult years of rejection in Vienna.[15] In fact, he offered

---

[11] Namely, Schoenberg's's *Die Jakobsleiter* and Sibelius' first version of the Fifth Symphony.

[12] Matti Huttunen, "The National Composer and the Idea of Finnishness: Sibelius and the Formation of Finnish Musical Style," in *The Cambridge Companion to Sibelius*, ed. Daniel M. Grimley (Cambridge: Cambridge University Press, 2004), 7–21.

[13] In *Finlandia, the Götterdämmerung*'s funeral march comes to mind.

[14] Tawaststjerna, *Sibelius, Volume II*, 213.

[15] Wilhelm Bopp; see Tawaststjerna, *Sibelius, Volume II*, 214, and Mäkelä, *Jean Sibelius*, 71.

Schoenberg a similar job that year, which was also turned down. Sibelius also tasted rejection in Vienna: while his First Symphony and Violin Concerto won some recognition, his Fourth Symphony, scheduled in Vienna for the 1912 season, was withdrawn from the programme. Sibelius' interest in Schoenberg's *Harmonielehre*, published in 1911,[16] emphasises the contrast between Schoenberg, as a great mind in music theory, and Sibelius, who apparently did not care about teaching music but was fully aware of new tonal concepts and sonic innovations, as we will see later in this essay.

The year 1914 may be considered the most important regarding Sibelius' interest in Schoenberg. At the beginning of the year he stayed in Berlin, composing one of his most-innovative scores, namely the "Yale version" of *The Oceanides*, and listening to a number of Schoenberg music performances. He listened to the Op. 10 Quartet and in his diary expressed his enormous interest in the quartet.[17] In an interview six months later he said that he "greatly admired Schoenberg," an expression he never used again while referring to any other living composer.[18] He also acquired Schoenberg scores and studied them thoroughly. Quoted in Levas, Sibelius said in 1930 that it was Busoni who advised him to purchase the scores, claiming that he nevertheless did not learn anything from them.[19] Mäkelä counts the list of scores found in Sibelius' estate, including the *Gurrelieder*, the first Chamber Symphony, the Opp. 11 and 19 piano pieces, and the Op. 16 Five Orchestral Pieces (including *Farben*, Op. 16 No. 3, to be discussed later), as essential for the study of Schoenberg and the rise and development of twentieth-century music, even among music students today. Sibelius most likely expressed his admiration of the *Gurrelieder* owing to its sonic merits.[20]

Vocal music and art song in particular played an important role in both Schoenberg's and Sibelius' stylistic development. The first opus numbered publications of both composers were song collections.[21] They both made use of the genre as a laboratory for experiments later to be expressed in wider-scale works. We also know that one of Schoenberg's pieces that

[16] Sibelius' diary, May 8, 1912, 138–9; see Mäkelä, *Jean Sibelius*, 251.
[17] Sibelius' diary, February 9, 1914, 185.
[18] Mäkelä, *Jean Sibelius*, 253; *Musical Courier*, June 10, 1914.
[19] Mäkelä, *Jean Sibelius*, 251.
[20] See also in Ibid.
[21] Schoenberg's's opp. 1–3 (1898–1903), and Sibelius' Op. 13, Runeberg Songs (1892).

made a deep impression on Sibelius in Berlin, January 1914, was a solo song (probably from his Op. 2 or Op. 3).[22]

Sibelius set Victor Rydberg's poem *På verandan vid havet*, Op. 38 No. 2, in September 1903[23] while he was extensively involved with the *Euterpe* Swedish-speaking artistic group in Helsinki, which was evidently one of the most important catalysts in his transformation process from national symbolism to Nordic expressionism. The opening phrase of Op. 38 No. 2 is known as one of Sibelius' most chromatic passages. Apparently, its construction can be identified as suspended tonality, where ten different chromatic pitch-classes are condensed in one short phrase, actually forming a row. The missing complementary 11th and 12th tones, namely A and E flat, form a tritone, thus seemingly denying any attempt to reach its resolution to B flat. In fact, one can refer to the opening F as the root of a dominant of the same tonal centre, while the two opposite chromatic lines lead into a minor sixth (B flat and G flat at the beginning of bar 3). This is, in fact, an elliptical Neapolitan chord, that does not resolve to its intended tonic (F), but rather is interpreted as part of diminished third/augmented sixth chords in bars 3–4 as subdominants to the target key B flat minor (where the vocal melody starts).[24]

Example 1. Sibelius, *På verandan vid havet*, Op. 38/2

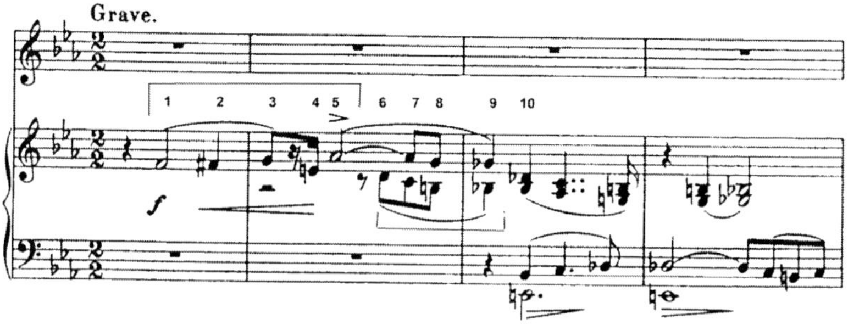

[22] Mäkelä, *Jean Sibelius*, 251.

[23] Tawaststjerna, Erik, Jean Sibelius, Volume I: 1865–1904 (Helsinki, 1965), (Layton, Robert, tr.) (London, 1976), p. 274, and Barnett, Andrew, Sibelius (New Haven, 2007), p. 156.

[24] The song's debt to Wagner becomes evident as the beginning of the vocal line of the song, with its strong tritone impact, is almost identical with the very first vocal line of *Tristan*, namely the unaccompanied sailor's song.

Working with chromatic segments, even less than 12 pitch-classes, has been pointed out by Schoenberg and his disciples in certain musical works of the past, from Bach to Wagner, aiming to advocate the 12-tone method as an inevitable stage in the progress of Western (essentially German) music.[25] "Before we knew about the law, we were obeying it. This proves that it really did develop quite naturally," testified Anton Webern in 1932.[26] "We sensed that the frequent repetition of a note, either directly or in the course of a piece, in some way 'got its own back,' that the note 'came through'.[27]" From here came the conscious necessity of the Second Viennese School composers to eliminate the sense of tonality. Webern admitted that while composing his *Bagatelles for String Quartet* (1911) he "wrote out the chromatic scale and crossed off the individual notes"[28] to make sure all 12 tones of the chromatic scale occurred before a repetition. Almost every piece Schoenberg wrote during his first tonal period obeys this still-unformulated rule of utmost chromaticism. In his second period ("free atonality"), one may find this principal even more precisely, as in the opening song of *The Book of the Hanging Gardens*, Op. 15 No. 1, composed in 1907–8.

---

[25] See, for example, Hans Ferdinand Redlich, *Alban Berg, the Man and his Music* (New York: J. Calder, 1958), 27–31 (abridged version of the original 1955 Universal Edition).

[26]Anton Webern, *The Path to the New Music*, ed. Willi Reich (Bryn Mawr: Theodore Presser, 1963), 52.

[27] Ibid., 51.

[28] Ibid.

Example 2. Schoenberg, *Unterm Schutz von dichten Blättergunden* Op. 15, No. 1 from *Das Buch der hängenden Gärten*

Sibelius shared the conflict of advanced composers of the period regarding the validity of tonal tradition. In the opening phrase of *På verandan vid havet* one hears, as described above, an elliptical Neapolitan chord and ambiguous series of augmented sixth chords against a descending chromatic melodic progression. A similar progression also characterises an essential part of early Schoenberg writing, as in *Verklärte Nacht*.[29]

In the beginning of Schoenberg's *Schenk mir deinen goldenen Kamm* Op. 2, No. 2, we witness his method of building chromatic segments vertically as well as melodically. Thus, a chromatically descending melody (similar to the previous examples) is accompanied by an unusual chord progression that leads to a supposedly subdominant seventh chord of a distant tonality of C minor (bar 2). This progression is practically unanalysable in traditional harmonic terms. However, pitch-class organisation of the chords, exploiting all 12 tones, provides a new analytical approach to this beautiful example of early tonal Schoenberg.

During Sibelius' turn-of-the-century transition from national symbolism to pan-Nordic expressionism, one can identify quite a

[29] Schoenberg, *Verklärte Nacht*, Op. 4 (Universal Edition) p. 8 letter E.

substantial number of melodic structures that blend his well-established modal writing and new chromatic row principle. The following example (also written in 1903) displays a 12-tone set in which the first five notes belong to a D sharp harmonic minor mode, while the next five notes are complementary to an absolute chromatic field. The two final notes of the row are again part of the opening mode.

Example 3. Sibelius, *Höstkväll*, Op. 38 No. 1

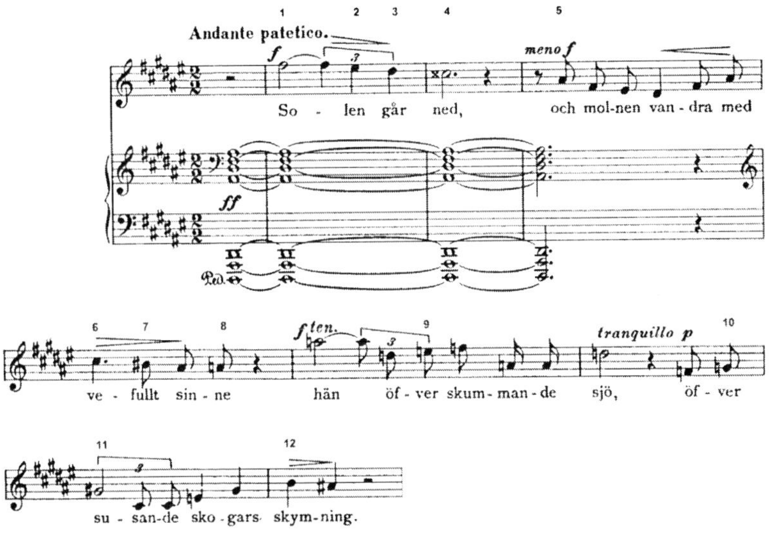

The next example, taken from the coda of *Pohjola's Daughter*, also balances Sibelius' modal writing (this time, clearly evocative of his national-symbolist period in the 1890s) and the chromatic row technique typical of the transitional period. The seven pitch-class set of the Dorian mode is followed by the complementary set of the five remaining notes. The harmonic progression, an elliptical Neapolitan cadence in essence, is a result of the row-like chromatic thinking.

Example 4. Sibelius, *Pohjola's Daughter*, four bars after P

This passage, highlighting Sibelius' turn-of-the-century stylistic transformation in a nutshell, suggests Alban Berg's peculiar treatment of the dodecaphonic row, as late as 1929, in his orchestral song *Der Wein*, in which all seven pitch-classes of the harmonic D minor scale precede the five complementary pitch-classes, making up a full 12-tone set.

Example 5. Berg, *Der Wein* (bars 15–18)

Moreover, Schoenberg's technique of condensing the row into vertical structures is presented in Sibelius' *Pohjola's Daughter* in its preliminary form, where the complementary non-mode pitch-classes are shaped as an *ostinato*, establishing the exceptionally mysterious conclusion of the piece.

Example 6. Sibelius: *Pohjola's Daughter*, one bar before R

One can compare this to the opening bars of *Der Wein*, where Berg employs an *ostinato* at the lower voice, thus establishing a greater contrast between the diatonic mode and the non-diatonic pitch-classes, creating, in fact, a polytonality of scale tones versus non-scale tones.

Example 7. Berg, *Der Wein*, beginning

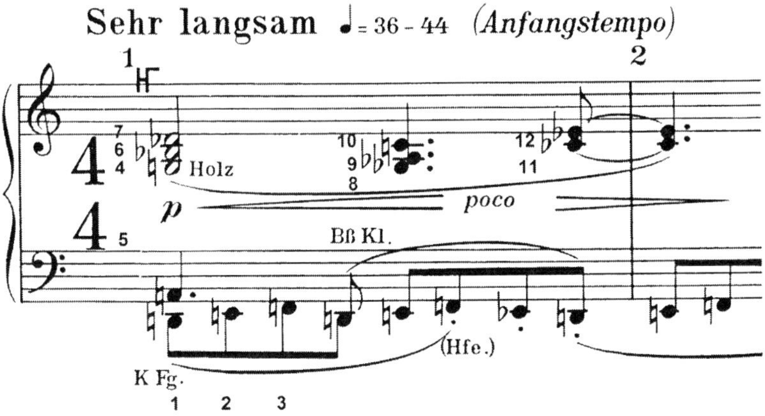

While Wagner's *Tristan* is undoubtedly a forerunner of early Schoenberg, evidenced by its chromaticism, dramatic content, and orchestration, it seems that Sibelius' major attraction to Wagner was fully manifested in the parameter of sonority. The term "sonority" may be defined as the subtotal of musical features which are not in the realm of "primary musical parameters," such as melody, harmony. and metric rhythm. Thus, sonority includes characteristics such as timbre, dynamics, registration, and density. As primary parameters identified with tonal functionality declined around the turn of the century, sonority gradually moved to the frontier of musical perception. Certain moments of intensified sonic experience are expressed in Wagner's music, as well as in his writings, mainly as a depiction of the power of nature, as is evident in the final part of his *Music of the Future*:

> The forest's visitor sits down to ponder; when … he girds the forces of his soul to a new power of observing … As if hearing with new senses, he listens more and more intently—he perceives with ever greater plainness the infinite diversity of voices waking in the wood. Ever and ever a new, a different voice peers forth. A voice thinks he has never heard as yet; as they wax in number. They grow in strange distinctness; louder and louder rings the wood; and many though the voices be, the individual strains he hears, the glinting. Over brimming stream of sound seems again to him but just the one great forest-melody …[30]

While some commentators refer to this passage as an evocation of the *Waldweben* from *Siegfried*, second act, the translator of the first English edition points towards the *Rheingold Prelude* as an example of "silence growing more and more alive."[31] This famous prelude is known for being comprised of one single E flat major chord all the way through. In terms of tonal-functional harmony, which is based on narrative progression, such a chordal stasis denies functionality. Yet, listening to the *Rheingold Prelude* we experience a narrative flow, a depiction of the gradual intensification of the Rhine. This is a result of Wagner's use of sonority as the main narrative element of the piece. Moreover, Wagner builds a number of sonic layers (or *sonic groups*),[32] accumulating one on top of the other, thus intensifying the richness and the complexity of the texture. We can take the first example, right at the beginning of *Das Rheingold*, where, on top

---

[29] Richard Wagner, "Zukunftsmusik," in *Richard Wagner Prose Works, Vol. III*, trans. William Ashton Ellis, 2nd ed. (London: Kegan Paul, Trench, Trübner &Co., 1907), 339.

[31] Ibid.

[32] A term employed by me in analysing Sibelius' (and other composers') sonic structures. See my "Sonic Design in Jean Sibelius' orchestral Music," in *Sibelius Forum II: Proceedings from the Third International Jean Sibelius Conference Helsinki, December 7–10, 2000*, eds. Matti Huttunen, Kari Kilpeläinen, and Veijo Murtomäki (Helsinki: Sibelius Academy. Department of Composition and Music Theory, 2003), 216–26.

of the prolonged bass sound, played by double basses and bassoons, he adds the imitative texture of the eight horns.[33]

Wagner was thoroughly aware of the sonic groups he constructed as well as the visual quality of his score. This is apparent in the placement of the bassoon section, which is situated, oddly, on the first page below the horns, next to the double bass section, and is later moved next to the flutes, at the top of the score. Together, they start a new sonic group, to be marked at the next example as *group 1. Group 2* is comprised of the imitating oboes and clarinets. The horns form *group 3*, while the strings play the semiquaver note patterns that form *group 4*. The double basses, trombones, and tuba create *group 5*, which continues to hold the prolonged sound of the beginning. Each of the five sonic groups comprising the entire score develops independently, and thus the general texture can be described as a "sonic counterpoint."[34]

Sibelius' use of sonority as a primary parameter is evident from his earliest works. This can be attributed to his affinity for nature as well as his unique views on incorporating Finnish folk music into art-music.[35] Listening to Wagner in Bayreuth in 1894, ambiguous experience as it was,[36] undoubtedly reinforced Sibelius' confidence in the role of sonority in the formation of Wagner's musical drama, as well as in his own path. This led him directly to his most original and advanced musical achievements. The opening storm music of *The Tempest* incidental music, composed in 1925, can be considered a case of absolute musical liberation from its traditional components of melody, harmony, and metric rhythm into new, strictly sonic artwork.

The score of the Prelude to *The Tempest* consists of a multi-layered sonic structure similar to *Das Rheingold*. The static harmony is comprised of a sequence of "French chords" (seventh chords, containing augmented sixths or diminished thirds, based on the whole-tone scale), played in parallel motion by the four upper string sections (violins I and II, violas and cellos).[37] The bassline moves independently, frequently adding a fifth tone to the vertical whole-tone structure.[38] The chord's lengthy time span

---

33 Wagner, *Das Rheingold*, Dover reproduction of first edition (Mainz, 1873), 1.

34 Ibid, 10.

35 Jean Sibelius, "Some Viewpoints Concerning Folk Music and Its Influence on the Musical Arts," in *Jean Sibelius and His World*, ed. Daniel M. Grimley (Princeton: Princeton University Press, 2011), 318–25.

36 Tawaststjerna, *Jean Sibelius, Volume I*, 152ff.

37 See also Grimley's harmonic analysis in *Jean Sibelius and His World*, 211–13.

38 Sibelius, *The Tempest,* Prelude, Op. 109 No. 1, Wilhelm Hansen Edition, 1.

prevents any kind of expectation for resolution, similar to Wagner's prolonged E flat major chord.[39]

No fewer than six sonic groups accumulate intensively on top of the initial string passages. The intensity and density of the new groups are much greater in this piece than in *Das Rheingold*, as all sonic groups are constantly present, occasionally uniting, splitting and changing their inner textures.

It should be stressed that this sonic group structure (as depicted in Example 8) [40] was by no means unique to *The Tempest* Prelude, but was a unifying feature and composition method for nearly all of Sibelius' mature output.[41] Example 8 presents two score pages together in order to emphasise the sense of continuity required to grasp the composer's intentions. One can count the flute and piccolo *group 1* imitating canonically the oboe and clarinet *group 2*. The horns' outburst events are marked as *group 3*. This group is, in essence, a sequence of "non-chordal" events, narratively developed, as we will also see in our Schoenberg example later. The so-called brass *pedal group*[42] (*group 4*) and the independent timpani *group 5* are considered to be the centrals features of Sibelius' mature orchestral writing. The opening string group described above is *group 6*, while the independent bassline (untypically doubled by the bassoons) is marked as *group 7*.

---

[39] Sibelius did resolve the chord to an unexpected unison on E in the first orchestral suite version (Op. 109 No. 1), arranged by him after the premiere of the theatre play where the *Tempest* Prelude is placed as the final movement.

[40] Also displayed in Grimley, *Jean Sibelius and His World*, 212.

[41] See Weidberg, *Sibelius Forum II*, 216–26.

[42] My own terminology used in the above-mentioned article.

Example 8. Sibelius, *The Tempest,* Prelude, Op. 109 No. 1, bars 2–4

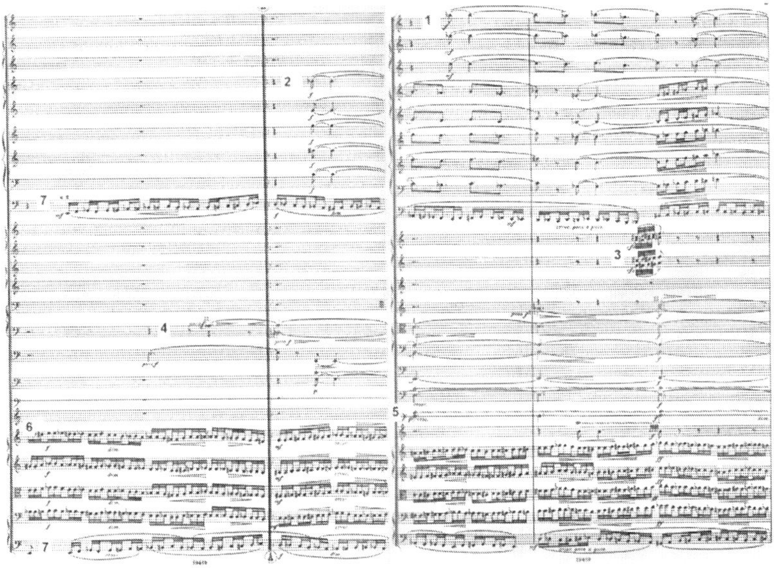

The pedal group (group 4) reveals an important feature of the piece's sonic design. Example 9 isolates this group, beginning with bar 6 (letter B in the score). The five-part chord[43] changes its transposition in a gradual process which can be described as a "mensuration canon." Each of the brass instruments descends one tone by means of imitation. Hence, the change of the chord structure resembles a sonic transformation, rather than a harmonic one.

[43] Dominant seventh chord with doubly augmented octave, and the lowered fifth is in the bass.

Example 9. Sibelius, *The Tempest,* Prelude, Op. 109 No. 1, bars 6–10, the pedal group (brass only)

The harmonic transformation technique via mensuration canon is typical of most of Sibelius' mature works. The formidable transition at the beginning of his Seventh Symphony from the initial A flat minor chord into an F major chord is done by means of a mensuration canon, simulating harmonic progression as sonic process. The origin chord also dissolves into the destination chord dynamically by means of sonic "cross fade."[44]

Schoenberg's interest in sonority might have originated directly from Wagner, similar to the way it appealed to Sibelius. Schoenberg's setting to George's *Entrückung* ("Ich fühle Luft von anderem Planeten"), as the fourth movement of his Second String Quartet, often considered his breakthrough into atonality, is essentially a sonic fantasy. The composer deliberately dismisses tonal tensions and resolutions in the quest for an alternative sonic system. One can understand Sibelius' positive reaction to the piece when he first heard it in Berlin in 1914, undoubtedly identifying the same sort of sonic thinking that he himself used to cultivate during his creative life. At the same time, he brought those sonic principals to their peak by working on the Yale version of *The Oceanides*.

The introductory bars of *Entrückung* depict a variety of sonic events. Schoenberg comes very close to the concept of *sonic phrase*,[45] as examined in Wagner's *Rheingold* and Sibelius' *Tempest* above. The sensation of harmonic progression is weakened by the complete unity of motivic and harmonic structures, as if the whole section consists of only one chord, along with a construction of distinctive sonic groups, in a

[44] Sibelius, Seventh Symphony Op. 105, Wilhelm Hanson Edition (Revised 1980), bars 3–5, p. 3.

[45] See footnote 31 above.

sequence of events that endows the piece with an exceptional, imaginary, narrative quality.[46]

Some scholars, including Mäkelä, called for a comparison between Sibelius' *The Tempest* Prelude and Schoenberg's orchestral piece *Farben*, Op. 16 No. 3, composed in 1909.[47] While the sonic structures of *The Tempest* crowned Sibelius' lifetime investigation of the problem of sonority, Schoenberg approached the sonic experience as a subject to be explored mainly scientifically. His term *Klangfarbenmelodie*[48] assumed that sound timbres can be theoretically systemised in a way analogous to the systemisation of melody and harmony. One can attribute Sibelius' critical 1912 "artificial river" expression[49] to this *Klangfarbenmelodie* concept. Considering that Schoenberg was a painter as well as a composer, *Farben* can be regarded as an attempt to unify the visual and sonic arts according to Wagner's concept of *Gesamtkunstwerke*, as well as unifying the ideals of *Der Blaue Reiter*, Schoenberg's artistic cycle at that time. Hence, idealistically, Schoenberg expected the listener to hear the music in the same manner as they would view a piece of art. In order to achieve this, Schoenberg called for the same measure of stasis that was also necessary in Wagner's *Rheingold* and Sibelius' *Tempest*. Accordingly, *Farben* is essentially based on one prolonged chord, in which the sensation of movement lies mainly in its constant changes of orchestral timbre.[50]

Charles Burkhart's 1973 definitive article on *Farben*[51] outlines its vertical structure as a five-part chorale, organised in three distinctive phrases. The chord (regardless of its orchestration) is constantly transformed and transposed by means of short melodic patterns imitating one another in the form of a mensuration canon, not unlike Sibelius' mensuration canons in *The Tempest* and the opening of the Seventh Symphony, discussed above. Burkhart's graphic description of the first phrase of the five-voice chorale successfully demonstrates similarities

---

[46] Schoenberg, String Quartet, Op. 10, Dover reproduction of Philharmonia No. 229, Universal Edition, fourth movement, bars 1–15, pp. 118–21.

[47] Among Schonberg's *Five Pieces for Orchestra* (1909), Op. 16, the first (*Vorgefühle*) is probably the most sonically designed in accordance with the principals Sibelius employed in his music, also reflected in *Entrückung*.

[48] The term *Klangfarbe* first appeared in Hugo Riemann's *Musik-Lexikon*, 5th ed. (Leipzig: Max Hesse's Verlag, 1900), 571–2, as a substitute for the French term *timbre*.

[49] Mäkelä, *Jean Sibelius*, 247.

[50] Schoenberg, *Farben*, Op. 16 No. 3, Edition Eulenberg No. 1328, first bar, p. 29.

[51] Charles Burkhart, "Schoenberg's *Farben*: An Analysis of Op. 16, No. 3," in *Perspectives of New Music* 12 (1/2) (Autumn 1973–Summer 1974): 141–72.

between Sibelius and Schoenberg regarding their transformation techniques of the static chord. The five chord voices act as independent sonic layers, whose slow temporal, dynamic, and register changes leave the necessary space to perceive the essential changes in timbre.[52]

Unlike Sibelius, Schoenberg did not "paint" his sonic layers with wide strokes of pure colour. Instead, he allowed small spots (or "points") of colour, thus forming a five-part mixture. The five-voice chord undulates between two combinations of colour mixtures. While all the sonic structures that we met in previous examples (Wagner, Sibelius, and Schoenberg's introduction to *Entrückung*) experience the constant flow of individual homogeneous sonic groups, *Farben* seemingly strives towards an opposite goal—reaching complete stasis via the non-directional use of timbre changes. It is supposedly in this context that one may understand Sibelius' famous saying that he "serves pure cold water" while his contemporary modernists "offer cocktails."[53]

Following the first phrase of the three "chorale" phrases, more mixtures develop in an ever-growing density of melodic, harmonic, and timbre changes, reaching a total of 87 different combinations of colouring in an extremely short span of time.[54] While the decision as to which colour should follow the preceding one seems to be arbitrary, there are, nonetheless, three organising principles which Schoenberg employs meticulously, all of which reveal astonishing parallelism to Sibelius' *Tempest* Prelude.

The first organising principle lies in the traditional A–B–A' phrase division of the chordal ground. Phrase B is by far the most adventurous in terms of chord transformations and colouring changes, while the concluding phrase A' echoes much of the opening static chord changes. It is noteworthy to follow Sibelius' outlines of the *Tempest* Prelude, discovering a similar A–B–A' division (with the addition of a coda in the incidental music version, depicting the subsiding storm). Thus, bars 1–10 (up to rehearsal number C) form the initial A-part, bars 11–21 (rehearsal numbers C to F) form the hyper-adventurous B-part, while bars 22–31 (rehearsal numbers F to H) form the A'-part, which is in many respects parallel the initial A-part.[55]

---

[52] See Burkhart's transcription in Ibid., 144–5.

[53] This famous unauthorised Sibelius quotation originated in Erik Furuhjelm's biography, 1916, and is repeated in Cecil Gray (1935); see Mäkelä, *Jean Sibelius*, 43.

[54] Data taken from Burkhart, "Schoenberg's *Farben*," 160.

[55] Analysed in Daniel M. Grimley, "Storms, Symphonies, Silence: Sibelius' Tempest Music and the Invention of Late Style," in Grimley, *Jean Sibelius and His World*, 212.

Paying tribute to the old forms and subordinating them to new sonic principals characterised both Schoenberg and Sibelius.

The second organisational principle of *Farben* was first exposed by scholars during the 1970s.[56] It became evident that Schoenberg used a palindrome structure of colours right at the climactic point of part B of the piece. Knowing this fact in advance, it is easy now to locate and identify this forward-backward (and forward again) motion of the colours solely by examining the score. This serialism of colours (nothing to do with 12-tone serialism) is supported by an increasing-decreasing dynamic plan.[57]

One may wonder whether Sibelius was acquainted with such serial techniques while still in the midst of his intensive creativity. Surprisingly, the *Tempest* Prelude does contain a long palindrome principle, for the whole string section of part A' (bars 21–31) repeats part A (bars 1–10) backwards! Hence, Sibelius, even as late as 1925, affiliated himself with the most up-to-date Viennese school production, such as Berg's *Chamber Concerto* or *Lyric Suite*, both famous for their palindrome constructions.[58]

The third organisational principle in *Farben* is also most fascinating, referring to all sound events heard throughout the piece that are not integral parts of the chordal structure described above. They neither take part in the A–B–A' form, nor in the palindrome structure found in the B part. Although they apparently do not contribute to the *Farben* concept, it would be hard to imagine the piece without them. They constitute two categories: the first group is in low register and the second one in high register. They are treated as two sonic groups similar to the way they are handled by Sibelius (such as in *The Tempest*) and in Schoenberg's introduction to *Entrückung*. While the low-register sonic group is based on a two-note motif steadily developed in canon-like structures throughout the entire piece (regardless of its subdivision into three parts), the high-register group does not obey motivic characterisation and appears as a series of bright, randomly splashed colours on a canvas that is otherwise strictly organised. Summarising all the appearances of the high-register

---

[56] In Jan Maegaard's *Studien zur Entwicklung des dodekaphonen Satzes bei Arnold Schönberg* (Copenhagen: Wilhelm Hansen, 1972); see also Burkhart, "Schoenberg's *Farben*," 164.

[57] Schoenberg, *Farben,* Op. 16 No. 3, Edition Eulenberg No. 1328, bars 25–28, p. 32. In fact, only the four upper voices of the "five-part chorale" participate in the above-described structure, while the bass keeps its own serial features. For further details see Burkhart "Schoenberg's *Farben*."

[58] I am grateful to Daniel M. Grimley, whose remark at the 2015 Sibelius conference in Hämeenlinna triggered my search for palindrome structures in *The Tempest* Prelude.

group throughout the piece illustrates how the seemingly unrelated events are organised in a constant development of the sonic materials. It is worth mentioning that, in the 1949 edition of Op. 16, most of these non-chordal elements appear with the H- (*Hauptstimme*) marking. Surprisingly, Schoenberg never marked the H on the 5-voiced chord itself.[59] One can see the importance Schoenberg himself attributed to this chain of developing events in the central narrative of the piece. This can be compared to non-chordal events that are presented in Sibelius' *Tempest* Prelude. One can recall the horn's short outbursts (sonic group No. 3 in example 9), followed by a chain of scale-like patterns of the horns and woodwinds, becoming ever denser, longer, and louder as the piece advances, mainly in part B.

Conclusion

This chapter outlines a wide range of discussion topics regarding Sibelius and Schoenberg, referring to both as early expressionist composers of the twentieth century, still in debt to Richard Wagner. In analysing the scores of Sibelius and Schoenberg, one can find many more similarities and parallels between the two composers than might have been expected. Sibelius is, surprisingly, shown experimenting with chromaticism up to the limits of the tonal system, while one can trace Schoenberg's works from a sonic point of view, mirroring Sibelius' experiments in sonority. *Farben* is frequently highlighted as a unique experiment that did not last as a mainstream tool for the Second Viennese School. Other works that successfully absorbed "Sibelian" sonic principals are Schoenberg's *Entrückung* movement of the String Quartet, Op. 10 and *Vorgefühle*, Op. 16 No. 1, as well as Berg's pre-dodecaphonic works, *Altenberg Lieder,* Op. 4, and his clarinet pieces, Op. 5. On the other hand, Sibelius evidently adopted serial techniques such as the palindrome, typical to the Second Viennese School. Later, pointillist approaches were successful in the total serialism of the post-Second World War avant-garde. The penetration of aleatory elements, Xenakis' calculated graphical scores, and the impressive reception of the purely sonic masterpieces of Penderecki and Ligeti by the end of the 1950s changed the artistic climate towards sonic practices, of which Sibelius and Schoenberg were indisputably regarded as being among the most representative pioneers.

---

[59] An observation made already by Burkhart "Schoenberg's *Farben*," 148.

JEAN SIBELIUS: PROGRESSIVE OR MODERNIST?

TIM HOWELL

December 8, 2015 was a significant anniversary: 150 years since the birth of Sibelius. By curious coincidence, it was also my birthday, though I should add I'm somewhat younger than 150 (despite appearances). Birthdays are of course a time for reflection, a pause for thought, so what follows is, inevitably, a rather personal contemplation of Sibelius' legacy. Hopefully, this is permissible on such an important occasion, especially as 2015 also marked exactly 30 years since the completion of my PhD thesis, *Jean Sibelius: Progressive Techniques in the Symphonies and Tone-Poems*.[1] This was the first doctoral dissertation to apply modern analytical approaches to Sibelius, so the use of the term "progressive techniques" relates to both composer and analyst alike. By now, many other studies have followed in its wake, and some may have superseded it, but my conclusions at that time are a useful starting point here. In 1985 I suggested that Sibelius, as a leading exponent of the twentieth-century symphony, was neither a reactionary nor a revolutionary but—on balance—a progressive. Now, in 2015, it's time to reconsider that view—and from a very different perspective, given that my research during the intervening period has mainly focused on contemporary music in Finland. Looking back on Sibelius' work, having seen how Finnish music has moved on after him, offers a particularly fruitful vantage point from which to reconsider his achievements: it casts new light on his shadow.

On the face of it, to claim that Sibelius was a progressive may not seem a particularly daring assertion, especially today. But back in 1980, when applying to universities to begin this PhD, there were some who thought that Sibelius was just not worthy of serious study; his music was too traditional, too conventional: simply too old-fashioned. Of course that

[1] Tim Howell, *Jean Sibelius: Progressive Techniques in the Symphonies and Tone-Poems* (PhD thesis, University of Southampton, 1985); published in the "Outstanding Dissertations in Music from British Universities" Series (Garland Press: New York, 1989).

was the very prejudice I sought to challenge, and there were open-minded people (like Arnold Whittall and Peter Evans) who were willing to take it on. (It was, after all, Arnold Whittall who defined Sibelius' *Tapiola* as "structurally concentrated and emotionally paralysing,"[2] which sums up very well the chapter you're about to read!) But back in the 1980s, there were other events within the UK that assisted my cause. The breath-taking performances and recordings conducted by Sir Simon Rattle allowed us hear this music in a totally different way. Also, the contemporary British composer Peter Maxwell Davies regularly discussed the idea of Sibelius being an influence on him, especially with regard to the manipulation of timescale. Of course, that comment has stood the test of time—but so too have Simon Rattle's Sibelius interpretations. I was privileged to hear him with the Berlin Philharmonic in February 2015 during their London residency, when they performed the Fifth, Sixth, and Seventh Symphonies together in a single, absolutely stunning concert. What Rattle so vividly conveyed (along with some interesting details I had never heard before) was an awareness of shape, direction, and energy in this music; it reminded me of just how modern Sibelius' sense of timescale is, thereby prompting some of the thoughts to be explored now.

So the idea of Sibelius being a progressive was a view that I held sincerely in 1985, and is something I want to revisit in order to question and interrogate it afresh. As a result, this updated perspective seeks to outline a case that he was rather more than just a progressive: to examine the possibility that he was—perhaps—a modernist. But the immediate problem is how to define the term "modernism," especially in this particular context, as this has been the subject of a lengthy and very complex discourse. A can of worms, Pandora's Box, even a box of delights: there is no intention of entering that particular minefield here. The potential debates and conflicted opinions are far too wide ranging and entrenched to be accommodated within the scope of this modest essay. But in trying to keep things simple and engaging, let's begin with a more open (but not especially serious) philosophical question: "How many psychotherapists does it take to change a lightbulb?" The answer is: "only one—but the lightbulb has really got to want to change." Now, if we reinterpret this old (and not especially funny) English joke—and become more serious—then the question becomes: "How many musicologists does it take to define modernism?" The answer again is just one—but all the other musicologists have got to want it to be defined. (We could take

---

[2] Arnold Whittall, "Sibelius' Eighth Symphony," *Music Review* 25 (1964): 239–40.

things further and ask: How many musicologists would it take to define "*post*-modernism?" In fact, it can only be one—but that's because if you put two musicologists together and ask them to define postmodernism, they'll inevitably disagree and, in any case, it's quite likely that one would try to kill the other.)

Consequently, I ask that we enter into a spirit of collective responsibility given that these views were outlined on a particular anniversary: so here goes. For (birthday) present purposes I would suggest that musical modernism is a creative process—a way of thinking—whereby the composer sets out to challenge tradition. So my question can now be simplified: does Sibelius' music challenge tradition? And, as a sneak preview, the answer is "yes"... and "no," because it depends on how you look at it.

Tonality can be something of a stumbling block for those seeking modernist credentials. Atonality and serialism seemed the way forward in the early twentieth century, despite Schoenberg's oft-quoted assertion that there was still plenty of good music to be written in C major—and our appreciation that Sibelius' Seventh certainly fits that bill. Today we could make the case that Sibelius' Symphony in C holds its own alongside that of its namesake by (the undisputed modernist) Stravinsky, for instance. And by now, many contemporary figures (in Finland, Magnus Lindberg would be a good example) are perfectly happy to employ some kind of pitch centre in their truly modernist works: so perhaps Sibelius was ahead of his time? What is certainly true is that Sibelius' mature harmonic language marks a considerable advance on its origins within nineteenth-century chromaticism—by way of tonal ambiguity, a renewed interest in modality, whole-tone organisation, and octatonicism—and the Fourth Symphony is perhaps the best example of what might be termed "modern tonality." But to try to illustrate this fully would take more time and detail than currently available, and there is no getting away from the fact that tonality—however rarefied and individual its usage might be—plays an equally significant part in both Sibelius' compositional language and the armoury of those who might wish to categorise him as a progressive rather than a modernist.

Formal Processes or Processing Form

As a consequence, my current concerns move away from the specifics of compositional language, especially with regard to pitch organisation, in order to address something more global: aspects of form. More particularly, the focus here is on the construction of multi-level formal schemes that seem highly characteristic and significantly original: forms that challenge the very term "symphony." Sibelius' formal processes seemingly offer contrast and conflict—yet ultimately coincide and complement—in a very intriguing manner. It all starts with an interest in economy. We're not talking finance here (Sibelius was not good with money after all), but the idea of using the minimum of compositional material to generate a maximum of effect. As a result, there is a creative engagement with the concept of formal compression and—most notably—a very particular attitude to musical timescale. Let's start with the most obvious example of formal compression and one where there is undisputable evidence that this was a consciously worked-out process by the composer. Looking at the original (1915) version of the Fifth Symphony—what was then the ending of its first movement—we find evidence of a composer who is perhaps not quite in control of his material. Given that birthday events are something of a trope for this chapter, it's worth reminding ourselves that the piece was written for Sibelius' 50th celebrations, and there's no doubt that he rather hurried it for that occasion. (Meeting deadlines was not necessarily his strong point it seems; rather higher forms of time management were at stake here, after all.) There is a sense, therefore, that this is a piece where the composer is not quite yet fully in control of his material.

If you listen to the "closing" moments of the original first movement (bars 95–106), you'll hear a transitional passage into what was then a coda—followed by a rather abrupt ending that includes a "new" rhythmic figure (*pizzicato* strings)—just at the end. If we were now to make a comparison from the corresponding place in the final (1919) version, we hear music that leads into a climactic restatement of material that gradually gives way to dance-like figures, using that tiny, dotted-rhythm, shape that "ended" the original first movement; the passage in question is from the *Largamente* (bar 92ff). The paradox here is that as the musical gestures have grown, the form has been compressed: a linear process of expansion has resulted in a vertical architecture that has contracted. Symphonically, two separate parts have been joined together, as familiar shapes adopt the characteristics of a scherzo. They continue to form the second "half" of a single structure offering—at one and the same time—a sense of restatement (of earlier material) yet something new, a dance-like episode. There is a very skilfully achieved balance between old and new. For the listener, such a shift in focus and perspective on essentially the "same" material is a highly economical process, as a number of effects are derived from a single source.

Of course, this much we all know; many of us have discussed these examples and studied the compositional techniques involved. Nevertheless, it's worth noting in passing that what emerges here is the kind of metrical modulation of which any contemporary composer would be proud—but it's a bit debatable (with such a blaze of B major ringing in our ears) that unequivocal claims for true modernism would seem really convincing. But what we're talking about is a very sophisticated kind of temporal articulation: a rather special transition. As mentioned above, formal compression here is the result of an essentially *linear* process—it emerges over time, we experience it as a journey. However, the result of that process is a formal architecture (two-movements-in-one) of *spatial* significance. It is this interplay between time and space that helps us in any quest for more modernist credentials.

Temporal Delineation and Continuity

The passing of (musical) time is an elusive concept. Composers often exploit the idea of temporal ambiguity, creating pieces that appear to subscribe to one timeframe while in fact suggesting a range of alternatives. This gap between compositional reality and listener perception—between the actual and the apparent—is quite intriguing. Traditionally, tonality was a powerful force in articulating musical time, generating both an ongoing sense of continuity yet delineating the various stages that shape an architectural outline. Does Sibelius challenge that formal tradition? Well, possibly not (or not very much) in the Fifth Symphony, though he is certainly experimenting with that kind of thinking, while acquiring significant technical advances in how to construct formal and temporal transitions. The Seventh Symphony takes this up most directly but, as an aside, it's worth considering the Sixth for a moment, as the "Cinderella of the series"[3] so often tends to get overlooked. Described by Sibelius as "pure, cold water"[4] (a comment we need to take quite seriously coming from a man who understood only too well the pleasures of alcohol), he himself sets up the work as offering an alternative to the (modernist) "cocktails" of other contemporary pieces.

Seldom performed and least well understood, the Sixth Symphony might appear to be somewhat regressive in terms of form: it is in four discrete movements, in apparently separate, clearly delineated periods of

[3] An expression first coined in Gerald Abraham, "The Symphonies," in *Sibelius. A Symposium*, ed. Gerald Abraham (Oxford University Press: London, 1952), 31.
[4] Cited in Cecil Gray, *Sibelius* (Oxford University Press: London, 1935), 56.

time. However, the piece offers a special challenge in terms of the listener's perceptions because if you expect these movements to be self-contained, if you attempt to predict closure, you will find this rather frustrating. Sibelius plays on our expectations. Quite simply, the first three movements of the piece end abruptly and unexpectedly. It's almost as if Sibelius follows the advice given by the King to the White Rabbit in Lewis Carroll's *Alice in Wonderland*: "begin at the beginning and go on until you come to the end—then stop." This suggests a degree of *discontinuity*: an immediate sense of disruption where a new idea begins before the old one has found completion. But, if the compositional potential of that earlier idea has not been fully achieved—and the listener is subtly made aware of this—then there is an *implicit* sense of continuity; there is a need for something further to happen which is also present. It is less a process of disruption, more one of delay, and an inevitable sense of delay (or a delay of the inevitable), that we come to experience. Perhaps initial frustrations give way to ever-growing anticipation as we come to know the piece better over time.

Therefore, I would suggest that Symphony No. 6 is not really in four separate movements (in the traditional sense) but offers us four different perspectives—a succession of meditations—all on the same object. Certainly, we're allowed to pause along the way, perhaps to have a sip of cold water, but these are four stages in a single journey. By simply comparing the very opening of the work with that of its last "movement," we hear the same material re-imagined in time: a temporal variation no less. (Respectively marked *Allegro molto moderato* and *Allegro molto*, they seem to stand in some kind of a temporal counterbalance; but notational differences allow events at the very opening of the piece to unfold at a much slower rate, despite the prevailing tempo.) Moreover, since the initial gestures of the finale serve to generate a more local series of variations, the cumulative sense that the opening proposition of the work is being channelled towards its final conclusion, especially given the lack of conclusive gestures so far, begins to emerge.

Overall, Sibelius' epithet is quite profound. In its simplicity of materials, stylistic elegance, and refinement there is something "pure" about this work. (Indeed, its consistently projected interaction between the C major scale and the Dorian Mode on D natural—both white-note collections and variants of one another—contributes to that sense of purity.) Meanwhile, the gestural restraint and economy of expression here result in an emotional temperature best described as "cold'; and, above all, in a symphony that does not resolve its prevailing musical argument, its tonal resolution, until the very end—holding back an accumulation of energy until its closing stages—the analogy with the channelling of "water," even the metaphor of a dam (a build-up of resistance that may be washed away), seems appropriate.

Restraint and moderation do not appeal to everybody. The concert-going public has never been renowned for drinking cold water just for the fun of it: they'd rather have a cocktail. Yet the unpopularity of the Sixth Symphony, reflected in the relative rarity of performances and its limited audience appreciation, stands in directly inverse proportion to the admiration and respect with which it's held by subsequent generations of Finnish composers. My more-recent research considers this influence. "After Sibelius" refers not just to a succession of later composers in chronological sequence, but also to the extent to which they "pursue," "imitate," and write "in the manner of" this highly influential figure.[5] Despite a hugely varied range of later compositional styles, an impressively consistent view cited the Sixth Symphony as *the* directly most-influential work emerged from my studies. People like Joonas Kokkonen, Einojuhani Rautavaara, Aulis Sallinen, Paavo Heininen, Magnus Lindberg, Usko Meriläinen, Mikko Heiniö, Kalevi Aho, and Olli Kortenkangas—to name but nine—are all on record as holding up the Sixth Symphony as having a particular significance for them. Once again, potentially modernist traits, the positive legacy of Sibelius' shadow, seem apparent in music that superficially might not seem a likely source of influence upon contemporary thinking. The degree of sheer musical concentration, the distillation of time in this piece, has perhaps achieved the opposite of what the composer thought it might. Rather than acting as a mere counterbalance to the cocktails of the emotionally charged, rhetorical angst of (so-called) 1920s modernism, it has paved the way for more recent modernist engagements with elements of pure timescale. In a sense, the piece has become more modern over time—rather than less so.

Spatial Architecture: Tonal Destinations

Recalling the Berlin Philharmonic concert at the London Barbican Centre in February 2015 provides us with a telling link. Having conducted an incredibly impressive, rousing, ecstatically received interpretation of the Fifth Symphony, Simon Rattle after the concert interval presented Symphonies Six and Seven without a break between them. One work seamlessly flowed into (and out of) the other, offering the audience a rather novel experience in terms of musical continuity. For a moment, the

[5] Tim Howell, *After Sibelius: Studies in Finnish Music* (Ashgate: Aldershot, 2006).

Fig. 1. Sibelius, Seventh Symphony—Formal and Tonal Architecture

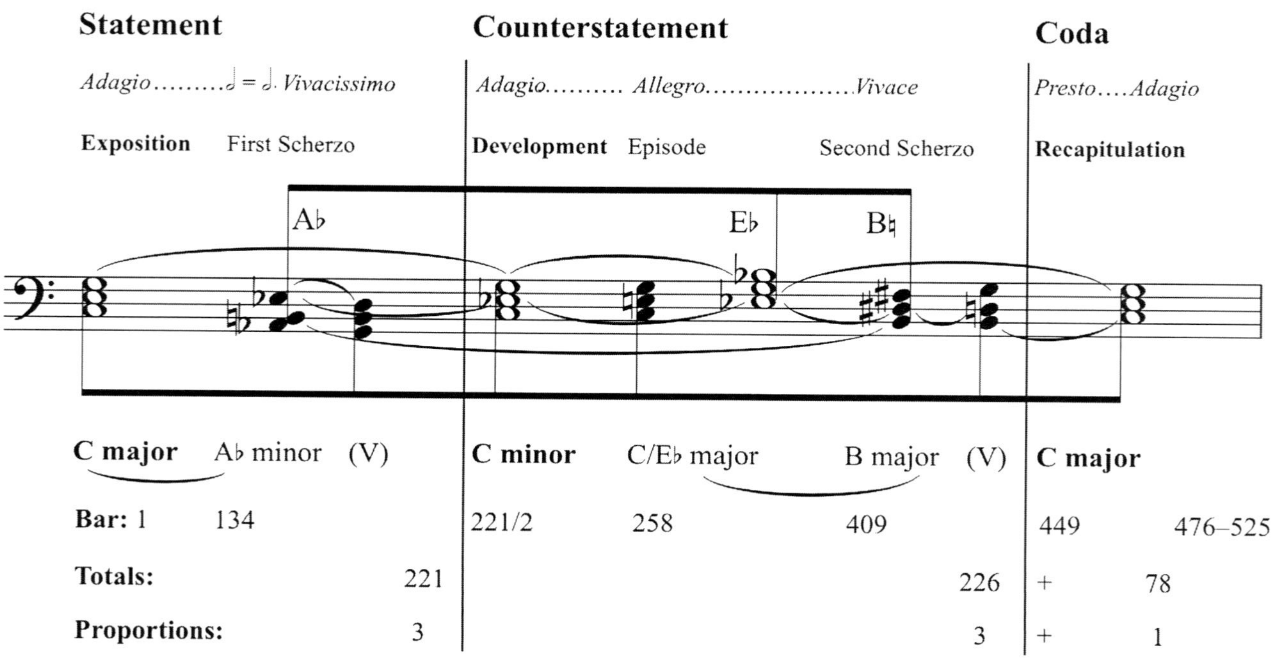

radical, one-movement Seventh Symphony was the natural outpouring of the highly restrained, purified Sixth. Nevertheless, in the context of the whole concert (and in terms of compositional technique and stylistic expression), the Seventh makes a particularly direct advance on the kind of structural and temporal compression exhibited within the Fifth Symphony. Apparently distinctive and independent structural levels have now been synthesised. Rather than adopting a linear, transitional process in order to physically join one movement on to the end of another, the Seventh strikingly *superimposes* these levels of activity: horizontal concerns are realigned vertically; multiple structures now operate simultaneously (rather than successively). Indeed, the sheer scale of this advance is perhaps more fully understood by appreciating the subtle temporal articulations of the intervening Sixth Symphony. It is possible to view the structural novelty of the Seventh as a horizontal reconfiguration of the vertical shifts associated with the so-called "separate" movements of its predecessor; each work offers different yet complementary perspectives on matters of continuity and timescale.

In the Seventh Symphony, the most immediate way of demonstrating this kind of thinking is to show Sibelius' handling of an organic structure through an ongoing succession of tonal centres, tempo changes, and thematic contrasts; collectively, these form a clearly-balanced structural design, as shown in Fig.1. The architectural shape outlined here to some extent evokes, yet reinterprets, a degree of traditional symphonic structure (with references to sonata and multi-movement formal categories) within an overarching framework of a "Statement/ Counterstatement" balance. Its tonal process is beguilingly simple and appealing. The C major–(developmental) C minor–C major (resolution) of the strategically placed *Adagio* trombone statements forms a structural skeleton; these are the bones which other tonal areas then flesh out. Whilst the E flat major (as the relative major of C minor) of the *Allegro* episode can be seen as a further variation of such mediant-related, major/minor considerations (especially as it is a transposition of a temporarily regained C major centre), it is also part of a trio of such connections, all underpinned by their characteristically fast-music identity. The initial *Vivacissimo* in A flat minor is counterbalanced by the later C flat/B major *Vivace*, and they surround this central E flat *Allegro.* Systematically, then, this succession of middle-ground events—A flat/G sharp, E flat, C flat/B—arpeggiates the pitch centre of the very first element in that sequence: the A flat minor possibility presented as the first main tonal conflict of the piece. What was a vertical harmonic/tonal event has evolved, over time, to become a horizontal sequence of secondary tonal centres.

Consequently, the immediacy of something potentially disruptive has found large-scale resolution through temporal prolongation. But most pertinent to the current discussion is the idea that what appears to offer multi-movement contrasts (fast music, *Vivacissimo* in a different tonal area) actually comes to subscribe to the single-movement continuity of this very special design. An A flat minor *Vivacissimo* might appear to be something "new," but actually it comes to function as a Neapolitan to the dominant, thereby *preparing* for a return to a C natural centre—albeit that of the minor mode—with the attendant temporal stability of its *Adagio* pace. Conversely, the B major element of its counterweight partner, *Vivace*, ultimately acts as a chromatic neighbour-note to the dominant: it prepares for a final C major (*Adagio*) resolution of the piece.

Temporal Continuity: Formal Journeys

Essentially, this kind of organic tonal thinking in the service of strikingly effective formal compression informed my findings in a doctoral thesis of some 30 years ago. It remains potentially helpful to anyone seeking to uncover the pitch-based, linear process behind the temporal continuity of Sibelius' carefully judged, single-movement construction. However, by being so deeply rooted within the multi-functioning nature of the tonal system, this type of analytical account is not going to serve us well here: it may be progressive, but it's not especially modernist. We now have to look beneath the specifics of compositional technique to more perceptual concerns: what is the *effect* of all of this? In so doing, what might be uncovered could be of interest to a modern-day composer working in a contemporary musical language. Certainly, the alignment between slow-tempo stability and fast-tempo diversity—and the conflict/relationship between the two—is clearly significant. So, if we start to separate out these two elements, focusing on temporal matters rather than key centres—on journeys, rather than destinations—this might initiate a different understanding; indeed, not only might it have some bearing on current compositional practice, but it could also suggest a degree of modernist thinking.

One of the main elements of contrast within a multi-movement symphony is that of tempo: at its most basic, the difference between slow and fast music. In the case of the Seventh Symphony, there is a single, underlying, slow-moving layer of material that seems to be carrying on in the background, regardless of whatever else is played on top of it. This structural underpinning is overlaid by faster-paced events which, at the time you hear them, sound new. However, in hindsight, with the benefit of time passing, they actually help to prepare for those slow-paced events that make up the formal pillars of a unified design. These formal pillars are of course those three versions of the trombone theme, each notably in a slow tempo, acting as structural signposts for the listener seeking any sense of architectural shape. To consider the last appearance—and the temporal transition that leads into it—we experience the sense of fast music giving way to slow music: a triumphal moment of resolution. If you listen from the *Presto* (bar 459) through the passage marked *Poco e poco rallentando*, what you perceive is a sense that foreground eventfulness gives way to background structure. It is this process of integration—a temporal variation that transforms fast, contrasting activity into slow, unifying confirmation—that is fundamental here. The listener begins to realise that the illusion of multi-movement symphonic contrasts is actually occurring within the reality of a single–movement entity.

Sibelius' Seventh Symphony simultaneously explores connections between these two contrasting frames of temporal impulse, and this process accounts for much of the dynamism of the piece. The way in which they interact—as a counterpoint of time segments—involves faster, apparently distinctive material actually being used to articulate the large-scale formal scheme: surface "disruptions" come to subscribe to an underlying continuity. This is less of a multi-movement form and more the sense of compositional multitasking. A tiny example, one of many such figures, helps to illustrate this larger point. Material that initiates the first scherzo music—at the relatively early stages of the work—returns much later as part of the closing moments of the piece (you will need to compare from the upbeat to bar 170ff with the events from bar 500ff). This is clearly the same material, but presented in radically different timeframes: it moves from foreground contrast to background resolution.

By now, we are moving away from an architectural view of form as a spatial phenomenon towards the idea that musical form is also a temporal process. This is a significant step, and one that will enable us to place (conceptual) observations about Sibelius alongside the (structural) preoccupations of a contemporary composer. Perhaps this all-important distinction between space and time is best clarified by way of a metaphor. The earlier diagrammatic summary of (tonal) continuity in the Seventh Symphony is a spatial realisation of a potentially temporal phenomenon; in the latter sense, it's woefully inadequate: it doesn't show how we experience events over time. If, for instance, you were to look at a map of Finland, you could see at a glance the distance—the spatial relationship—between the capital, Helsinki, and Sibelius's birthplace, Hämeenlinna. A map, rather like Fig. 1, allows the viewer to assimilate a larger picture, a sense of proximity, distance, and even direction: a snapshot that offers an overview. But it is an abstraction; you could imagine making the journey between these two destinations, but this is not in any way a *real* experience. It is the perceptual engagement with musical form as something fluid that unfolds over time, rather than the spatial representation of its tonal destinations that allows us to take a more conceptual perspective: a formal journey.

A New *Era*

Well, just how modern is any of this? To try and answer that, let's fast forward almost a century and consider something from a very different era; indeed, to consider a piece of that very name: the orchestral work *Era* by Magnus Lindberg (2012). If you just listen to the beginning of this piece, assuming you're familiar with Sibelius' Fourth Symphony, then you'll begin to realise its relevance. These opening bars are directly reminiscent of the initial gestures of Sibelius' Fourth. This kind of referential process is part of a larger picture. *Era* is another birthday piece. It was a commission to mark the 125 years of the Concertgebouw in Amsterdam—both the building and its orchestra—and the title refers to events over this period, centred within that place. Translated into a single composition, *Era* is undoubtedly written in a contemporary idiom, but it consciously makes reference to the past: Sibelius, Schoenberg, Stravinsky, Mahler, Debussy, and Strauss, to cite the most obvious, are all pressed into service. Snapshots of modern music are somehow distilled into a single piece: a kind of "rogues gallery," if you will. As a temporal narrative, though, this is less of a family album and not even a photo-montage, but something altogether more cinematic. Essentially, *Era* is the twentieth century distilled into 20 minutes: a kind of time capsule. It definitely forces us to question the passing of time. Lindberg himself comments on the overt reference of his opening gesture to that of Sibelius's Fourth Symphony, and as we experience the piece overall these initial gestures generate an organic unfolding of subsequent events. What is so fascinating is the way in which that direct evocation of Sibelius gradually subsides: *Era* ends, very clearly, in the style of its creator. It charts something of a stylistic journey, from early twentieth-century Sibelius to thoroughly contemporary Lindberg. [6]

---

[6] For my detailed analysis of the work see Tim Howell, "Magnus Lindberg: Narratives of Time & Space," in *Musical Narratives: Studies in Time and Motion*, ed. Tim Howell, *Contemporary Music Review* 33 (4) (2014): 355–72.

Once again, it is the interplay between time and space that is of interest here. Fig. 2 provides a diagrammatic summary of the formal outlines of the piece, a guide for anyone seeking to grasp a sense of the work as a whole. Identifying architectural blocks of differing characters (within and between component sections) is a plausible way of gaining a spatial overview; it offers a personal interpretation, though one that is easily verified by other listeners when followed through with a score. On the largest scale, there are three main sections of essentially equivalent duration (at about six minutes each). Yet, the ambiguities surrounding our perception of musical (rather than "clock") time become immediately apparent, and even counting up bar numbers is not really useful given the fluctuating tempi involved. Perceptually, the nature and density of events contained within those three "equivalent" time-spans vary considerably. Qualifying these formal stages in terms of statement, fragmentation, and synthesis helps to differentiate in this regard, with each metaphor having a distinctive functional character and tempo implication. For instance, the slightly "shorter" final section (in terms of bar numbers and duration) actually feels far more spacious; overall, the piece seems to slow down more and more towards its close. The drawing together of various elements—in a deliberately illusory, non-explicit, and contemplative manner—has the effect of stretching temporal assimilation at this stage. Reminiscences take time. Conversely, the relative discontinuities of a central passage feel more eventful in their fragmentation of earlier materials and may create the illusion that time is speeding up. However, these disruptions to any flow of ideas make it difficult to gauge any overall pace or even put down some markers, so our assimilation of time passing is challenged by a situation where any sense of continuity seems so fractured.

Any such surface discontinuities are mediated by way of more deep-rooted temporal concerns. Lindberg tells us that the structure of *Era* explores the interaction of two levels of motion: a single tempo used throughout, and a relatively faster degree of foreground activity that overlays this underlying pulse. There is a dynamic interplay between these two frames of temporal impulse that are working in conjunction with one another. So, beyond the gestural use of Sibelius' Fourth Symphony on its surface, the whole conceptual framework of *Era* evokes that of the Seventh Symphony, embedded in a structural outline that is hidden from view. While there are certainly some architectural parallels between these orchestral works that balance contrast and continuity within a single expanse of music (compare Figs. 1 and 2), it is an underlying process of timescale that seems to provide the real modernist connection here.

Fig. 2. Magnus Lindberg, *Era*—Formal Overview

SECTION I Bars 1 – 140 STATEMENT						SECTION II Bars 141 – 283 FRAGMENTATION				SECTION III Bars 284 – 392 SYNTHESIS		
A1 1–45 = 84	**A2** 46–57 = 126	**B1** 58–95 = 84	**A3** 96–115 *a tempo*	**B2** 116–30 = 126	**A4** 131–40 *Tutti*	**C1** 141–49 *a tempo*	**C2** 150–239 *a tempo*	**D1** 240–249 = 126	**D2** 250-283 = 84	**A5** 284–318 = 126	**B3** 321–369 *a tempo*	**Coda** 370–392
Main material presented in two stages;		Scherzo -like; contrast	*Tutti* arrival;	Scherzo recalled	*(Poco rall.)*	A number of tempo changes articulate a sense of development		Fragmentation; more block-like. Emphasis on linearity		Sense of return yet continuity: GP at 318	Scherzo-like; prolonged *Tutti* (350ff)	Fragmentation and resolution

Section I	Section II	Section III
Overall characteristics: Gestural shapes forming registral arches, define spatial character of the work initially. Give way to more arpeggiated figures, associated with a faster, scherzo-like tempo. Small number of motivic elements being constantly reworked.	More fragmentary, discontinuous feel to this central section. Material deployed is often familiar but placed in new contexts: sense of variation and development overall. Generally more linear and chamber-music like.	Sense of return initially but this is only fleeting: a different chain of events ensues (though with references to earlier shapes). GP marks a point of culmination: silence and space used to dramatic effect. Coda both refers to Section II and offers overall resolution: idea of synthesis.
Motivic shapes and significant recurrences: **(a):** bars 1/8/18/31/46/68/96 **(b):** bars 7/14/23/30/37/52/58ff/99/116ff **(c):** bars 15/24/39/95/106/112/130 **(d):** bars 49/74/104	**(a):** bars 163ff **(c):** bars 199ff **(d):** bars 144ff/158/175/228/250	**(a):** bars 284/308/370 **(b):** bars 321/377/386 **(c):** bars 302/350ff **(d):** bars 311ff/337/358
Dynamics: ***f*** ***ff*** ***p*** *sub.* ***ff*** (*Tutti*) ***mf*** ***ff*** (*Tutti*)	***f*** ***p*** / ***f*** ***f*** ***ff*** (*Tutti*)	***fff*** (*Tutti*) ***p*** – ***mp*** – ***ff*** (*Tutti*) ***p*** – ***f*** (*Tutti*)

But is this true? Well, I asked Lindberg whether the temporal and formal processes of *Era* significantly commented on those of the Seventh Symphony, and he was happy to confirm this.[7] The fact that Sibelius' final solution to matters of symphonic compression (the single-movement entity of the Seventh) plays such a highly influential role in the music of a truly contemporary generation helps to bolster the modernist case in this discussion. As an aside, we could speculate what Sibelius might have done next. After a symphony in just one movement, it could be argued that he took a completely logical next step, the ultimate in formal compression: an Eighth Symphony in no movements at all! Resisting the Cagean resonances of that kind of thinking (though it should be noted that a full 30 years of silence rather outdoes a mere four minutes and 33 seconds), it is of course *Tapiola* that capitalises on the concept of using a single idea to derive multi-level music, exploring a unique balance between linear and circular time, but there's (ironically) not time now to explain the full story. (You can read my thoughts on this piece in a chapter—even more ironically—called "Sibelius the Progressive."[8])

This brings me full circle and I return to my original question: Jean Sibelius—progressive or modernist? Well, ultimately, that's up to you to decide. But, as I get older (and birthdays are a reminder of that), and having now studied so much contemporary Finnish music, I increasingly find Sibelius' music to be more modern, especially in relation to his manipulation of timescale in the interest of structural economy. As a footnote, though, the labels of "progressive" or "modernist" are of course just words, and as Hans Christian Andersen reminds us: "Where words fail, music speaks." Consequently, you are encouraged to listen again to the Seventh Symphony—it takes about as much time as reading this chapter. That's where you'll find your own answer to my question, and where you'll have a far richer experience than anything mere words can offer. If you're feeling particularly adventurous and want to adopt a more modernist position, then you might just preface this by listening to the Sixth Symphony first. Such a journey may seem to take rather less time than you'd expect, but its effect will be significantly more expansive than you might have imagined.

---

[7] I am grateful to Magnus Lindberg for agreeing to meet up (in Helsinki, October 2013) to discuss his recent work and especially the compositional processes involved in this piece.

[8] Tim Howell, "Sibelius the Progressive," in *Sibelius Studies*, ed. Timothy Jackson and Veijo Murtomäki (Cambridge University Press: Cambridge, 2001), 35–57.

III

ANALYSIS AND INSTRUMENTAL PRACTICES

1. MODALITY AND COMPOSITIONAL TECHNIQUES

A TRADITIONAL SEQUENCE PATTERN SIBELIANISED

JUHANI ALESARO

As far as I can see, the analytic practice usually conducted in the domain of Sibelius analysis seems to hold the opinion that the music of Sibelius is bound to be based on a scholarly four-part *Satz*. Is this opinion correct? It is in part; in the music of Sibelius there are indeed numerous passages that are based on a four-part *Satz*. However, there are also passages that exceed its limits. These appear in abundance, e.g. in bars 354–496 in the first movement of Sibelius' Fifth Symphony, Op. 82 (1915/1916/1919). Explaining these as scholarly four-part *Satz* throws them into a Procrustean bed and prevents us from grasping the whole.

Describing harmonic constructions that exceed the principles set out in the common textbooks of harmony necessarily brings forth some seemingly new concepts. As a matter of fact, some of these principles (e.g. superposition and supposition) have already been established in the course of the history of music theory. Another concept of great importance, three-voice framework, has its roots in organ point *Satz*,[1] although the term is new. In connection with a statutory organ point, there are mostly two harmonic possibilities: either the organ point is a chord-member of a chord above it, or not. The third possibility, an organ point and a harmony above it that together build a wider chord-formation (e.g. a ninth chord), is here called three-voice framework.[2] This device is present in the music of Wagner and Bruckner.

---

[1] The term "organ point," an older equivalent of the term "pedal point," is a direct translation from German (*Orgelpunkt*) and French (*point d'orgue*); see C. P. E. Bach, *Essay on the True Art of Playing Keyboard Instruments*, trans. and ed. William Mitchell (London: Eulenburg Books 1985), 319–21; *Versuch über die wahre Art das Clavier zu spielen*, Zweyter Theil (Berlin: Georg Ludwig Winter, 1762), 181.

[2] In case of those two first-mentioned harmonic possibilities I shall use the term "organ point," while in connection with the third harmonic possibility, three-voice framework, I shall use the term "pedal point." Thus, in my article those two terms operate in different contexts.

My aim is not to scrutinise the whole section mentioned above bar by bar, but select some details that illuminate the application of these old "new" concepts in the most convenient, approachable and systematic way. Through their application it becomes possible to attain a simple overall plan of the section. Consequently, what emerges in the music of Sibelius are sections which cannot be exhaustively described in terms of major-minor tonality, and sections that utilise different scale-structures, many of which are modal.[3]

In bars 354–496 in the first movement of Sibelius' Fifth Symphony there is a chromatic transitional section comprising 143 bars. Here, the opening horn motif (bars 1–2) is powerfully restated by the trumpets and timpani (in bars 455–462).[4] The following concluding section (bars 497–586), as well as the preceding one (bars 298–353), are firmly rooted in E flat, whereas this transitional section mostly uses a chromatic harmonic sequence.[5] The initial pattern of this sequence could have been written by any composer of the tonal era, and the chromatic sequential processes are commonplace amongst composers from Beethoven to Sibelius. Thus, the originality of this section does not depend on its harmonic material, but on the ways in which the pattern is diversified. In bars 354–470, 473–478, and 481–486 this is achieved in various ways that "Sibelianise" this traditional sequence, to give it a flavour that is peculiarly Sibelian. The main emphasis of this paper is on these ways of diversification.

In the Sibelius literature, this section has already come under scrutiny, yet the results are not uniform. According to Simon Parmet in this "some kind of working-out section … Sibelius is working with quite simple harmonic sequences which, however, it is by no means easy to find."[6] Perhaps for this reason Parmet admits that his reconstruction "logically derived from notation" in Ex. 48, which covers the music between the rehearsal letters J and K, "is not necessarily final." Although Parmet finds his "Harmonic scheme" (the lower staff of Ex. 48) "relatively correct,"[7]

[3] See Juhani Alesaro, "Sibelius—'a Composer Made for Modes'," *Musurgia* XV (1–3) (2008): 7–16.
[4] This can be seen later in Fig. 4a.
[5] In the first version of the Fifth Symphony (1915) this transitional section is shorter; it occupies bars 291–391 of the second movement. In the handwritten copy of the score (Helsinki: Helsingin yliopiston kirjasto 1991, 25) from the rehearsal letter K to eight bars after O this section takes pp. 59:7–65:8. A comparison of the versions falls outside of the scope of this article.
[6] Simon Parmet, *The Symphonies of Sibelius. A Study in Musical Appreciation*, trans. Kingsley A. Hart (London: Cassell & Co., 1959), 73.
[7] Ibid., 74.

the reader cannot help noticing that in Ex. 48:1–2, 5–6, and 9–10 some minor sixth chords are replaced by major sixth chords. Finally, in Ex. 48:12–13 in this "Harmonic scheme" a correct minor sixth chord (A-rooted) precedes a major triad without a fifth (B-rooted). Unfortunately, in the following bars in Ex. 48:14–15, 16–17, and 18(–19), Parmet then takes this pair of chords as a starting point for a sequence outlined by him. This no longer matches with the content of the "Text of the score" written above it. Yet, Parmet's invention is not without grounds, only misplaced. From Parmet's sequential point of view his metric division in Ex. 48 is problematic, because in his bar-grouping 4+4+2+4+4 the two-bar unit in Ex. 48:9–10 leans on a single chord that—if corrected to a minor sixth chord—only with the addition of the following chord (Ex. 48:11) would form a pattern in the outlined sequence. Parmet does not discuss an overall plan of this "working-out section."

According to Veijo Murtomäki, a "harmonic module X … is the basic unit of the entire development and which was introduced in passing on B level in the Trio as the chordal progression B minor–C sharp major–A minor–B major (42:7–43:3)."[8] In his analysis, Murtomäki calls the section "Development 2" and considers this harmonic module or cell "circular in character." In it, "the only change that takes place is that the opening minor chord is changed into a major chord."[9] Thus, Murtomäki at first seems to deviate from Parmet's sequential principle: "The modules are not modulated in themselves, but as they are moved down by major thirds the effect resembles modulation."[10] Yet, Murtomäki later concedes: "However, this analysis of development 2 is not without it[s] problems. Although the first module in terms of its chordal content would appear to prolong E flat level, most appearances of the module—although not every one—refer to a structure of two pairs of chords rather than to an entity of four chords."[11] Murtomäki defines the harmonic content of those pairs like Parmet, namely as half cadences ii7–V and minutely describes the appearances of his module X throughout the section, showing an overall plan (see Fig. 77). Here, however, the four-bar modules are considered more important than the chord-pairs.

---

[8] Veijo Murtomäki, *Symphonic Unity. The Development of Formal Thinking in the Symphonies of Sibelius*, trans. Henry Bacon (Studia musicologica universitatis Helsingiensis 5) (Helsinki: University of Helsinki, Department of Musicology, 1993), 169.

[9] Ibid.

[10] Ibid., 169–70.

[11] Ibid., 170.

Although James Hepokoski does not consider any harmonic details of this section, he nevertheless seems to represent a third kind of tonal opinion in his view of this "second interpolated section" as an "extended, rustling mini-development of fragments that dissolve any clear sense of tonal pull."[12] But Hepokoski does not offer an overall plan of the section.

What lies behind these differences in defining the length and the tonal character of the initial pattern of the sequence? Why did Parmet consider that those "quite simple" harmonic sequences were "by no means easy to find"? With Murtomäki the Schenkerian approach seems responsible for favouring the concept of "prolongation" in modules or harmonic cells instead of sequences established by the chord-pairs.

The Initial Pattern

At the beginning of the section (bars 354–361) the initial pattern appears in its barest form, as two dissolved triads. While in agreement with Parmet, I have chosen another way of "logical derivation from notation" and presented them as a minor triad and a major six-four chord (see Fig. 1). The dissolving motive comes from the opening bars (218–219) of an earlier trumpet theme (bars 218–230), while the rhythmic form of the initial four-bar pattern (bars 354–357) has appeared before (in bars 342–345). In describing the initial pattern a key is chosen where these triads ("A" and "B") function as the subdominant and dominant, in the manner of a half cadence, although the initial pattern appears over an elongated terminating note (E flat: I3). In the sequential process the pattern is transposed down by a major second (or by a diminished third, as is the case in the melody in bars 358–359). In the sequence between chord B and the first chord (A1) of the transposed next pattern (AB–A1B1), the third of the chord (B) never ascends in the manner of a leading-note, but always proceeds downwards in the manner of a deceptive cadence.

---

[12] James Hepokoski, *Sibelius: Symphony No. 5* (Cambridge: Cambridge University Press, 1993), 69.

Fig. 1. The initial pattern and its sequential process. Op. 82:I:354–361

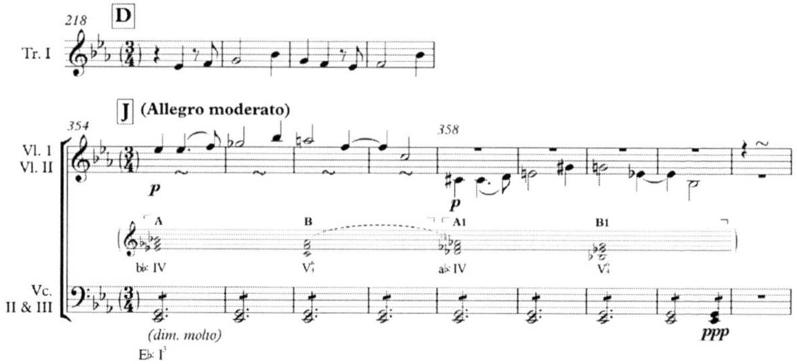

Superposition and Supposition

In addition to its melodic character (see Figs. 1 and 2), the initial pattern is diversified harmonically and contrapuntally. Harmonic diversification is achieved by means of *superposition* and *supposition*.[13] In superposition a seventh is added to the triad (see Fig. 2a). An addition to the first triad A makes it a minor seventh chord. Spatially, this added-seventh here occurs below triad A, which makes it an inverted seventh chord (Fig. 2b [Op. 82:I:473, 475]). A seventh added to the second triad B makes it a dominant-type seventh chord. Spatially, this added-seventh may occur above triad B (a root-position seventh chord), below it, or in the middle (which makes it an inverted seventh chord; see Fig. 2b [Op. 82:I:474, 476]).

[13] These devices may be traced back to the audition lecture held by Sibelius in 1896; see Juhani Alesaro, *The Apparition from the Forest. A Treatise on* Satz *in the Music of Jean Sibelius* (Studia Musica 66) (Helsinki: University of the Arts Helsinki, Sibelius Academy, 2015), 30–3, 77–9, also at http://ethesis.siba.fi/showrecord.php?ID=483626.

Fig. 2a–b. Superposition. Op. 82: I:473–476

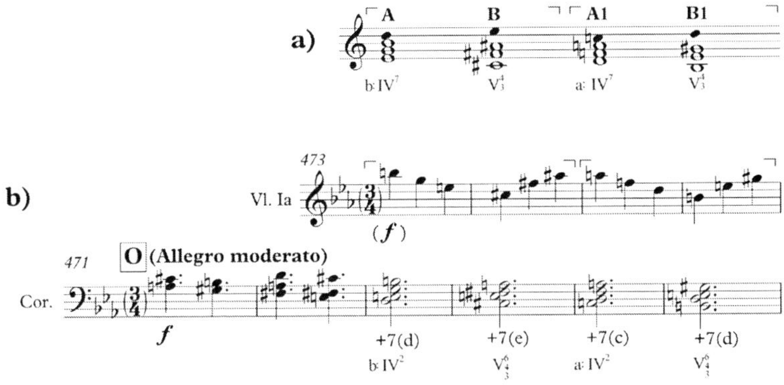

In supposition, a note is added a minor third below the root of the triad, and an added-root seventh chord is created. Here, the root of the original triad becomes the third (1 → 3), the third of the original triad becomes the fifth (3 → 5), and the fifth of the original triad becomes the seventh (5 → 7) of the added-root seventh chord. By means of supposition, the first chord A in the first contrapuntal adjustment of the pattern turns from a triad to a half-diminished seventh chord (in bar 365; see Fig. 3a). Spatially, this added-root may occur below triad A (a root-position seventh chord; see Fig. 3b), as well as above it, or in the middle (which makes it an inverted added-root seventh chord). Supposition is not applied in connection with chord B. The combination A (half-diminished seventh chord) – B (triad) is the most common pairing in this transitional section and may be considered to be its standard form (see Murtomäki above).[14] In Fig. 3a, it can also be seen that the duration of chord A or B in a pattern is not fixed and, although the most common duration of the pattern AB is two bars, three-bar (rarely) or four-bar patterns may exist.

---

[14] The very same standard form also appears in the finale of Sibelius' Fourth Symphony (Op. 63:IV:201–208). There, the harmonic sequence was also Sibelianised (Alesaro, *The Apparition from the Forest*, 281–2), even in a more complicated way than a few years later in the first movement of the Fifth Symphony. Thus, the later application offers a clearer opportunity for scrutiny of the methods of Sibelianisation.

Fig. 3a–b. Supposition. Op. 82: I:362–366

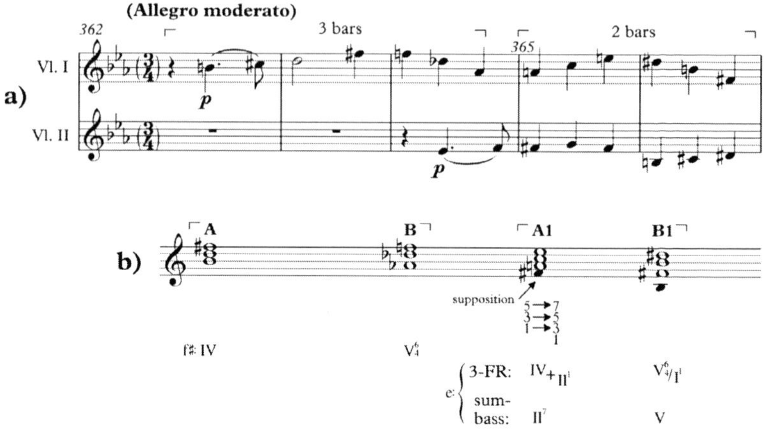

Finally, both superposition (to chord B) and supposition (to chord A) may be applied in a pattern. Yet, this combination (half-dim7–dom7) is not very common.[15]

Additional Counterpoints

Contrapuntal diversification is achieved by means of contrasting counter-themes and counterpoints.[16] The restatement of the opening motif

---

[15] Supposition to chord A and superposition to chord B (half-diminished 7th chord–dominant 7th chord; here as well as in the footnotes below a lowercase letter with 7 denotes a half-diminished 7th chord): bars 371–375 (f sharp7–B2), 404–405 (e7–A7), 406–407 (d7–G six-five), 423–424 (d sharp7–G sharp7), 431–432 (a7–D7), 447–448 (g7–C7), 451–452 (c sharp7–F sharp7), 463–464 (b four-three–E7), and 485–486 (g four-three–C7).

[16] According to Murtomäki, "The arrival on the dominant B flat is a turning point. Although the harmonic labyrinth will still return, it will yield to more significant melodic material" (*Symphonic Unity*, 173). This "yielding" may of course take place in the listener's mind, but in the domain of the *Satz* this "more significant melodic material" has the status of a counterpoint in relation to the ongoing sequential basis. With Hepokoski, the contrast between the sequential basis and its counterpoints is depicted even more markedly: "In bar 455 Sibelius reaches into the *uncentred fragments* [italics mine] to seize control with three unison trumpets sounding the upward-surging incipit motto. This … reclaims the hegemony of E flat …" (*Sibelius: Symphony No. 5*, 69).

mentioned above (bars 455–462) may be considered a contrasting counter-theme (see Fig. 4a). The *tutti*-turn culminating to *ff* presented twice earlier (in bars 28–30, 62–64) is used twice in a modified form as a second counter-theme only allotted to the horn group (bars 471–478; see Fig. 2b, 479–486). The third non-modified statement, again as a *tutti* in the last eleven bars of this transitional section (bars 487–496), dispenses with the sequence pattern; the same is true for the opening bars 471–472 (see Fig. 2b) and 479–480 of the first and the second statements of this second counter-theme (see the end of Fig. 7).

The melodic contours of the contrapuntal lines are quite simple. As a matter of fact, according to the classical models, the first example is not proper counterpoint at all. The descending segment of a chromatic scale that is embellished by upper auxiliary notes is merely a heterophonic version of the middle part of the pattern (see Fig. 4b). Yet, this is made distinctive by means of rhythm, registration, and orchestral colour. Firstly, it is presented as a tiny two-bar motif passed from one instrument to another,[17] but soon it is lengthened to three bars.[18] In the latter part of the section it covers four bars,[19] and finally five of them (bars 482–486), framing the whole *Satz* in the highest and lowest registers.[20]

The second contrapuntal line only enters in the latter part of the section (from bar 439ff). It is a rising scale-like formation compiled of successive trichords. It may also frame the whole *Satz*.[21] In bars 439–446 and 457–463 (see Fig. 4c) every other trichord contains the root and third of an accompanying subdominant added-root seventh chord (see Fig. 3b), whereas every other trichord contains the root and third of an accompanying dominant triad. (Later in bars 467–471, 472–474, 479–480, when the second counterpoint shortens and is submitted to the first one, the harmonic relation to the pattern is different). Besides occurring separately, these counterpoints may also occur together (bars 457–459, 459–462, 462–463; see Fig. 4).

---

[17] Heterophonic part functioning as a two-bar counterpoint: bars 389–390, 391–392, and 393–394, also later in bars 408–409, 410–411, and 444–445.

[18] Heterophonic part functioning as a three-bar counterpoint: bars 396–398, 399–401, 412–414, 415–417, 417–419, 419–421, 421–423, 441–443, and 457–459.

[19] Heterophonic part functioning as a four-bar counterpoint: bars 459–462, 462–465, and 467–470 in Cb. part, 475–478.

[20] Heterophonic counterpoint framing the *Satz*: bars 467–469, 475–478, and 482–486.

[21] Scale-like counterpoint framing the *Satz*: bars 443–446, 472–474, and 479–481.

Fig. 4a–c. The sequence and its counterpoints. Op. 82:I:455–465.

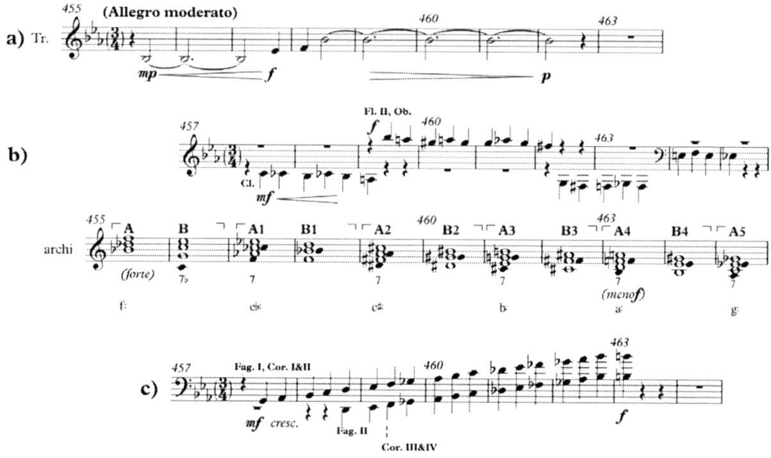

The Three-voice Framework

The harmonic and contrapuntal means of diversification are combined in increasing the first chord A into a dominant-type ninth chord by means of supposition. This may be achieved by a combination of two triads (min+maj) that have a pivot note (see Fig. 5 [Op. 82:I:369–370]),[22] or by a combination of a half-diminished seventh chord and a single note a major third below it (see Fig. 6 [Op. 82:I:423–430]).

---

[22] See also bars 380–381 (a fifth-related combination of f+B flat). In bars 376–377, a combination of two fifth-related triads (g+C six-four) is made over an organ point A (see the next footnote). In bar 383 a fifth-related combination e flat+A flat is inverted (the 1st inversion). Combining fifth-related minor and major triads may also be traced back to the audition lecture held by Sibelius in 1896 (see Alesaro, *The Apparition from the Forest*, 38–9).

Fig. 5a–b. A dominant-type ninth chord achieved by means of supposition. Op. 82:I:365–371.

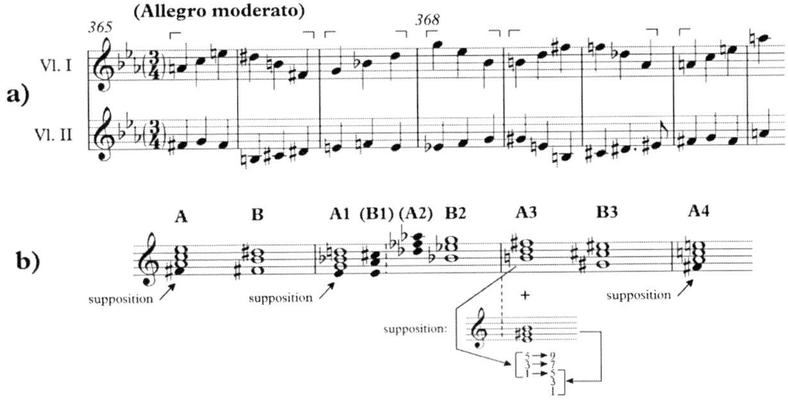

In both cases, but especially in the last one (see Fig. 6a), the lowest note of the upper chord does not lose its identity and turn to an inner part, but maintains its structural character even when a proper bass note is added below it. In this kind of *Satz* there are thus three framing parts: soprano, an assisting bass (the lowest note of the half-diminished seventh chord), and the bass. Their combination may be called the *three-voice framework*. The situation may also be described as though the framing parts (soprano and bass) of a two-voice framework are supplemented by a third "framing" part that operates above the bass and below the soprano.

Fig. 6a–b. Three-voice framework in interruptions. Op. 82:I:423–439.

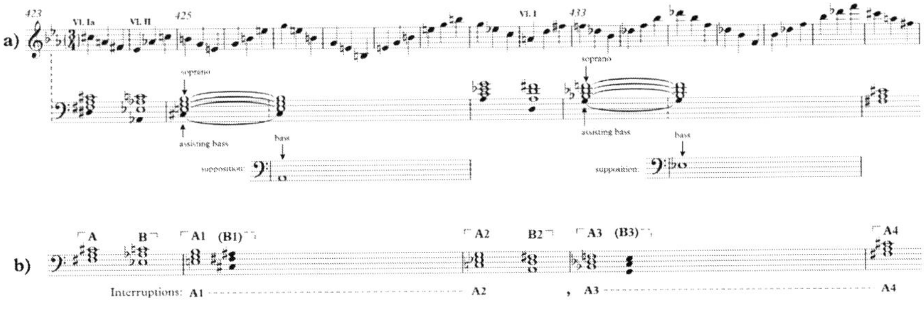

However, this was not invented by Sibelius. The concept of the three-voice framework (though not this term) was already established by C. P. E. Bach in connection with an organ point *Satz* where there is an organ point below a two-voice framework (see Fig. 1).[23] In principle, this device made possible the additive harmonies discussed above, although in the late Baroque era they emerged only exceptionally. In connection with a proceeding (non-stationary) bass part the three-voice framework containing additive harmonies was already utilised by, for example, Wagner and Bruckner.[24]

Guiding Whole-note Scale and Splitting the Pattern

As mentioned above, in the sequential process the pattern is transposed down by a major second (see Fig. 1 [Op. 82:I:354–361]). If this is done consistently, all the roots of the B-chords (the goal chords of the half cadence-pattern) gather into a collection of whole-notes. Although on the surface level of the music there are no traces of a whole-note scale, in its harmonic reduction a sequence is *guided* by a whole-note scale. Furthermore, the principle of a *guiding whole-note scale* is not new. The seeds of this principle may already be found in some modulating sequences of the Classical era.[25]

Yet, this transposing down of the pattern is never done endlessly. At the latest point before reaching the lower octave of the initial pattern, the sequential process is always interrupted and then started again at another level. In an interruption the pattern is always split, which means that the

---

[23] See C. P. E. Bach, *Essay on the True Art of Playing Keyboard Instruments*, 319–21. With Sibelius, a three-voice framework may be further extended by adding an organ point below it (see Alesaro, *The Apparition from the Forest*, 105–7). This device is also utilised in the transitional section under discussion (see bars 369, 376–7). However, for reasons of space, the extended three-voice framework is not discussed in this paper.

[24] Assisting bass+bass (as sustained note+proceeding part): Bruckner: IV Symphony 2. mvt. bars 3–6 (assisting bass: Vle., bass: Vc.; in bar 6 the *Satz* continues as a two-voice framework); Assisting bass+bass (as proceeding part+proceeding part): Bruckner: VII Symphony 3. mvt. bars 41–48 (assisting bass: Vl. II, bass: Vc., Cb.; in bars 39–40 there is still a two-voice framework).

[25] A guiding whole-note scale in a descending sequence: Mozart: Fantasy in C minor KV 475, bars 74–82 (in bars 75–76 and 77–78 there is a three-chord pattern in e flat:–c sharp:–, bars 79, 80, and 81 show a three-chord pattern in b:–a:–g:–, in bar 82 there is a two-chord pattern in F, of which the length is a half bar. The guiding scale is thus e flat–c sharp–b–a–g–F. After this, in bars 82–83 the two-chord pattern is sequentiated, but no longer according to the previous whole-note scale:–e:–d:–C:. We see that, in his own way, Mozart also avoids continuing the guiding whole-note scale to the lower octave of its beginning. In bar 82 there is a succession F:–e: instead of F:–E flat: or F:–e flat:.

last chord in a split pattern is chord A. Also in an interruption, a split pattern may be followed by a whole pattern, or by another kind of a split pattern. In the first case (e.g. A---A1B1), two different "A" chords follow each other (see Fig. 6b [Op. 82:I:425–431] e–c: A1---A2B2, [Op. 82:I:433–439] b flat–f sharp: A3---A4[B4]).[26] In the latter case, where a split pattern is followed by another kind of split pattern where the only chord left is B (e.g. A---B1), "A" and "B" chords from different patterns follow each other (see Fig. 5b [Op. 82:I:367–368] e7–E flat: A1---B2]).[27] In this latter kind of interruption there is the possibility that a listener may begin to perceive the harmonies in a reversed order to the original (i.e. as the pattern A---B1A2–B2A3 etc.).[28]

An Overall Plan of the Section

Fig. 7 presents a reduction of the whole transitional section (Op. 82:I:354–486). Regarding the guiding scales it divides into two halves, the first 61 bars (354–414) are guided by the whole-note scale F–E flat–D flat–C flat=B–A–G, whereas the last 72 bars (bars 415–486 out of the total 415–496) are guided by the whole-note scale E–D–C–B flat–A flat–G flat=F sharp.[29] From the point of view of the transitional function of this section, it is appropriate that the latter whole-note scale lacks the tonic E flat of the first movement; due to a longish absence, the tonic chord and its key are far from being a spent force in the ensuing concluding section.[30]

---

[26] Interruption A---A1: bars 414–415 (f sharp7–b7), 449–451 (f7–D flat9–c sharp7), 453–455 (b7–b flat7), and 465–467 (a7–F7–a flat).

[27] Interruption A---B1: bars 385–386 (b flat7–A), 398–399 (b flat7–A), 394–395 (h–G), 402–403 (c7–H7).

[28] In their analyses, Parmet and Murtomäki do not take into consideration the possibility of splitting the pattern. Neither does Hepokoski, for the reasons explained above.

[29] According to Murtomäki, "The development … is divided into equal halves according to the number of bars at the point where for the first time during the development a chord is supported by the bass. This chord 'happens' to be the trinote dominant A (bar 426, 52:8)" (*Symphonic Unity*, 170).

[30] In the latter half of the transitional section the tonic key is of course vaguely hinted at through the dominant chord of the parallel key E flat minor in bars 422, 458, and 468.

Fig. 7. Structures resulting from the roots of B-chords. Op. 82:I:354–496

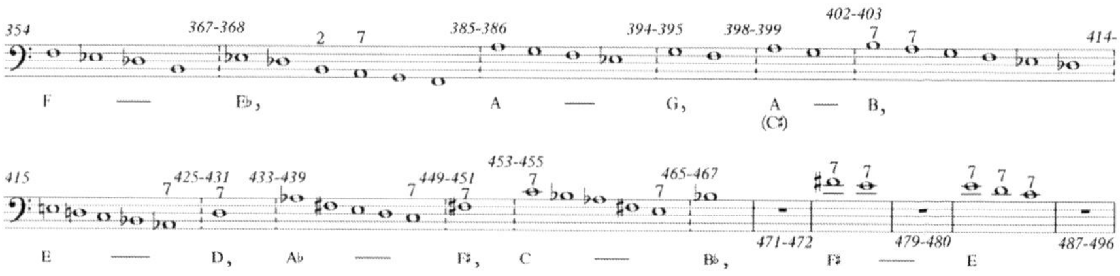

In both halves, one can also detect some hyper-sequences. In the first half the first notes of the fragments of the guiding scale are F–E flat, A–G, A–B (an exact three-unit hyper-sequence would have been F–E flat, A–G, C sharp–B). In the second half, the equivalent pitches are E–D, A flat–F sharp, C–B flat, F sharp–E. Here, the exact three-unit hyper-sequence that was implied during the first half is now realised. The lengths of the guiding scale segments also match. The fourth unit (F sharp–E) again avoids the re-presentation of the first unit (E–D) that would result from following the pattern exactly.

Conclusions

We have seen that in diversifying his harmonic material Sibelius has used the full capacity of his imagination and compositional tools. In grasping the harmonic and tonal logic of this transitional section, I find the three-voice framework to be an essential feature. In Sibelius' music there are more techniques in the domain of *Satz* than, for example, a Schenkerian approach would be apt to take into consideration.

According to Hepokoski, "The very length and seemingly 'gravity-free' chattering of the passage suggest how fragile is the survival, even at this late point, of the E flat tonic."[31] As mentioned at the outset, this transitional section stands between sections that are firmly rooted in E flat. The "survival" of the E flat tonic is thus less fragile and more secure. In my opinion, the term "gravity-free"—or "seemingly gravity-free"—does not do justice to the tonal architecture of this section. To my mind, the two structural arches of the guiding whole-note scales (see Fig. 7) are no less free from "gravity" than more traditional major- or minor-scale structures.

[31] Hepokoski, *Sibelius: Symphony No. 5*, 69.

JEAN SIBELIUS AND THE MODES OF LIMITED TRANSPOSITION

AARE TOOL

My aim in this chapter is to provide a short overview of the modes of limited transposition used in Jean Sibelius' music. The term "mode of limited transposition" originates in Olivier Messiaen's book *The Technique of My Musical Language* published in 1944—one of the best-known early treatises to address questions concerning non-major/minor scales.[1] Messiaen describes seven different modes, providing examples from his own compositions. Here, the discussion focuses on three modes that can be considered as the most widely used in the nineteenth and early twentieth centuries: octatonic, hexatonic, and whole-tone scales. Admittedly, the phrase "widely used" might be somewhat misleading, because it is their rarity, the very specific context in which they are deployed, that makes them a worthwhile research topic. Although it is almost common knowledge that octatonic passages can be encountered, for example, in several works of Rimsky-Korsakov,[2] and whole-tone harmonies are a frequent feature of Debussy's music, the real magnitude of nineteenth- and twentieth-century octatonic, hexatonic, and whole-tone practices is still waiting to be scrutinised in music-theoretical writings.

Recently, interest in the relatively obscure area of octatonicism and hexatonicism has been revived, partly due to the new developments in music theory associated with the term "transformational theory" (or "neo-Riemannian theory"). In transformational theory, octatonicism and hexatonicism have emerged as one of the most widely discussed topics, even though the range of composers mentioned in connection with those scales tends to be rather small. From a transformational viewpoint, hexatonicism and octatonicism serve as the ultimate manifestations of

---

[1] Olivier Messiaen, *The Technique of My Musical Language*, vol. 1., trans. John Satterfield (Paris: Alphonse Leduc, 1956 [1944]), 58–61.

[2] Richard Taruskin, "Catching Up with Rimsky-Korsakov," *Music Theory Spectrum* 33 (2) (Fall 2011): 175.

voice-leading efficiency due to their symmetrical structures. Apart from thoroughly investigating the special mathematical properties of these scales, transformational theories have also contributed to our understanding of the wider cultural context in which the modes of limited transposition occurred in the late nineteenth and early twentieth centuries. Richard Cohn notes that in the so-called Freudian age, hexatonic progressions of major/major triads were often used to signify certain "uncanny" topics related to misery, fear, confusion, and death.[3] Observations about the gloomy connotations of hexatonic progression, however, also hold true for the other modes. In the music of Rimsky-Korsakov, octatonic passages occur in connection with sorcery and exoticism, as in *Sadko*, and chords of the whole-tone scale (augmented triads) are a prominent feature of Franz Liszt's late piano pieces, such as *Unstern!*[4] In the context of nineteenth-century common-practice tonality, occasional whole-tone, hexatonic, and octatonic passages functioned as the musical "other" and, accordingly, suggested a wide array of topics concerning estrangement. During the first half of the twentieth century, as non-major/minor scales became more common, their initial "Freudian" connotations were gradually abandoned.

In Olivier Messiaen's treatise, the term "first mode of limited transposition" stands for the whole-tone scale, and his "second mode" is known today as the octatonic scale—a term proposed by Arthur Berger in the 1960s.[5] The hexatonic scale is a six-note subset of Messiaen's "third mode." To demonstrate the genesis of the octatonic scale, the following scheme can be used (see Example 1a): every side of the triangle stands for one transposition of the diminished seventh chord. By combining the pitches of any two sides, one transposition of the octatonic scale (one octatonic collection) can be produced, and, therefore, there are three octatonic collections in total.[6] The sides of the triangle (and the according

---

[3] Richard Cohn, "Uncanny Resemblances: Tonal Signification in the Freudian Age," *Journal of the American Musicological Society* 57 (2) (Summer 2004): 285–6; see also Richard Cohn, *Audacious Euphony. Chromaticism and the Triad's Second Nature* (Oxford: Oxford University Press, 2012), 21–3.

[4] Larry R. Todd, "The 'Unwelcome Guest' Regaled: Franz Liszt and the Augmented Triad," *19th-Century Music* 12 (2) (1988): 114.

[5] Arthur Berger, "Problems of Pitch Organization in Stravinsky," *Perspectives of New Music* 2 (1) (1963): 20. For further information about the origins of the term "octatonic" see Arthur Berger, *Reflections of an American Composer* (Berkeley: University of California Press, 2002), 186–8.

[6] Richard Cohn defines the octatonic scale (or collection) as "the union of two distinct diminished seventh chords" and the hexatonic scale as "the union of two adjacent augmented triads" (*Audacious Euphony*, 212).

diminished seventh chords) are marked as "0", "1," and "2." "0" corresponds to the diminished seventh chord {C,D#,F#,A} (as it contains pitch-class {0}), "1" to {C#,E,G,A#}, and "2" to {D,F,G#,B}. An analogous scheme can be produced to demonstrate the genesis of hexatonic and whole-tone scales (Example 1b). Every side of the square stands for one transposition of the augmented triad (marked as "0," "1," "2," and "3"). By combining the pitches of any pair of adjacent sides, one transposition of the hexatonic scale can be produced, and the opposite sides of the square generate one transposition of the whole-tone scale. All the transpositions of the octatonic, hexatonic, and whole-tone scales can be denoted as OCT_0,1, OCT_1,2, and OCT_2,0; HEX_0,1, HEX_1,2, HEX_2,3, and HEX_3,0; WT_0,2 and WT_1,3. Each of the two integers following the abbreviation represents one constituent chord of that transposition (diminished seventh chords in OCT and augmented triads in HEX or WT). For example, the octatonic scale {C,D,D#,F,F#,G#,A,B} is OCT_2,0, as it consists of diminished seventh chords {D,F,G#,B} ("2") and {C,D#,F#,A} ("0").

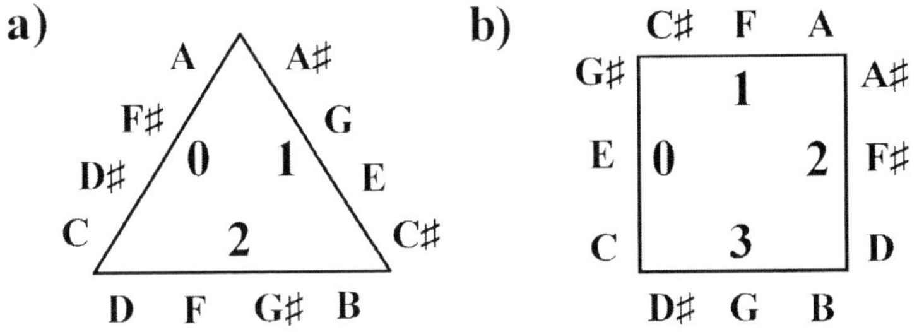

Example 1. Diminished seventh chords as generators of octatonic collections (a); augmented triads as generators of hexatonic and whole-tone collections (b)

Of Jean Sibelius's works, the Fourth Symphony has probably been the most often discussed in connection with octatonic and whole-tone sonorities (or, more generally speaking, the tritone—a dyad characteristic of both scales).[7] It is initiated by a whole-tone figure {C,D,F#,E}, and the

[7] The role of the tritone in the Fourth Symphony has been analysed in Veijo Murtomäki, *Symphonic Unity. The Development of Formal Thinking in the Symphonies of Sibelius*, trans. Henry Bacon (Studia musicologica universitatis helsingiensis 5) (Helsinki: University of Helsinki, Department of Musicology, 1993), 86–7. See also Elliott Antokoletz, "The Musical Language of the Fourth

whole-tone scale is prominent in what follows. For example, at the beginning of the mid-section of the first movement (from bar 54 onwards), there are octatonic implications, and from bar 71 onwards extensive whole-tone passages appear, played by the strings *sulla tastiera*. It is very characteristic of Sibelius to underline the "otherness" of octatonic or whole-tone passages further by means of special string-playing techniques, such as *sulla tastiera (sul tasto)*, *tremolo*, or *sul ponticello*. In his music, these techniques often appear in the context of the otherworldly topics, as in *Lemminkäinen in Tuonela* from the *Lemminkäinen* Suite, although the modes of limited transposition are not always manifest in those cases. In the second movement (*Allegro molto vivace*) of the Fourth Symphony from *Doppio più lento* (rehearsal letter K) onwards, an ascending octatonic passage {C#,D,E,F,G,Ab,Bb,B} (OCT_1,2) appears in the lower strings. Although the Fourth Symphony has been associated with the whole-tone and octatonic practices probably more than any other of Sibelius' work, there are even more eloquent examples of these scales to be found elsewhere in his music.

Nowhere is Sibelius's whole-tone practice exemplified as strikingly as in the music written in 1909 for Mikael Lybeck's play *Ödlan* (*The Lizard*). The plot, with its underlying motives of mystery, seduction, mental breakdown, and death, provided Sibelius with the pretext for delving into the depths of gloomy musical imagery. One needs to keep in mind that *The Lizard* was never intended to be played as a concert piece, and the music is tightly interrelated with the spoken text. The most appropriate label for the genre of Sibelius' work would be "melodrama."[8] The music for *The Lizard* consists of two pieces: a relatively short one written for Scene No. 1 and a considerably more extensive one to accompany Scene No. 2. In the concluding bars of the first piece, a passage based on octatonic collection {G#,A#,B,C#,D,E,F,G} (OCT_1,2) occurs, played by the solo violin, the personification of one of the characters. In the music for the second scene, whole-tone harmonies are prominent. In bars 13–14, semitonally ascending augmented triads appear, not dissimilar to those used by Franz Liszt in his sinister piano piece *Unstern!*, for example. Descending whole-tone passages eventually lead to a "whole-tone canon" (rehearsal letter F), in which all the voices are exclusively based on WT_1,3 (Example 2). Such extensive whole-tone harmonies are rather

---

Symphony," in *Sibelius Studies*, eds. Timothy L. Jackson and Veijo Murtomäki (Cambridge: Cambridge University Press, 2001), 302–3.

[8] Jeffrey Kallberg, "Theatrical Sibelius: The Melodramatic Lizard," in *Jean Sibelius and His World*, ed. Daniel M. Grimley (Princeton: Princeton University Press, 2011), 74.

exceptional in Sibelius' oeuvre, and *The Lizard* can be considered as the most eloquent manifestation of his whole-tone practice. In the nineteenth century, whole-tone harmonies were one of the main devices to suggest a wide range of otherworldly topics. Whole-tone passages (or chord types characteristic of that scale) typically appear in connection with death, but also in pieces of programme music concerned with diabolic visions, such as the original 1867 version of Modest Mussorgsky's *Night on the Bare Mountain*.

Example 2. "Whole-tone canon" in *The Lizard* (Scene No. 2)

Although the Fourth Symphony and *The Lizard* are undeniable landmarks in the development of Sibelius' musical language, the modes of limited transposition were by no means unprecedented in his earlier music. Hexatonic and octatonic chord relations also appear in his works written in the 1890s. Octatonic relations are those in which chords of the same type (either major/minor triads, half-diminished seventh chords, minor seventh chords, or dominant seventh chords) are transposed by three or six semitones. Hexatonic relations occur as the result of transposing major/minor triads by four semitones. Occasional hexatonic chord relations can be encountered in Sibelius' first orchestral piece, the Overture in E major written in 1891 during his studies in Vienna. In bars 92–97 there is a sequence of minor triads related by four semitones, initiated by a progression of D sharp minor and G minor triads. Thus, from the very beginning, Sibelius demonstrated an affinity to the Lisztian-Wagnerian harmonic practice, with octatonic and hexatonic chord relations as one of its characteristics. It is worth noting, however, that hexatonic (or octatonic) progressions of minor triads are somewhat more common in Sibelius' music than progressions of major triads—a feature that distinguishes his harmonic practice from that manifest in several works of Liszt (consider, for example, the hexatonic relationship of A major and F major triads at the beginning of his Second Piano Concerto).

Sibelius has tackled the topic of the otherworldly in several of his works, often in connection with mythological themes. The gloomy connotations of hexatonic chord progressions are underlined in *Kullervo*, a work concerned with guilt and revenge. The third movement, entitled *Kullervo and his Sister*, concludes with a section known as *Kullervo's Lament* (*Kullervon valitus*), in which the anti-hero recognises the irretrievable harm he has caused ("Woe my father, woe my mother, woe to you, my aged parents ..."). In the passage in question (from bar 525 onwards), octatonic chord relations are prominent, as F minor triads alternate with A flat minor triads. In *The Swan of Tuonela* from *Lemminkäinen*, hexatonic and octatonic chord relations appear: in bars 7–9, a hexatonic progression of B flat minor and F sharp minor triads occurs, and from bar 44 onwards half-diminished seventh chords {B,D,F,A}, {D,F,Ab,C} and {F,Ab,Cb,Eb} of one and the same octatonic collection (OCT_2,0) are used. Similar relations of half-diminished seventh chords are the hallmark of the Prelude to Wagner's *Tristan und Isolde*. *The Swan of Tuonela* almost comes across as a Sibelian paraphrase of probably the most celebrated musical treatment of the love-and-death-topic—not least because of the cor anglais used to a great effect in both works. A further example of the modes of limited transposition used in connection with death can be encountered in Sibelius' song *Come away, Death*, Op. 60 No. 1, on words from Shakespeare's *Twelfth Night*. In that song, hexatonic progressions of minor triads are notable: at the beginning, an E minor triad is followed by a G sharp minor triad in order to emphasise the word "death," and it is the G sharp minor triad that concludes the song, despite the apparent E minor key.

In Sibelius' earlier works, with the exception of *The Lizard*, these modes usually appear in conjunction with other (major/minor) scales, and extensive passages of only one transposition of the octatonic or whole-tone scale are relatively rare. However, in the 1920s, such passages became much more common. Let us consider the third piano piece *Forest Lake* from Op. 114, for example. In the middle section (bars 14–23), the pitches of only one octatonic collection OCT_1,2 ({Db,D,E,F,G,Ab,Bb,Cb}) are used, and in bars 24–29 and 30 half-diminished seventh chords {B,D,F,A} and {F,Ab,Cb,Eb} related by a tritone (and thus belonging to one and the same octatonic collection OCT_2,0) appear. Therefore, *Forest Lake* is a good reminder that, in Sibelius' music, the modes of limited transposition also signify the mysterious and sublime qualities of nature.

Octatonicism is manifest in the incidental music written for *The Tempest* by Shakespeare, completed in 1926 and thus one of Sibelius' very last orchestral works. No. 9 is entitled *The Oak Tree* (*Ariel Plays the Flute*) and accompanies the scene where the survivors of the shipwreck curse their fate, as they have landed on a desert island. The octatonic flute melody, mostly based on OCT_0,1 ({E,F#,G,A,A#,C,C#,D#}), is accompanied by chords of the same octatonic collection played by the harp, harmonium, and violins (as in the original version—the instrumentation is somewhat different in the orchestral suite). The particularly extensive degree of strictly used octatonicism in *The Oak Tree* is definitely unusual in Sibelius' output. The "otherness" of hexatonic and octatonic chord relations is emphasised in *Caliban's Song*: in bars 13–16, a hexatonic progression of G minor and B minor triads appears, followed in bars 17–20 by an octatonic progression of G minor and C sharp minor triads (see Example 3). Traits of octatonicism are also to be found in No. 23 entitled *The Rainbow*: a six-note subset {B,C,D,Eb,F,Gb} of OCT_2,0 is played by the cellos and violins, combined with descending whole-tone passages {C,Bb,Ab,Gb} from the double basses in bars 7–10. Whole-tone harmonies are extensively used in the Prelude to *The Tempest* (especially in bars 32–35), depicting the shipwreck.

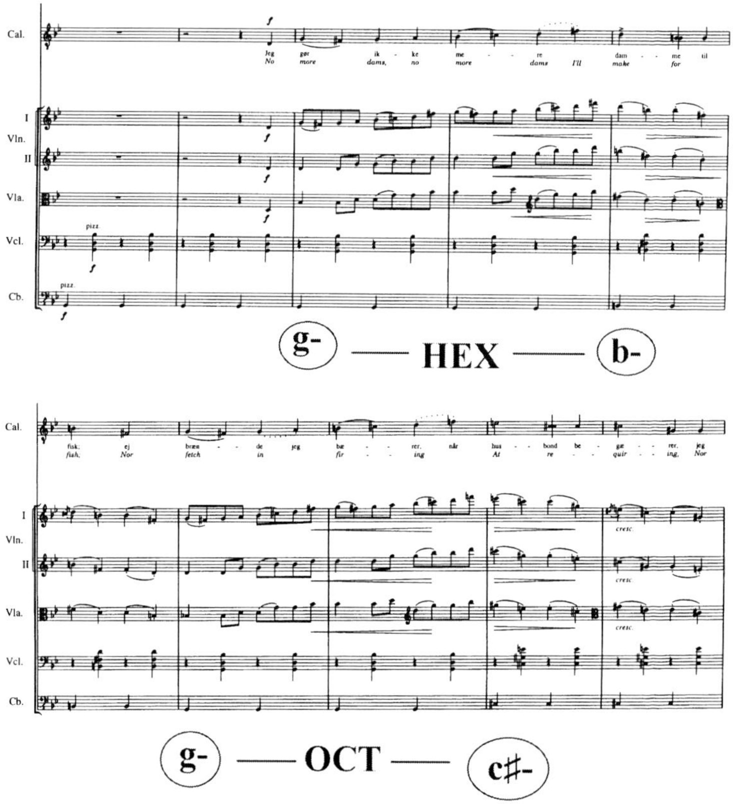

Example 3. Hexatonic and octatonic chord relations in *Caliban's Song* from *The Tempest*

To bring things to a conclusion, some remarks on the use of the modes of limited transposition in Estonian music are useful. Many of the composers who entered the musical scene in the first half of the twentieth century have, not surprisingly, mentioned Sibelius as one of the main sources of inspiration, and there are some similar compositional tendencies in their use of these collections. Whole-tone and octatonic scales first appeared in Estonian music during the first decade of the twentieth century. *Nineveh's Turn from Evil* from the oratorio *Des Jona Sendung* (1909) by Rudolf Tobias (1873–1918) is arguably one of the first instances of octatonic progressions in Estonian music (see Example 4). The oratorio is based on the Biblical story of the Prophet Jonah, who was to announce the doom of

Nineveh. In *Nineveh's Turn from Evil*, a children's chorus calls for repentance: "Let neither man nor beast taste anything, and cry mightily unto God. Who can tell if God will turn and repent, and turn away from his fierce anger, that we perish not?" An A minor triad leads to those of C minor and E flat minor, which, by being related by three (six) semitones, belong to one and the same octatonic collection. Very much like Sibelius in *Kullervo's Lament* or *The Swan of Tuonela*, for example, Tobias operates within the late nineteenth-century tradition of tonal signification, with octatonicism and other modes of limited transposition as its main markers for sinister topics. The first Estonian to use the octatonic scale more extensively was Eduard Oja (1905–50). During the first half of the 1930s, he produced a number of works largely based on octatonicism, such as the piano cycle *Silent Moods* (*Vaikivad meeleolud*) and the Piano Quintet.[9] Although there are several other early twentieth-century composers (most notably Alexander Scriabin) whose music could have influenced the emerging octatonic trends in Estonia, the guiding role of Sibelius should not be ruled out.

---

9 For an analysis of the *Silent Moods* see Aare Tool, "Aspects of Octatonicism in the Music of Eduard Oja," *Lietuvos muzikologija* [*Lithuanian Musicology*] 16 (2015): 24–31.

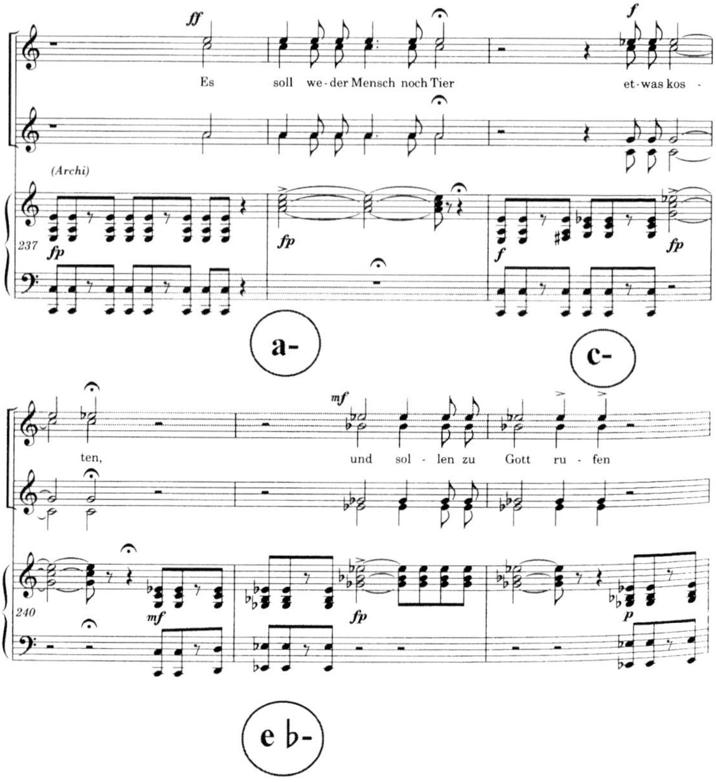

Example 4. Rudolf Tobias's oratorio *Des Jona Sendung* (1909): *Nineveh's Turn from Evil*

Sibelius' oeuvre, spanning from the 1890s to the 1920s, eloquently reflects how using the modes of limited transposition changed during that period of turmoil: occasional octatonic and hexatonic chord relations in the vein of Liszt and Wagner, and often in connection with some very specific gloomy or exotic topics, gave way to more extensive passages based on those scales. Sibelius can be considered as one of the crucial links between the *fin-de-siècle* harmonic practices and the modernist trends that emerged in the 1920s.

DORIAN DEPARTURES: MODALITY IN SIBELIUS' SIXTH SYMPHONY

LES BLACK

Admirers of Jean Sibelius' music typically appreciate the balance of sheer sensuous beauty and structural logic in his works. For music theorists, the latter is usually a priority, though it is impossible to separate the intellectually satisfying devices that unify works from their expressive energies. Sibelius seems to guide listeners away from overly technical approaches to his works in this quote regarding his Sixth Symphony.

> You may analyze it and explain it theoretically. You may find that there are several interesting things going on. But most people forget that it is, above all, a poem.[1]

So, before beginning my analysis, I'd like to reveal the poem I hear in Sibelius' Sixth Symphony, lest I forget. While opinions vary concerning the effect of the endings of the exterior movements, I have always heard the final measures of the first movement as resilient and confident. The final melody rises to the characteristic D-Dorian pitch B, and then settles on the mediant note F, emphasising the D-Dorian tritone and proudly proclaiming that the mode is alive and well. The finale, on the other hand, is a complete surrender. Not only has the Dorian B been abandoned for Aeolian B flat, but the melodic energy collapses, confined to a non-syncopated, lifeless version of the cadence gestures from the beginning of the movement.

As shown in Example 1, the final melody of the last movement might be heard as a weak echo of the passage to D Dorian in the first movement, where a powerful ascending motion C–D–E in the trumpets is followed by a D minor arpeggio in the clarinet that neatly places D in the middle of the C-E space, setting the stage for the ascent to B.[2] This gesture announces

[1] Harold E. Johnson, *Jean Sibelius* (New York: Alfred A. Knopf, 1959), 192.

[2] Jean Sibelius, *Symphony No. 6*, rev. ed. (Copenhagen: Wilhelm Hansen AS, 1981). All musical examples are based on this edition.

the Dorian ending with confidence, while its counterpart in the finale simply settles on D, unable to seek out the Dorian B natural after B flat has taken hold. It is clear that the departure of the Dorian mode leaves the music mourning for its unique sonic identity as it submits to the silence of the void.

Example 1. Sibelius, Symphony No. 6, I: 258–266, IV: 249–256

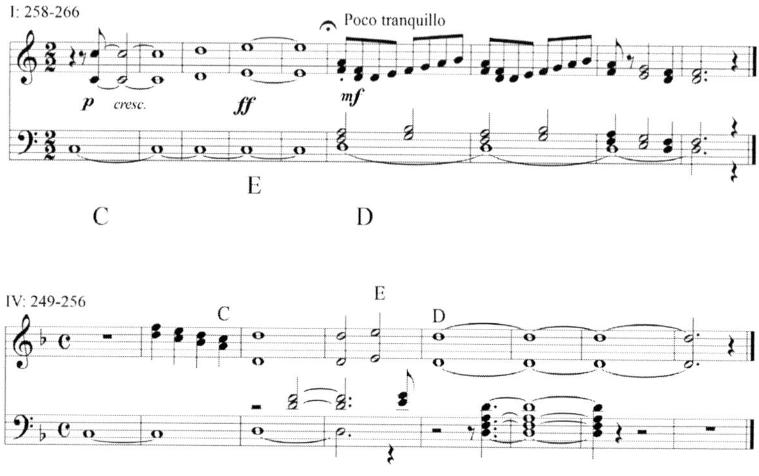

The transformation in tone that I hear in these endings depends mostly on the modal colouring. Previous analyses of this work, particularly Veijo Murtomäki's treatment, have correctly pointed to the many critical appearances of B flat and B natural that support the modal transformation.[3] Subsequently, James Hepokoski's analysis of the finale as a rotational structure identifies an ultimate goal moment or *telos* for the movement, derived from the earliest sketches for the symphony.[4] This *telos* summarises the tonal journey from D Dorian, through C major, to D Aeolian. The ultimate victory of D Aeolian is secured in the finale at a point Hepokoski identifies as "the crisis." I believe this crisis point, the

[3] Veijo Murtomäki, *Symphonic Unity: The Development of Formal Thinking in the Symphonies of Sibelius*, trans. Henry Bacon (Studia Musicologica Universitatis Helsingiensis 5) (Studia musicologica universitatis helsingiensis 5) (Helsinki: University of Helsinki, Department of Musicology, 1993), 193–241.

[4] James Hepokoski, "Rotation, Sketches, and the *Sixth Symphony*," in *Sibelius Studies*, eds. Timothy L. Jackson and Veijo Murtomäki (Cambridge: Cambridge University Press, 2001), 322–51.

moment when the finale's *telos* is utterly lost, is also the *telos* moment for the symphony as a whole. A series of ideas, initiated in the opening of the first movement, coalesce at Hepokoski's crisis point, assuring the transformation of mode.

Four principal ideas emerge in the opening pages of the first movement. Most important initially is the relationship between the notes D and C. The formal ambiguity of the movement allows these notes to evolve from rivals to allies, a situation that will be reflected by a counter-alliance in the finale. The source of this counter-alliance is the second idea, which may be characterised as a steady growth in the status of B flat. It becomes clear through the work that neither the pitch B flat nor chords built on B flat have the power to overcome D Dorian. The magic talisman for D Aeolian turns out to be a breakthrough to the key of B flat. This breakthrough might be compared to the routine of breaking through to the dominant of the dominant in sonata-form transitions. The extra turn to the sharp side assures that the music will settle comfortably in the dominant key. Likewise, in this symphony, attaining the diatonic collection with two flats assures that the music can comfortably settle back into the one-flat collection, securing D Aeolian. The third idea from the first movement is symmetry, which is the natural source of power for the Dorian mode since D is one of the points of the axis of symmetry of the natural-note collection. The fourth and final idea is a characteristic resolution of half-diminished seventh chords first suggested in mm. 61–66 of the first movement. The basic voice-leading is shown in Example 2.

Example 2. Half-diminished seventh chord resolutions in mvt. 1

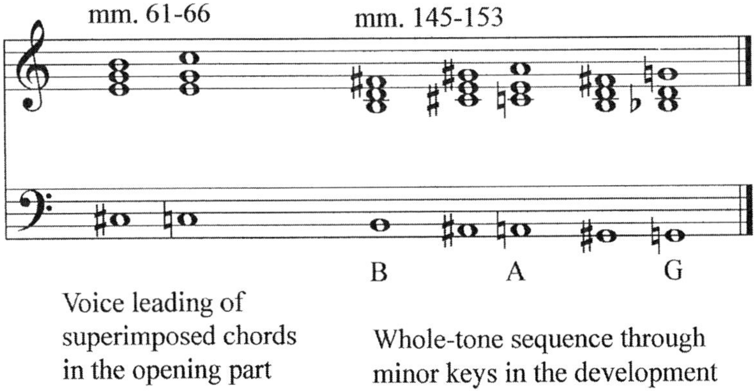

In the first passage, a C sharp half-diminished seventh chord in the strings and woodwinds is replaced rather brutally by a superimposed C major harmony in the brass. There is no actual voice-leading motion in this succession of sounds, since the two chords overlap with C major simply outlasting the other chord. However, as Tim Howell has pointed out, the implied resolution is a seventh expanding to an octave with two common tones, as shown in Example 2.[5] Another presentation of this voice-leading idea occurs in the whole-tone sequence of minor keys during the first movement's development section, also shown in Example 2. However, the essential occurrence of this progression unfolds in the finale at the crisis point.

To uncover the evolution of these ideas, the contentious issue of form in the first movement must be addressed. Analysts have expressed different opinions regarding the identity of the first theme of this movement, with most identifying m. 29 as the start of a modal form featuring D Dorian, but with a few selecting m. 67 as the start of a C major tonal form.[6] Even for those expounding the modal form, the opening must contain some introductory material since the primary theme does not appear at the outset. The feeling of an introduction is clearly announced by the subdued texture, and relatively slow note values. In the same way, Beethoven in his Ninth Symphony and Brahms in his Second Symphony generate the impression of slow introductions despite consistent meters and tempos between the apparent introduction and exposition sections.

Sibelius' opening is certainly in no hurry to establish D as a centre. In fact, the initial gesture that unfolds over mm. 1–4 appears to present both C and F as possible centres. Note that the pitch content in these measures is the hexachord from C to A, thus withholding the nature of the complete diatonic collection. The first chord could be tonic in F major moving to a dominant chord, or a subdominant moving to a C major tonic. The unfolding of a complete C major triad in mm. 3–4 briefly secures C major, a conclusion that is supported in m. 5 when B natural enters to complete

---

[5] Tim Howell, *Jean Sibelius: Progressive Techniques in the Symphonies and Tone Poems* (New York and London: Garland Publishing, 1989), 78.

[6] Howell, *Jean Sibelius*, 80; M. Stuart Collins, *The Orchestral Music of Sibelius* (PhD dissertation, University of Leeds, 1973), 346–60; Simon Parmet, *The Symphonies of Sibelius. A Study in Musical Appreciation*, trans. Kingsley A. Hart (London: Cassell & Co., 1959), 99–102. Howell takes the C major theme of m. 67 as the beginning of the exposition. Collins treats this section as a second theme, but identifies C major as the main key of the movement. For a complete survey of the literature see Murtomäki, *Symphonic Unity*, 215–21.

the diatonic collection within a very prominent idea consisting of step-wise motions through thirds sequenced down by a step.

Although B flat never appears in these measures, the mere possibility of its appearance within F major seems to provoke a strong compensatory reaction in the music. A C sharp^{o7} chord soon locates D as a tonic through its leading tone energy, and suggests Dorian colouring with its seventh. Note also the F sharps, leading to persistent arrivals on E minor triads. All this sharp-side energy erupts in the music to counter what must be termed at this point an imagined threat from the flat side. These events set the stage for the D Dorian theme at m. 29, which enters in a manner that fails to project the type of opening-out energy usually associated with primary themes. Note that the violins begin a third rendition of the melody from m. 5 just before the D Dorian theme begins. Thus, there is a sense of an idea "in progress" at this moment, and when the idea from m. 5 is not sequenced but rather directed down an additional step to a resting point, the opening gesture of the D Dorian theme takes on a closing feel.

The continuation of the theme in the flutes at mm. 33–37 could be heard as a varied expansion of the abandoned third attempt at the idea from m. 5. Later events clarify that this is the primary theme of the movement. However, the music in mm. 29–37 simply does not sound like music aspiring to be a main theme. Of course, Sibelius is under no obligation to compose his primary theme in a manner that clearly announces its function. My suggestion is that the weakness of this D theme opens the door to the initial perception that it is not a theme at all, but simply more spinning out of introductory ideas. Thus, Sibelius gets his modal form under way while at the same time extending the feeling of introduction to the end of m. 66, allowing the C major theme that follows to sound like the event that launches the expository phase of a tonal form.

The C major theme at m. 67 (letter B in the score) clearly has the opening-out energy of a primary theme. The note values and overall activity increase giving the impression of a change to a faster tempo, and the melody unfolds in a clear sentence form. I am sure it has also been noticed by many listeners that this theme seems to reference the opening of Beethoven's "Waldstein" Sonata with the top line using a sharpened fourth scale degree and the bass following a lament pattern that introduces B flat into the texture for the first time as a chromatic detail. Referencing one of the most famous primary themes in common-practice literature strikes me as a clear invitation to hear this theme as the launching point of a sonata form. Thus, Sibelius sets up his game of simultaneously unfolding modal and tonal sonata forms. Listeners hearing a tonal form now expect a second theme, while modal listeners hear a completed modal exposition that sets D Dorian against C Ionian.

Extending the possibility of both forms is manageable since both models now require a relatively unstable passage. Modal listeners are expecting a development, while tonal listeners are expecting a transition to the second theme. Example 3 presents a sketch of this passage, from approximately mm. 97–144. An extension of the whole-tone sequence idea from the beginning of the theme connects the final C major cadence with G flat major. For most of this passage, G flat and C major triads are juxtaposed in eighth-note string figurations. When the music moves from these chords the motion is by whole-tone steps.

Example 3. Sibelius, Symphony No. 6, I: 97–144 (sketch)

The whole-tone progressions essentially fill the space between G flat and C, leading to the impression that the music is simply fixated on these notes and the triads and dominant-seventh chords built upon them. In conventional harmonic syntax, major triads a tritone apart suggest the progression Neapolitan to dominant. Because of the symmetry of the tritone within the octave each chord may have either function, meaning that this progression can be directed to the major or minor keys on B or F. In fact, both of these possible goals are clearly suggested in the figuration around m. 110, where V^7 chords with roots on G flat and C resolve to C flat and F major triads. Thus, this entire passage builds energy for an arrival on one of these keys. As it turns out, this incredibly strong signpost is preparing both of these goals. B minor appears at m. 144 to begin a long development of the D Dorian theme, and F major appears at m. 190, bringing with it the enigmatic new theme of the recapitulation. Listeners expecting either form to clearly dominate are disappointed by these arrivals.

Tonal listeners are disappointed first. While it is conceivable that an unusually long transition is still in effect at m. 143, the B minor arrival clearly seems to indicate that we are already in the development section. While the key relationship of C major to B minor for a second theme is certainly not a problem, having been explored by Sibelius in his Third Symphony—the material is the Dorian melody from m. 29. When this material is spun out into a whole-tone sequence, it is clear that Sibelius is combining the material of m. 29 with the sequential whole-tone bass pattern of the C major melody and thus engaging in classic developmental behaviour. So, modal listeners may gloat for a few measures as the following passage unfolds, and an apparent recapitulation begins at m. 168.

Unfortunately, listeners convinced that the modal form will prevail suffer a setback when the new melody emerges in F major at m. 190. This melody provides a long-anticipated second theme for the tonal form. Though it lacks the expected cadence, this theme does appear in a new key, and Sibelius seems intent on pointing out the significance of this key by changing the key signature for the only time in the movement. Considering that the new signature persists for only nine measures, the motivation for its appearance seems to be more semiotic than practical.

When the natural-note collection returns, we immediately hear the new theme transposed to C major, followed by the closing ideas of the C major music from the exposition, still in the key of C. All of this is disastrous for those expecting the modal form, in which the C major material functions as the second theme and therefore should be transposed to D Dorian.

Instead, C major persists to the end of the recapitulation, acting more like the key of a primary theme. Furthermore, the contrast of keys expected in tonal works has occurred, even though the two versions of the secondary theme have been presented side by side in the recapitulation. In the end, it appears that neither model is sufficient. The movement is the offspring of a modal mother and a tonal father, sharing characteristics with both but necessarily growing into a unique individual.

If we accept the idea of two potential forms unfolding at once, it becomes possible to speak of two independent, large-scale functions also unfolding within this movement. The modal form raises the issue of pitch centricity in the symphony, pitting C against D. While these tones compete in the modal form they are allies in the tonal arena, since their specific scale formations, C Ionian and D Dorian, belong to the same diatonic collection. The tonal form presents an old-fashioned key contrast, bringing F major and the one-flat collection into the mix. This key replaces the usual dominant in order to elevate B flat from a chromatic detail in the C major theme to a diatonic pitch. However, the flat-side energy is not yet strong enough to overcome the natural-note collection.

The F major music is immediately neutralised by a transposition to C major. At this moment, we come to understand how useful the alliance with C is for the main D Dorian mode. C major takes on the role of a champion, vanquishing challenges from the flat side. The champion role re-emerges in the coda. The passage at m. 255 returns the signpost gesture from the development section, except with major-minor seventh chords separated by a semitone. Since this type of progression usually suggests a German-sixth to V^7 progression, the G flat and F seventh chords invite a move to the key of B flat.

The following scale ascends from D flat through the notes of B flat minor. However, this attempt to solidify the key is immediately undermined by a roll on C in the timpani, reinforced with Cs and Gs in the brass section. When the scale reaches C, the trumpets take over with the aforementioned C–D–E gesture. The top note is not only a sonic highpoint but also the key moment in vanquishing B flat as a key, since both B flat major and minor require the pitch E flat. Now, the Dorian final simply settles into the middle of the major third. I believe this is a defining moment for the whole modal argument in the work. Consider that C major dominates the recapitulation, taking on the role of the principal key, vanquishes the only tonal challenge within the main form, and overcomes a late challenge in the coda. C major is incredibly strong, and yet it simply cedes the final cadence function to D Dorian. This clearly presents C major as an ally of D Dorian, an ally that D Dorian seems dependent upon in the struggle against the flat-side collection.

For its own part, D Dorian is bolstered by the appearance of symmetrical structures. The brief but formally important arrivals on B minor in the development and F major in the recapitulation locate the extreme notes of the natural-note collection, which are symmetrical around D. Another important symmetry is shown in Example 4. After the long whole-tone sequence breaks in the development, Sibelius touches on the harmonies C sharp minor, B flat major, F sharp minor, and E flat major. The roots of these notes are symmetrical around D, preparing the moment of recapitulation.

Example 4. Chord root symmetry around D, I: mm. 157–168 (sketch)

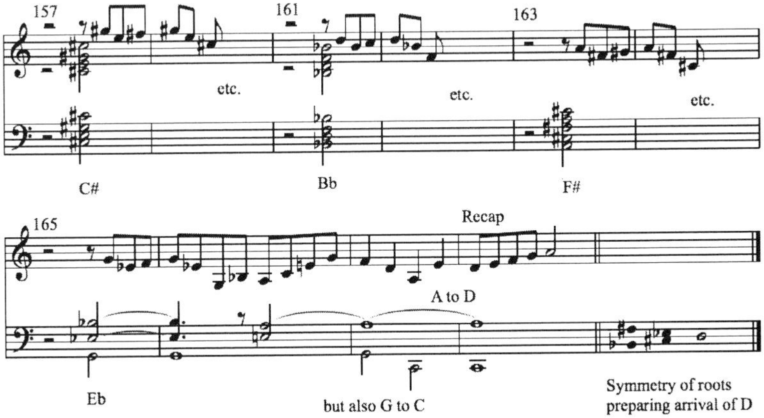

Finally, the powerful C–D–E trumpet idea that prepares the final D Dorian arrival is symmetrical around D. Taking this idea of symmetry forward into the middle movements, we find that the second movement is written in the two-flat collection and appears to be in G minor. However, melodic minor scale formations are ubiquitous, even in the final cadence of the movement. Thus, it could be argued that the reference collection for this movement is actually the unique melodic minor scale pattern, and, as shown in Example 5, this scale, like the natural-note collection, is symmetrical around D.

Example 5. Common symmetry of D-Dorian and G-Melodic-Minor

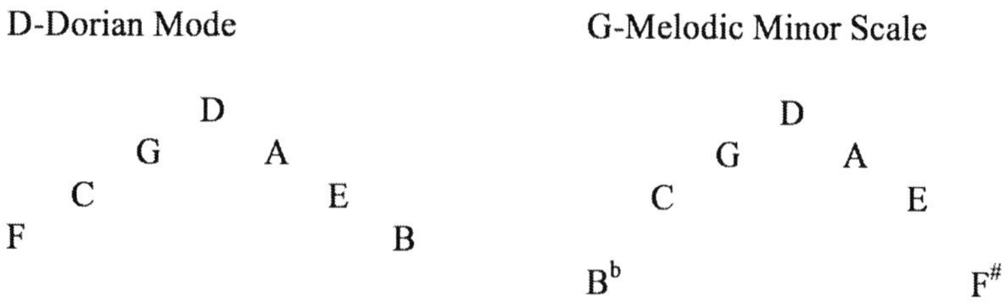

The pitch D is occasionally featured as a local tonic in this movement, most prominently in the important violin melody that sounds in m. 17, m. 51, and finally at m. 90. In the final version, the initial chord is a glorious breakthrough to B flat major. Unfortunately for the talisman of the flat keys, a cadence is not in the works. Sibelius quickly shifts to D minor and then A flat major, the axial partner of D in symmetrical relationships. As with previous versions, the final part of the melody arrives on a D major triad, sounding as a dominant of G minor. So, in this movement, we might hear D taking on the role of the champion, vanquishing B flat when it attempts to rise to the status of stable key. Perhaps here, D is made to appear secure enough to survive without its ally C major.

This notion is advanced in the following movement, in which D Dorian appears to dominate. Example 6 shows the general layout of this movement. The primary section modulates to A Dorian on the sharp side, but is then followed by a long contrasting section in G Dorian, thus exploring the one-flat collection. When all the ideas cycle through a second time, all modulations are abandoned, leaving D Dorian to dominate. So while there is a balance of sorts with appearances of both flat and sharp side Dorian modes, I would point out that the setting of the larger contrasting section in G Dorian results in far greater emphasis on the flat-side collection. Thus, while symmetry is prevailing in the middle movements, there is a growing bias for the flat side. The key of B flat almost emerged in the second movement, and the one-flat collection receives its longest presentation of material in the third movement.

Example 6. Formal diagram of movement 3

A			
	Intro	mm. 1-8	D Dorian
	a	mm. 8-22	D Dorian
	transition	mm. 23-32	D Dorian to A Dorian
	b	mm. 32-52 (ends with intro refrain)	A Dorian
B			
	c	mm. 53-99	G Dorian/F major
	retrans	mm. 99-110	G Dorian to D Dorian
A_1			
	a	mm. 110-124	D Dorian
	transition	mm. 124-134	remains in D Dorian
	b	mm. 134-154 (ends with intro refrain)	D Dorian
B			
	c	mm. 154-203	D Dorian
	retrans	mm. 203-217	remains in D Dorian
A_2 (Coda)			
	a	mm. 218-225 (cadence with first idea)	D Dorian

Having arrived at the finale, it can certainly be argued that Sibelius has nurtured D Dorian, strengthening it with ideas of symmetry. However, one might wonder if the Dorian is strong enough to survive without its ally and champion, C major, considering B flat and the flat-side keys have been gaining strength as well. As if reacting to this uncertain situation, the repeated and varied phrases at the beginning of the finale tend to launch from A minor triads, provisionally settle on E minor triads, and then cadence in C major, returning D Dorian's ally. The feigned motions to E minor present a slight sharp-side colouring, recalling the sharp-side motions at the beginning of the first movement, and perhaps also suggesting a path to Dorian preservation.

If the sound of this finale had persisted in the use of sharp-side colouring, perhaps emulating the sound of the finale of the Third Symphony, the flat-side incursions may have been put back. However, the initial sharp-side sounds are neutralised by the main theme of the middle part of the movement, which launches in D Aeolian with Phrygian colourings in the form of repeated E flat major to D minor progressions.

Murtomäki correctly identifies the ascending idea that powerfully projects D Dorian in m. 64 as "the basic motive of the movement and the entire symphony."[7] This brings us to Hepokoski's perfect version of his finale *telos*, shown in Example 7. It begins with a slightly extended form

[7] Murtomäki. *Symphonic Unity*, 227.

of the basic motive, with the important addition of a G-sharp to A motion. The addition of G sharp to the natural note collection maintains the symmetry around D, producing the Sibelian-Dorian collection, a sound featured prominently in the opening of the Violin Concerto, a work infused with many layers of symmetry around the Dorian final.[8] The *telos* clearly presents this strong D Dorian with its companion C major joining in before the emergence of D Aeolian. Thus, the *telos* suggests that D Aeolian may have the final word, a conclusion that is finally confirmed at the moment of truth.

Example 7. Sibelius, Symphony No. 6, IV: 72–83 (Hepokoski's *telos*)

Example 8 summaries the events of the crisis passage from mm. 144–154. This passage occurs at the point in the form where the *telos* had occurred

8 Les Black, "Symmetry as Modal Abstraction: The Evolving Language of Sibelius's Violin Concerto," in *Sibelius in the Old and New World: Aspects of His Music, Its Interpretation, and Reception*, eds. Timothy L. Jackson, Veijo Murtomäki, Colin Davis, and Timo Virtanen (Frankfurt am Main: Peter Lang, 2010), 171–84.

previously. The passage begins with a gigantic B$^{\varnothing 7}$ chord, a sound that could be characterised as the essential D Dorian *klang*. While C-sharp$^{\varnothing 7}$ has the power to locate D Dorian as a dominant function chord, the B$^{\varnothing 7}$ collects all the essential sounds of the mode: the D minor triad along with a raised sixth scale degree. In works such as *En saga*, Sibelius harmonises complete Dorian melodies with this sound alone. Unfortunately, the desperate Dorian outburst of the crisis is not followed by its ally and champion, C major. Instead, variations of phrases from the opening of the movement are presented. Note that the descending phrase moves from high A to low A using the notes of the two-flat collection, generating a very unstable Locrian sound.

Especially telling is the inclusion of the chromatic note C flat, which performs two key functions. First, it denies the pitch C a place in the initial melodic descent, emphasising the absence of the D Dorian ally. Second, it enharmonically recasts B natural, the essential Dorian pitch. B natural gives up its B nature and becomes a lowered C that must resolve down to its rival B flat. In addition, C sharp, the leading-tone to D, appears as D flat, resolving down to C within the F chord at the end of the first phrase. Thus, all upward energy is neutralised, preparing the soft upper tetrachord of D Aeolian. The ascending phrase that follows confirms victory for the flat side by providing the long awaited cadence in B flat. As in the opening, the voice-leading resolution of the half-diminished seventh chord does not appear as a surface event. However, the sketch shows how one might hear this passage governed by the same expanding contrary motion that transformed C sharp$^{\varnothing 7}$ into C major in the first movement.

Example 8. Sibelius, Symphony No. 6, IV: 144–154 (sketch)

Having truly achieved the two-flat collection with a cadence, the music settles back into the one-flat collection. The subsequent key signature change is followed by the return of several phrases from the opening, slightly varied and transposed to the one-flat collection. This is the only place in the symphony where a block of music originally set in the natural-note collection is transposed one degree to the flat side, giving final confirmation of the flat-side victory.

In the final pages, it is uncertain whether F major or D Aeolian will conclude the tonal journey. With C major vanquished at the crisis, F major now takes on the role of champion. Since F major and D Aeolian share the same pitch collection, they may work as allies. Thus, the sudden shifts into both flat and sharp keys in the coda are invariably directed to the major third F–A, the first sound of the symphony. F major becomes the final champion and, as was the case with C major in the first movement, does so on behalf of D, but now Aeolian, the key to which it willingly cedes the last word.

On reflection, the formal ambiguities of the first movement invite us to hear the complete symphony as a confrontation of both modal pitch centres and diatonic collections. The modal contrasts evolve into alliances, bringing the contest of pitch collections to the fore. Despite the presence of symmetrical ideas that bolster the Dorian, the relentless strengthening of B flat from a mere suggestion in the opening to a chromatic detail, to a diatonic pitch, to a potential key, to a key confirmed by a cadence, points out the path to the inevitable victory of the one-flat collection and D Aeolian. But this victory is only confirmed when the ally and champion of D Dorian, C major, departs from the scene, and the striking treatment of the half-diminished seventh chord heard in the opening passage is applied to a chord that defines the sound of D Dorian. All the strands of thought initiated in the first movement have a role in the evolution of the final sonic landscape, transforming the confident Dorian into a passive Aeolian.

That is the poem I hear. Of course, my words fall far short of the poetry in Sibelius' music.

2. Instrumental and Notational Practices

JEAN SIBELIUS AND THE CELLO

JORMA DANIEL LÜNENBÜRGER

Of all of the instruments that he did not play himself, Jean Sibelius was most familiar with the cello. Many scholars have noted his command of the violin as well as his improvisational abilities on the piano, and have connected these activities with his compositions for the two instruments. The role of the cello is less well known, although this instrument was important in Sibelius' biography. His compositions include a series of solo and chamber works with cello as well as the frequent employment of the cello in his orchestral music. Sibelius tended to project disappointments as well as unrealised plans and dreams upon his compositions for the cello. Although a passage from a letter written on March 31, 1888 initially invoked an impression to the contrary, it also contained hints of the reasons for his failure to succeed in this area of endeavour:

> Yesterday I finished the first movement of a cello concerto for Kitti (*à mon frère*). Kitti seems to think there are too few technical bravura passages and difficulties, but in my opinion they sound abominable on the cello whose strong point is precisely its cantilena.[1]

Two conclusions may be drawn from these comments:

- In his early years, Sibelius composed extensively for his brother's instrument.
- He valued the cello more for its capacity for cantilena than for its virtuosity.

These conclusions are not only valid for the early cello compositions, as although Sibelius never wrote a cello concerto, he nevertheless used the cello repeatedly as a solo instrument in his orchestral works. For the most part, he invented lyrical passages for the cello.

---

[1] Glenda Dawn Goss, *Jean Sibelius. The Hämeenlinna Letters. Scenes from a Musical Life 1874–1895* (Esbo: Schildts Förlags Ab, 1997), 95, 174.

First Cello Experiences

Perhaps it is only a coincidence that Sibelius was given instruction in violin rather than cello. It is commonly known that he first began formal violin instruction in the late summer of 1881, yet, shortly before, in a letter to his uncle, Sibelius expressed a desire to study the violin ("I want so much to learn to play the violin"), followed a little later in the same letter by "I would also like to learn to play the violoncello."[2] However, because Sibelius himself had no cello and his uncle made a violin available to him, he learned this instrument. It is possible that his poor school grades and the necessity of repeating a school year just at this point (1881) prevented him from being able to learn both instruments simultaneously.[3]

The cello later became the instrument of his younger brother, Christian, often called Kitti, though it is not known whether and when Kitti's formal instruction might have begun. In letters from the year 1884, Sibelius reported that his brother practised diligently and made progress.[4] It is probable that, following his older brother's example, he also had begun to play the cello much earlier. However, whether or not Sibelius' (presumably) first composition *Vattendroppar* JS 216 (1881?) could have been actually played by both brothers is questionable.

Sibelius was able to garner first impressions of the cello only from amateur musicians. His uncle Pehr, a merchant by occupation, was a music enthusiast who apparently also played the cello.[5] Sibelius' first experiences with chamber music in Hämeenlinna involved his playing together with the pharmacist and amateur cellist Hugo Elfsberg. Because his violin teacher Gustav Levander also taught his brother Christian cello, Sibelius often included this instrument in his numerous chamber music compositions.

With the exception, however, of the *Andantino*, JS 40 for cello and piano from the year 1884, it was some time before Sibelius would compose for the cello as a solo instrument. Subsequent to his assumption in 1886 of the artist name "Jean" and his shift of priorities to the study of composition, Sibelius wrote several cello pieces. The compilation below summarises known works from the 1880s.

---

[2] Ibid., 47, 134f., letter from June 19, 1881.

[3] Jorma Daniel Lünenbürger, *Zwischen Kreativität und Traditionsbewusstsein. Jean Sibelius' Kammermusik vom Frühwerk zu* Voces intimae (Frankfurt am Main etc.: Peter Lang, 2015), 48f.

[4] Goss, *Jean Sibelius*, 64, 149, letter from February 24, 1884.

[5] Ibid., 57f., 144, letter from December 22, 1882.

1884	JS 40	Andantino C major	Vc, piano [6]
1885–9		Moderato F major	Vc solo
1887	JS 36	Andante molto	Vc, piano
1887	JS 193	Tempo di valse [I]	Vc, piano
1887	JS 196	Theme and Variations D minor	Vc solo
1887–9		[Mazurka] G minor	Vc solo
1888	JS 22	Allegretto E flat major	Vl, piano [7]
1888	JS 76	[E flat minor]	Vl or Vc, piano
1888	JS 91	[B minor I]	Vc, piano
1888/89	JS 92	[B minor II]	Vc, piano
1888/89		Andante molto B minor	Vc, piano
1889	JS 15	Adagio F sharp minor	Vc, piano
1889	JS 79	Fantasie	Vc, piano
1889	JS 194	Tempo di valse [II]	Vc, piano

Three Cello Pieces from 1887 and Other Works until 1889

Three at least partially preserved pieces from the year 1887 provide interesting insights into Sibelius' compositions for the cello. He wrote these works for his brother Christian, who in addition to his medical studies also studied cello at the Music Institute, beginning in 1888.[8] The *Andante molto* in F minor, JS 36, for cello and piano, explicitly dedicated to his brother, demonstrates how deeply familiar the two were with this instrument: Jean as composer and Christian as interpreter. Next to its lyric cantilenas, the *Andante molto* contains a virtuoso passage for the cello. It is possible that the "consertino" [*sic*] mentioned by Christian Sibelius to a friend in 1887 was a reference to the *Andante molto*.[9] Its modulations followed by a subsequent virtuoso passage create the impression of an

[6] All information is taken from Fabian Dahlström, *Sibelius-Werkverzeichnis. Jean Sibelius Thematisch-bibliographisches Verzeichnis seiner Werke* (Wiesbaden: Breitkopf & Härtel, 2003).

[7] Autograph of a cello part as a sketch in the Finnish National Library HUL 0532b, see Dahlström, *Sibelius-Werkverzeichnis*, 503.

[8] Fabian Dahlström, *Sibelius-Akademin 1882–1982* (Helsingfors: Sibelius-Akademins publikationer, 1982), 464.

[9] Vesa Sirén, *Aina poltti sikaria. Jean Sibelius aikalaisten silmin* (Otava: Helsinki, 2000), 60, 637; Andrew Barnett, *Sibelius* (Yale: Yale University Press, 2007), 30, 355.

extraterritorial island within the "Tchaikovsky-influenced melancholy of the composition," according to Tawaststjerna.[10]

Similarly, the *Theme and Variations* in D minor, JS 196, was created explicitly with his brother Christian in mind. Presumably the first opus for cello solo in Finland, it also contains Sibelius' most extensive variations for the instrument in a single work. An introduction encompassing four bars is followed by a theme and seven sixteen-bar variations, which are in turn resolved by a twelve-bar coda. Faithfully following classical models, changes of key, metre, tempo, and character are used to increase intensity until the end of the sixth variation. The last variation then echoes elements of the earlier introduction, with the coda providing a conclusion to the piece. This *Theme and Variations* contains the most extended virtuoso passages of all cello compositions by the young Sibelius. Its style and harmonic structure reveal models extending from Bach to Beethoven and pieces by contemporary cellists. During his years as a student at the Music Institute of Helsinki, concert programmes included a number of works by Georg Goltermann. Furthermore, references to compositions by Felix Mendelssohn Bartholdy, Wilhelm Fitzenhagen, Franz Neruda, Auguste Franchomme, Bernhard Romberg, David Popper, and Alfred Pester were presented.[11] Jean Sibelius had certainly heard some of these pieces. It is possible that Georg Goltermann's *Romanze*, Op. 90, in the same key, served as one of his models.

Of the third piece from 1887, the *Tempo di valse* in G minor, JS 193, only the cello part remains. This composition was most probably the "Walse fantastique," presented to his uncle as his Opus 1. For this purpose, he hoped for a tour of the cellist Jaromír Hřímalý to include Hämeenlinna: "He will surely have a full house."[12] Sibelius had occasionally played string quartets with Hřímalý, the cello professor at the Music Institute.[13] Unfortunately, Sibelius' plans were not realised, and for some time no composition had the label "Opus 1" with its symbolic significance. It is interesting that his simplest piece from the year 1887 became a candidate for an opus number. Neither the virtuoso passages from the *Andante molto* nor the *Theme and Variations* but rather the cantilenas of the *Tempo di valse* were to receive this honour. Sibelius himself emphasised his preference for lyric cello passages six months prior to the letter quoted above. Interestingly, his largest chamber music piece

---

[10] Erik Tawaststjerna, *Jean Sibelius*, vol. 1 (Berkeley etc.: University of California Press, 1976), 50.

[11] Dahlström, *Sibelius-Akademin*, 344, 352ff.

[12] Goss, *Jean Sibelius*, 89, letter from September 27, 1887.

[13] Ibid., 86; Dahlström, *Sibelius-Akademin*, 353.

from 1887, the "Korpo" piano trio, JS 209, contains several striking cello cantilenas and virtuoso passages that find no counterparts in other works from the same period.

"Yesterday I finished the first movement of a cello concerto." With this quote, Sibelius leads us into the year 1888.[14] Indeed, a number of shorter pieces from this time still exist, though some of them only as fragments. Three of these pieces are in the key of B minor, leading to the speculation that they may have belonged together in a cyclical context. The larger portion of these compositions, however, was devoted to the lyric cantilena, and there is little evidence of a cello concerto in the classical sense, a form usually characterised by virtuoso passages. Although the triplets in *Andante molto* are technically demanding, they are far removed from the virtuoso passages of some of the violin compositions. Upon examination of surviving material, it is hardly imaginable that the "Cello Concerto" from 1888 existed in this form at all. At the same time, the importance of his brother's instrument is revealed in several smaller pieces for cello and piano (an alternative cello part was composed for the pieces JS 22 and JS 76 for violin and piano[15]). In addition to smaller undated works, two pieces in F sharp minor were composed in 1889, the *Adagio*, JS 15, and the *Tempo di valse* (II), JS 194, also known as the "Lulu Waltz."

The *Fantasie*, JS 79, from 1889 is worthy of closer examination; with its five movements, it is Sibelius' most extensive work for the cello. Unfortunately, only fragments remain, as we can see on the last of the eight pages of the manuscript. The piano part is missing entirely, and the construction of the transitions and the conclusion remains unclear. The characteristics of tempo, key, metre, etc. give us an overview.

- *Moderato* C minor 6/8–*Vivo* 3/4–*Tempo I* 6/8–*Presto* C major 4/4–short cadence–*Tempo I* 6/8
- *Tempo di valse. Moderato* G major 3/4, middle section in A minor (?)
- *Alla polacca* G minor 3/4, middle section in G major, cadence
- *Alla Marcia* C major 4/4, middle section in F major
- [leggiero] A minor 4/4, conclusion open

The succession of the movements in different keys is reminiscent of early cyclical chamber music works, in which the cyclical integrity is loose. The

[14] See the first citation in this article (Goss, *Jean Sibelius*, 95).
[15] Dahlström, *Sibelius-Werkverzeichnis*, 503, 536.

missing piano part also means that the relationship between movements remains unclear; however, the work must have been complete, as it was performed repeatedly in Loviisa in August 1889.[16] Just prior to this occasion, the violin sonata JS 178 was completed, and shortly thereafter Sibelius left for Berlin on his first international journey.

The Cello as an Orchestral Instrument

The equal importance given to the cello in Sibelius' early chamber works, such as the piano trios, the string quartets, and the piano quintet, makes it difficult to draw conclusions with respect to particular compositional characteristics.[17] Several prominent cello passages in the first three movements of the Piano Quintet, JS 159, may be regarded as precursors of later cello solos in the orchestral works, as many passages in the quintet were composed in an orchestral manner.[18] It is much easier to discover the compositional particularities by considering the numerous orchestral works composed after 1890. Although Sibelius treated the cello as an independent entity, it was often doubled by the double bass or played the middle part together with the viola. Frequently, themes or motifs were assigned to the cello alone. Sibelius readily chose to double the main melody of the first violin with the cello at the interval of an octave, but seldom at the interval of two octaves. Examples of such "cantilena" passages may be found in all of the symphonies and in the famous compositions like *Finlandia*, Op. 26 (1900) and *Valse triste* from Op. 44 (1904). Many passages may also be found in which all strings, with the exception of the double basses, play in unison.

In addition, notable roles for the cello in the following categories can be identified, though the differences between them are not especially great:

- The cello solo, sometimes also of central importance at the beginning of a work
- The cello group combined with wind instruments
- The cello group voices divided as a choir, sometimes supplemented by violas or double basses ("cello chorus")

---

[16] Tawaststjerna, *Jean Sibelius*, 54.
[17] See Lünenbürger, *Zwischen Kreativität und Traditionsbewusstsein.*
[18] Ibid., 127ff.

Even if Sibelius' cello concerto failed, he nevertheless favoured the use of the instrument for its soloistic qualities, most commonly for "cantilena" passages. In some cases, the instrument is used at the beginning of a composition, as in the *The Swan of Tuonela*, Op. 22 No. 2 (1900). Here, a musical soundscape is presented wherby the initial theme of the major solo instrument, the cor anglais, is followed by the solo cello which, so to speak, "opens the curtain" (bar 7ff.).

A particularly significant cello solo at the beginning of a piece is to be found in the Fourth Symphony, Op. 63 (1909–11). Starting in bar 6, the solo cello is the leading voice for at least seven further bars. Thereafter, within its entire 20-bar length, it is partially doubled by other strings. This passage is a rather austere cantilena, far removed from any virtuosity. Further cello solos at the beginning of orchestral movements occur in combination with the other aforementioned types. In *Pohjola's Daughter*, Op. 49 (1905–6), the cello solo appears in combination with the cello group *divisi* (bar 1). The cello solo at the beginning of the *Spring Song* (*Vårsång*), Op. 16 (1902), merges with the clarinet and the viola group, creating an unusual and special timbre (bar 5). Considering solo passages amongst the pieces, we find that in both *Lemminkäinen and the Maidens of the Island*, Op. 22 No. 1 (bar 268) and *Lemminkäinen in Tuonela*, Op. 22 No. 3 (bar 211) structurally similar solos exist. In both cases, a soundscape is generated primarily by the strings, or supplemented in the second case by the winds, in order to provide a basis for the cello solo.

Various combinations with wind instruments are also to be found where the classic example, as in the violin concerto, is that of the bassoon in relation to the cello (first movement, fig. 2). In *En saga*, Op. 9 (1902), the distinctive combination of *pizzicato* celli and bassoon is notable (bar 34ff.). Shortly thereafter, the celli are complimented by the horn (bar 58ff.), as found already in *Kullervo*, Op. 7 (third movement, bar 242ff.) and later in the Second Symphony, Op. 43 (third movement, bar 298). This cello-horn combination is also supplemented by woodwinds, either with the bass clarinet as in *Pohjola's Daughter*, Op. 49 (letter M), or with several woodwinds as in *Lemminkäinen in Tuonela*, Op. 22 No. 3 (bar 67ff.) or *Lemminkäinen's Return*, Op. 22 No. 4 (fig. 12). Rarely, a combination with the oboe as briefly as in *Lemminkäinen and the Maidens of the Island* (after letter I), or with the flute and later the clarinet as in the Sixth Symphony Op. 104 (first movement, letter H), may be found. This symphony contains a section in which the celli and the woodwinds alternate in dialogue whilst the high strings accompany them (first movement, letter F). In all cases, the passages are decidedly lyrical, never virtuosic in nature.

The combination of clarinet and bassoon with viola and cello in the narrowly-voiced, four-part texture within the Second Symphony (second movement, letter K) is an important step towards the later chorale-like cello passages. This development can be demonstrated in the Third Symphony, Op. 52 (1904–7), which opens with the classic combination of cello and double bass, although shortly thereafter the celli take up the melody (fig. 3). In the second movement there is a short cello section with divided parts (fig. 6), followed by a longer cello chorus in the finale (fig. 13). Although in this final passage the cellos are supplemented by violas in the middle voices, the cello sound clearly dominates because it plays the upper voice. Similar distributions of parts exist in short passages in the Fourth (first movement, letter C) and Sixth Symphonies (first movement, letter L), *The Bard*, Op. 64 (beginning and letter C) and *Tapiola*, Op. 112 (bar 199ff.). The cello either plays the upper voice or merges with the viola in a single-voiced upper line. Only in the example out of the Seventh Symphony, Op. 105 (after letter B), does the viola lie above the cello. In all of the "cello chorus" passages, the use of divided voices invokes a more intense cello sound. These sections are also primarily characterised by their sustained and cantabile lines.

Malinconia

Once Sibelius began to compose orchestral works, he produced very few chamber music compositions and almost no pieces for the cello, with the exception of a single piece originally written for cello and piano. Several other works were composed for violin or cello, partially with orchestral accompaniment:

1900	Op. 20	*Malinconia*	Vc, piano
1914/15	Op. 77	Two Serious Melodies: Laetare anima mea (Cantique) Devotio. Ab imo pectore	Vl or Vc, orchestra (piano)
1915/17	Op. 78	Four Pieces: Impromptu Romance Religioso Rigaudon	Vl or Vc, piano

Malinconia, Op. 20, was composed in March 1900 within a very short period of time—though probably not in three hours, as has been suggested.[19] The piece was originally entitled "Fantasia," resulting in associations with the 1889 piece of the same name. Tawaststjerna's assumption that this work represents an outpouring of grief over the death of the composer's 14-month-old daughter Kirsti on February 13, 1900[20] is elaborated by Tomi Mäkelä:

> The musical ideas, brilliant piano cascades on the one hand and cello melodies on the other hand, are an elaborate representation of an inner emptiness and a deliberate speechlessness in spite of the consciousness of language. Speechlessness is consistent with the aftermath of Kirsti's death. Sibelius apparently never again spoke the name of his daughter.[21]

However, referencing a letter dated March 17, 1900, Mäkelä questions earlier speculation with respect to the motivation for this work.[22] Shortly after the premiere of "Fantasia," the composer had written a rather business-like letter to his wife with regard to the potential success of the composition.[23] In March 1900, under the original title "Fantasia," the piece had been completed and performed for the first time in Helsinki.[24] Several changes of title were explored before it was finally published in 1911 by Breitkopf and Härtel as *Malinconia*, Op. 20. [25] According to Mäkelä, the change of title signified a "specification as well as a reduction of weight in terms of its historical genre."[26] In the course of time, the generic title "Fantasie" had become increasingly weighty for Sibelius, while the Italian title *Malinconia* utilised a *topos* with a lengthy history in literature and the arts. Beethoven's string quartet movement *La Malinconia* from the last

---

[19] Dahlström, *Sibelius-Werkverzeichnis*, 81.
[20] Tawaststjerna, *Jean Sibelius*, 224f.
[21] Tomi Mäkelä, "Jean Sibelius' Malinconia d-Moll op. 20—finnische Fantasie oder Ballade der Sprachlosigkeit?" in *Facetten I: Symposien zur Kammermusik von Jean Sibelius, zum Liederkomponisten Max Kowalski und zur Liszt-Rezeption* (Musikwissenschaftliche Schriften der Hochschule für Musik und Theater München, Bd. 6), ed. Joachim Brügge (Tutzing: Schneider, 2014), 72. I am grateful to Judith Schmidt for her assistance in translating this quotation as well as the entire text.
[22] Ibid.
[23] SuviSirkku Talas (ed.), *Tulen synty. Aino ja Jean Sibeliuksen kirjeenvaihtoa 1892–1904* (Suomalaisen kirjallisuuden seura: Helsinki, 2003), 182; letter from March 17, 1900.
[24] Dahlström, *Sibelius-Werkverzeichnis*, 81.
[25] In approximately 1905 the piece was mentioned under the title "Fantasia" Op. 25, then at the latest in 1910 under the title *Malinconia*, Op. 20; see Dahlström, *Sibelius-Werkverzeichnis*, 682, 689.
[26] Mäkelä, "Jean Sibelius' Malinconia d-Moll," 76.

quartet in Op. 18, occasionally performed by the violinist Sibelius,[27] provided a musical reference point, though both historically and in terms of its genre classification it stood in a different context.[28]

The premiere of *Malinconia* was given by Georg Schnéevoigt, who was unjustly accused of being no more than a passable instrumentalist.[29] In his defence he had studied under Julius Klengel[30] and was apparently one of the leading cellists of his time. As of 1895 he was the solo cellist at the Helsinki Philharmonic Society Orchestra,[31] taught at the Wegelius' Music Institute from 1896,[32] and in the following years was a soloist in frequent concert appearances in Finland.[33] There are probably two reasons for the fact that Georg Schnéevoigt's reputation as a cellist was fading: firstly, the Europe-wide piano career of his wife Sigrid Sundgrén-Schnéevoigt, with whom he had played the first performance of "Fantasia," was blossoming: the concert including the premiere of *Malinconia* (Fantasia) was announced as a musical portrait of the pianist, and included primarily piano compositions.[34] Secondly, Schnéevoigt himself later gained much more prominence in his career as a conductor.

Late Compositions for Cello

Sibelius' closest approximation of a cello concerto may certainly be found in his *Two Serious Melodies*, Op. 77. The two pieces *Cantique* and *Devotion* were premiered in reverse order by the solo cellist of Kajanus'

---

[27] Sibelius played the second violin in Beethoven's Quartet, Op. 18 No. 6, including the movement *La Malinconia*, with the string quartet of the Helsinki Music Institute on April 22, 1887 and five years later on November 7, 1982. See Dahlström, *Sibelius-Akademin*, 354 and 359.

[28] With respect to the Beethoven movement, Friedhelm Krummacher refers to old discussions of the question of whether the designation *La Malinconia* is to be applied only to the introduction or to the whole movement. He favours a conscious choice to leave the question unresolved in order to preserve the "enigmatic character of the music." See Friedhelm Krummacher, *Geschichte des Streichquartetts*, vol. III (Laaber: Laaber-Verlag, 2005), 246.

[29] Mäkelä, "Jean Sibelius' Malinconia d-Moll," 68.

[30] *Uusi Suometar*, July 26, 1895, 3.

[31] Ibid.

[32] Dahlström. *Sibelius-Akademin*, 334.

[33] I used the database http://www.hri.fi/fi/dataset/helsingin-kaupunginorkesterin-konsertit, and checked many of the concerts at http://digi.kansalliskirjasto.fi /sanomalehti.

[34] *Hufvudstadsbladet*, March 8, 1900, 4, and *Uusi Suometar*, March 10, 1900, 2.

orchestra, Ossian Fohström, in 1916.[35] Although he was two years older than Schnéevoigt, Fohström was engaged as his successor in the Helsinki Philharmonic Orchestra. Schnéevoigt himself had long since shifted his focus to his conducting career, and Fohström was also active as a conductor.

A performance of the violin version of Op. 77 within Sibelius' lifetime is not documented.[36] Despite the fact that the first publication of this piece was for violin and orchestra, it was nevertheless dedicated to the cellist Fohström. Though Op. 77 from 1914/15 (again) failed to evolve into a true cello concerto, it (once more) contains many lovely cantilenas for this instrument. On the basis of their dedication and their first performances, these two pieces may rightly be designated as Sibelius' only cello compositions with orchestra.

It is interesting to compare the two solo voices, especially as the *Cantique*, Op. 77 No. 1, with the subtitle *Laetare anima mea*, reveals changes made to accommodate the cello instrument. In general, many double stops are removed, and more significantly the *pizzicati* in bars 35ff and 82ff are replaced by sustained tones. In addition, a multifaceted use of octave transpositions is employed so that it almost appears as if an entirely new piece has emerged; some 37 out of 93 bars are played at the same pitch as the violin, while 40 measures are notated one octave lower, and 6 bars are two octaves below the violin voice.[37] The "sul G" violin passages are generally played by the cello at the same pitch. Perhaps the performance indication for the violin was an attempt to achieve an imitation of the cello sound. The version for cello in *Devotion*, Op. 77 No. 2, with the subtitle *Ab im pectore*, is more conventional. In this case, 10 of the 57 bars are played at their original pitch, 38 bars are notated one octave lower, and 8 bars two octaves lower.

As in the case of Op. 77, the *Four Pieces*, Op. 78, for violin and piano were not composed as a cycle, and thus varied in their origins. For these pieces, alternative cello versions may also be found. The *Impromptu* (No. 1) was initially intended to include an orchestral accompaniment. Sibelius also offered his publisher an orchestral accompaniment for the *Romance* (No. 2). Except for the *Rigaudon* (No. 4), which is played by the cello completely one octave lower, there are again different octave transpositions.[38] In conclusion, the impetus for *Religioso*, Op. 78 No. 3,

---

[35] Dahlström, *Sibelius-Werkverzeichnis*, 338.
[36] Ibid.
[37] The missing bars are explained by rests and the replacement of *pizzicati*.
[38] *Impromptu* (No. 1): 15 of 56 bars at the original pitch and 37 bars one octave lower; *Romance* (No. 2): 18 of 50 bars at the original pitch, 24 bars one octave and

must be mentioned. Long after the student Sibelius had composed numerous works for his brother, among them the failed "cello concerto," the dedication of this mature work was to set a memorial to his sibling: "To Prof. Dr. Chr. Sibelius" appears on the title page. In contrast to the markedly virtuoso passages in *Malinconia*, which impressively displayed the potential of his brother's instrument, Sibelius now concluded his career as a cello composer with cantilenas.

6 bars two octaves lower; *Religioso* (No. 3): 21 of 79 bars at the original pitch, 37 one octave, and 12 bars two octaves lower.

On the Instrumentation of Melody Lines in Sibelius' Early Orchestral Works (1892–4)

Charris Efthimiou

Sibelius' stay in Vienna in 1890–91 was of fundamental importance to his future compositional development. Up until that point, he had almost no experience of writing for orchestra, yet he went on to compose a series of orchestral works which are considered as standard in the concert repertoire today. He finished his first two orchestral pieces (Overture in E major and *Scène de ballet*) in Vienna, and the first versions of *En saga*[1] and *Kullervo*[2] were also conceived there.[3] These works show the compositional maturity that Sibelius had already achieved by 1891, especially with regard to the use of motivic development and instrumentation. While a whole set of musicological treatises deals with formal, harmonic, and motivic aspects of his early orchestral oeuvre, analysis of aspects of instrumentation and tone-colour in Sibelius' works, especially regarding his early pieces, has received little attention by music theorists.[4] The aim of this chapter is to look at the

[1] On the creation of the two versions of *En saga* see Tuija Wicklund, *Jean Sibelius's En saga and Its Two Versions: Genesis, Reception, Edition and Form* (Studia Musica 57) (Helsinki: Sibelius Academy, 2008), 9–21.

[2] On the creation of *Kullervo* see Glenda Dawn Goss, "Vienna and the Genesis of *Kullervo*: Durchführung zum Teufel!" in *The Cambridge Companion to Sibelius*, ed. Daniel M. Grimley (Cambridge: Cambridge University Press, 2004), 22–32.

[3] A conference devoted to his stay there was held in Vienna in 2002; see *Jean Sibelius und Wien*, ed. Hartmut Krones (Wiener Schriften zur Stilkunde und Aufführungspraxis), ed. Hartmut Krones, Sonderband 4 (Wien, Köln and Weimar: Böhlau Verlag, 2003).

[4] An exception are the following papers by Ron Weidberg: "Comparing the 1915 and the 1919 Versions of Sibelius's Fifth Symphony: From Sonic Experimentalism to Functional Synthesis," in *Sibelius in the Old and the New World. Aspects of His Music, Its Interpretation and Reception*, eds. Timothy L. Jackson, Veijo Murtomäki, Colin Davis, and Timo Virtanen (Interdisziplinäre Studien zur Musik, eds. Tomi Mäkelä and Tobias R. Klein, Band 6) (Frankfurt am Main: Peter Lang,

design of melodic lines in Sibelius' early orchestral works (1892–4) from a music-analytical perspective. The following features are examined in detail: instrumentation of recurring themes, instrumentation of the bassline and octave doublings of the melody line within a movement, alongside the participation of the low strings and the brass section when playing the melody. The two versions of *En saga* will be the main focus of this music-analytical discussion, though the other symphonic poems of the same period will be briefly considered using the same analytical approach for the purposes of comparison.

En saga

Both the earlier (1892) as well as the later (1902) versions of *En saga* belong to the most interesting symphonic poems of the last decade of the nineteenth century, and they have been analysed by several musicologists to date.[5] Ernst Tanzberger devoted an entire chapter to *En saga* in his 1943 monograph on Sibelius' symphonic works where he ordered its many themes, tried to connect them to the characters in the legend of *En saga*, and gave an overview of its entire form.[6] In her treatise on the form and content of the symphonic works by Sibelius, Brigitte Pinder gives an overview of the symphonic works in general,[7] and *En saga* in particular.[8] What is striking is the difference of opinion between different music analysts, especially in connection with aspects of the overall form of this work.[9] The same is true about the cataloguing of its diverse themes and

---

2010), 239–67; "Sonic Design in Jean Sibelius's Orchestral Music," in *Sibelius Forum II. Proceedings from The Third International Jean Sibelius Conference Helsinki, December 7–10, 2000*, eds. Matti Huttunen, Kari Kilpeläinen, and Veijo Murtomäki (Helsinki: Sibelius Academy. Department of Composition and Music Theory, 2003), 216–26.

[5] Not only from a formal, thematic, and harmonic point of view, but also in the field of semiotics; see Veijo Murtomäki, "The Problem of Narrativity in the Symphonic Poem *En saga* by Jean Sibelius," in *Musical Signification. Essays in the Semiotic Theory and Analysis of Music*, ed. Eero Tarasti (Berlin & New York: Mouton de Gruyter, 1995), 471–94.

[6] Ernst Tanzberger, *Die Symphonischen Dichtungen von Jean Sibelius* (Triltsch: Würzburg, 1943), 8–24.

[7] Brigitte Pinder, *Form und Inhalt der Symphonischen Tondichtungen von Sibelius* (Berlin: Wissenschaftlicher Verlag, 2005), 20–3.

[8] Ibid., 43–7.

[9] Cf. Tanzberger, *Die Symphonischen Dichtungen von Jean Sibelius*, 24 with Robert Layton, *Sibelius: The Master Musician Series* (Oxford: Oxford University Press, 1992), 63–4.

their interrelationships. Although Pinder derives almost all themes of the first 196 bars from the opening material (bars 1–8),[10] Tuija Wicklund[11] sees two thematic areas (bars 1–89, 90–196) and Robert Layton[12] identifies four such areas (bars 1–34, 35–95, 96–149, and 150–196). Examples 1a and 1b give an overview of the main themes of the first two versions of *En saga*.

Ex. 1a. *En saga*, 1892 version: main themes

[10] Pinder, *Form und Inhalt der Symphonischen Tondichtungen von Sibelius*, 50–5.
[11] Wicklund, *Jean Sibelius's En saga and Its Two Versions*, 177.
[12] Layton, *Sibelius: The Master Musician Series*, 64.

Ex. 1b. *En saga*, 1902 version: main themes

In her monograph, Wicklund compares both versions with respect to form, motifs, and harmony, and shows how much they differ from one another in these respects. Although *En saga* has been analysed thoroughly from this perspective, there has been no discussion about the instrumentation and tone-colour of the various themes of this symphonic poem. The development of the tone-colour of all these main themes will be explored in order to determine similarities and differences between the two versions. This results in a huge amount of data which makes it extremely difficult to gain a sense of overview; it is, therefore, necessary to develop a system that illustrates the course of such tone-colour processes.

The abstraction of sound dispositions in tabular form has the advantage (in terms of the large-scale form) of clearly displaying timbral processes. Such tables can provide information about long-term trends of the instrumentation of the melody line that would otherwise remain hidden because of the size of an orchestral movement.[13] Alternatively, the description of the tone-colour combinations of the melody line through symbols has the advantage that one can compress all this data into only a few lines. However, any review of these processes becomes much more difficult as the data compression increases.

Consequently, it becomes necessary to develop a system which compresses as many tone-colour constellations onto a single-page table in as clear a way as possible. As a result, long-term tendencies are visible, something which would not be possible through the many different changes of instrumentation as they occur throughout a movement. Different colours and symbols are introduced for the representation of the different places where the melody is doubled or/octave-doubled. The colour black is used when a melody doubles another one (Example 3a: violas and cellos are doubling the first bassoon), the colour grey represents the octave-doubling of a melody (Example 2a: the first and third horn double the bassoon), and the symbol "X" signifies that a melody is played two octaves higher (Example 5, bar 271: piccolo and flute play the melody of the second bassoon two octaves higher). The colours give no information about the register, but describe the final relation that two melodies have. The instruments are listed from bottom to top, according to the arrangement of a modern score.

Example 2 shows the instruments which play the introductory theme (in both versions). In order to achieve a clear overview (and save some space), the rest of the instruments are not denoted. Because the horns play the melody an octave higher than the bassoons, they are shown in grey. In the later version, Sibelius exchanges the first and the second bassoon, a change that is minimal and not comprehensible at the time.[14]

[13] Jan Beran, *Statistics in Musicology* (London: Chapman and Hall/CRC, 2004).

[14] Only after the listing of all tone-colour constellations of both versions and the subsequent transfer in tabular form will the reasons for this minimal exchange of bassoons be recognisable.

Exx. 2a and 2b. *En saga*: introductory theme, bars 1–4

Exx. 3a and 3b. *En saga*: first appearance of the main theme a (MA), bars 38–40 (version A) and bars 34–36 (version B)

Ex. 4. Tone-colour constellations of the melody line of Exx. 2a, 2b, 3a, and 3b in tabular form

Version	**A**	**B**	**A**	**B**
Bar	**1**	**1**	**38**	**34**
Bsn. 1	■		■	▒
Bsn. 2		■		■
Hn.1	▒	▒		
Hn. 3	▒	▒		
Vla.			■	
Vc.			■	▒
Kb.				■

The instrumentation changes of the first appearances of the main theme A (MA) between the first and later versions are essentially bigger than those of the opening theme. In the 1892 version, three instruments play this material (bassoon 1, viola, and violoncello), while in the 1902 version the composer introduces an extra instrument. Noteworthy here is the change of density in the music (four instead of three instruments), and also the change in tone-colours (bassoons with low strings instead of bassoon 1, viola, and violoncello). Example 4 presents all four tone-colour constellations in a table. The advantages of presenting the melody line with symbols are now clear: no two tone-colour constellations are identical, even though the number of instruments is limited. Also, all four themes are played in octaves. As the number of constellations increases, the more difficult it is, firstly, to document the tone-colour changes in the two versions, and secondly to discern Sibelius' system behind these changes. Example 5 shows all the appearances of the six main themes (Example 1b) in his later version of *En saga*. The first row shows the current formal section, the second gives the bar number where the theme begins, and the third shows which theme is played.

Ex. 5. *En saga*, 1902 version: complete tone-colour constellations of all six themes

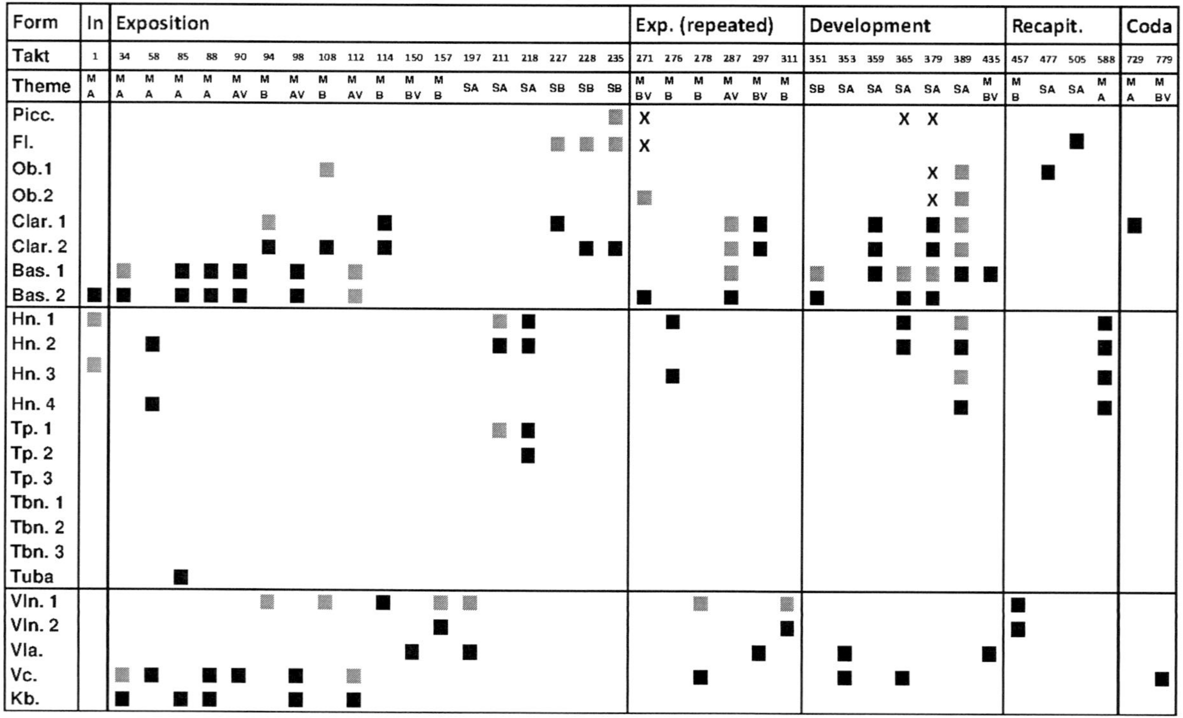

The following results are evident after examining Example 5:

- The instrumentation of all six themes changes 38 times
- Some instruments play the melody line more often than others. The tone-colours of the strings and some of the woodwinds (bassoons and clarinets) dominate, while flutes, oboes, and violins are used sparingly
- The tone-colour of the brass instruments is often present. The first two horns appear more often than the rest of the horns and the first two trumpets, while the remaining horns and the lower brass instruments almost never appear
- Sibelius avoids doublings in two octaves (symbol "X" [Example 5: bars 271, 365, and 379] appears only three times in the 1902 version). The number of combinations in unison (shown in black only) is not significantly different than that of constellations in octaves (grey)
- Surprisingly, a theme which is played by only one instrument appears more frequently (five times), though he generally prefers mixed sounds
- Sibelius avoids repetitions of tone-colour constellations. From a total of 38, only one is repeated (bar 88 correlates with bar 99). Although the two bassoons and lower strings play many themes alone (the number of instruments is very limited), Sibelius tries to obtain maximum differentiation
- The development introduces themes in tone-colours with different density (compared to the exposition). In this section, many instruments play the melody line doubled in two octaves

Ex. 6. *En saga*, 1902 version: complete tone-colour constellations of all six themes separately

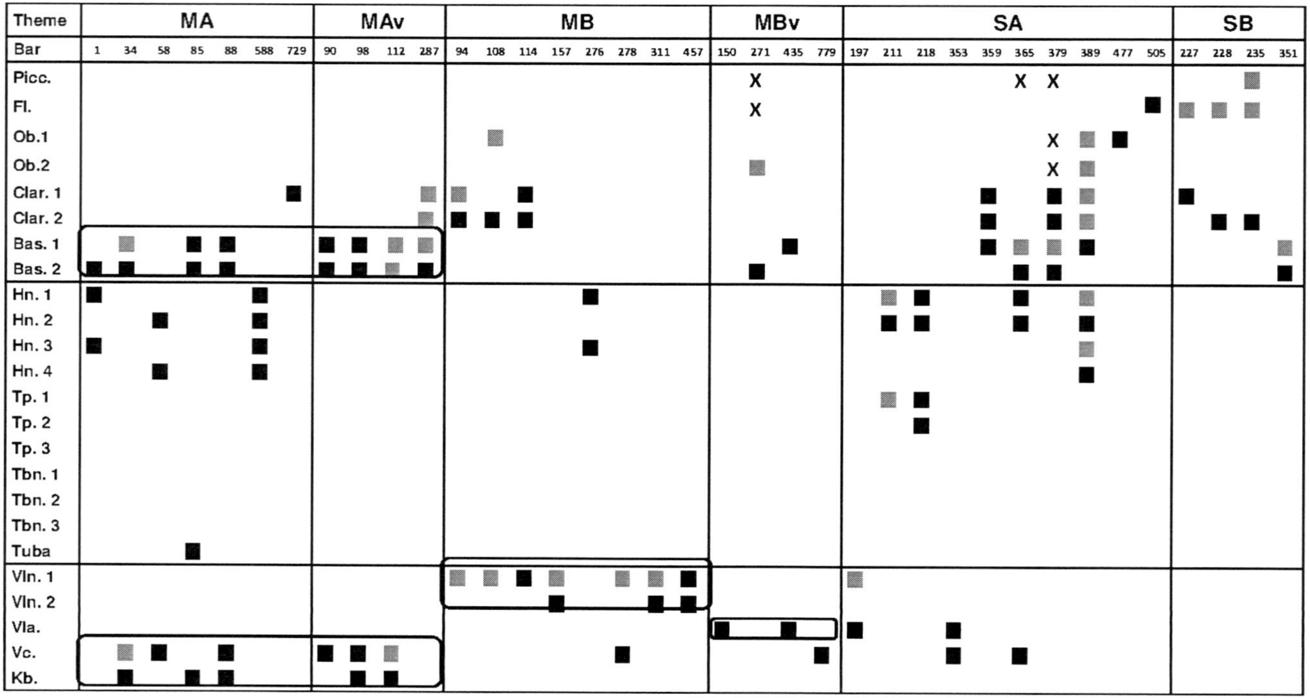

Example 5 documents all constellations of all six themes throughout the whole composition, while Example 6 lists all the appearances of the themes. The second column shows all the appearances of the main theme A (MA) from beginning to the end of *En saga*, and the third column the appearances of main theme A varied (MAv) etc. Example 7 shows the following:

- Particular instruments dominate the sound of MA and MAv (bassoons with lower strings). With the exception of the horns, both themes have a very similar tone-colour. He does not try to separate MA and MAv from each other with respect to tone-colours
- The exact opposite is true for MB and MBv. Although the first two themes are very similar from a motivic point of view, they are very different in their tone-colours. The clarinets, horns, and violins pause at MBv
- The same is true for MAv and MB[15]
- Although the main themes (MA, MAv, MB, and MBv) and the secondary themes (SA and SB) have similar tone-colours (horns), the differences overweigh these similarities. In the secondary themes, the woodwinds and brass instruments dominate, while the strings mostly pause. Sibelius' purpose was not only to separate the main and secondary material thematically and harmonically, but also to create a clear distinction in terms of their instrumentation

After a closer examination of Examples 5 and 6, we can see that Sibelius' skills as an orchestrator had become very acute by 1902. He was not only able to master the tone-colour characteristics of various instruments, but also to sketch and carry out a long-term plan for the instrumentation. These are properties of a composer with a significant degree of experience in instrumental writing. Example 7 shows all tone-colour constellations of the first version of *En saga* in tabular form, revealing the following results: the earlier version is 142 bars longer (17.5% more bars). At the same time, however, there are 45 more instances of a change in tone-colour in the melody line (118.4%).[16] The number of constellations increases more than tenfold. Thus, the tone-colour of the melody line

[15] There are obviously some instruments which play in almost all themes. The themes MA, MAv, MB, and MBv never have absolutely different tone-colours. Between MAv and MB and between MB and MBv there is, statistically, a more intense tone-colour change than the one between MA and MAv.

[16] Only the six main themes are calculated, which are identical in both versions.

changes more frequently in the earlier version than in the latter, and Sibelius reduces the number of appearances of the six main themes in the final version of the work. Also noteworthy is the fact that, from a total of 73 constellations (1892 version), only one is repeated (bar 38 correlates to bars 409, 890, and 921). Almost every combination of instruments is unique in this symphonic poem, something which again has not happened merely by chance. Sibelius most probably composed each constellation in such a way as to ensure it was not repeated. Such processes are only discernible by looking at the work from an overall perspective.

Ex. 7. *En saga*, 1892 version: complete tone-colour constellations.

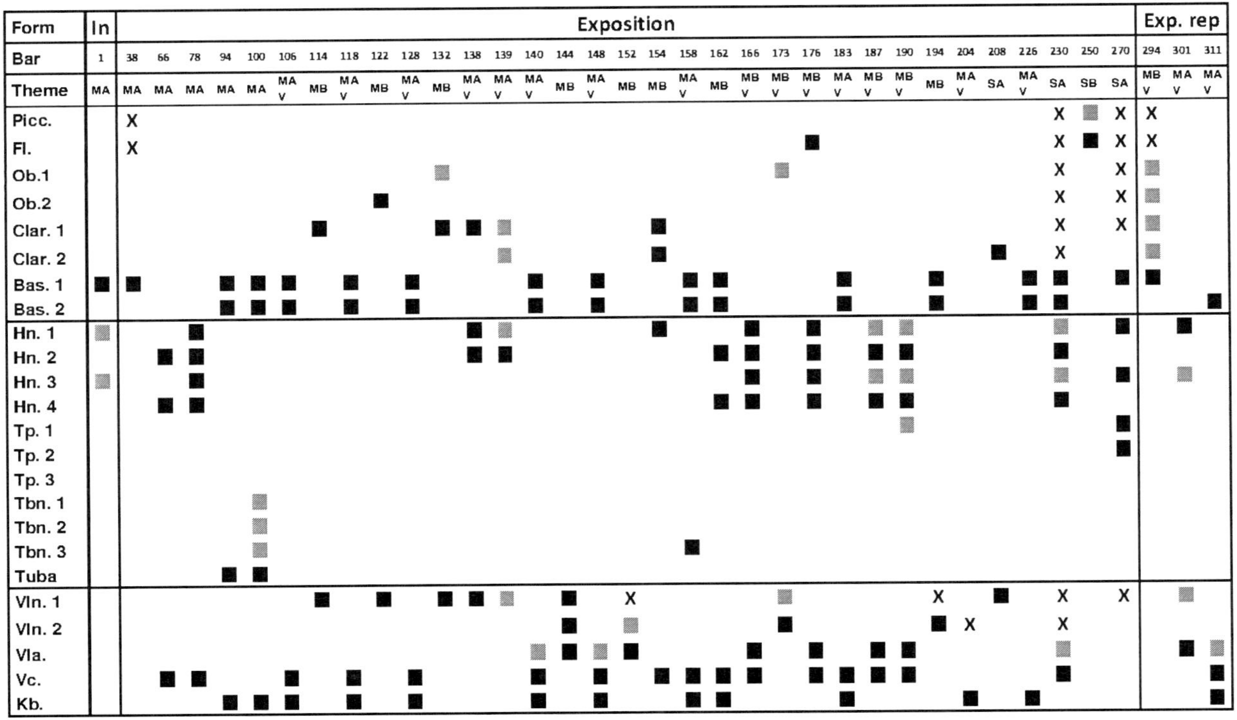

The behaviour of melodies in unison (black colour) and melodies in octaves (grey) is similar to the one in the earlier version. Similarly as in the 1902 version, there are constellations with different densities (melodies are played on between one and eight or nine different instruments), yet in the early version there is a greater percentage of melodies which are doubled in octaves (symbol "X"), and the group of brass instruments is present in almost all formal sections. So, in the first version, a differentiation in tone-colour prevails. It would probably be logical to think that Sibelius tries to create a sound which is more complex, more contrasting, and more varied in the second version. The opposite is true, however. A bigger differentiation in tone-colours does not enhance the quality of a composition, though Sibelius' processes in his handling of instruments in the 1892 version show the extent of his compositional talent. The later version was exceptionally well received both by the public and the critics,[17] and was considered for many decades to be the standard version. Examples 8 and 9 try to shed some light on this preference.

---

[17] Wicklund, *Jean Sibelius's En saga and Its Two Versions*, 26–30.

Ex. 8. *En saga*, 1892 version: complete tone-colour constellations of the themes MA and Mav

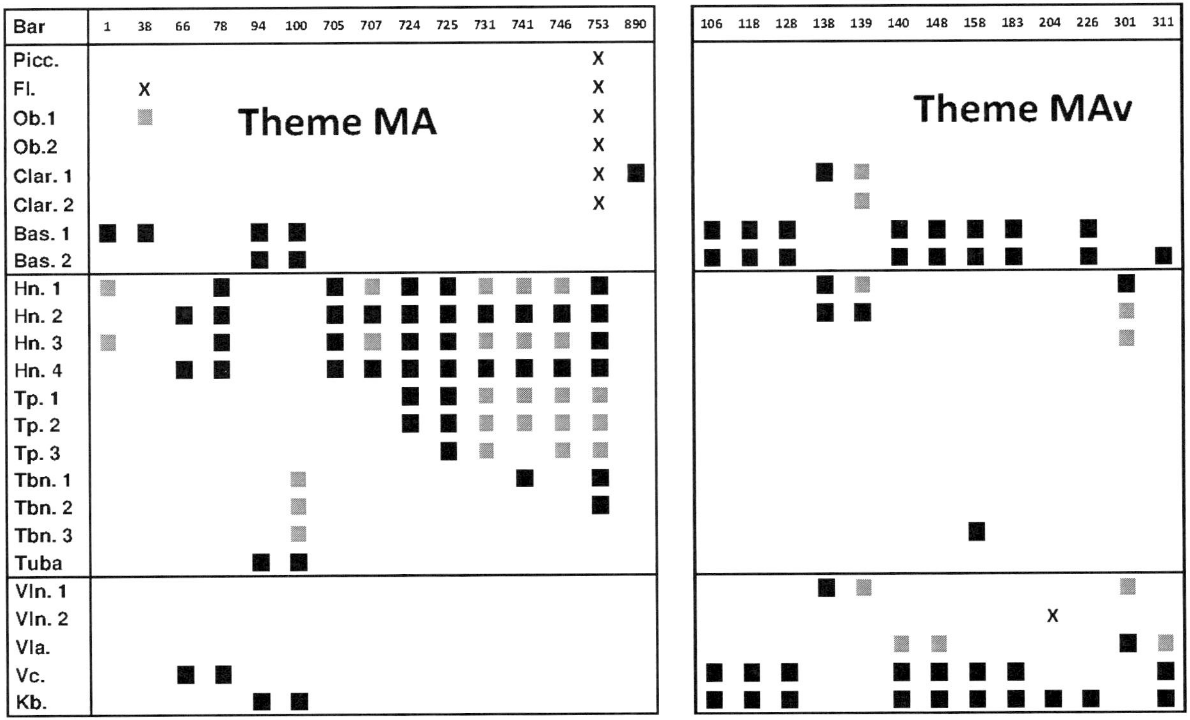

Ex. 9. *En saga*, 1892 version: complete tone–colour constellations of the themes MAv and MB

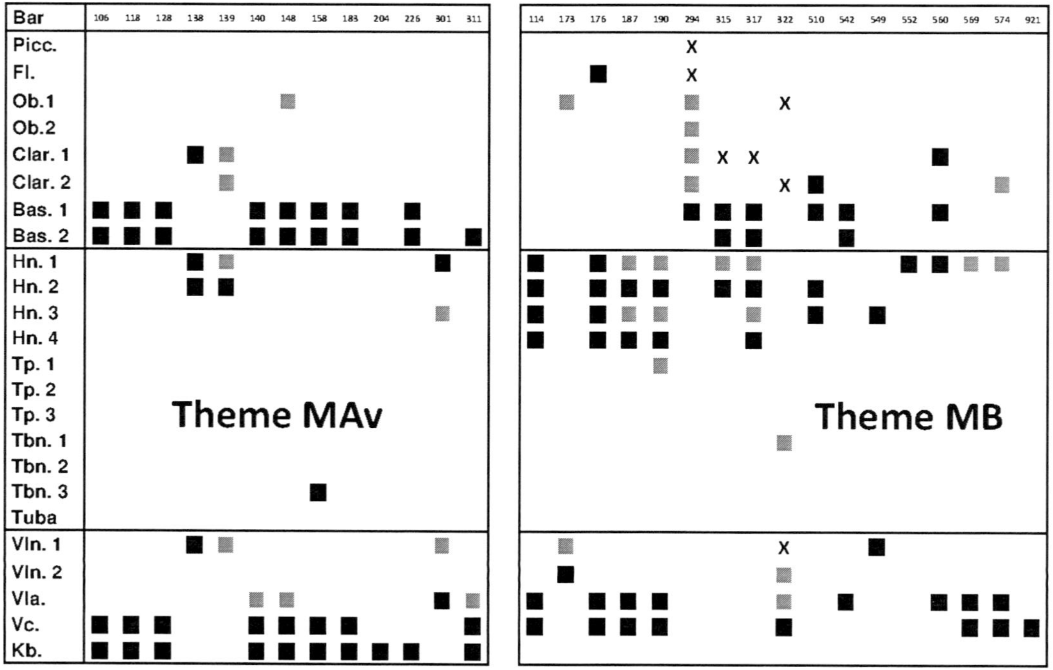

The themes MA and MAv (1902 version) have very similar tone-colours, but significant differences exist between MAv and MB as well as between MB and MBv (see Example 7). For the listener, it is relatively easy to separate the tone-colours of MA from those of MB. A completely different situation is present in the early version where, with the exception of bars 705–753, the rest of the work has a relatively clear degree of tone-colour distinction between MA and MAv. While in the latter version the tone-colours of two themes are similar, the image changes in the earlier version (see Example 9). Example 10 describes a similar situation, as it is difficult to see a real distinction between MAv and MB. In all three themes (MA, Mav, and MB) most instruments are used (with the exception of the lower brass instruments and the trumpets), so it is particularly difficult for the listener to separate the tone-colours of one theme from another; the very high number of constellations makes it even more difficult (in the earlier version). In summary, both versions of *En saga* have a high degree of timbral differentiation, as each instrumentation of the six themes is essentially unique. Overall, Sibelius explores as much variety as possible here. Different combinations in density and the use of brass instruments and specifically of the lower strings in the melody lines are some of the characteristic tone-colours of *En saga*.

Kullervo (Introduction)

This work, which is something between a symphony and symphonic poem, was composed, like *En saga*, in Vienna[18] and is a large-scale piece of some 70 minutes' duration. The first part (Introduction) has a similar form to *En saga*, and the theme played by the strings in bars 23–26 (see Example 10) dominates the entire first movement, like the six main themes of *En saga*.[19]

---

[18] See Glenda Dawn Goss, "Wien und die Entstehung von Sibelius' Kullervo," in *Jean Sibelius und Wien*, ed. Hartmut Krones (Wien, Köln and Weimar: Böhlau Verlag, 2003), 79–91.

19 Considering the large-scale form of the introduction of *Kullervo*, see Satoru Kampe, *Jean Sibelius's* Kullervo *and* Lemminkäinen. *Form, Image and Musical Narrative* (Acta Semiotica Fennica XXI. Approaches to Musical Semiotics 8) (Helsinki: International Semiotics Institute at Imatra & Semiotic Society of Finland, 2005); see also Timothy Jackson, "Brucknerian Models: Sonata Form and Linked Internal Auxiliary Cadences," in *Sibelius Forum II: Proceedings from The Third International Jean Sibelius Conference Helsinki, December 7–10, 2000*, eds. Matti Huttunen, Kari Kilpeläinen, and Veijo Murtomäki (Helsinki: Sibelius Academy. Department of Composition and Music Theory, 2003), 155–71.

Ex. 10. first part of *Kullervo*: theme of bars 23–26

Example 11 shows that this theme appears 16 times in total, and this frequently-appearing material is orchestrated in an equivalent way to the six themes from *En saga*:

- The variety of tone-colours is considerable. Only two tone-colour constellations are repeated (bar 23 correlates with bar 335 and bar 130 with bar 234)
- There are combinations of different densities (bars 172, 173, 232, and 552: played by only one instrument; bar 446 played by six instruments)
- Almost all instruments appear in the orchestration of this theme

Ex. 11. First movement of *Kullervo*: complete tone-colour constellations of the theme of bars 23–26

Bars	5	23	128	130	172	173	228	232	234	269	310	327	335	495	499	552
Fl. 1														▒	▒	
Fl. 2											■					
Ob.1											■			▒	▒	
Ob.2																
Clar. 1	■				■											■
Clar. 2						■										
Bas. 1							■									
Bas. 2																
Hn. 1	■							■		■					■	
Hn. 2										■						
Hn. 3	■									■					■	
Hn. 4										■						
Tp. 1			■											■	■	
Tp. 2			■												■	
Tp. 3																
Tbn. 1				■					■							
Tbn. 2				■					■							
Tbn. 3																
Tuba																
Vln. 1		▒											▒			
Vln. 2		▒											▒			
Vla.		■					■					▒	■			
Vc.		■										■	■			
Kb.																

There are also deviations which can be seen:

- Doublings in two octaves (symbol "X") are nowhere to be seen
- Unison combinations dominate here, while in both versions of *En saga* the percentage of such combinations is lower

After examining all the timbral combinations of both works (*En saga* and *Kullervo*'s introduction), it is clear that the young Sibelius always tries to explore as much variety of instrumentation as possible. These were not the only orchestral works composed in this period, and the Overture of *Karelia* (op. 10) and the Ouverture in E major also emerged from this very productive time in Sibelius' life and therefore need to be considered.

Karelia Overture, Op. 10

Right at the beginning of the *Karelia* Overture we hear two themes (A[20] and B[21]), which recur through the entire composition (Example 12).

Ex. 12. *Karelia* Overture: Theme A (bars 1–2) und B (bars 8–9)

From a thematic point of view, both are relatively closely connected to one another, as is also the case regarding tone-colour. Example 13 gives an overview of all the appearances of the two themes in tabular form and shows the following results:

- The brass instruments are almost completely absent[22]
- The bassoons and double basses are not used[23]

[20] Bars 1 and 2, played by the first clarinets, violas, and the first half of the cellos.

[21] Bars 8 and 9, played by the second violins and the first violins in octaves.

[22] See also Ex. 7 (*En saga*, 1902 version: MAv, MB, MBv, and SB) and Ex. 9 (*En saga*, 1892 version, MAv).

- Many appearances of the themes are played in one (grey) or two (symbol "X") octaves[24]
- As in the works analysed above, he tries to achieve a high differentiation in tone-colour so there is little by way of repetition in this regard (only bar 61 correlates with bar 96 and bar 202 correlates with bar 210)
- As with most of his works from the time, Sibelius tries to orchestrate his themes with different densities. There are combinations with only one instrument (bars 35 and 235) as well as with more (bars 15, 61, 92, 96, 198, and 22)

---

[23] In both versions of *En saga*, Sibelius uses the tone-colours of the bassoons and double basses very often, something which is not the case here. See also Ex. 10 (*Kullervo*).

[24] See Ex. 7 (*En saga*, 1902 version: SA and SB) and Ex. 8 (*En saga*, 1892 version: bars 230–368).

Ex. 13. *Karelia* Overture: complete tone-colour constellations of the themes of bars 1–2 (theme A) and 8–9 (theme B)

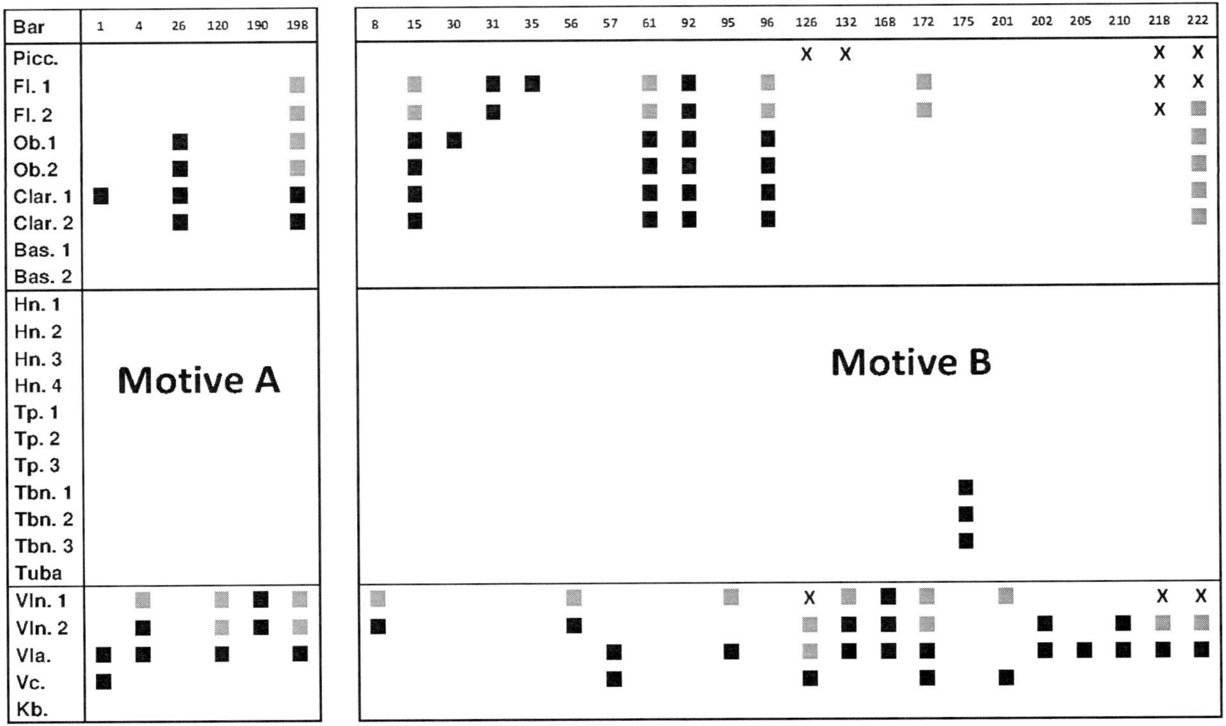

Overture in E Major

Sibelius' first orchestral composition has gained relatively little attention in terms of published scholarly research. There are actually no music-analytical references to the instrumentation of the Overture in E major, so it seems important to put the very first steps of this great symphonist under the microscope. Do the instrumentation properties found in *En saga*, the introduction of *Kullervo*, and the *Karelia* Overture also exist in this very first orchestral work? Sibelius himself talks about a duality of the two most important themes (Example 14) of his Overture in E major.[25] Does he separate the tone-colours in the instrumentation of these two themes? Or does he follow another path?

Ex. 14. Overture in E major: theme A (bars 1–2) and B (bars 44–45)

Example 15 shows all the appearances of the two themes in tabular form. There are parts of the Overture where neither theme A nor B appears. There are three blocks to this orchestral work (bars 1–35, 97–197, and 274–322) in which theme A occurs, and two (bars 45–56 and 218–306) for theme B. In order to make these blocks clear, the table for theme A is divided into three parts, and that of theme B into two.

[25] Veijo Murtomäki, *Introduction to the Orchestral Score* (Helsinki: Edition Fazer, 1997).

Ex. 15. Overture in E major: complete tone-colour constellations of the theme A (bars 1–2) and B (bars 44–45)

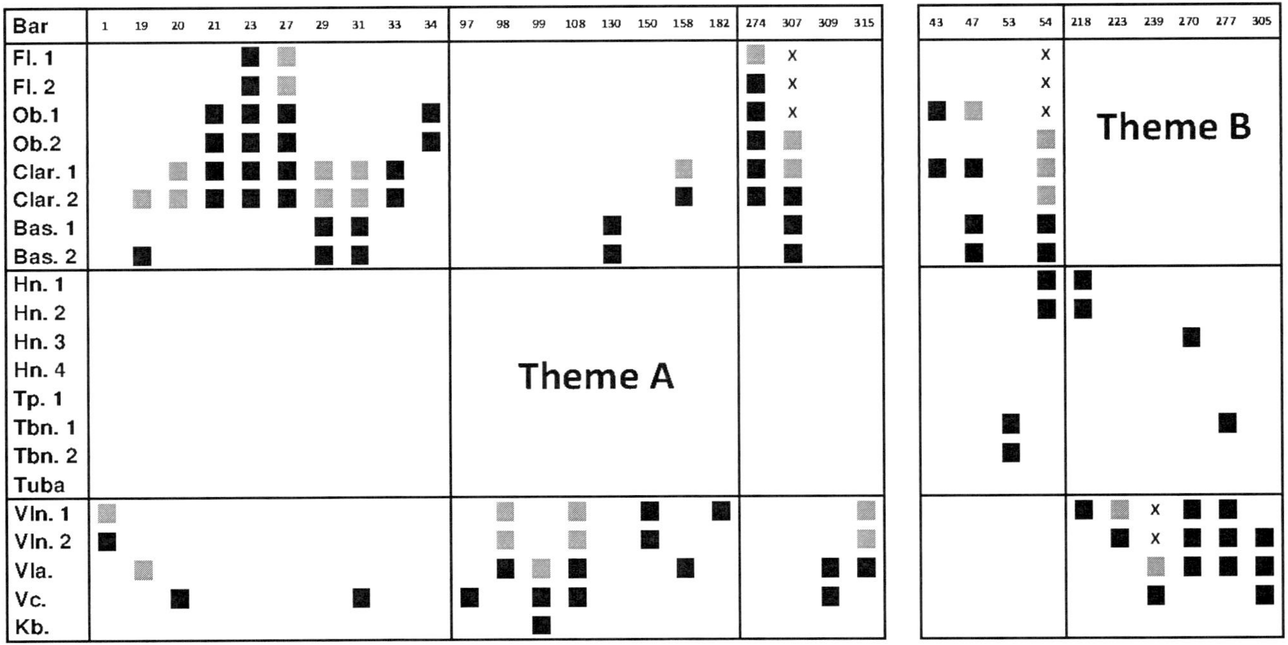

All the tone-colour properties of the previously analysed works are actually present here as well: doubling in one and two octaves, a large variety in density, and no timbral repetitions. Through the use of brass instruments (the texture of the first theme makes the usage of brass instruments enormously difficult) and by leaving out the strings (first block of theme B), Sibelius distinguishes the tone-colours of the two themes from each other. Their separation into different blocks unveils another strategy that the young Sibelius uses in order to develop the entire sound of the Overture in E major, given that each block uses a different combination of instruments. In the first and third blocks of theme A the woodwinds dominate, while in the second a more blended orchestral sound dominates. In a similar fashion, the brass instruments dominate the first block of theme B, and ultimately the strings, along with the brass, take over in the second block.

In summary, Sibelius orchestrates the melody lines of his early instrumental works with an astonishing maturity, which more typically would only be found in composers with a long experience of writing for orchestra. He was not only able to use combinations of instruments which created a well-balanced sound, but also to regulate the enormous number of such combinations, giving each a very specific character. Moreover, Sibelius manages to avoid timbral repetitions, despite the high number of such combinations. It would be of great interest to observe the development of these characteristic tone-colours in his later tone poems and symphonies in order to discover long-term developments. This chapter offers a different perspective on matters of instrumentation and tone-colour in the early works of Sibelius, showing his mastery of such elements even at the start of his compositional career.

Indication of Articulation and Accentuation in Sibelius' Notation. Sources and Background

PEKKA HELASVUO

During the seventeenth and eighteenth centuries, the notation of pitch and rhythm was supplemented with dynamic markings and hairpin signs, which often had a broader meaning than strictly showing changes in dynamics. Signs expressing exceptional emphasis, accent, or length of sound gradually began to be used, although universal standards explaining their meaning had not been developed, except for some well-meant attempts. Sibelius—as well as his contemporaries—had in principle a ready-made notation system in use, which he could adopt from the sources he was exposed to during his early years. We know for sure that Sibelius was aware of the composition treatises by Adolf Bernhard Marx and Johann Christian Lobe, the instrumentation guide by François-Auguste Gevaert, as well as violin tutors he used and compositions he played from his youth. The most common signs of articulation were essentially going to mean the same to him as for most other composers whose musical educations were based on the practices of classical masters. Because some signs, as always, can be interpreted in different ways, I have tried to trace the foundations of Sibelius' concept of articulation signs in order to try and sort out what they actually meant to him.

About the Common Use of Articulation

From the metre of music, it follows that certain beats of the bar are emphasised more than others. Accents falling on divergent parts of the bar can be marked with signs, which often have a double meaning: the sign emphasising a note may, at the same time, also indicate lengthening or shortening of the duration of the sound. Most articulation signs are not problematic: the interpretation of a common hairpin accent (>) or *sforzato* (***sf***), as well as expressing the length of notes with a combination of note values and rests, is fairly clear and explicit. Using verbal expressions like *staccato*, *martellato*, etc. may inspire discussion about the degree of shortening or accentuating the notes, but it seldom causes questions about the meaning of the word. However, the dots and horizontal articulation lines, often called tenuto-lines, can be ambiguous. Combinations of slurs and accents, dots, or lines form a special group. The problem of multiple interpretations of certain signs is a very real issue when discussing the music of Sibelius: horizontal lines and repeated ***f*** and ***ff*** signs especially need further examination.

When dealing with bowed string instruments, many signs are also read as bowing instructions. In most orchestration guides, the presentation of articulation styles has been addressed in connection to string instruments, and is associated with two issues: firstly, the bowing styles and articulation are essentially attached to each other, and secondly, almost all classical instrumentation treatises underline the central role of the strings in the orchestra.

In the course of history, a dot upon or under the head of a note has meant different things depending on time, place, and composer. Often, dots were used just to ensure that the notes should not be played *legato.* It was equally common (as it is today) to use the dot to indicate a short articulation. Although Marx writes that "the exact amount of time that is to be subtracted from the original value remains undecided," he instructed that quavers with dots on are about one quarter shorter than real ones, and those with dashes about half of their value.[1] When expressing a bowing style such as *spiccato* or *ricochet*, the dots have double meanings: they impact not only the bowing style but also act by shortening the notes.

Vertical dashes (ˡ) or wedges (▼) above or under the notes generally express short articulation, often also meaning accentuation. The horizontal line or articulation line (–) has usually been interpreted in two, partly conflicting ways: either the notes should be gently emphasised in performance, or they are to be played evenly with the same intensity throughout (as *tenuto line*).

Actually, the ideal of a tone sounding evenly from its beginning until the end has never been self-evident. Instead, the articulation of the beginning of the note has always been considered important, and the use of slurs has multiple significance. Apart from indicating *legato* or bowings of stringed instruments, slurs have been employed to show articulation, in

---

[1] Adolf Bernhard Marx, *The Universal School of Music* (orig. *Allgemeine Musiklehre*), trans. A. H. Wehrhan (London: Robert Cocks and Co., 1853), 76.

which case the beginning of the slur is articulated more strongly and towards the end the notes become softer and lighter. This is especially notable when the slurs form syncopations.

Nicolaus Harnoncourt writes in his *Musik als Klangrede*:[2]

> there is namely also an old rule, which says that every note should fade away. The note arises, and fades out—about like the sound of a bell—it ends "disappearing." One cannot hear the precise end of it, because the illusion, the phantasy of the listener, continuing the sound, cannot be set apart from the real hearing experience.

It is not possible to name a "best-before date" for this rule. When writing polyphonic textures, even contemporary composers follow this rule, probably without noticing it, because their education is based on the polyphony of Bach and other classical composers. This convention, obvious in classical music, was probably the basis for Sibelius' way of handling articulation and phrasing.

The importance of this matter should not be underestimated because the meaning of articulation for the dynamic and balance of an orchestra or ensemble performance is crucial. By means of articulation it is possible to accomplish a polyphonic texture in which the parts can be differentiated by individual articulations, thus letting the different thematic characters stand out independently. It is quite common to try to achieve balance by dynamic means: diminishing the volume of the secondary parts and increasing the force of more important ones. In this way, the elements of polyphonic structure often remain hard to differentiate, and the music sounds more like a melody and accompaniment. The final climaxes of Sibelius' symphonies are brilliant examples of how important an appropriately characteristic articulation is. If the notes of brass instruments are played like an organ, with the same volume from the beginning until the end, it is impossible to distinguish the individual lines of the texture.

[2] Nicolaus Harnoncourt, *Musik als Klangrede* (Salzburg and Wien: Residenz Verlag, 1982), 36: "es gibt nämlich auch eine alte Regel, die besagt, daß jeder Ton ins Nichts verklingen muß. Der Ton entsteht und verklingt—etwa wie der Ton einer Glocke—, er endet 'sich verlierend,' man kann das präzise Ende nicht hören, weil die Illusion, die Phantasie des Hörers, die den Ton fortspinnt, nicht von der realen Hörerfahrung zu trennen ist."

The Sources of the Meaning of Articulation Marks in Sibelius's Compositions

In general, the most significant factor to shape Sibelius' musical ideas was probably his intuition and imagination. However, behind the intuition lie an unexplored number of influences, out of which the regularities of a composer's musical world are made. The sounding environment of a child in Hämeenlinna at the end of the nineteenth century consisted of countless experiences of hearing and playing music. Exploring Sibelius' intuition or his musical experiences, with the exception of some references in his letters, is not practical. It is however possible to make some assumptions on the grounds of those literary sources which are known to have been available to him.

Sibelius learned violin playing by using the Carl Henning violin school and studies by Heinrich Ernst Kayser, Jacques Féréol Mazas, and Rodolphe Kreuzer.[3] Apart from slurs, there are no articulation marks in the first part of the *Praktische Violinschule* by Carl Henning. Dots are only used for two purposes: to show notes not belonging under slurs and, within dotted rhythms, to show that two notes connected with a slur should be played *non legato*. In No. 69, short *staccato* notes are notated by using an alternation of quavers and quaver rests, as employed by Sibelius in *Kullervo*, Op. 7, for instance. In the second part, dots as well as hairpin accents are used in more diverse ways. The third part, from No. 9 onwards, contains more ambitious compositions and symbols accordingly: dots expressing the shortening of notes and also in combination with slurs in the meaning of one bow *staccato* and *portato*.

On the last page of the first part of the studies by Kayser[4] there is an "explanation of signs" in German, French, and English. After multiple signs indicating the use of different parts of the bow, horizontal lines and dots over the notes are explained: singing *staccato* and hammered *staccato*. It is not possible to know if there was an equivalent chart in the edition Sibelius was using, but in any case the basic concept was that dots and lines meant different grades of *staccato*.

The expressions *staccato* and *détaché* basically indicate the opposite of *legato* in relation to bowed string instruments. They mean separate, detached, which suggests that the notes are played with separate bow

---

[3] Glenda Dawn Goss, *Jean Sibelius, The Hämeenlinna Letters* (Esbo: Schildts Förlags Ab, 1997), 136 (Henning) 139, 150 (Kayser) 155–156 (Mazas), 150, 156, 164 (Kreuzer).

[4] Edition by C. Nowotny.

strokes but do not necessarily mean that the sounds should be separated from each other by shortening them. Nevertheless, because the dot is occasionally meant to indicate exactly that, these signs can often be interpreted in many ways. Clive Brown[5] quotes a definition of *staccato* or *détaché* in *Musikalisches Wörterbuch* by J. D. Andersch,[6] an older contemporary of A. B. Marx: "Deliver the notes short and somewhat prominently, without, however, making their separation strikingly perceptible to the ear." There are no explanations of signs in the studies by Kreutzer[7] and Mazas,[8] though many types exist. Sibelius must have made a decision about how to interpret these when practising the studies of Kayser from 1882 on, Kreutzer from 1884 on, and Mazas from 1885 on.[9]

Erik Furuhjelm[10] writes that during his school years Sibelius borrowed the composition guide by Adolf Bernhard Marx[11] from the school library. Glenda Goss[12] assumes that, in a letter to his uncle Pehr, Sibelius possibly meant Marx's book when he referred to the harmony book.[13] If that is the case, the book Sibelius found in the school library was presumably the first volume of *Die Lehre von der musikalischen Komposition.* This information, which originates from the discussions between Erik Furuhjelm and Sibelius in 1916, has been published in most biographies which describe the composer's youth.[14] However, there is no trace of this in the Sibelius letters, and it is thus possible that he actually meant some other treatise on harmony. Furuhjelm states: "He studied masterpieces so keenly that he was able to assert: 'Everything was approximately clear to

---

5 Clive Brown, *Classical & Romantic Performance Practice 1750–1900* (New York: Oxford University Press, 1999), 217.

6 Berlin 1829, article "*Abstossen.*"

7 Ed. Ferdinand David, ca. 1850.

8 Ed. Hermann, 1882.

9 Goss, *Jean Sibelius, The Hämeenlinna Letters,* 139, 150, and 155.

10 Erik Furuhjelm, *Jean Sibelius, hans tondiktning och drag ur hans liv* (Borgå: Holger Schildts förlag, 1916), 23.

11 Adolf Bernhard Marx, *Die Lehre von der musikalischen Komposition I–IV* (Leipzig: Breitkopf & Härtel, 1837–1847).

12 Goss, *Jean Sibelius, The Hämeenlinna Letters,* 27.

13 "Harmonielära," ibid., 142 and 144.

14 Karl Ekman, *Jean Sibelius, Taiteilijan elämä ja persoonallisuus.* (Kustannusosakeyhtiö Otava: Helsinki, 1935), 32; Santeri Levas, *Jean Sibelius, Muistelma suuresta ihmisestä* (Porvoo, Helsinki and Juva: WSOY, 1986), 46; Erik Tawaststjerna, *Jean Sibelius I* (Helsinki: Otava, 1965), 8.

me—i.e., the forms—when I started my studies in Helsinki'."[15] Later, Sibelius studied at least the third part of Marx's guide during his studies in Berlin in 1889–90.

What was the role of the book by Marx in comparison with studying works by great masters? Tawaststjerna mentions, with reference to Furuhjelm, that Sibelius emphasised the latter. When he acquired the *Lehrbuch der musikalischen Komposition* by J. C. Lobe,[16] Sibelius wrote enthusiastically to his uncle Pehr in February 1884 that he had already read the first 44 pages from this book in German.[17] The guides by both Marx and Lobe use examples from classical masterworks, a fact which, according to Furuhjelm, supported what Sibelius actually did: he studied masterworks.

On the subject of articulation, neither of the two extensive books contains much information, unlike *Neue Instrumenten-Lehre*, the German translation by Hugo Riemann (1885) of *Traité général d'Instrumentation* by François-Auguste Gevaert[18] which Sibelius had in his library (now preserved in the National Library of Finland). There is a stamp in the book: Emil Berte, Wien,[19] which suggests that Sibelius possibly purchased it while studying in Vienna in 1890–1. Among all the literature Sibelius had at his disposal, the chapter about the violin contains the most extensive presentation of bowing styles and articulation markings – more thoroughly than in the classical *Grand traité* by Berlioz.[20] This treatise may thus have had considerable influence on all Sibelius' orchestral works. In Gevaert's book, as well as in most orchestration guides, the presentation of articulation styles has been addressed in connection with string instruments. This reveals two things: firstly, the bowing styles and articulation are essentially inseparable, and secondly, all instrumentation treatises underline the central role of the strings in the orchestra.

---

[15] Furuhjelm, *Jean Sibelius*, 23: "Mästerverken studerade han så ivrigt, att han kunnat försäkra: 'Allt var mig i stort sätt bekant—d.v.s. formerna—då studierna i Helsingfors togo vid'."

[16] Johann Christian Lobe, *Lehrbuch der musikalischen Komposition I–IV* (Leipzig: Breitkopf & Härtel, 1850–67).

[17] Goss, *Jean Sibelius, The Hämeenlinna Letters,* 149.

[18] Françoise-August Gevaert, *Neue Instrumenten-Lehre* (*Traité général d'Instrumentation*, Gent, 1863), trans. Hugo Riemann (Paris and Brüssel: Henry Lemoine & Co, 1887).

[19] Tomi Mäkelä, *"Poesie in der Luft;" Jean Sibelius. Studien zu Leben und Werk* (Wiesbaden: Breitkopf & Härtel, 2007), 187.

[20] Hector Berlioz, *Grand traité d'instrumentation et d'orchestration modernes*, rev. ed. (Paris-Bruxelles: Henry Lemoine & Cie, 1855).

The 36th paragraph begins:[21]

> The different possible ways of gripping the strings with the bow are extremely important and affect the sound and character of melodies and phrases in a particular way … The attack of the bow for down bow as well as up bow gives the sound of the instrument a distinct articulation, equal to the one, which a consonant gives to the beginning of the syllable in singing. As this articulation emerges more with down bow than with up bow, the player organizes [the bowings] so that, if possible, the accented beats of the bars, or at least notes, which should have a heavier accent, will fall on the down bow.

One of the oldest and most common signs to have had a great number of meanings during history[22] is a dot upon or under the note. According to Gevaert,[23] it is used with multiple meanings: to show that the notes should be separated from each other with a short rest, as well as for *grand détaché* and for different kinds of light bowings like *spiccato*. In connection with slurs, dots are also used to show "even if not legato, still with one stroke of the bow," or light bowings like *ricochet*, one bow *staccato*, and *arpeggiato* or "undulating tremolo" (*das wogende Tremolo*), which could be described today according to Harnoncourt[24] as *Bogen-vibrato* ("bow-vibrato").

Gevaert[25] describes the horizontal line (–) as follows:

---

[21] Gevaert, *Neue Instrumenten-Lehre*, 24: "Die verschiedenen möglichen Arten des Angriffs der Saiten durch den Bogen sind von grosser Wichtigkeit und beeinflussen in eigenartiger Weise den Klang und den Charakter der Melodien und Passagen … Der Ansatz des Bogens zum Herunterstrich wie zum Hinaufstrich giebt dem Ton des Instruments eine wohlunterscheidbare Artikulation, analog derjenigen, welche der eine Silbe beginnende Konsonant dem Ton der Singstimme giebt. Da diese Artikulation beim Herunterstrich hervortretender ist als beim Hinaufstrich, so richtet sich der Spieler so ein, dass möglichst die schweren Takttheile oder doch die einen gewichtigen Accent bekommenden auf den Herunterstrich fallen."

[22] Brown, *Classical & Romantic Performance Practice*, 168.

[23] Gevaert, *Neue Instrumenten-Lehre*, 24–9.

[24] Harnoncourt, *Musik als Klangrede*, 191.

[25] Gevaert, *Neue Instrumenten-Lehre*, 25: "Will der Komponist, dass in einer getragenen und singenden Phrase jeder Ton artikuliert wird, so tut er gut … durch eine ergänzende Vorschrift wie *cantabile, sostenuto* oder 'Bogen auf der Saite' vorzubeugen. Man verwendet jetzt in gleicher Bedeutung einen kleinen Strich über oder unter der Note."

> If the composer wants every note in a calm and singing phrase to be articulated, he does well ... to add additional indication like *cantabile*, *sostenuto* or "on the string." Nowadays one uses a short line upon or under the note for that same purpose.

This means that a note must follow the preceding one without a rest, but that every note should be articulated.

The music Sibelius was studying and playing during his early years probably had more influence on the way that different signs should be interpreted than the explanations in violin tutors and composition guides. His repertoire consisted of piano trios and string quartets by Haydn, Mozart, Beethoven, Mendelssohn, and Schumann as well as contemporary composers and solo violin music by Bériot, Kreutzer, Vieuxtemps, and Viotti.

Sibelius's Typical or Atypical use of Articulation Signs

When dealing with articulation signs and their impact on the music, it cannot be ignored that in order to understand their meaning some comprehension of the basics of phrasing, alongside the relevant articulation and dynamics, has always been required. A musician without such background knowledge cannot distinguish the meanings of the same signs in different contexts. The case resembles the situation with verbal analogies where a word can be understood differently according to its context (for example, to *play* the violin or to watch a *play* in the theatre).[26]

What conclusions can be drawn concerning other orchestral instruments or piano? It is quite clear that discussion about *portato* or *martellato* between a pianist and trombone player may result in a lot of confusion. However, the articulation signs used for different instruments are generally consistent, and Sibelius is in this sense no exception as he often used different signs for winds and strings; sometimes, one or the other instrument group has been left without any markings, which shows his awareness of the individual character of different instruments.

The world of the musician at the end of nineteenth century was influenced by the maxims of that era, which, in Sibelius' case, meant primarily the German cultural heritage of the time. Adolf Bernhard Marx was appointed professor of music in Berlin University in 1830, a position he held until his death in 1866. The concepts he discussed in his

[26] For the use of the vertical stroke in the meaning of shortening and lightening the final note of a phrase versus a common type of staccato mark, see, for instance, Brown, *Classical & Romantic Performance Practice*, 143.

Allgemeine Musiklehre (1839) and *Die Lehre von der musikalischen Komposition* probably still formed the basis for every music student when Sibelius was studying in Berlin from 1889 to 1890. From that period, handwritten Swedish translations exist of the third part of Marx's composition guide in a notebook by Sibelius.

The impression of Sibelius' intimate relationship with nature has become something of a cliché. Nevertheless, when the sounds of nature were singing in his ears so vividly, it is reasonable to assume that he occasionally pursued such effects in his music and thus used rather innovative markings. One could quote as an example the lines, accents, and *messa di voce* signs (<>) in connection with slurs in *Kullervo*, Op. 7. Such markings, which appear especially nuanced in the early orchestral works, are rather rare elsewhere. In corresponding cases, slurs and dots have commonly been used, a practice which had been introduced in many books.[27] However, Sibelius' use of the common *hairpin accent* (>) is not different from its normal use.

The use of slurs together with different kinds of emphasising signs in his earlier works is a good example of Sibelius' own way of using articulation marks according to what was appropriate for that moment. In such matters, one could well imagine that the composer did not wish to bother leafing through books in order to find the commonly accepted sign. On the other hand, in the first 75 bars of the solo part of the Violin Concerto, Op. 47—depending on the interpretation—there are almost one hundred articulation marks: lines, hairpin accents, negative accents, long accents, and *rinforzandos*. This shows that it was very significant for Sibelius to show how the notes were to be performed or articulated.

Some points of Sibelius' typical or atypical use of articulation signs can be listed as follows:

- Marking of tone length only is most simply and unambiguously done by using note values and rests. See, for example: Cl. I–II, Fg. I–II, Cor I–IV, Vl. I-II and Va. in *Kullervo*, Op. 7, third movement, bb. 93–102 (Jean Sibelius Works [JSW] I/1.2, p. 142)
- Dots are used not only for shortening the note, but sometimes clearly for lightening the sound as well. A good example of this can be found in the oboe and flute solos in *Lento e soave* sections in the third movement of Symphony No. 2 Op. 43, bb. 147–149 and 295–297 (JSW I/3, pp. 116, 137–138)

---

[27] See, for example, Marx, *The Universal School of Music*, 273, examples 360 and 361.

- The long accent or "large hairpin"[28] employed by Sibelius in many works has also been discussed in relation to music by Schubert and Brahms, for example. It is often difficult to draw conclusions about whether the hairpin means *decrescendo* or accent, but, nevertheless, in many cases it is quite clear that it is a matter of a long accent.

Example 1. *Rakastava* Op. 14, early version, third movement, bb. 51–54; see the Viola part. Copied from the autograph manuscript (NLF 0488) preserved in the National Library of Finland

A single or repeated short *crescendo* hairpin could be called a negative accent in some cases.

[28] Brown, *Classical & Romantic Performance Practice*, 107.

Example 2. *Suite mignonne*, Op. 98a, first movement, bb. 49–52, see Fl. I–II, Vl. I–II. Copied from the autograph manuscript preserved in the Sibelius Museum, Åbo-Turku, Finland

Also, the meaning of this sign may be to avoid a normal structural accent. See, for example: Solo violin part, b. 37 in the first movement of Violin Concerto, Op. 47 (JSW II/1, p. 131).

The articulation line can be interpreted in almost all cases as a gentle, emphasising accent. In the string parts, a slur with lines is merely a bowing sign, and there is usually not a slur in the equivalent wind part at the same time. See, for example: Ob. I, Cl. I, and Vl. I in the first movement of Symphony No. 1, Op. 39, bb. 295–296 (JSW I/2, p. 35). However, the slur needs to be considered as a phrasing or articulation mark as well, at least in most cases.

With dotted rhythms, lines or accents are often used on the long notes, which suggests the interpretation that Sibelius liked to emphasise the common metrical accentuation in these instances. Consequently, this means that the small notes should not be particularly emphasised. See, for example: solo violin in Violin Concerto, Op. 47, b. 26 (JSW II/1, p. 131).

At some point after 1910 Sibelius started to occasionally use wedges in string parts, though very sparingly. One can presume that he was meaning an exceptionally short or strongly accentuated articulation. See, for example: Symphony No. 5, Op. 82 (Edition Wilhelm Hansen [WH] 17538, pp. 29 and 49), *Rigaudon*, Op. 78/4 (WH 18201, violin part in the piano score, p. 4), *Humoresque III*, Op. 89a (WH 26420, p. 24), and Symphony No. 7, Op. 105, bb. 246, 249–250 and 253 (JSW I/8, p. 38).

Repeated ***f*** and ***ff*** marks, very typical for Sibelius, originate from a practice before the time ***sf*** or ***rf*** markings were in use. Clive Brown[29] gives an example of the development from the Overture to *Orfeo ed Euridice* by Gluck: in the version from 1762 repeated ***f*** marks on the first beats of bars 6–10 were used, and in the 1773 version these were replaced with ***sf*** marks. A third version, a contemporary piano score by Rellstab, uses ***rf***. In the string quartets by Beethoven, which Sibelius performed during his studies in Helsinki, only in Op. 59 No. 2 (see the fourth movement, bars 231–234 and 239–242) are repeated ***f*** and ***ff*** marks used. This is more common in Beethoven's symphonies, although he used plenty of repeated ***sf*** markings as well (see, for example, the end of exposition in the first movement of Symphony No. 9, bars 146–157). Repeated ***f*** and ***ff*** marks were still used by Schumann.[30] All this is further evidence that Sibelius based his way of using markings not only on books but actually on the music he used to play, and that he continued this tradition.

Example 3. The end of *Andante festivo* for string quartet, JS 34a. Copied from the autograph manuscript preserved in *Keski-Suomen Museo*, Jyväskylä, Finland.

According to the evidence of recordings from the early twentieth century, it seems that a major change has occurred in terms of interpretation. The execution of printed notes has become more slavish, the natural breathing of phrases has often disappeared just like *portamentos*, and the treatment

[29] Brown, *Classical & Romantic Performance Practice*, 63–4.
[30] Ibid., 66.

of dotted rhythms has changed.[31] All these wide-ranging matters are relevant to the music of Sibelius. Is it possible to draw conclusions about the origins of the signs and expressions of articulation in order to make use of them in the interpretation of Sibelius' works as a whole? This question cannot be answered with a simple yes or no. There are countless different situations, so no universal rules can be applied. Indeed, on the contrary, every case needs careful consideration because there always seems to be a rational explanation for using a sign or verbal expression. Nevertheless, the cases discussed above may suggest something of a typical interpretation of articulation and accentuation markings in Sibelius' music.

[31] A good piece of evidence of this is the dotted rhythm of the first violins in b. 44 (fifth bar after letter C) in *Andante festivo* (JS 34b, 1938). In the autograph of the string quartet version (JS 34a, 1922) the rhythm is double dotted, and in the recording of the string orchestra version 1.1.1939 conducted by Sibelius the rhythm is executed clearly as double dotted, even though it is written with one dot only.

3. Analytical Essays

UNCONFIRMED PASTORAL TOPIC AND DENIAL OF THREAT IN THE SLOW MOVEMENT OF SIBELIUS' FIRST SYMPHONY

LAURI SUURPÄÄ

Sibelius' first orchestral works, composed in the early 1890s, can all be associated with an extramusical programme. In these works, the programme is either clearly stated, as in the *Lemminkäinen* Suite, whose topic derives from the Finnish national epic *Kalevala*, or is more unspecified, as in *En saga*.[1] The First Symphony, composed in 1898–9, is the first orchestral work that was published without any descriptive or programmatic title. However, the drafts show us that, when planning his first symphony, Sibelius also thought of basing this work on a programme. He even called the drafted symphony a "Musical Dialogue," giving all the movements individual titles. But the tonal plan of the draft also indicates that the sketched work considerably differs from the finished First Symphony.[2] When publishing the Symphony, Sibelius had abandoned all programmatic references, or at least decided not to make them public.

---

[1] In spite of the lack of a specific programme, some authors have interpreted quite concrete extramusical associations in *En saga*. For a detailed discussion of the various programmatic interpretations of the work, see Tuija Wicklund, *Jean Sibelius's En saga and Its Two Versions: Genesis, Reception, Edition, and Form* (DMus diss., Sibelius Academy, University of the Arts Helsinki, 2014), 31–47.

[2] The draft has been discussed, for example, in Erik Tawaststjerna, *Sibelius Volume 1: Years 1865–1905,* trans. Robert Layton (Berkeley: University of California Press, 1976), 200; and in Timo Virtanen, Preface to *Sibelius, Symphonie Nr. 1 e-moll, op. 39: Studienpartitur, Urtext der Gesamtausgabe Jean Sibelius Werke* VI (Wiesbaden: Breitkopf & Härtel, 2009). Tawaststjerna doubts whether these sketches were related to the published First Symphony, primarily because of the differences between the tonal layout in the sketches and that of the finished work. Virtanen, by contrast, argues for the possibility of a closer connection, writing that, "as some of the sketches for the *Allegro* theme of the first movement are written in F major, it is entirely possible that the key scheme was closely related to the First Symphony plans."

The lack of a specific programme does not mean, of course, that the First Symphony does not have a narrative quality. Indeed, James Hepokoski, for example, has spoken about the work's "clear allusion to, then deformation of, the standard *per aspera ad astra* symphonic plot."[3] This essay will trace some narrative aspects of the symphony's slow movement, making a programmatic reading without an extramusical programme, if you will. I trace the movement's narrative course through alleged experiences felt by a "virtual musical persona," to use the term coined by Edward T. Cone.[4] In Cone's view, the music's expressive states and temporal trajectories can be elucidated through references to a kind of imaginary protagonist; if we say, for example, that music expresses joy or sadness, we can say that these affective states are experienced by the virtual musical persona. Likewise, if we say that the music is aiming at a goal—say a cadential confirmation of a key—we can argue that the musical persona is aspiring towards a state he or she would like to reach. And conversely, if an anticipated goal does not arrive we can say that the musical persona departs from the assumed path.

As a general interpretative context, let us first very briefly consider the framework provided by the entire symphony. At the most fundamental level, the work's narrative outline can be boiled down into the musical persona encountering a tragic threat; that is, the protagonist is aware of a negative danger he or she would like to avoid or overcome. Apart from the Scherzo, which in a way stands outside this narrative framework, each of the Symphony's movements seems to react differently to threat. To oversimplify, in the first movement the musical persona attempts to resist or challenge fate, while in the finale the protagonist accepts the unavoidability of fate, occasionally dwelling in a reverie that temporarily moves threat into the background. In the slow movement, the topic of this essay, the musical persona seems to deny this fate, or to avoid encounters with it directly. My analysis will concentrate on ways in which the slow movement displays threat, whose significance the music, or the virtual musical persona, then downplays.

---

[3] James Hepokoski, "Sibelius," in *The Nineteenth-Century Symphony*, ed. D. Kern Holoman (New York: Schirmer Books, 1997), 421.

[4] Cone discusses in detail the concept of a "musical persona" in his influential book *The Composer's Voice* (Berkeley: University of California Press, 1974); for a more recent, thorough discussion of musical persona that situates the concept in a

Table 1. Sibelius, Symphony, op. 39, II, chart of form.

Rotation 1

P (mm. 1–33), E♭ major, with hints of C minor
P^1 (mm. 1–25); P^2 (mm. 26–33)

TR (mm. 34–84)
Roving harmony (mm. 34–71) → c: V (m. 72–79) → A♭: V^6_5 (m. 83–84)

E^1 (mm. 85–113), A♭ major
A♭: V–I (mm. 85–98)

Rotation 2

P (mm. 114–141)
P^1, a♭: V^6_4, resolution to $^5_3$ elided (m. 114–126) → C♭: I^6–V^7–I (= PAC) (mm. 127–130)

E^2 ⇒ TR (mm. 142–239), based on thematic material from TR in R^1
Roving harmony (mm. 142–223) → c: V (mm. 224–239)

Rotation 3

P (mm. 240–274), C minor → E♭ major
P^2 (mm. 240–249), c?; P^1 (mm. 250–274), c: I^6 (m. 250–252) → E♭: I (m. 253–274)

Legend

P	= primary theme
TR	= transitory section
E	= episode
R	= rotation
⇒	= functional transformation, "becomes"

Table 1 is a formal chart that provides us with a preliminary orientation of the movement. I have divided the overall form into three rotations, each of which begins with the movement's primary theme.[5] My analysis

wide philosophical context, see Jenefer Robinson and Robert Hatten, "Emotions in Music," *Music Theory Spectrum* 34 (2) (2012): 71–106.

[5] The term "rotation," which is one of the key concepts of the recent and highly influential sonata theory by James Hepokoski and Warren Darcy, was used earlier by Hepokoski in an examination of the peculiarities in Sibelius' formal thinking; see *Sibelius: Symphony No. 5* (Cambridge: Cambridge University Press, 1993), 23–6. The slow movement of Sibelius' First Symphony departs from a paradigmatic rotational form in that the rotations are mainly identified through the

concentrates on the three occurrences of the primary theme as well as the manner in which the theme's returns have been prepared at the outset of rotations 2 and 3. In addition, I will discuss the "episode" that closes the first rotation, a passage whose musical quality clearly departs from the rest of the movement. Together, these excerpts give us a chance to chart the overall narrative, the path traversed by the virtual musical persona.

As Table 1 shows, the primary-theme material that opens the first rotation can be subdivided into two units: P^1 in bb. 1–25 and P^2 in bb. 26–33. The primary-theme area establishes the key of E flat major, and one of its characteristic features is the pitch E flat that sounds throughout in the bass. Example 1 is an analysis of bb. 1–25, the P^1 section. I have divided this section into three phases, which I label sentences owing to their associations with a Classical sentence. The cadential closure of each sentence is weakened by the pedal-point E flat in the bass, which omits the root-position dominant. That is, there is no perfect authentic cadence (PAC), hence the designation "quasi PAC" in Example 1.[6]

---

primary-theme material that begins them, while their later thematic material is distinct in all respective rotations.

[6] Principles of the classical sentence are thoroughly described in William Caplin, *Classical Form: A Theory of Formal Functions for the Instrumental Music of Haydn, Mozart, and Beethoven* (New York: Oxford University Press, 1998), 35–48. The most notable departure from these sentence-paradigms in the Sibelius is the avoidance of unequivocal cadential closure.

Example 1. Sibelius, Symphony, op. 39, II, mm. 1–25 (P[1]), analytical sketch.

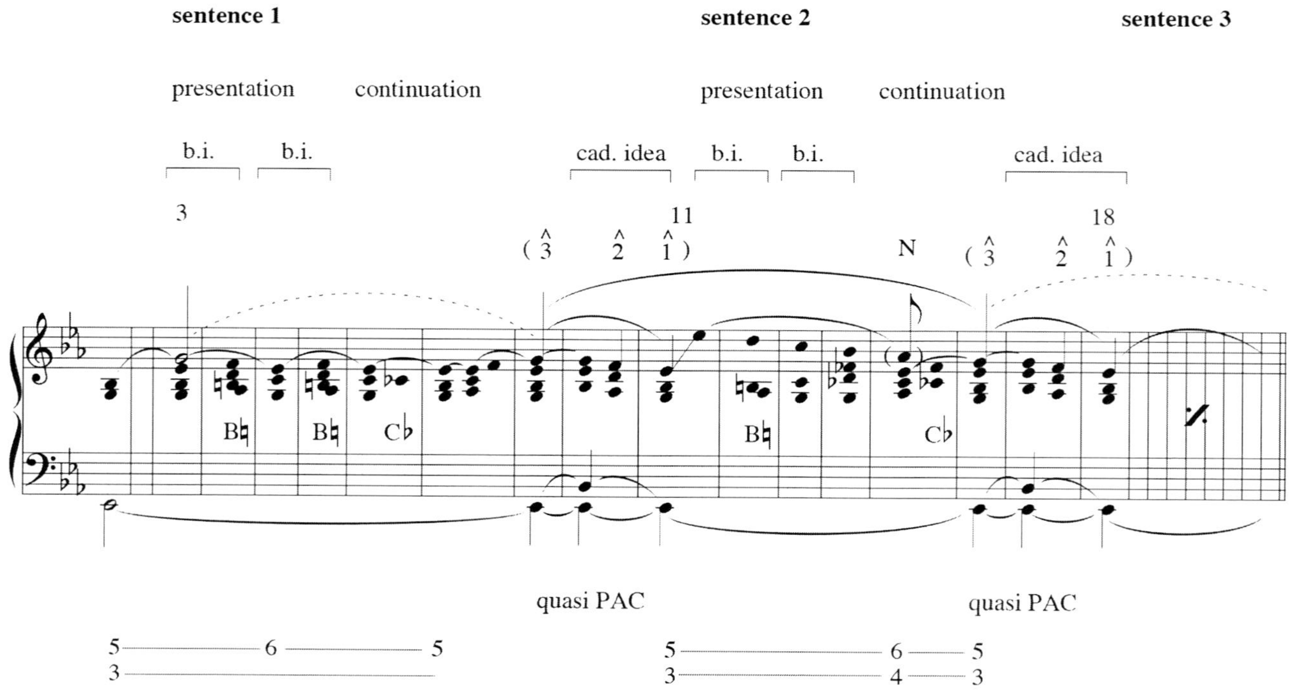

The first sentence includes two issues important for our virtual musical persona's journey. The first is the characteristically Sibelian chromaticised 5–6–5 motion in bb. 3–8.[7] Owing to this progression, the music juxtaposes E flat major and C minor triads. Example 1 shows that the B–C progression is heard twice, so the C-minor six-three chord receives quite a bit of emphasis. In bb. 7–8, a passing C flat brings the music back to the E flat major triad, however, and the "quasi PAC" then confirms this chord. C minor, which the first sentence fleetingly refers to, will later function significantly in the movement. I will argue that C minor represents the threat I spoke about earlier. But rather than openly facing threat, the musical persona always avoids a direct confrontation, thus in a way denying the existence of threat.

The first occurrence of the denial of C minor can be seen in the second sentence (see Example 1). The B–C flat pair again appears in the music, but this time B natural is a local passing tone within a progression preparing an A flat major six-four chord reached in b. 15. That is, B natural does not lead to a C-minor triad, and consequently the neighbouring chord prolonging the E flat major tonic is now a six-four chord, not a C-minor six-three sonority as in the first sentence. And as the second sentence is immediately repeated, the phrase that avoids B natural's function as a preparation of a C-minor triad is emphasised.

[7] This phenomenon in Sibelius' music and its reception in the scholarly literature has been discussed, for example, in Anna Pulkkis, *Alternatives to Monotonality in Jean Sibelius's Solo Songs* (DMus diss., Sibelius Academy, University of the Arts Helsinki, 2014), 61–4.

Example 2. Sibelius, Symphony, op. 39, II, mm. 26–34 (P²), analytical sketch

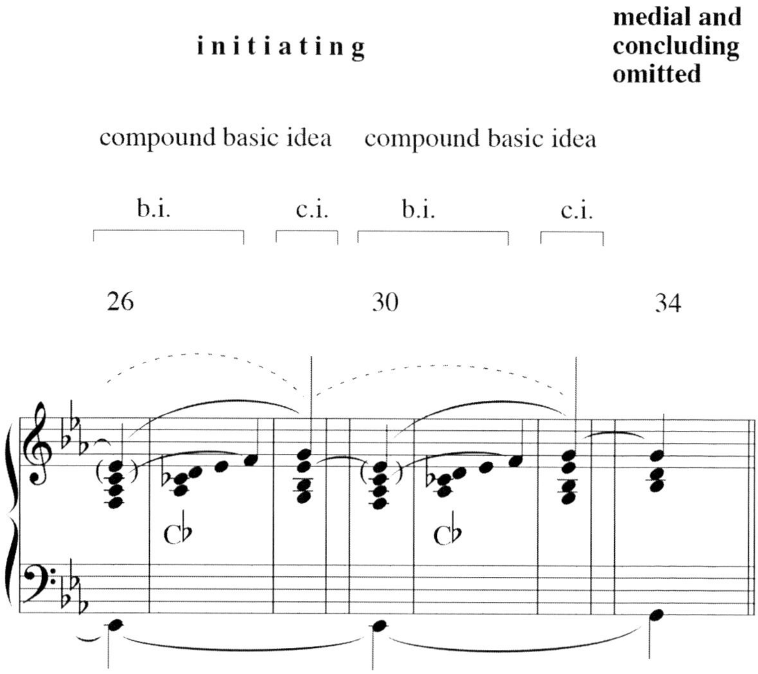

The second unit of the primary-theme area, P^2, brings the denial of threat further. As Example 2 shows, P^2 features C flat, but not its enharmonically equivalent B natural, the pitch that introduced, in the movement's opening sentence, the C minor six-three chord. So the C minor as an option is at least temporarily wiped off, an outcome that the music's more declamatory quality seems to emphasise. Phrase-structurally, P^2 seems to begin a more extended unit than the sentences heard so far; bb. 26–33 twice sound a modification of what William Caplin might call a "compound basic idea," and thus it seems that the music could be starting a sixteen-bar sentence.[8] But this attempt is cut short; medial and concluding phases are completely omitted, and immediately in the ensuing b. 34 a transition follows whose beginning is governed by roving harmonies.

---

[8] For a clarification of the concepts of "compound basic idea" and "sixteen-measure sentence," see Caplin, *Classical Form*, 61 and 69, respectively.

In spite of its phrase-structural and harmonic clarity, the primary-theme material avoids firm tonal closure: the somewhat hesitant P^1 sounds an unsatisfactory closure, a "quasi PAC," three times, while the more declamatory P^2 fails to reach any closure, its more determined quality notwithstanding. This unconfirmed quality creates expressive associations. The primary theme is governed by a pastoral topic, which in the music of the Classical and early Romantic eras often refers to the eternally lost Arcadia, a golden past that has been lost for good.[9] Raymond Monelle has spoken about the significance of the pastoral in arts generally: "Originally set in in a sunlit meadow where shepherds engaged in singing contests, it took on a yearning for the Golden Age, which could be associated with the Christian heaven."[10] Monelle also associates such qualities with music:

> But music is much nearer to its final signification than literature, because it does not have to stop at concepts. The pastoral is about finding perfection in innocence, heaven in the uncorrupted, true morality in the irresponsible, the mystic vision of maturity in the allegory of youth and simplicity. These are the meanings universally expressed by composers of all ages, from the pellucid Monteverdi to the overheated Strauss, from the clear-edged Vivaldi to the lyric Brahms, from the fragrant Scarlatti to the picture-postcard Respighi, from the pious Bach to the atheist Janáček.[11]

In Sibelius' Andante, the primary-theme material can be associated with such general aspects associated with the pastoral topic, its avoidance of cadential confirmations enhancing the unobtainable, yearning quality of the pastoral.

---

[9] Several scholars have argued that in addition to Classical repertory, topic theory provides a valuable perspective to nineteenth-century music as well, but also warned analysts to be cautious when applying it to nineteenth- rather than to eighteenth-century music; for further discussion see Kofi Agawu, *Music as Discourse: Semiotic Adventures in Romantic Music* (New York: Oxford University Press, 2009), 41–50; and Julian Horton, "Listening to Topics in the Nineteenth Century," in *The Oxford Handbook of Topic Theory*, ed. Danuta Mirka (Oxford: Oxford University Press, 2014), 642–64.

[10] Raymond Monelle, *The Musical Topic: Hunt, Military and Pastoral* (Bloomington: Indiana University Press, 2006), 271.

[11] Ibid., 271.

Example 3. Sibelius, Symphony, op. 39, II, mm. 72–98 (end of TR and beginning of E[1]), analytical sketch.

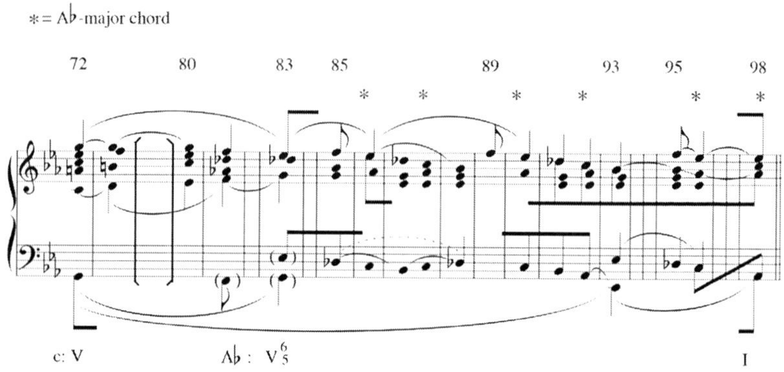

The transition that begins in b. 34 avoids firm tonal centres until b. 72, where the music reaches a dominant of C minor. Once again, C minor is not established, but the music rather starts to move toward A flat major, which will gradually establish itself as a tonal centre, clearly confirmed in the first episode beginning in b. 85. The music sounds quite directionless in bb. 72ff. As Example 3 shows, the high woodwinds oscillate around the dominant of C minor, whose bass is sounded in the timpani. A solo cello recalls the primary theme, as if the musical persona was lamenting the fate that is now unequivocally represented by C minor. It seems that threat is about to materialise—that the C minor fleetingly referred to at the movement's beginning is about to be confirmed. But the musical persona continues to deny the threat. Example 3 shows that the root-position dominant of C minor is, in b. 83, contrapuntally transformed into a dominant six-five of A flat major; that is, the bass pitch G assumes a new guise and a new direction. The threat of C minor is again denied.

In b. 85, with the onset of episode 1, the music undergoes drastic changes which affect its tempo, time signature, and texture. The 6/4 time signature and the broad thematic ideas of the horn can be associated with the pastoral topic heard at the movement's opening, this time even more clearly than earlier. But yet, the pastoral remains also here somewhat insubstantial, its strong textural emphasis notwithstanding. As Example 3 shows, the music has difficulty in reaching a firm A flat major tonic. The asterisks indicate that an A flat major chord is heard several times, but prior to the one in b. 98 these are all contrapuntal elements within the prolonged dominant. And when the tonic finally arrives in b. 98 it sounds gesturally almost like an afterthought, rather than the goal of a deliberate motion. The pastoral here resembles a reverie, a positive state occurring without a solid foundation.

Later in the episode, the music attempts to establish A flat major through more exuberant rhetoric, and thus provide a solid foundation for that key. But this process is interrupted by the unexpected return of the primary theme, significantly in A flat *minor* rather than major. Example 4 is an analysis of bb. 109–130. Starting in b. 109, the music begins to build a cadence in A flat major, moving from the tonic to a pre-dominant, prolonged in bb. 112–113. The next step, the dominant, does arrive as a cadential six-four chord, but in an unexpected guise and in a strange manner. First, the fermata above the bar line between bb. 113 and 114 gesturally detaches the pre-dominant from the dominant; second, the key is no longer A flat major but rather its parallel minor; third, the thematic material brings the primary theme back in b. 114, so we seem to be dealing, from the thematic perspective, with a new initiation rather than with the end of a cadential progression. As a result, the music fails cadentially to confirm the key of the episode; or, from a narrative perspective, the musical persona must face the fact that the pastoral topic here remains only an unconfirmed illusion.

Example 4. Sibelius, Symphony, op. 39, II, mm. 109–130 (end of E^1 and beginning of R^2), analytical sketch.

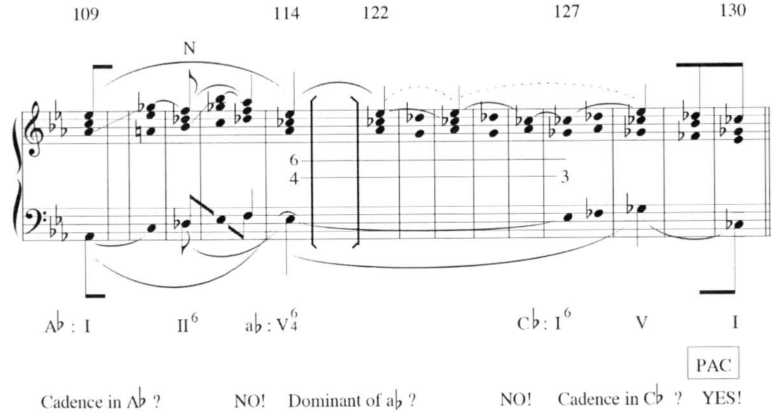

In the same way that our protagonist is willing to dwell in delusion and denial, A flat minor also remains unconfirmed. Ultimately, the six-four chord of bb. 114 ff. does not function as a cadential element. Rather, as

Example 4 shows, it is first prolonged until b. 126, after which its bass-pitch E flat is reinterpreted as $\hat{3}$ in C flat major, a key that is cadentially confirmed in bb. 127–130. Poetically, it is as if the musical persona did not immediately know what to do after the six-four chord in A flat minor has brought the opening theme back, suggesting a new, tragic beginning. The extended prolongation of the six-four sonority can be seen to reflect the confusion, and only the brief C flat major cadence provides the protagonist with a way to deny the threat of A flat minor.

But again, the avoidance of threat—that is, the omission a cadential confirmation of a minor key—has no lasting effect. Towards the end of the movement, the music reaches a powerful dominant of C minor, which seems to proceed, via a detour, to the tonic of this key. Yet, once more, the musical persona denies the threat, and the primary E flat major returns, although again in a non-confirmed guise.

Example 5. Sibelius, Symphony, op. 39, II, mm. 224–274 (end of R[2] and R[3]), analytical sketch.

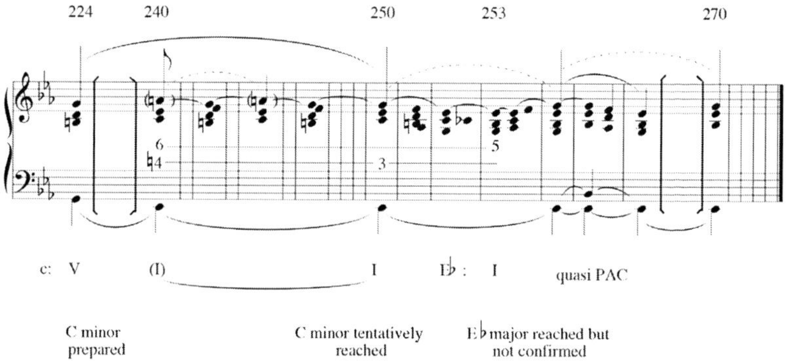

Example 5 is an analysis from the arrival at the dominant of C minor in b. 224 until the movement's end. The dominant's bass-note G moves in b. 240 to E flat, and this pitch is then sounded without interruption until the end. Apart from some fleeting local sonorities, the bass E flat fundamentally supports three chords: a dissonant six-four (bb. 240 ff.), a C minor six-three (bb. 250 ff.), and an E flat major five-three (bb. 253 ff.). The six-four sonority begins the movement's final, third rotation by bringing back the primary theme's P[2] material. With the arrival of the six-three chord in b. 250 the P[1] material returns; at the same time, we probably assume that the C-minor triad will bring along the key of C minor, a key that has so far been mainly represented by its dominant. But the musical persona again denies the threat of C minor, and in b. 253 the preceding C minor six-three chord is transformed into an E flat major five-three chord, a sonority that then extends until the movement's end. But, significantly, the key of E flat major is not cadentially confirmed, just as it has never been in the movement. Thus, it remains somewhat insubstantial: the musical persona is able to deny the threat of C minor, but at the same time he or she is unable to fully confirm the pastoral of E flat major.

All the musical excerpts that we have discussed prominently feature in the movement's overall structure, shown in Example 6b.[12] I will point out only two aspects in this example that are significant for the overall narrative. First, the top voice prolongs $\hat{3}$ throughout. So, at the largest level, the top voice does not signify progression but rather stasis. In the harmonic structure, in turn, there is no structural dominant. The strongest sonority with a dominant flavour is the G major chord in b. 224, the apparent dominant of C minor, which functions, in the global context, as a chromatically altered mediant in the primary key of E flat major. So, the harmonic structure lacks an overarching progression within a tonic–dominant axis, and thus also suggests, at a very abstract level, a kind of stasis.

Yet, the movement includes an implication of a strongly goal-directed progression, clarified in Example 6a, a hypothetical and uncompleted progression in C minor. Up to the arrival at the dominant of an apparent C minor in b. 224, the music might consist of an auxiliary cadence aiming at a C minor tonic, with the top voice descending from $\hat{5}$ towards $\hat{1}$.[13] But the concluding C minor tonic is of course omitted, and thus this progression is

---

[12] Joseph Kraus' reading of the movement's middleground structure is very close to Example 6b, the only notable difference being the greater emphasis he gives to the C-minor six-three chord in bb. 250 ff.: "The middleground structure of Mvmt. II consists entirely of a descent into the inner voice from g^1 to c^1, the latter functioning as upper neighbor to b flat"; see Kraus, "The 'Russian' Influence in the First Symphony of Jean Sibelius: Chance Intersection or Profound Integration?" in *Sibelius Forum*, ed. Veijo Murtomäki, Risto Väisänen, and Kari Kilpeläinen (Helsinki: Sibelius Academy, 1998), 150. In his essay, Kraus only discusses the deep middleground.

[13] The term "auxiliary cadence" refers to goal-directed, cadential harmonic progressions, which lack a firm opening tonic as a five-three sonority. If a firm C minor tonic had arrived at the end of the Andante, we would have a III–VI–V–I auxiliary cadence in C minor. For a thorough discussion on this concept see Poundie Burstein, "Unraveling Schenker's Concept of the Auxiliary Cadence," *Music Theory Spectrum* 27 (2) (2005): 159–85.

also thwarted. That is, the avoidance of a C minor tonic also has global significance, transforming the goal-directed progression towards the materialisation of threat (C minor) into the return of the initial reverie of the unconfirmed pastoral topic (E flat major). For the present, the musical persona has been able to deny the threat of fate, only to encounter it in a devastating and unavoidable manner in the Finale.

Example 6. Sibelius, Symphony, op. 39, II, a hypothetical C-minor framework (6a) and an overview (6b).

a)

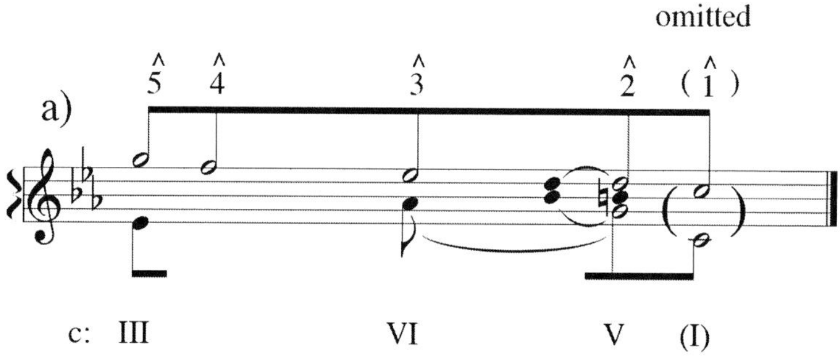

b)

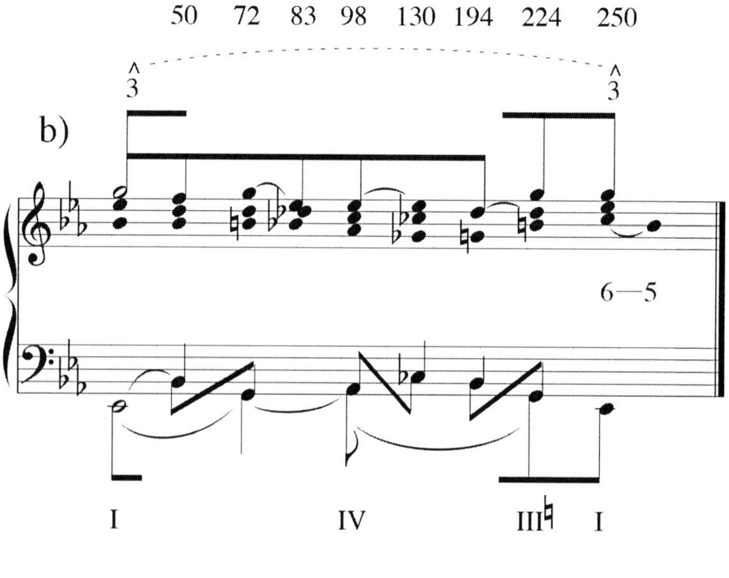

SIBELIUS' SKETCHES FOR THE VIOLIN CONCERTO

TIMO VIRTANEN

Sibelius' earliest reference to a sketch for a violin concerto appears in a letter he wrote to his fiancée, Aino Järnefelt, in Vienna in October 1890.[1] The surviving manuscripts shed no light on the reference or the sketch. In 1898, Sibelius returned to the plan of composing a concerto for violin in a letter to his friend, writer Adolf Paul; two years later, in June 1900, Sibelius' friend and patron Axel Carpelan enquired about a violin concerto.[2]

Carpelan's initiative of summer 1900 began to materialise two years later. Sibelius spent the late summer and early fall of 1902 on the coast at Tvärminne in southern Finland. In Tvärminne, he worked on the revision of *En saga*, Op. 9, for an upcoming Berlin performance in November. In addition, in a letter he wrote to Aino, he first mentioned his new large-scale composition: "I have got wonderful themes for the Violin Concerto."[3] One of these themes might be the idea in E flat minor that eventually appears in the first movement of the Concerto (bb. 147ff.).[4] The sketch is written in blue ink and crossed out in lead pencil. It is—exceptionally—dated (September 23), and accompanied by a drawing by the composer (see Example 1).[5]

---

[1] Sibelius' letter to Aino Järnefelt, dated October 29, 1890 (National Archives of Finland, Sibelius Family Archive [=NA, SFA], file box 94).

[2] Sibelius' letter to Adolf Paul, dated September 2, 1898 (photocopy in the National Library of Finland [=NL], Coll. 206.62); Axel Carpelan's letter to Sibelius, dated June 7, 1900 (NA, SFA, file box 18).

[3] Sibelius' letter to Aino Sibelius, dated September 18, 1902 (NA, SFA, file box 95): "Olen saanut ihania teemoja viulukonserttiin."

[4] In the present article, all bar numbers related to the Violin Concerto are given in accordance with the 1905 version of the work.

[5] The year 1902 becomes evident from the date *Tminne 22 Okt* [Tvärminne, October 22] written on the other side of the folio, although the month (October) is probably incorrect.

Example 1. HUL 0450, p. [2], staves 3–6

Sibelius' correspondence and other literary documentation only sparsely describe the compositional process of the Concerto. The surviving musical manuscript material for the work, however, is extensive,[6] and comprises a variety of documents from preliminary thematic sketches and elaborated drafts to score fragments both for violin and piano and for violin and orchestra. Yet, the manuscripts provide no overall picture—chronological or otherwise—of the development of the musical ideas or the compositional process as a whole. The focus chosen for this article concerns the connections between the Violin Concerto and other works by Sibelius as revealed in the sketches—the manifestations of the Sibelian "mosaic method" in the sketches related to the Concerto.[7]

As is typical of Sibelius' large-scale works, the Violin Concerto belongs to a group of compositions planned in parallel and completed over a period of several years, either before or after the Concerto. The manuscripts reveal that some of the ideas that appear in the Concerto were written down years earlier, before Sibelius' stay in Tvärminne in 1902. Provisional ideas for the third-movement themes appear in the memoranda, including thematic ideas that eventually appeared in the

---

[6] For a complete list of sketches for the Violin Concerto see Timo Virtanen (ed.), Jean Sibelius Works. Series II, *Works for Solo Instrument and Orchestra*, Volume 1: Violin Concerto in D minor, Op. 47 (Wiesbaden: Breitkopf & Härtel, 2014); Jean Sibelius Works. Series II, *Works for Solo Instrument and Orchestra*, Volume 1A: Violin Concerto in D minor, Op. 47, Version for Violin and Piano (Wiesbaden: Breitkopf & Härtel, 2016).

[7] For the "mosaic method" see Timo Virtanen, "From Heaven's Floor to the Composer's Desk: Sibelius's Musical Manuscripts and Compositional Process," in *Jean Sibelius and His World*, ed. Daniel M. Grimley (Princeton: Princeton University Press, 2011), 58–73.

Music for the Press Celebration Days of 1899 and the song *Vilse* (Op. 17 No. 4). Thus, the earliest ideas apparently date back to 1898 or 1899.

The earliest sketch for the opening theme of the Concerto's first movement likely originates from 1901. Above the sketch, Sibelius has written an annotation *Allegretto Klockorna i Rapallo* ("Bells in Rapallo"), and probably notated a tune played by church bells which he heard in Italy in early 1901. Furthermore, above the annotation Sibelius has notated a sketch for the opening of the second movement of the Second Symphony.

Example 2. HUL 1550, p. [4], staves 5–11

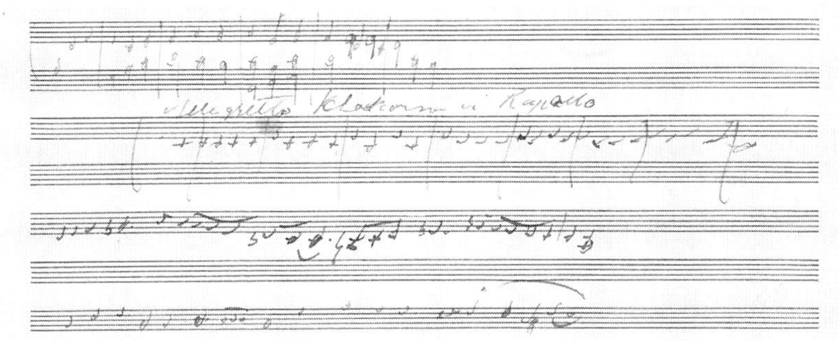

After the previous sketch in an implied G minor, in the manuscripts the opening theme of the first movement also occurs in G sharp minor, C sharp minor, and E minor. The keys of C sharp minor and E minor are present in the manuscript, where Sibelius first notated his opening ideas for the Concerto in C sharp minor, then continued in E minor with material that ended up in the Symphonic Fantasy *Pohjola's Daughter* in 1906 (bb. 9–12). The chordal writing in the *Pohjola's Daughter* passage, marked with strong red/orange pencil lines, is entirely playable as multiple stops on the violin.

Example 3. HUL 1580, p. [2], staves 6–14

The connection between the Violin Concerto and *Pohjola's Daughter* becomes evident in two or three sketches, but the connection between the Concerto and *Cassazione*, Op. 6, appears to be particularly close: the two works were composed in parallel and first performed in the same concert in February 1904. *Cassazione* ideas occur especially in connection with materials for the third movement of the Concerto, but the following two-page draft also reveals that Sibelius planned to use material that appears in *Cassazione* in connection with the Concerto's second movement. In this draft, labelled with the tempo marking *Adagio sostenuto*, the slow-movement material of the Concerto, page 1, is cast in A major, followed by the *Cassazione* idea (bb. 48ff.) on page 2, following a key change to C sharp minor (Ex. 4a). After the cadence in A major in the last bar of p. 1, Sibelius drew a line leading to staves 5 and 6 on p. 2 where the C sharp minor key signature appears, but he later crossed out the planned continuation. Also, he drew lines to staves 9 and 10 which feature an idea that can ultimately be heard in the cantata *The Captive Queen* (appearing for the first time at rehearsal letter F, in the orchestra). The draft also suggests that the passage beginning in b. 102 in the first movement of the Concerto derived from the original second-movement material (see Examples 4a and 4b).

Example 4a. HUL 0471, pp. [1] and [2]

Example 4b. HUL 0471, p. [1], staff 9, bb. 1 and 2

Example 4c. Violin Concerto, movement I, bb. 122–124 (Vl. solo)

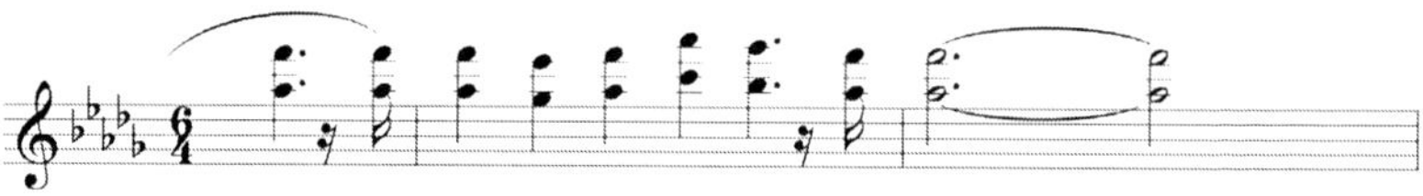

If one can assume that Sibelius at some stage planned the first movement of the Concerto in C sharp minor, then the key of the second movement of the previous draft (A major) would have had the same (major) third key relationship that prevails in the completed Concerto in D minor (the second movement being in B flat major). Moreover, the submediant key relationship would be between the sketches for the first movement in E minor and the sketches for the second movement in C major.

The manuscript page annotated "*Violin Concerto* | *Finale*" by Sibelius' son-in-law, conductor Jussi Jalas (who identified a large number of the composer's sketches), reveals a highly interesting combination of the openings of the finale movements of the Concerto and the Second Symphony. After three bars of ostinato accompaniment, the draft begins with the opening theme of the Concerto's third movement, in B major. At this stage, nothing refers to solo violin writing. The draft, however, contains several references to orchestration: *Trä* ("woodwind") and *Str.* (on staff 5), *Corno* (staff 7/8), *Pauke* (staff 10/11), and *Arpa* (staff 12). The idea annotated for strings and horn(s) in the last bar of staves 5 and 6 refers to the fanfare-like passage in the horns in the finale of the Symphony (for the first time in bb. 9–12). In addition, the ostinato accompaniment at the opening, in 3/2 metre, is related to the corresponding accompaniment in the Symphony's finale. Almost like a jigsaw puzzle, the ascent of a ninth from A to B, and the following downward leap from B to C sharp, build a connective element between the finale themes of the Symphony and the Concerto (see Examples 5b and 5c).

Example 5a. HUL 0477, p. [1]

Example 5b. Violin Concerto, movement III, bb. 19–21 (Vl. solo)

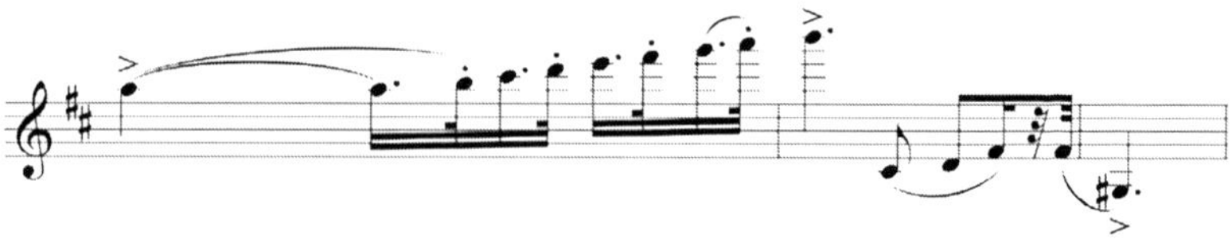

Example 5c. Second Symphony, movement IV, bb. 12–15 (Vl. I)

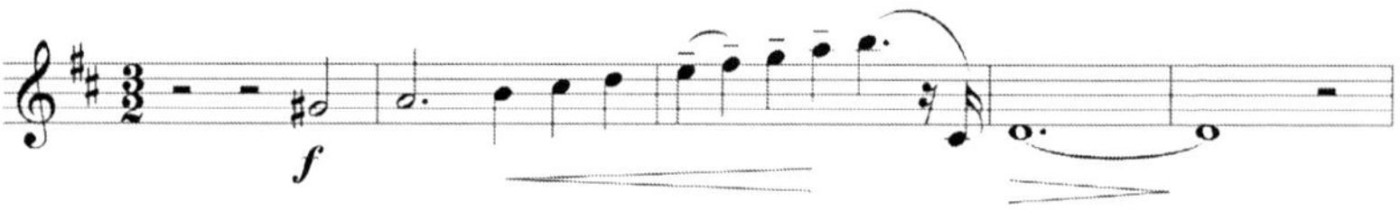

In addition to the works discussed above, ideas which appear in *Cortège* (JS 54, 1906; bb. 9ff., cf. Ex. 6, staves 5 and 6), *The Captive Queen* (cf. Ex. 6, staves 7 and 8), and in the last movement of the Fourth Symphony (1911; bb. 159–167, cf. Ex. 6, staves 1 and 2) appear on the manuscript pages containing material for the Concerto (the opening of movement III, in C major; see Ex. 6, staves 5 and 6).

Example 6. HUL 0472, p. [1]

The Roman numerals *II* and *IV*, added on this manuscript page in red pencil, probably imply that Sibelius planned to use the ideas within the same compositional scheme. In addition to *Cortège*, *The Captive Queen*, and the Fourth Symphony, the same manuscript bifolio contains ideas for *Cassazione* and *Pan and Echo* (Op. 53a, 1906). Roman numerals *I* and *III*, also in red pencil, appear in connection with the *Cassazione* materials.

The Violin Concerto was completed, first as a version for violin and piano, in late summer 1903. After having completed the version for violin and piano, Sibelius continued working on the orchestral score and, on December 19, announced to Carpelan that two movements were already orchestrated and that he was beginning to orchestrate the last movement. Thus, the orchestration of the third movement was probably completed at the turn of the year (1903–4). Ernst Röllig copied the orchestral parts for the upcoming first performance, which took place in February 1904. Today the autograph orchestral score of the 1904 version is preserved in the National Library of Finland, and the parts in the Sibelius Museum in Turku. The manuscripts for the revised version are few, probably because Sibelius worked on the revision in Berlin, and the whereabouts of the autograph score of the 1905 version remains unknown.

Sibelius' sketches for the Violin Concerto are not limited to those written in 1898/9–1905 (thus including the sketches related to the revision in the winter and spring of 1905). In 1930–1, nearly 25 years after the publication of the piano score and the orchestral score of the Concerto, Lienau suggested some notational changes to the orchestral score. Sibelius accepted Lienau's suggestions without question (although they were not implemented in later printings of the score), but the composer's reply to the publisher also contained new ideas: "Naturally, I agree with the suggested changes. I would still like to alter the orchestral accompaniment. It is too heavy. Like a symphony. Please write to me what you think about it."[8] In his reply, Lienau agreed about the "symphonic" character of the orchestral accompaniment in the Concerto and expressed his satisfaction with Sibelius' decision to revise the work. The publisher sent a printed score copy to Sibelius to be used as a template for the revision.[9]

Sibelius' correspondence with his publisher sheds no further light on the revision plan, but in the score, which Sibelius later donated to Jalas, the composer indeed planned changes to the orchestration. He pencilled circles around certain passages in the trumpet and trombone parts, and also around some passages in the woodwind and horn parts. In the first two

[8] Sibelius' letter to Lienau, dated December 22, 1930 (private collection of Rolando Pieraccini, Helsinki): "Selbstverständlich bin ich einverstanden mit den vorgeschlagenen Aenderungen. Die Orchesterbegleitung möchte ich doch anders machen. Die ist zu schwer. Wie eine Symphonie. Bitte mir zu schreiben was Sie darüber denken."

[9] Lienau's letter to Sibelius, dated January 7, 1931 (NA, SFA, file box 46).

movements he outlined woodwind and horn parts for the first violins and clarinets (see Example 7).[10]

Example 7. Violin Concerto, movement II, bb. 27–29; p. 36 of the printed score. Private collection of Satu Jalas (Parma, Italy). © Robert Lienau Musikverlag, Erzhausen

[10] Today, the score is in the possession of Jussi Jalas's daughter, Satu Jalas (Parma, Italy). I am deeply indebted to her for the opportunity to inspect the extremely interesting score copy.

Jalas later wrote:

> Pencilled markings, appearing in his own score, reveal that the composer evidently intended to omit the heavy brass instruments from the first and second movements, i.e., the trombones and trumpets. Around these parts, in every passage, he drew a dividing line and lightly assigned their tasks to other instruments. This supposedly derives from his own experiences as a conductor of the work, because at that time, with the exception of elite orchestras, the brasses tended to overpower the rest of the orchestra and drown out the soloist. Because of the general development in the skills of the wind players in the orchestras, which improved the balance between instruments, he no longer needed to follow through with his revision plan.[11]

However, because the composer circled only some of the passages in the trumpet and trombone parts, whether he actually intended to exclude the "heavy brass instruments"—as Jalas calls them in his book on Sibelius' symphonies—from the score entirely remains unclear.

As a matter of fact, Sibelius' experiences as a conductor of the work were not significant; after the few performances of the early version in 1904, he only conducted the revised version once, in 1924. More likely than this experience is that the negative reviews and comments about the instrumentation had worked their effect: even after the first performances of both the early and the revised versions, critics had complained about the orchestration, which they considered too heavy. The conductor of the revised version, Richard Strauss, even found the Concerto "badly orchestrated" ("schlecht instrumentiert").[12] These kinds of verdict, and the rather tame success of the Violin Concerto during the two first decades after its first performances as a whole, made Sibelius doubtful about the

---

[11] Jussi Jalas, *Kirjoituksia Sibeliuksen sinfonioista. Sinfonian eettinen pakko* (Helsinki: Fazer, 1998), 113: "Hänen omassa partituurissaan nimittäin on lyijykynämerkintöjä, jotka kertovat, että säveltäjä nähtävästi aikoi jättää ensimmäisestä ja toisesta osasta pois raskaat vaskipuhaltimet, pasuunat ja trumpetit. Näiden osuuden ympärille hän on joka kohdassa aina piirtänyt rajan ja kevyesti hahmotellut niiden tehtäviä muille soittimille. Arvatenkin tämä johtuu hänen omista kokemuksistaan teosta johtaessaan, sillä niinä aikoina, valio-orkestereita lukuunottamatta, vasket pyrkivät dominoimaan muuta orkesteria ja saattamaan solistin peittoonsa. Orkestereiden puhallinsoittajen taidoissa tapahtuneen yleisen kehityksen vähitellen korjatessa soitinten välistä tasapainoa hänen ei enää tarvinnut toteuttaa muutossuunnitelmaansa."

[12] Robert Lienau, *Ich erzähle. Erinnerungen eines alten Musikverlegers*, unpublished manuscript dated "Christmas 1942" (Archives of Robert Lienau Music Publishers, Erzhausen, 1942), 44.

future of the work. However, even without the planned new revisions, the Concerto's breakthrough began only a few years later in the 1930s, when Jascha Heifetz and other remarkable virtuosos started to make it famous with their performances and recordings.

SIBELIUS' REVISION OF THE FIRST MOVEMENT OF THE VIOLIN CONCERTO: REMOVING TONAL CLICHÉS, STRENGTHENING TONAL STRUCTURE

OLLI VÄISÄLÄ

There were doubtless several reasons why Sibelius revised his Violin Concerto, and many of them have been suggested in the previous literature.[1] In this paper, I shall focus on reasons that concern Sibelius' relationship with conventional tonality, an issue that has attracted less concentrated attention, despite its crucial stylistic and aesthetic implications. Confining my purview to the first movement, I will argue that Sibelius' revision manifests two basic aims that relate to the resources of conventional tonality. Paradoxically speaking, Sibelius both weakened and strengthened the status of such resources. To be more precise, he weakened the role of overly conventional *surface* elements, to which I refer as tonal clichés, but strengthened the *large-scale* tonal structure, an issue I will address through Schenkerian analysis.

---

[1] The suggested reasons for Sibelius' revision of this movement include improving its temporal proportions (Minna Lindgren, "'I've got some lovely themes for a violin concert'," *Finnish Music Quarterly* 3–4 [1990]: 25–31), reducing the amount of virtuoso material (Erkki Salmenhaara, "The Violin Concerto," in *The Sibelius Companion*, ed. Glenda Dawn Goss, Westport [Connecticut: Greenwood Press, 1996], 103–20), increasing motivic coherence (Jukka Tiilikainen, "The Genesis of the Violin Concerto," in *The Cambridge Companion to Sibelius*, ed. Daniel M. Grimley [Cambridge: Cambridge University Press, 2004], 66–80, see especially 77), and providing a "symmetrical" key scheme reflecting the Dorian mode (Les Black, "Symmetry as Modal Abstraction: The Evolving Language of Sibelius' Violin Concerto," in *Sibelius in the Old and New World: Aspects of his Music, its Interpretation, and Reception*, eds. Timothy L. Jackson, Veijo Murtomäki, Colin Davis, and Timo Virtanen [Frankfurt am Main: Peter Lang, 2010], 173–88).

When approaching the aesthetic significance of this apparent paradox, we might start by citing James Hepokoski, who describes the closing cadences in the Fifth Symphony as "no mere default conclusions but hard-won victories of tonal clarification."[2] Though Hepokoski emphasises how specific the connotations of tonality in that symphony are for the time of its composition (1915–19), his expression captures, I would suggest, something of an aesthetic attitude that had begun to emerge much earlier and had already motivated the revision of the Violin Concerto (1904–5). Sibelius strived for more strongly individualised compositional solutions, so as to serve the specific expressive ends of each particular moment in each particular work.[3] Consequently, it became less satisfactory for him to employ conventional tonic–dominant-based harmonic resources "by default," or as ready-made clichés, in cadences and elsewhere. While he did not entirely dispense with such resources, the revision demonstrates two tendencies that manifest a desire to endow them with a new kind of significance, going beyond that of conventional default procedures. First, he excised several passages that feature such resources, confining their use to special moments with particular formal, dramatic, and expressive significance, the most significant of which are the form-defining perfect authentic cadences. Second, as will become evident in our survey of cadences, even in such special moments he preferred to employ tonal resources in ways that do not just adopt clichéd "default" formulas, but colour, modify, and even deform them in individualised ways, underlining their specific expressive functions.

Owing to these tendencies, the role of conventional tonality becomes more sharply identified as a counterforce to other, less conventional elements in the final version. Though there are fewer moments featuring tonic–dominant relationships, the remaining ones—cadences, primarily—assume a renewed and heightened significance in large-scale organisation owing to their greater rarity and stronger opposition with contrasting forces. This, again, suggests the potential for the renewed significance of the tonal relationships that arise between the harmonies highlighted through such special moments. Indeed, it seems possible that Sibelius' removal of tonal surface material made him sense all the more vividly the structural implications of the remaining points of tonal clarification, thus

---

[2] James Hepokoski, *Sibelius: Symphony No. 5* (Cambridge: Cambridge University Press, 1993), 110.

[3] This agrees with Hepokoski's statement about the revision of the Violin Concerto: "The versions show a composer extremely careful about what he writes, wanting not to write standard things, demanding the highest originality everywhere" (Lindgren, "'I've got some lovely themes for a violin concert'," 26–7.)

prompting him to strengthen the tonal large-scale structure and giving rise to the apparent paradox.

The Opening

Before exploring how Sibelius' revisions affected the position of conventional tonality in this movement, it is useful to take a look at some of its contrasting, less-conventional features. Example 1 shows the opening passage, which is essentially similar in both versions. Though the music is mostly diatonic, its organisation has been characterised as modal rather than tonal.[4] A crucial "non-tonal" characteristic is the avoidance of the dominant, which, of course, contrasts with the eventual cadences. Moreover, individual voices move with considerable independence from each other, giving rise to dissonances that have an uneasy relationship with the conventional norms of dissonance treatment. For a listener who approaches this passage from a tonal perspective, several events appear to allude to conventional procedures but refuse to comply fully with them.

[4] Among others, Erik Tawaststjerna, *Jean Sibelius* II (Helsinki: Otava, 1967), 274, and Black, "Symmetry as Modal Abstraction," have characterised the opening as Dorian with an additional emphasis on the sharp 4. degree (G sharp).

Example 1. Sibelius, Violin Concerto, opening

Leaving aside the non-normative 6/4 position of the opening tonic triad, the very first G in the solo violin poses a problem concerning its status as a non-harmonic note. Of course, we might label it as an ascending *appoggiatura*, but there is conventionally no upward pull from $\hat{4}$ to $\hat{5}$. To account for the ascending motion, Example 1 models this G as a passing tone coming from an implicit F, but there is, of course, nothing to imply such an F before the G appears. The poetic effect of this G relies on the sense in which it "comes out of nowhere" or just appears there, with no apologies for its existence.

The subsequent events may suggest, for the tonally oriented listener, a tonicisation of A minor and a return to D minor.[5] In both cases, however, only some of the voices participate in these suggestions, whereas others remain static, creating further dissonances with less conventional behaviour. The A minor allusion is supported by the G sharps in the solo violin and by the C6–D6–E6 peak-tone progression (bb. 9–10), which suggests a transposed realisation of the previous implicit F5–G5–A5. While the D5–C5–B4–C5 inner-voice counterpoints the peak-tone progression in a fairly conventional way—D–C resolving a suspension and B–C forming archetypal parallel tenths—the stationary F5, dissonant against E6, contradicts the A-minor implications, and neither dominant nor tonic in that key materialises.[6] The retonicisation of D, in turn, is effected by the restatement of the opening G–A–D motif in the lowest voice, hinting at the IV–V–I formula, but with immobile upper voices. Reinforcing its unapologetic character, G appears here while the solo melody is still occupied with the G sharp–A relationship, creating a bold overlap between the two suggested key areas.[7]

---

[5] Black observes that "the opening S-Dorian [= Dorian with added sharp $\hat{4}$] may initially sound like a D minor piece that is pushing toward its dominant" ("Symmetry as Modal Abstraction," 178).

[6] As conventional harmonisations in A minor for the melody in b. 10 one might imagine $VII°6/5–I^6$ or, on the other hand, $II^2–V^6$.

[7] Some features in the opening events relate interestingly with the thoughts in Sibelius' 1896 lecture about the harmonisation of Finnish folk songs based on the Dorian mode (a term he did not use). That he writes no fully-fledged modulations to and from A minor is consistent with his unfavourable attitude towards such modulations in folk-song harmonisation, and the "unapologetic" return of G in b. 11 momentarily realises the ninth-chord sonority he seems to favour as a harmonic framework; see Jean Sibelius, "Några synpunkter beträffande folkmusiken och dess inflytande på tonkonsten—Joitakin näkökohtia kansanmusiikista ja sen vaikutuksesta säveltaiteeseen," trans. Ilkka Oramo, *Musiikki* 10 (1980): 86–105, especially 98. For an extensive discussion about the relationship of this lecture and Sibelius' compositional technique, see Juhani Alesaro, *The Apparition from the Forest: A Treatise on Satz in the Music of Jean Sibelius* (PhD Dissertation, Helsinki: University of the Arts Helsinki, Sibelius Academy, 2015).

The apex F6 of the violin melody (b. 20) is marked by what comes closest to a conventional chord progression in this opening passage: a sequential pattern in descending thirds (I–V, VI–III) leading to VII°4/3–I^6. While this progression is, of course, far from cadential with respect to its power to establish a "victory of tonal clarification," it illustrates more subtly, and in a smaller context, how conventional progressions can assume a renewed character through their opposition with unconventional *Satz*.[8] This progression is not neutral "default" material, but has the special function of underlying the melodic turning point (F6, which I shall take as the *Kopfton* in my Schenkerian readings in Examples 3 and 7). Its temporary nature is signalled by the prominent reappearance of the opening dissonant G—marked by a change in the violin melody's sequential design—as soon as the I^6 is attained (b. 23).

While this G might be regarded as a passing note moving to the demisemiquaver F, its rhythmic and gestural strength suggests a more prominent function as an anticipation of the ensuing Neapolitan II^{6b} (b. 24). Whereas the Neapolitan conventionally leads to the dominant, as sketched in the lowest system of Example 1, Sibelius lets the tonic follow immediately, producing a direct II–I succession. From the tonal perspective, this combination might be conceived of in terms of a suppressed dominant (V6/5), of which the accented, tersely dissonant C sharp leading-tone (b. 27)—the first C sharp in the solo violin—might be considered as a residue.

By describing the modal opening from the tonally oriented perspective, I do not wish to suggest that the pertinent modal phenomena could not or should not be approached in their own right. The II–I succession, in particular, is a characteristic part of Sibelius' modal vocabulary in general, and it would be questionable to assert that it should always be understood as implying the presence of a suppressed dominant.[9] My purpose in focusing on the relationships and differences between the opening *Satz* and conventional tonality has been to give an idea of the compositional dimension based on their polarity. As will be illustrated below, Sibelius'

---

[8] Following Alesaro, *The Apparition from the Forest*, xviii, I use the German word *Satz* as a term that "covers all aspects of harmony and counterpoint" and especially "the interdependence between them."

[9] Alesaro, in *The Apparition from the Forest*, lists I^6–II^6–I^6 progressions as characteristic closures in several modes, including Phrygian and Ionian. See also my discussion of II6/5–I6/5 alternation in the first movement of the Fifth Symphony in Olli Väisälä, "*Ursatz* taivaan permannossa?—huomioita satsitekniikasta ja lineaarisista arkkityypeistä viidennen sinfonian avausosan muotoutumisen taustatekijöinä," *Musiikki* 41 (2011): 197–226.

ability to move across this dimension is crucial for organisation and expression in this movement, and also its revision. Though Sibelius' II–I progressions doubtless did not, in general, emerge from the concrete suppression of pre-existent dominants, this movement includes a crucial moment which he did revise through just such a suppression, suggesting that he actively exploited this dimension for depriving conventional tonality of its "default" position.

To be sure, the variety of material within this movement involves richer dimensions than just the one based on a simple modal–tonal polarity. Apart from the characteristically Sibelian modal diatonicism, conventional major–minor tonality is challenged by advanced chromaticism, relating to more general Late Romantic trends. The primary-theme zone already combines these two elements, as the modal opening with its static character is followed by radical chromatic activation (see especially bb. 42 ff.), before the eventual cadential clarification (b. 77). Moreover, modal implications are absent from the "nostalgic, fully romantic" secondary theme—to cite Jukka Tiilikainen's expression—which features a II–V9/7–I progression in D flat major before a chromatic continuation (final version: bb. 102 ff., *Largamente*).[10] This theme, incidentally, provides another example of the "non-default" use of tonal resources, as Sibelius employs the cadential II–V–I formula in an opening rather than closing function, effecting an abrupt modulation (from B flat major to D flat major), and intensifying the moment's expressivity through the soloist's dissonant high suspensions (F6 referring back to the *Kopfton*; see Example 3 below).[11] For reasons of space, however, I will not try to describe all pertinent stylistic elements in detail, but will rather proceed to a comprehensive survey of authentic cadences in the two versions to see how their disposition and formation manifest tendencies in Sibelius' revision.

---

[10] Tiilikainen, "The Genesis of the Violin Concerto," 79, notes that, "In the final version the movement's basic dilemma is the tension between the first subject and its modal sonority and the nostalgic, fully romantic second subject."

[11] On the distinction between "cadential content" and "cadential function" in more traditional music, see William Caplin, "The Classical Cadence: Conceptions and Misconceptions," *Journal of the American Musicological Society* 57 (2004): 51–116.

Survey of Authentic Cadences

Exposition

In the Final Version (hereafter FV), there are two perfect authentic cadences (PACs) in the exposition section, shown in Examples 2 and 3. The first PAC closes the primary-theme zone in the main key of D minor (b. 75), and the second brings about the Essential Expositional Closure in B flat minor (b. 127), to use Hepokoski's and Darcy's terminology.[12] In addition, the latter cadence is followed by a set of weaker, non-perfect authentic cadences, further confirming the "victory of tonal clarification" (bb. 154, 164, 166).

Example 2. Cadence to D minor closing the primary-theme zone (FV: bb. 49–75)

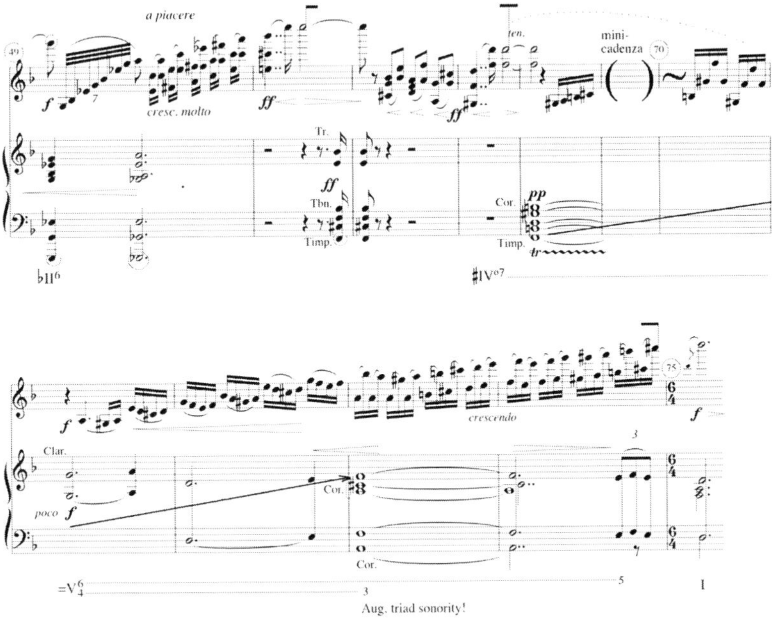

12 James Hepokoski and Warren Darcy, *Elements of Sonata Theory* (Oxford: Oxford University Press, 2006), xxv–xxviii.

Example 3. Cadence to B flat minor effecting Essential Expositional Closure (FV: bb. 116–127)

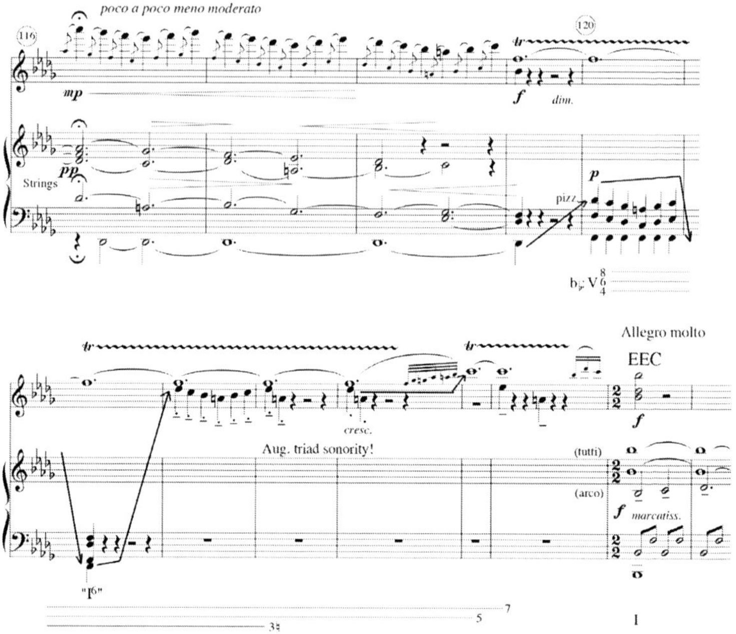

The way to EEC: A Schenkerian sketch

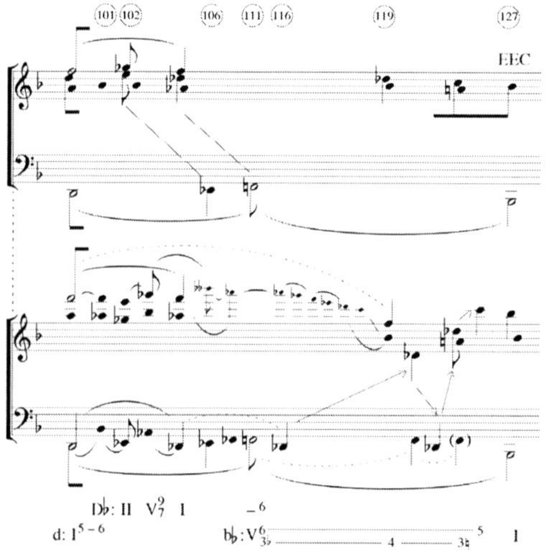

The Early Version (hereafter EV) contains, apart from counterparts to these cadences (EV: bb. 75, 138, 165, 175, 177), an intervening PAC to B flat major (b. 113), shown in Example 4. The removal of this cadence served, I would suggest, Sibelius' aesthetic aims in two ways. It made, of course, the remaining cadences all the more exceptional, adding especially to the freshness of the B flat minor cadence as the sole cadential establishment of B flat. Moreover, since the B flat major cadence merely adopts an entirely conventional harmonic formula (I–VI–IV–V–I) with no original modification, it exemplifies the kind of clichéd "default" procedure that had become unsatisfactory for Sibelius.[13]

Example 4. The removed cadence to B flat major (EV: bb. 109–113)

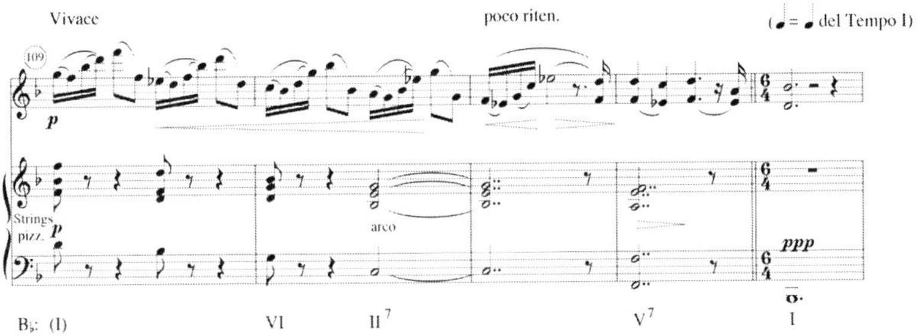

The D minor and B flat minor cadences are much more sharply individualised to serve the particular expressive aims of this particular music. While ultimately yielding to the V–I progression, they show a dramatised opposition between the motion towards the V and contrasting forces. As indicated by arrows in Examples 2 and 3, both cadences involve complex voice-leading in which the V is preceded by a prominent $\hat{3}$ (of the upcoming key) in the bass, which is ultimately transferred to become an upper voice in a $\hat{3}$–$\hat{2}$–$\hat{1}$ descent.[14] After this transfer, the suspended $\hat{3}$

[13] In a larger context, the passage in Example 4 serves to elaborate the resolution of the preceding extended cadential 6/4 (EV: bb. 103–108).

[14] The participation of a bass $\hat{3}$ in upper-voice voice-leading has a long history in tonal tradition. See, for example, William Rothstein, "Transformation of Cadential Formulae in the Music of Corelli and His Successors," in *Essays from the Third International Schenker Symposium*, ed. Allen Cadwallader (Hildesheim: Olms, 2006), 245–78.

(V^{6-5}) produces, in both cases, an emotionally charged augmented-triad sonority, which further highlights the resistance $\hat{3}$ creates against the motion towards the dominant.

The bass V is not stated as a matter of course in either cadence, but is problematised in ways that highlight its expressive function as a counterforce to previous elements. In the D minor cadence, the sharp IV^7 ($VII^{\circ 7}$ of V) at the end of the solo violin's mini-cadenza (Example 2, b. 70) creates the expectation of an imminent dominant, but whether this expectation is fulfilled is at first ambiguous. The violin figuration can be heard as composing-out the cadential 6/4 (bb. 71–72), but the concurrent reference to the opening motif in the clarinets, with the tonic D as the lowest pitch, momentarily suggests the kind of dominant-avoiding *Satz* that characterised the opening (see especially bb. 11–12 [Example 1]). It is only the ensuing explicit dominant (b. 73) that retrospectively resolves this ambiguity.

In the B flat minor cadence, the bass V is problematised by its conspicuous absence at the crucial cadential moment (Example 3, bb. 122–126). Since the solo violin clearly expresses the dominant harmony—with the trill on $\hat{2}$ as a particular nod to tonal tradition—the omission of the bass V has no modal implications but implies, nonetheless, that the dominant has lost its position as a self-evident "default." Instead of a tonal–modal polarity, the approach to this cadence dramatises a more-conventional opposition between relative keys. The salient tonicisation of D flat major (starting from the II–V9/7–I in bb. 102–104) is followed by a chromatic bassline ascent to F (E flat–F flat–F natural, bb. 103–111), but the D flat bass is restated (b. 116) and competes with F even when the sense of key has shifted toward B flat-minor (bb. 118–120), until the solo violin decides, having been left alone by the orchestra, their rivalry in favour of V of B flat. The Schenkerian sketch in Example 3 summarises these events, suggesting that the D flat is, despite its initial prominence, ultimately subsumed within the motion towards B flat as an inner-voice chromatic passing note—a reading that tallies with the poetic idea of D flat major as representing happy reverie rather than sustainable reality.[15]

---

[15] As indicated by slanted lines and overlapping slurs, my Schenkerian sketch is complicated by reading successive events as standing for simultaneous ones. The upper-voice combination of G flat 6–F6 and B double flat 6–A flat 6 is similar to one of Schenker's types of unfolding; see Heinrich Schenker, *Free Composition*, trans. and ed. Ernst Oster (New York: Schirmer, 1979) Fig. 43b4. Moreover, reflecting the association between the hypermetrically accented E flat basses in bb.

While the removal of the B flat major cadence was Sibelius' most significant revision for the exposition's cadential disposition, the D minor and B flat minor cadences also underwent some noteworthy changes. In both cases, the changes strengthened the dramatic opposition between the cadence and preceding counterforces. In EV, the first cadence does not involve a root-position V, but the horns' G3–A3–C sharp4 chord is sandwiched between the two registers of the doubled $\hat{3}$–$\hat{2}$–$\hat{1}$ motion.[16] While this is a rare example of a *less* conventional detail in EV, the normal root-position V in FV serves more effectively the larger aim of establishing a clear polarity between the opening dominant-avoiding *Satz* and conventional tonality. As for the B flat minor cadence, the passage starting from the soloist's trill (EV: b. 130, FV: b. 119 [Example 3]) is quite similar in both versions, but the preceding events in EV reveal much less emphasis on D flat major (and no chromatic ascent to F), yielding a much milder dramatic opposition between the relative keys.[17]

In both PACs of FV's exposition, the tonal drama involves the sharp individualisation of both the soloist and orchestra's roles, which doubtless suggests rich potential for narrative interpretation. Without delving into this issue, a brief comment may be needed about the description of cadences as "hard-won victories of tonal clarification" cited above. Given the sense of struggle in the approaches to cadential dominants, this expression seems apt, but owing to the minor modes of the cadential goals the victorious power does not convey positive implications. The B flat minor goal, in particular, has the effect of something unwanted but unavoidable—fate or a difficult decision, perhaps—which the soloist-protagonist must face without external support after the happy D flat major reverie.

Development and Recapitulation

The two cadential closures in FV's exposition reappear as modified transpositions to articulate the most significant subsequent formal junctures. In both versions, the development ends and the recapitulation

---

102, 104, and 106, I read the E flat–D flat motion as ultimately relegated to an inner-voice status above the structurally decisive E flat–F motion.

[16] Another prominent difference is that in EV the bass $\hat{3}$ is explicitly sustained by the orchestra during the passage that became the mini-*cadenza* in FV (bb. 55–72).

[17] In EV there are just four bars of D flat major (bb. 123–126, corresponding to FV: 102–105), followed by a motion through the Neapolitan II^{6b} to the cadential 6/4 of B flat minor.

begins in the subdominant key, whose establishment refers back to the first cadence, as illustrated by vertical alignment in Example 5. In FV, moreover, Essential Structural Closure is achieved through a modified transposition of the EEC, but EV shows a weaker parallelism in this respect.

Example 5. The first cadence to D minor compared with the establishment of G minor at the joint between the development and recapitulation in EV and FV

(a) FV: Cadence to I closing the primary theme zone

(b) EV: Cadence to IV closing the development (solo cadenza) and leading to recapitulation

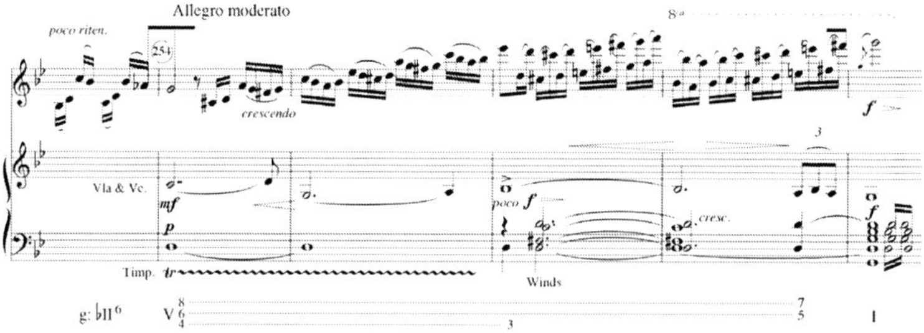

(c) FV: Corresponding passage

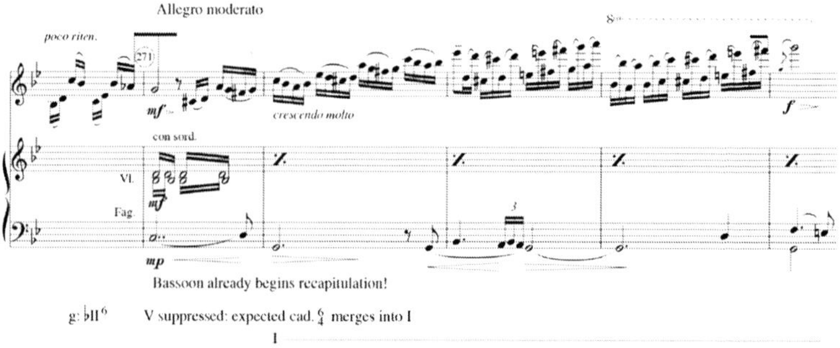

One of the most intriguing changes in Sibelius' revision concerns the establishment of the large-scale IV at the joint between the development and recapitulation, illustrated in Examples 5(b) and 5(c). In both versions, the cadenza that constitutes the main part of the development leads to the Neapolitan II^{6b} in G minor (EV: b. 253, FV: b. 270), which, like the sharp IV^7 in the first cadence (b. 70), creates the expectation of an ensuing dominant. In EV, this expectation is fulfilled by a cadence that largely parallels the first D minor cadence, but makes the dominant unambiguous through an explicit bass V both under the reference to the opening motif (bb. 254–255, timpani roll) and in the ensuing V^7. In FV, by contrast, the dominant becomes more ambiguous or, rather, is suppressed altogether. Though a listener may assume that the bassoon statement of the opening motif (b. 271) stands for the cadential 6/4, following the model of the first cadence, no dominant harmony ensues to confirm this assumption. Instead, the assumed cadential 6/4 directly merges into—or turns out to be—the G-minor tonic, whose premature entrance deprives the soloist's $\hat{7}$–$\hat{8}$ (F sharp7–G7) closure its harmonic support, leaving the leading tone as the only residue of the dominant. From a thematic perspective, the bassoon melody turns out to be not just a reference to the opening motif but the opening motif itself, starting the recapitulation four bars prior to the soloist's expected cadential closure.[18]

Sibelius' way of revising this cadence shows enhanced mastery in the purposeful exploitation of the tonal–modal dimension at the service of musical expression and drama. Whereas the root-position V of the first cadence negates the dominant-avoiding implications of the reference to the opening motif (bb. 71–72, Example 2), its G minor counterpart overturns that negation. The former cadence helps to establish the modal–tonal polarity through its contrast with preceding events, and the latter

[18] Though Sibelius' compositional solution does not lack originality, the resource on which it is based—the association between the tonic triad and the cadential 6/4, and the attendant potential of ambiguity and reinterpretation—has been employed for various effects by him and his Romantic predecessors. For an early example with a comparable formal function, consider Beethoven's Piano Sonata in E minor, Op. 90, first movement, in which the cadential 6/4 at the end of the development likewise seems to merge into the tonic of the recapitulation (though in the home key). In the Sibelius movement, the opening motif relates with ambiguous treatment of cadential 6/4 also in the canonic passage of b. 250 ff. Once again, there is a strong expectation of V (now of A minor) when the motif appears, suggesting cadential 6/4 at that point. But do the ensuing $\hat{3}$–$\hat{2}$ (C–B) motions resolve the 6/4 or already represent the tonic into which the 6/4 merges?

cadence—deformed, from the tonal perspective—re-establishes that polarity on the larger scale through its contrast with the first cadence. Locally, the revision may have been motivated by the fact that the passage in question is preceded by one of the most conventional surface progressions in this movement—g: I–(V)–VI–($\mathrm{VII}^{\circ 7}$ of IV)–IV–VII^{6}–I^{6}–II^{6b} (bb. 269–270, *Pesante*, *ravivando*)[19]—whose straightforward cadential completion, as in EV, would bring the music close to the clichéd idiom exemplified by the B flat major cadence. By suppressing the dominant, Sibelius refers in many ways back to the opening modal world, ushering in its recapitulatory return. The direct II^{6b}–I succession, with just a leading tone as the residue of an intervening dominant, recalls the events in bb. 24–32 (recapitulated in G minor in bb. 290–297). But there is also a more general aesthetic sense in which the appearance of the large-scale IV brings back the world of bold overlaps and unapologetic entrances that characterises the opening.[20]

To complete this survey of authentic cadences, it remains to ask how Essential Structural Closure relates to Essential Expositional Closure in the two versions. In FV, these events and their surroundings are bound together through an extensive parallelism covering both the pre-cadential passage in Example 3 and the weaker imperfect cadences in the closing zones (bb. 438, 448, 450).[21] The events that lead to B flat minor in the exposition reappear in the recapitulation transposed at the upper third, thus attaining the home key D minor. There are, however, changes and additions that strongly affect the expressive and dramatic implications of the ESC. Most significantly, the cadential dominant has an explicit, four-bar bass (bb. 417–420: horns, timpani) and is further highlighted through a new element of furious quaver figuration in the low strings—yielding the most emphatic dominant in the movement by far. After attaining the tonic,

---

[19] The structural hierarchy within the development is by no means self-evident. Perhaps the apparent G minor tonic that starts this chord progression functions as a passing chord between the A minor chord in b. 234 and the g: II^{6b} in b. 270, which are related through voice exchange.

[20] In their refusal to comply with the rules of normal conduct, both the opening $\hat{4}$ and the large-scale IV might, perhaps, be compared with natural phenomena or "apparitions from the forest," to quote Sibelius' characterisation of his compositional peculiarity. See Jean Sibelius, *Dagbok 1909–1944*, ed. Fabian Dahlström (Helsingfors: Svenska litteratursällskapet i Finland, 2005), 44.

[21] In bb. 395–420 each bar corresponds to a half-bar in bb. 114–126 (with some slightly shifted gestures); bb. 421–468 show a bar-by-bar correspondence with bb. 127–174; bb. 469–484 correspond to bb. 175–180 lengthening 6-bar units to 8-bar units.

the quaver figuration is taken over by the soloist to counterpoint the orchestral closing-zone material. In contrast to the EEC, the orchestra neither abandons nor overwhelms the soloist, but there is some sense of cooperation between the two—as if the soloist-protagonist had somehow come to terms with the bitter but inevitable cadential destination.[22]

In EV, the parallelism between EEC and ESC is much weaker, as it only concerns post-cadential closing-zone events and not the approach to the cadential dominant.[23] In this version, the cadential dominant follows the second cadenza (bb. 394–457)—whose removal is, of course, one of the most radical changes in Sibelius' revision. Since the cadenza ends on the dominant (b. 453) and can entirely be heard as prolonging that harmony, there is no sense of struggle in the approach to the cadential V, and the ESC thus comes close to being just a "default conclusion."

The Removal of the Second Cadenza

From the present perspective, Sibelius' removal of the second cadenza seems easy to understand. Apart from not offering any counterforce for the dominant of the ESC, the cadenza, whose beginning is shown in Example 6, is internally based on surface progressions, including the straightforward alternation of I and V chords, which sound unacceptably commonplace for the aesthetic aims that characterise the revision.

---

[22] The natural $\hat{7}$ in the ascending C–D–E figure in bb. 423–424 might be taken as a token of modal defiance against the victory of tonality.

[23] FV and EV show a pervasive bar-by-bar correspondence (albeit with several emendations in FV) from the quaver figuration that marks the cadential dominant to the very end (EV: bb. 458–540 ≈ FV: bb. 417–499).

Example 6. The removed second cadenza, beginning (EV: bb. 399–411)

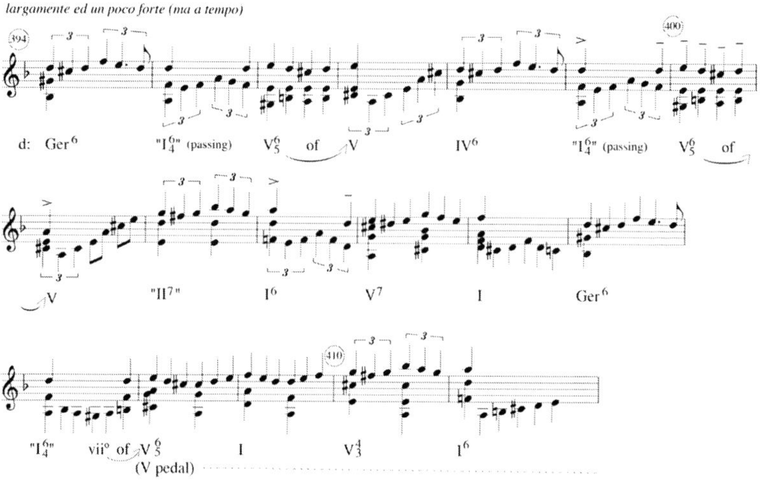

The removal of this cadenza is only part of the extensive revisions that Sibelius made in the recapitulation section. Some other removals can likewise be explained as reflecting Sibelius' desire to excise commonplace surface progressions—such as those in the D minor counterpart to the excised B flat major cadence (EV: bb. 368–371) and in the orchestral introduction of the cadenza's opening material (bb. 371–393). However, as I will argue in the following, Sibelius' revision of the recapitulation was motivated not only by the quest to avoid surface clichés but also by the more constructive aim of strengthening the overall tonal structure.

The Large-scale Structure: A Schenkerian View

Despite their differences, the two versions are guided by a similar harmonic large-scale pattern up to the beginning of the recapitulation. In the Schenkerian sketch of Example 7, the events common to the two versions are shown to the left of the dotted vertical line. In both cases, cadences to D, B flat, and G (including the deformed one in FV) help to articulate a descending arpeggiation I–VI–IV, which attains its goal IV at the beginning of the recapitulation—a pattern previously employed at least by Schubert.[24] In both versions, moreover, an untransposed quotation from the exposition follows, with a D pedal tentatively suggesting a tonic return (EV: b. 282, FV: b. 304; see Example 8). In comparison to the previous structural harmonies, however, this D is weakened by the lack of cadential confirmation.[25] Moreover, its function as a structural tonic is questioned, in both versions, by the ensuing progression to a powerful Phrygian cadence in G minor (II4/3–V; EV: b. 302, FV: b. 324), which reinterprets the bass D as the dominant of G minor, suggesting that the large-scale IV has not yet lost its governing position.[26]

Example 7. Overall structure

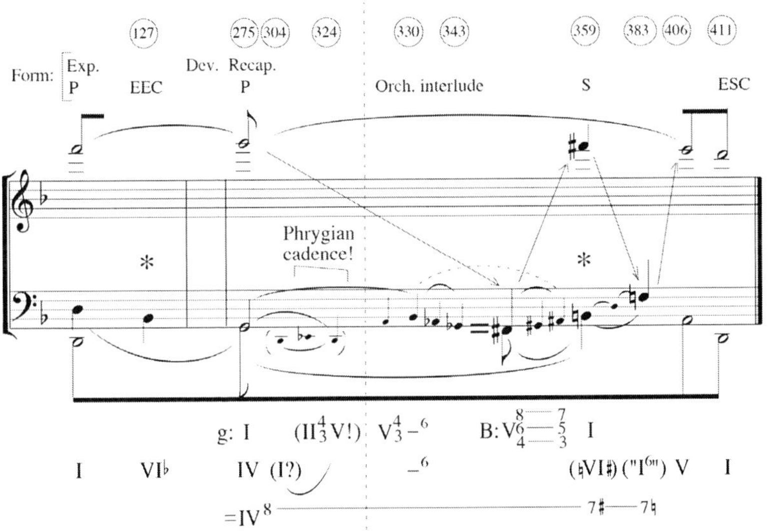

From this point onwards the two versions depart radically from each other. If, as I have suggested, Sibelius' removal of surface clichés was coupled with an enhanced concern for the large-scale tonal structure, several features in EV may have given him dissatisfaction in this respect. Though

---

[24] See, for example, Piano Sonata in A minor, D537, first movement. The remaining events in this movement are not analogous with the Sibelius.

[25] That the modulation from G minor to D minor before the D pedal is made by means of sequential repetition (bb. 292–303) also fails to support a strong arrival at D.

[26] In both versions, the G minor key signature extends until this point (and further), thus denying visual confirmation of the suggested tonic return.

the Phrygian cadence points to the ongoing influence of the large-scale IV, the subsequent events fail to fulfil its structural implications convincingly. The Phrygian cadence is followed in EV by an extended prolongation of the D-major chord with unstable key feeling (bb. 302–329), until a brief G minor chord follows (b. 330, first half), leading to the secondary theme in F major through II–V–I. While one might argue that this G minor chord still prolongs the large-scale IV, its short duration and tonal instability are far from ideal for clarifying its structural significance after the extended D-governed stretch (bb. 282–329). Moreover, the ensuing events do not complete the structure in a satisfactory way. The F-major area (= III) is followed by an assertion of another D pedal (b. 349) without any intervening dominant, and from there on the music never gets far from D minor, but repeatedly returns to I and V until the second cadenza. Overall, the recapitulation in EV is characterised by the abundance of Is and Vs, which bring back the tonic key in some way but leave their relationship with the previous structural pattern unclear.

Through his revision of the recapitulation, Sibelius created a much clearer and more effective overall structure. To clarify the large-scale prolongation of IV, he inserted a new orchestral interlude that takes up and tonicises G minor immediately after the Phrygian cadence. This, as illustrated in Example 7, is followed by a complex progression that attains the tonic only through the eventual ESC, whose emphatic cadential chords complete the archetypal I–VI–IV–V–I overall structure with no previous Is or Vs challenging their hierarchic superiority.[27]

Concretising the connection between the original IV and its resumption at the orchestral interlude, the latter begins with a variant of the opening motif, referring back to the beginning of the recapitulation. As illustrated in Example 8, the chain of associations is supplemented by the intervening passage above a pedal D (bb. 304–311), which likewise features the motif at the same transpositional level, suggesting small-scale tonicisation of G minor. Recalling that this passage is a literal quotation from the exposition, its original occurrence (bb. 33–40) can now be understood as a premonition of the structural IV, a relationship corroborated by quoting it in the new context. All these associations are aurally supported—and perhaps compositionally motivated—by the distinctive tone colour of the violin's G string.

---

[27] The locally tonicised D in b. 375 is clearly a middle element in the sequential ascent B–D–F.

Example 8. Associations between variants of the opening motif supporting subdominant prolongation

Whereas the first two motivic occurrences in Example 8 have a static-contemplative character—owing to modality in the first case and to the pedal in the second—the orchestral interlude adapts the opening motif to

fit a decisively tonal context, signalling an active desire to move forward in the tonal structure. Once again, the move towards conventional tonality is not just a "default" procedure, but one that gains particular significance through its contrast with the previous statements and its crucial function in the large-scale structure. Moreover, the heightened expressivity of this moment is underlined by chromaticism, complex voice leading, and cross relations. While the sharpening of $\hat{4}$ to sharp $\hat{4}$ (subtly foreshadowed in b. 311) renders it an unequivocal appoggiatura (C sharp–D), its clash with the simultaneous $\hat{4}$ (C natural) in the accompanying V6/5 intensifies the sense of struggle required by the reactivation of tonal forces.

After taking up G minor, the orchestral interlude heads towards B major—a new key in this version and one that did not feature at all in EV—for the start of the secondary-theme zone. Example 9(a) offers structural clarification for these events and 9(b) shows more detail. A key feature in this modulation is the enharmonic reinterpretation of B flat, the third of G minor, as A-sharp, the leading tone of B major. The bassline traverses a third down from B flat to G flat—which becomes F sharp, the dominant of B major—and back to what is now A sharp. The highest stave in Example 9(b) shows motivic statements that help to clarify structural relationships. Whereas the use of the opening motif helps to buttress the subdominant prolongation, its new syncopated continuation (bb. 328–329) is repeated so as to indicate subsequent upper-voice relationships.

Example 9. Orchestral interlude: modulation from G minor to B major (FV: bb. 275–359)

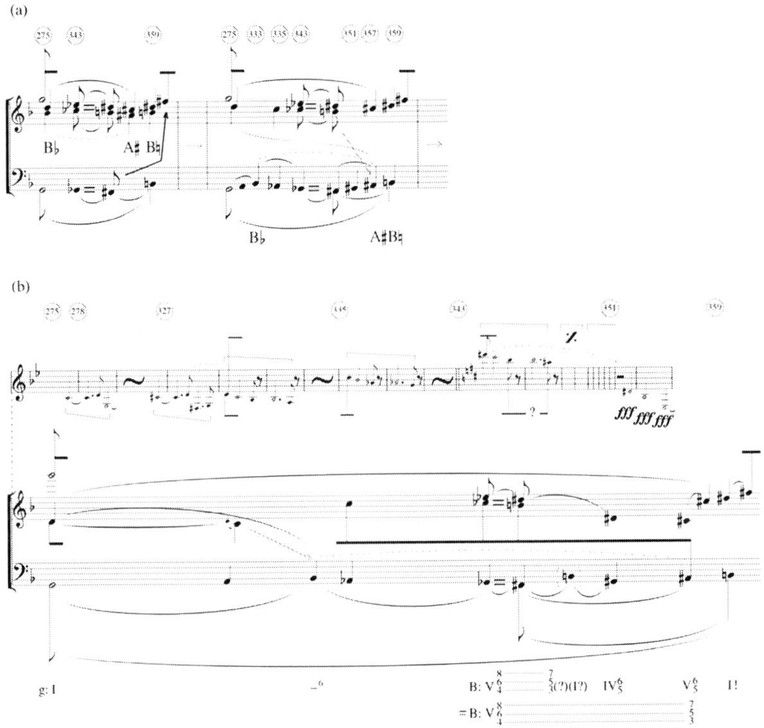

The arrival at B major key area is announced by a cadential 6/4 (b. 343), whose treatment requires some explanation. Instead of a "default" resolution, Sibelius again exploits the association between the 6/4 and the tonic triad to create ambiguity and tension in the approach to the harmonic goal. At first, there seems to be a V8/6/4–7/5/3 resolution in bb. 343–344 followed by I5/3: the beam on the highest stave in Example 9(b) is based on this initial impression. However, motivic repetitions question the decisiveness of the first I5/3. Since the V8/6/4–7/5/3 is followed by I5/3–V^7, sounding like its modified repetition (bb. 345–346), and the ensuing longer bass B, in turn, supports an extension of the previous syncopated motif, the effect of the I5/3s is far from cadential confirmation. The ensuing bass G sharp (b. 351), in contrast, is marked by a clear change in design by the extremely emphatic (*fff*) D sharp–B–E motif, suggesting a more decisive structural event and pointing to the F sharp–G sharp–A sharp bassline, as shown on the lower system of Example 9(b).[28] Under this reading, the first B major 5/3 chords represent anticipatory visions of the upcoming goal—expressing an eagerness to get there, as it were—rather than its structural attainment, and the 6/4 resolves conclusively only to the 6/5 on A sharp (b. 357).[29]

We can think of several reasons why Sibelius found it satisfactory to incorporate B major at this point of the form. From the Schenkerian perspective, the bass B prolongs IV as its modally altered third, offering consonant support for F sharp, a passing tone in the chromatic descent from G to E, as shown in Example 7. The asterisks in Example 7 highlight the large-scale contrast between two modally altered forms of VI, B flat minor and B natural major.[30] The aesthetically appealing aspects of such large-scale chromaticism include both its relationships with characteristic surface chromatics and its influence on the dramatic effect of the eventual structural completion. In several ways, the large-scale chromatic relationships recompose and amplify those introduced within the opening primary-theme zone. The motion from B flat to B natural through the B flat–A sharp (and G flat–F sharp) reinterpretation is featured on the surface right after the modal-static beginning, when B flat major 6/3 leads to B natural minor 5/3 (through G flat/F sharp major) at a striking moment of chromatic-enharmonic activation (bb. 41–44). As shown by circles and arrows in Example 2, the approach to the first cadence also involves a chromatic G–F sharp/G flat–F–E line, with F ($\hat{3}$) being transferred to the bass, as in the large-scale structure. The B major harmony provides temporary stability for chromatic elements that typically play an unstable role on the surface—and must, of course, ultimately yield to D minor also

[28] I am applying the all-important analytical principle formulated by John Rothgeb: "changes in surface design usually coincide with crucial structural points, and accordingly such changes must be given the most thoughtful attention in deriving or verifying an analysis." John Rothgeb, "Design as a Key to Structure in Tonal Music," *Journal of Music Theory* 15 (1971): 230–53 (231).

[29] Since the upper voice highlights B–A flat in bb. 343–344 and D sharp–C sharp in bb. 352–358, one might perhaps read here the kind of temporally disintegrated unfolding that was mentioned in note 15 above.

[30] In Aldwell's and Schachter's terminology, B flat minor represents *secondary mixture* and B natural major *double mixture*; see Edward Aldwell and Carl Schachter, *Harmony and Voice Leading*, vol. 2 (New York: Harcourt Brace Jovanovich, 1979). Black, "Symmetry as Modal Abstraction," relates the contrast between these keys to that between D minor and D Dorian.

in the large-scale structure.[31] Highlighting elements of D major in both of its outer voices (B natural and F sharp) and sharing no common tones with the surrounding G minor and D minor chords, the B major triad serves ideally for freshening the effect of the concluding D minor tonic.

Summarising Remarks

In comparison to EV, FV shows, in two ways, a more purposeful way of using tonal forces in large-scale organisation. There is, first of all, that aspect of organisation based on the opposition between tonality, centring on the I–V relationship, and contrasting—modal and chromatic—elements. In FV, there are three perfect authentic cadences (disregarding the "deformed" one), each of which has a clearly identified function in establishing and dramatising that opposition. At the end of the primary-theme zone, the first cadence (Example 2) establishes not only the home key but tonality in general as one of the forces pertinent to the overall drama. The second and third cadences articulate the EEC and ESC, respectively, and are followed by progressions closed by weaker imperfect cadences. Though space has not allowed a detailed description of all surface elements, these post-EEC and post-ESC progressions feature conventional tonality in a more straightforward and unproblematic way than anything else in the movement.[32] There is thus a sense of overt tonality being held back over most of the exposition and recapitulation, creating a tension whose relaxation at the EEC and ESC is then highlighted through these progressions. In order to create this large-scale effect, it was necessary for Sibelius to delete passages such as the B flat major cadence (Example 4) and the second cadenza (Example 6), which in EV feature straightforward surface tonality en route towards the EEC and ESC. The deformation of the G minor cadence at the end of the

[31] Related chromatic-enharmonic incidents include, for example, the introduction of G flat in b. 88 through a sequential pattern that leads one to expect an F sharp. This G flat resolves in parallel thirds with E flat to the upper notes of the B flat major triad, producing a detail of voice leading that the large-scale structure reproduces with enharmonic reinterpretation.

[32] Bb. 155–164 are based on B flat minor: (V6/5)–I–(V6/5)–I(–V6/5 of)–VI–(V6/5 of)–IV–V6/4–5/3–I, which is preceded by the same progression without (V6/5 of)–IV in bb. 147–154. These progressions reappear in D minor in bb. 441–459, albeit with partially changed chord inversions owing to the added solo part (suggesting a prolonged dominant in bb. 441–447). It may be no coincidence that most tonal surface progressions (including FV: b. 20 ff., 116 ff., 269 ff.; cf. also Example 4) as well as the large-scale progression feature descending thirds (I–IV–IV).

recapitulation (Example 5[c]) also prevented overt tonality from bursting out prematurely, and intensified the dramatic opposition between modal and tonal counterpoles.

A second aspect of large-scale organisation is based on relationships internal to tonality. Through his revision, Sibelius created a clearly articulated I–VI–IV–V–I overall structure, which involves an even larger tension span, ranging from the first cadence to the eventual ESC. Postponing the structural tonic return to the ESC is exceptional, though possible, within sonata-form tradition, and may to some extent explain the unusually strong dramatic effect of the ESC in this movement.[33] Even more significant, however, is that the two aspects of tension and relaxation coincide at the ESC. The closing cadence achieves not only the tonic return and the *Urlinie*'s arrival on $\hat{1}$, but also tonality's definitive victory, with the emphatic V contrasting with all previous moments of dominant avoidance. Despite its entirely conventional V–I, $\hat{2}$–$\hat{1}$ motions, the effect of Sibelius' closing cadence could hardly be farther from a "default conclusion." (Indeed, I find it difficult to think of a traditional example of an ESC or *Urlinie* completion with an equally strong dramatic effect.) This points to a particularly significant aspect of Sibelius' accomplishment. Not only was he one of the last masters inclined and able to employ the full structural potential of tonal resources, but, most importantly, he gave them new significance by involving them in a highly personal synthesis of contrasting forces.

---

[33] In traditional sonata (or concerto) form, the tonic harmony normatively returns prior to the *Urlinie* $\hat{1}$, beginning the second branch of the interrupted structure (Schenker, *Free Composition*). For exceptional cases of uninterrupted structures in sonata form, see, for example, Lauri Suurpää's analysis of Brahms's String Quartet in C minor in "The Undivided Ursatz and the Omission of the Tonic *Stufe* at the Beginning of the Recapitulation," *Journal of Schenkerian Studies* 1 (2005): 66–91.

EDITORS

Daniel Grimley is Professor of Music at the University of Oxford and a Fellow of Merton College. His research interests are in Nordic music, cultural geography, and the environmental humanities (with particular reference to landscape). His books include *Grieg: Music, Landscape and Norwegian Identity* (Boydell, 2006), *Carl Nielsen and the Idea of Modernism* (Boydell, 2010), and, as editor and contributor, *Jean Sibelius and his World* (Princeton, 2011). Future projects include a book entitled *Delius and the Sound of Place*, and an edited collection based on his Leverhulme International Network *Hearing Landscape Critically*.

Tim Howell is Reader in Music at the University of York, UK where he specializes in the analysis of new music. An internationally-recognized authority on the music of Sibelius, his research has now broadened to encompass contemporary Finnish music as reflected in two major publications: *After Sibelius: Studies in Finnish Music* and *Kaija Saariaho: Visions, Narratives, Dialogues.*

Veijo Murtomäki is Professor of Music History at Sibelius Academy in the University of Arts, Helsinki. He writes on music for the daily newspaper *Helsingin Sanomat* (1984–), and is member of the Editorial Board of the *Jean Sibelius Works* (1996–). His books include *Symphonic Unity. The development of formal thinking in the Symphonies of Sibelius* (1993), and *Jean Sibelius ja isänmaa* [Jean Sibelius and Fatherland] (2007). He is coeditor of *Sibelius Forum* (1998), *Sibelius Studies* (2001), *Sibelius Forum II* (2003), and *Sibelius in the Old and New World* (2010).

Timo Virtanen is editor-in-chief of the complete critical edition *Jean Sibelius Works* (JSW) in the National Library of Finland since 2004. He has been appointed as docent (adjunct professor) of music philology at Sibelius Academy in the University of Arts. In the series of Sibelius's collected works, he has edited Symphonies Nos. 1 and 3, the two versions of *Cassazione*, and the two versions of the Violin Concerto.